American Literary Studies

American Literary Studies

A Methodological Reader

EDITED BY

Michael A. Elliott and Claudia Stokes

New York University Press

NEW YORK AND LONDON

NEW YORK UNIVERSITY PRESS
New York and London

Library of Congress Cataloging-in-Publication Data
American literary studies : a methodological reader /
edited by Michael A. Elliott and
Claudia Stokes.
p. cm
Includes bibliographical references and index.
ISBN 0-8147-2215-6 (acid-free paper)—ISBN 0-8147-2216-4 (pbk. acid-free paper)
1. American literature—History and criticism—Theory, etc.   I. Elliott, Michael A.   II.
Stokes, Claudia, 1970–

PS25 .A445 2002
810.9—dc21   2002071904

Contents

A Note on the Text

In order to incorporate as many critical voices as possible into this volume, the editors have made small deletions to many of the essays reprinted here. However, the editors have attempted throughout to preserve for the reader the full sense of the contribution that the essays make to American literary studies. Deletions are marked in the text by three dots: •   •   •.

In addition, the editors have preserved the method of citation used by the essay in its original printing. Since a style of documentation is also a kind of decision about scholarly methodology, we have chosen this path rather than make all the selections consistent with one another.

Introduction
What Is Method and Why Does It Matter?

Michael A. Elliott and Claudia Stokes

The recent emphasis on interdisciplinary scholarship—manifest in the resurgence of institutional programs like American studies and publications in cultural studies—has relocated both the literary critic and the literary text to unfamiliar territory. This new interest in broaching disciplinary limits has proved to be exciting and invigorating. Literary critics have turned their attention to media other than the written text, and nonliterary specialists, such as historians and sociologists, have used literary texts to support their own research. This book is a response to American literary interdisciplinarity and attempts to raise, and address, the inevitable questions that emerge when disciplines collaborate: What can texts tell us about American culture or history? How can literary interpretive methods be adapted to other fields? What do literary texts evidence?

This volume responds to these questions by focusing attention on problems of *method,* specifically methods of integrating the study of American literature with other disciplines that study American culture. What does "method" mean in the world of literary studies? In reply to a query about research methods, a biochemist might respond by pointing to the materials used in the laboratory, the design and equipment of experiments, and the tools used to interpret raw data. When pollsters— a kind of social scientist—discuss their methods, they regularly refer to the number of people they poll, the type of questions they ask, and the manner in which they select their participants. In these instances, questions of methodology are anchored in underlying theories about how to gather and interpret information properly, and they entail tools such as statistical models, margins of error, and laboratory conditions that are tailored to suit these theories. We expect methods to be transferable from one setting to another; for this reason, we presume that they can be described in clear and exact terms. The word itself comes from the Greek roots "meta" (after) and "hodos" (a way). Method literally means the path that one takes as a scholar; it encompasses those things necessary for producing knowledge, the tools one uses to proceed on "the way after" scholarship.

Thinking about method forces scholars to consider the goals of their work and to ask how they should judge the best manner for proceeding toward them. These are the challenges that this volume poses to literary scholars currently working in the field of American literary studies. This book in no way intends to serve as an exhaustive primer of literary interpretative methods, a service ably performed by more than a few collections. Instead, we have sought to collect diverse examples of scholarship that address a shared set of methodological problems. These essays share a common denominator: They are committed to the integration of literary study with fields of knowledge and critical practices not typically associated with literary exegesis.

We have invited experienced scholars whose own work depends upon this integration to consider the implications, requirements, and choices related to methodology. Each of these scholars has selected and introduced a previously published essay that pairs textual analysis with an extraliterary source—for example, the conditions of popular dramatic performance, legal testimony, and Enlightenment philosophy—to illuminate a literary concern, whether a text, writer, or period. The obverse of this critical endeavor is the application of literary interpretive practices like close reading to the analysis of cultural spheres other than the literary one. For instance, this interdisciplinary practice, which generally goes under the appellation "cultural studies," is at work in Ann duCille's essay "The Occult of True Black Womanhood," reprinted here, which examines the conditions surrounding the labors of African American feminist scholars. In the essay, duCille, in effect, "reads" the literary academy itself and applies literary interpretive skills to the profession in which she works.

For many literary scholars in the United States, cultural studies has reinvigorated literary criticism by importing to it methods and texts from outside the discipline, as well as enabling literary critics to engage in new ways the world beyond the written page. For others, cultural studies has threatened English as a profession by altering the disciplinary limits that define this field and distinguish it from the work performed in other departments, such as history, communications, or philosophy. In his recent "autopsy" of literary criticism, for example, Mark Bauerlein names several of the components of cultural studies that its proponents have found attractive, only to contend that these very things render it an incoherent enterprise. "By studying culture in heterogeneous ways, by clumping texts, events, persons, objects, and ideologies into a cultural whole (which cultural critics say, is reality) and bringing a melange of which, logical argument, speculative propositions, empirical data, and political outlooks to bear upon it, cultural critics invent a new kind of investigation immune to methodological attack" (34–35). Bauerlein's point is that this interdisciplinarity risks making it impossible for literary studies to articulate the internal standards of judgment necessary for a discipline to evaluate the scholarship produced in its name. In other words, this practice is on the verge of turning English into everything and nothing at the same time.

We admit to being more sympathetic to the impact of cultural studies upon American literary criticism, but we also feel that the concerns Bauerlein articulates (and he is not alone) merit attention. This volume is an attempt to respond to that challenge by fostering a conversation within one field of literary criticism—American literature—about its methods and methodological judgments. Talking about method in this way will allow for the generation of standards of evaluation and will also serve the purpose of introducing beginning scholars to the disciplinary practices of their new peers. We begin by proposing that a method—any method—of criticism is comprised of three primary parts:

- the primary information subject to the critical enterprise, traditionally a written text or texts
- the engagement with one or more of the various professional categories used to group and classify literary texts; these organizational divisions include period, aesthetic movement, genre, geographical region, and social affiliation, whether in the writer's own membership in a social group or in the text's representation of a social group
- the strategies and assumptions that allow the critic to handle and interpret that information

This last point will serve as the primary focus of this volume, though the essays in this collection certainly challenge and reevaluate the two other components of criticism. Indeed, the interdisciplinary practices highlighted often call into question the first component of literary method—the centrality of a literary text—either by applying literary interpretive skills to nonliterary material, by omitting altogether the literary text per se from this critical enterprise, or by rendering the literary text secondary to a larger social critique.

Literature and Culture: A Brief History of Literary Methods

Our description of method is itself the product of a long-standing dialogue concerning the nature and function of literary study, a discussion produced by the institutionalization of literary scholarship over the last hundred years. As English-language literature—and, for the purposes of this study, American literature in particular—became a field of scholarly expertise and a pedagogical enterprise, literary interpretation became formalized and therefore acquired a shifting set of critical goals. Each of these goals, in turn, has led to a different set of interpretive assumptions and strategies. The result is a diverse and varied interpretive toolbox, one organized chiefly around the enduring critical discussion of the relation between the literary text and the culture(s) in which it is composed and, as some critics might venture, read.

One of the reasons we feel this volume to be necessary is the vast diversity of opinion in the history of American literary studies about this very relationship. This debate about the connection between literary studies and cultural analysis has a long and complex past—and making sense of it can be daunting to a beginning scholar. This volume does not aim to isolate particular interdisciplinary strategies and offer them as definitive answers for the questions that animate American literary studies. Instead, we hope to sharpen debates about the goals and practice of interdisciplinary literary studies by bringing into the foreground the methods by which such scholarship is produced. We see this volume as participating within a lengthy discussion about the relation of the literary text to the culture that surrounds it. Therefore, we offer a brief outline of past contributions to this discussion as a way of showing how current methods of American literary scholarship depart from and draw upon former models of criticism.

We begin our survey of literary criticism at the turn of the century, the very moment when American literature became a subject of scholarly analysis. In fact, the current interest in reading the literary text alongside other kinds of language and knowledge bears some resemblance to the "expressive realist" method common in literary criticism from the late nineteenth century to the Second World War (Belsey 7). In this method, broadly defined, "literariness" emerged as a special category of language, one distinguished by its direct correspondence with culture. As the product of the European and American literary realist movements, the category of literariness straddled the gulf between the elite and the common, a negotiation made possible by assigning special status to texts generally believed to chronicle accurately some essential truth about life. In effect, the documentation of the common caused the literary text both to be elevated above other linguistic forms and to be valorized for its ethical and aesthetic qualities, among them beauty and honesty. Operating within this idiom, the critic sought in the text evidence of verisimilitude and used the correlation between the literary text and the surrounding culture as evidence of a text's artistic achievement. Moreover, the expressive-realist method of literary criticism imparted special standing to the writer, who both reflected and stood apart from his or her historical surroundings. As such, literary interpretation often involved engagement in authorial biography in an effort to ascertain the correspondences between the literary text and aspects of the writer's own life.

During and after the Second World War, expressive-realist criticism was countered by an influential body of critics—including Cleanth Brooks, John Crowe Ransom, and Robert Penn Warren—who sought both to standardize literary interpretive methods for their students and, simultaneously, dispel the belief that other kinds of knowledge were necessary for a full understanding of the literary text. Born out of pedagogical needs and the professionalization of literary scholarship, the New Criticism touted the singularity of literary language and thereby formally dislocated it from other kinds of writing and fields of knowledge. Whereas the expressive-realist critics ascertained literariness precisely by a text's correspondence with culture, the New Critics famously offered a mode of interpretation predicated on the removal of the literary text from culture and designated as "fallacious" the interpretive reliance on authorial biography.

New Criticism argued that the text alone was all a scholar required for its interpretation. Any other information—biography, social context, speculation about the writer's intent, or the use of the reader's emotional response—figured in the New Criticism as unnecessary and even seriously misleading impediments to interpretation. In the place of these expressive-realist interpretive mainstays, the literary apparatus of the "close reading" emerged, which paid careful attention to language, structure, and form and appointed the unities and disunities of these qualities as repositories of meaning. Because of the New Critical insistence that the critic attend to the text alone, the literary text emerged after the postwar era as a haven from, and even elevated above, culture. Like the famous "well wrought urn" coined by Brooks in his interpretation of Donne's "The Canonization," the literary text in New Critical parlance is perfect in its formal qualities, the subject of awe, and untouched by the stains of time and space.

In the United States, New Criticism coincided with the development of American literary studies as an increasingly (though never completely) distinct enterprise, as literary critics sought to identify a national tradition commensurate with the mantle that the United States had assumed as the global defender of freedom and democracy. Within the academy, these efforts found support in the growth of "American studies" departments that benefited from the broader endorsement of "area studies" as a Cold War strategy for studying the world, as well as the more particular urgency of defining the nation. The confluence of New Criticism with these interdisciplinary programs produced what is now referred to as the "myth-and-symbol" school of American criticism, a label applied to works such as Henry Nash Smith's *Virgin Land* (1951), R. W. B. Lewis's *The American Adam* (1955), and Leo Marx's *The Machine in the Garden* (1964). On the one hand, these works of American studies differed from the more traditional New Criticism in that they placed literary texts within narratives of American history; they even relied upon nonliterary texts (dime novels, sermons, political speeches) as evidence. Yet these works treated history and culture much as New Criticism treated its texts: as an organic, unified whole.

Each of the books named in the paragraph above argues for a central myth, symbol, or pattern it considers to be at the center of American history—and then claims that the presence of this central element makes America an exceptional nation. This brand of scholarship concerned itself not with documenting literary histories of influence and biography, but with describing a coherent tradition. (Richard Chase's *The American Novel and Its Tradition* [1957] is a well-known example.) Unfailingly, these works found that tradition in the nineteenth-century writers whom we even now take for granted as the canonical figures of the "American Renaissance," the title of F. O. Matthiessen's 1941 study that influenced so many of these scholars writing in the 1950s and early 1960s. During this period, American literary studies came to be dominated by a method divorced from the empiricism that had characterized the earlier expressive-idealist literary scholarship. This endeavor aimed not to explain the history of literature, but to use literature to distill the character of American history itself. "No longer an object of historical investigation," one recent commentator has observed, "American literature was now an ideal order of eternal objects reflecting the mind of a whole people" (Shumway 337).

With the social and intellectual upheaval of the late 1960s, both New Criticism and the myth-and-symbol school came to be associated with a kind of political and academic conservatism. The intellectual underpinnings and origins of poststructuralism have been well documented elsewhere, though for our purposes the position of this diverse intellectual movement on the relation of literature to culture warrants some consideration. Whereas New Criticism distinguishes literary language from other forms of language and fields of culture, poststructuralist thinkers such as Roland Barthes, Jacques Derrida, Michel Foucault, and Julia Kristeva reconsidered language, and literary language in particular, as the carrier, enforcer, and product of a necessarily conservative, self-perpetuating, and often oppressive culture. The expansiveness and diversity of poststructuralism—which encompasses individual strains such as deconstruction, discourse theory, Lacanian psychoanalytic theory, and French feminism—render it difficult to address in this broad discussion. However, what is especially vital for our methodological concerns is the effort of poststructuralist literary critics to examine the literary text as an agent and envoy of social values so entrenched as to be practically invisible, a cultural function often denoted by the term "ideology."

Poststructuralist literary criticism directed much of its attention in particular to the texts that gave rise to the expressive-realist literary method: namely, literary texts that presumed a direct representational correspondence with an external social reality. Anchored in the apprehension of language and its subdivision, the discursive formation, as broadcaster of ideology, critics such as Roland Barthes and Jacques

Derrida attempted both to unravel the ideology at the center of these texts and consequently to demonstrate the constructedness of the text and of the reality presented there. At the same time, the poststructuralist belief in the entanglement of culture and language made it possible for literary scholars such as Roland Barthes to analyze nonliterary aspects of culture—popular entertainment, advertising, food—using literary interpretive methods, an analytical practice that collapsed the boundaries that distinguished the literary text from other fields of knowledge and culture and that paved the way for the current academic practice of cultural studies.

In spite of its attention to the involvement of the literary text in the workings of culture, poststructuralism drew criticism because of what some detractors believed was its inadequate attention to the precise conditions of both culture and the texts that it produces. Though it questioned the distinctiveness of the literary text and placed it in the larger context of cultural ideology, poststructuralism was found by some to be "hair raisingly unhistorical. There was no question of relating the work [of literature] to the realities of which it treated, or to the conditions which produced it, or to the actual readers who studied it" (Eagleton 109).

This characterization of poststructuralism as heedless of the social and political contexts of literature triggered the New Historicist interpretive method, which mixes the goals and tools of poststructuralism with historical materialism in order to be more specific about the ideological insights possible through literary analysis. New Historicism complicated the placement of the literary text among other fields of knowledge and cultural products with a sophisticated double move: in reading literary texts in the context of history, the New Historicist method applied literary interpretive skills to both fields of knowledge and in so doing muddied the boundaries between them. At the same time, New Historicism maintained the primacy and distinctiveness of the literary document, which communicates knowledge not simply about the ideology of the cultural moment that produced that text but most specifically about how this particular literary text responded to the conditions of its own production. The literary text in the New Historicist method is acutely social and cultural, and the determination of the precise nature of this engagement is what occupies the New Historicist critic, an endeavor deeply indebted to the goals of poststructuralism.

The basic claim that underwrites both poststructuralism and its descendant, New Historicism, is the belief that language both produces and maintains culture, a tenet that has allowed poststructuralist critics to analyze, or "read," nonliterary aspects of culture and New Historicist critics to designate history as a site of interpretation. The fundamental belief in the entanglement of language with the workings of culture has empowered literary critics to apply their skill of textual interpretation to culture not just as it appears in literature but in many of its products. In this intellectual arena, an ever-increasing multiplicity of cultural sites has become available to the critic: communications, social history, media studies, social science, popular entertainment, architecture, and urban planning (among many others) have become subject to methods of interpretation and analysis born out of literary interpretation. In turn, these fields have informed the analysis of literary texts.

These developments have also contributed to the redrawing of the institutional boundaries that have long distinguished literary study from other intellectual endeavors. The most obvious example of this phenomenon has been the reinvigoration of interdisciplinary programs such as American studies, cultural studies, and ethnic studies departments, which, in constructing curricula around shared methodological and intellectual goals rather than around literary texts, erode the boundaries that distinguish fields of knowledge at the broadest level. In short, the interdisciplinarity that has animated literary study in recent years has also caused a reconstruction of the academy itself.

At the same time, the integration of extraliterary sources into textual analysis has spawned discussion about the role of the literary critic. Whereas the New Critical method set clear goals for the project of textual interpretation and evaluation, the poststructuralist and New Historicist methods use the text to investigate the wider social order, whether in a text's capitulation to dominant ideology or in its engagement of the conditions of its own production. The literary critic using interdisciplinary methods often serves in the capacity of the social critic, using the literary text to launch an analysis of the social order reproduced or contested in its literary product. For example, is a critic like Sau-ling C. Wong, who interprets a literary text like Hualing Nieh's *Mulberry and Peach* within the context of Chinese diasporic identity, operating solely as a literary critic, or is her literary analysis in the service of a broader social critique? Indeed, as the incorporation of extraliterary sources into literary analysis has prompted the redrawing of disciplinary boundaries, it also causes us to reconsider the role that literary interpretation may play in the social realm. To integrate the literary text with another field of knowledge presumes some kind of belief in the social function of the critical act, a belief that literary interpretation has some use or meaning beyond the limits of the written page.

Such judgments proceed from an assumption, famously articulated by Edward Said, that "texts are worldly." Said stated in *The World, the Text, and the Critic* (1983) that "texts have ways of existing that even in their most rarefied form are always enmeshed in circumstance, time, place, and society—in short, they are in the world, and hence worldly" (35). Of course, what precisely it means for a text, as well as a literary critic, to be "worldly" remains a complicated matter. Insofar as critics are enjoined to consider how a text is "enmeshed in circumstance," both in the text's production and the moment of criticism, they are able and even obligated to speak to "worldly" problems. This premise, or some variation of it, underlies much contemporary scholarship of American literature, which attends to a now familiar litany of issues (race, gender, class, sexuality) emanating from questions of power our contemporary society has yet to address adequately. While the discipline continues to debate whether these issues dominate American literary studies to a fault, or whether they have yet to receive adequate attention, no one can deny that a relationship between literary interpretation and social commentary has become a received truth of this field. The goal of this inquiry, on the other hand, remains subject to dispute. Can, as some believe, the investigation into the "worldiness" of literary texts offer a means of staging some kind of political intervention in the very social dynamic it discerns in the literary text?

Explaining his selection of Lora Romero's essay for this volume, Ramón Saldívar argues that Romero does that very thing in her "attempts to understand the links between one's professional and political commitments" and that doing so requires her to think about "the relation between a scholar's community of origin and the community of learning she inhabits." In other words, Saldívar lauds Romero for taking account of a public that is situated beyond the academy, even if she does not address that public directly through the publication of that scholarship. Moreover, Saldívar implies that Romero has made methodological decisions based upon her vision of that public, a "utopian streak" that leads to her "courageous stand of refusing to see ethnic, gendered, and racialized writings as uniquely separate from the broader context of

American cultural patterns." In the essay reprinted here, Romero pursues this agenda by contending that Cooper's *Last of the Mohicans* is "enmeshed"—to use Said's term—in nineteenth-century judgments about the relationship of racial identity to gender, judgments that Romero believes continue to divide a public that she hopes to see united. As such, her literary inquiry attempts to constitute at once a social and professional intervention. Moreover, we have been struck by the number of scholars who have used the word "utopian" in introducing the essays reprinted here, a pattern that surely suggests a widespread belief in the power of textual study to effect social and political change.

Focusing on the methodology of a piece of literary scholarship like Romero's is not necessarily a matter of judging that scholarship to be right or wrong—though it may facilitate such judgments. Rather, it creates the opportunity to discuss the principles and decisions required of any work of criticism that are often left unarticulated. Scholars of American literature currently draw upon a continuously proliferating number of critical methods, including a variety of theoretical models and bodies of evidence, and combine them in new and challenging ways within a single article or book. Such changes invigorate the field and enable it to participate in interdisciplinary dialogues about questions crucial to the academy, but it makes it necessary that we begin a concrete and careful discussion of the methods that we employ. To fail to do so endangers our ability to communicate, among ourselves and to other disciplines, the skills and training that make American literary scholarship possible.

Using This Volume

Our volume departs from the standard essay collection format in that it pairs critical analysis with examples of interdisciplinary methods. Rather than ask scholars to submit an essay in which they plumb the depths of contemporary critical methods—a decision more characteristic of the academic essay collection—we asked these scholars to select an essay, whether from a journal or a book, that they felt employs a thoughtful and instructive method of interdisciplinary American literary study. In addition, each scholar has written a preface highlighting both the methodological insights offered by that essay and the intellectual decisions that underlie such strategies. It is our hope that this combination of examples of literary criticism with analysis will serve both as a pedagogical tool and as a critical resource.

Our task has been a delicate one: offering critical blueprints while preserving the methodological diversity that has made this kind of work both vastly appealing and vulnerable to attack. Of course, this volume is by no means complete in its inclusion of the many critical methods, intellectual practices, and kinds of texts available to the literary critic. The formal constraints of this collection (constraints we placed upon ourselves) compelled us to sacrifice thoroughness to honor the choices of our contributors. In so doing, we have not been able to dictate the final shape of this volume, though we attempted to manage this inevitable difficulty by asking a broad cross-section of scholars to contribute to this project in the belief that their own methodological affiliations and research interests would find their way into this volume. In most instances, this has proved true; at the same time, this volume includes some striking surprises: for example, the selection by Frances Smith Foster, a scholar widely known for her work on nineteenth-century African American literature, of Roy Harvey Pearce's 1962 essay on the pedagogy of popular culture.

The volume is divided into three sections that bring together essays with divergent approaches to similar methodological problems. Those essays included in the first section, "History and Literature in America," take up a challenge long familiar to students of American literature: How can one attend at once to the aesthetic object and to its historical context? In spite of the tradition of combining history and literature within American Studies, the methods of reading literature have never been fully congruent with those of historians. Carroll Smith-Rosenberg's essay, "Domesticating Virtue: Coquettes and Revolutionaries in Young America" approaches this methodological problem from a different angle, for Smith-Rosenberg is a historian by training who asks about the value of literature and literary ways of reading to historical inquiry. Lora Romero's "Vanishing Americans: Gender, Empire, and New Historicism" shows the operation of New Historicist criticism and its limits through a reading of James Fenimore Cooper's *The Last of the Mohicans*. The section then closes with a pair of essays, one by Laura Wexler and the other by Lauren Berlant, that examine the historical conjunction between racial and gender politics. In the case of Wexler, this project entails closely "reading" photographs as aesthetic objects in order to illuminate a historical moment. Berlant, on the other hand, brings nineteenth-century texts into the fractious late-twentieth-century debate over the nature of sexual harassment.

Scholarship such as Wexler's and Berlant's argues the necessity of applying literary forms of analysis to "culture," as well as the difficulty of defining the boundaries of that very thing. The essays that comprise the second section, "Reading 'Culture,'" address this problem. Roy Harvey Pearce's essay, "Mass Culture/Popular Culture: Notes for a Humanist's Primer," sounds an optimistic note about the possibility of literary scholars venturing beyond textual studies, even as it prefigures many of the conundrums that face those who do so. The three selections that follow Pearce's offer more specific examples of what such scholarship— proceeding from a convergence of American literary and cultural studies—might offer. W. T. Lhamon, Jr., carefully attempts to recover and decode the performances of black men "Dancing for Eels at Catherine Market" during the antebellum period. Paula A. Treichler insists that such methods can perform a crucial role in confronting the AIDS epidemic. And Ann duCille's "The Occult of True Black Womanhood" shows us that an inquiry into literary methods may yield insights into the culture of literary criticism within the academy itself.

For at least the last century, nationhood has played a central role in the organization of literary study. The rise of globalization both as a historical process and as a theoretical framework has forced scholars of U.S. literature to embark upon what one recent anthology calls "postnationalist American studies" (Rowe). "Nationalism Reconsidered," the final section of this volume, includes four essays that help to clarify the methodological challenges that this "post-nationalism" raises. Michael Warner's "The Mass Public and the Mass Subject" addresses both eighteenth-century texts and recent productions of popular culture to form an argument about the difficulty of thinking about the national "public" in any easy way. Elaine A. Jahner's scholarship on traditional Lakota narrative demonstrates how an understanding of Lakota nationalism at once complicates the designation of this literature as "American" and shows why concepts of national sovereignty may still matter a great deal in the criticism of Native American literary production. Sau-ling C. Wong, meanwhile, turns to a novel written in the Chinese language, but within the geographical borders of the United States, to show how the nation is no longer an adequate category for understanding literary production, even though it plays a necessary part in understanding literary *reception*. Finally, the discussion of "Americanization" written by the Dutch Americanist Rob Kroes forces us to reconsider the global implications of American literature, as he uses the study of literature to understand the relationship of American culture to the larger world.

Throughout, our goal has been to make this volume useful to scholars regardless of their familiarity with the field, from upper-level undergraduates learning for the first time the idiom of literary critics to more advanced scholars teaching in colleges and universities. The format of this text lends it to a variety of pedagogical uses. Teachers can use this volume in seminars for literature majors; in helping their students prepare to research and write undergraduate theses; in literary theory courses for both undergraduate and graduate students; and as supplements to American Studies courses with a literary orientation. Despite the Americanist focus of the essays included here, this collection can offer instruction to scholars of different fields who are interested in the practices and decisions involved in an interdisciplinary interpretive method, which has by no means been restricted solely to the scrutiny of American literary texts. Because the interest in aligning literary texts with nonliterary material has suffused literary study writ large—across disciplines demarcated by language, period, and nation—this volume may be of use to scholars interested less in the debates occupying nineteenth-century American literary exegesis than in the various methodological decisions made and examined here, which are doubtless applicable and transferable to other literary texts, fields, and projects. For example, Laura Wexler's study of antebellum representations of domestic labor may provide a useful interpretive model to the scholar working on nineteenth-century book illustration or 1980s photojournalism, to just name a few examples.

Most importantly, we hope that this book will encourage its readers to continue the dialogue that it has created among scholars of American literature about the choices that they make in producing literary criticism. Such a conversation can play a vital role in articulating the standards by which our scholarship should be judged, as well as the boundaries of our disciplinary reach. These questions matter not only for our own internal organization of the field, but also so that Americanist critics, as well as literary studies as a whole, can speak to those outside the discipline about the contribution that literary studies can make to an increasingly interdisciplinary academy. While such a conversation will no doubt bring us to moments of cacophony, the din of debate is preferable to the silence of a field ill-prepared to explain its own methods.

Works Cited

Bauerlein, Mark. *Literary Criticism: An Autopsy.* Philadelphia: University of Pennsylvania Press, 1997.

Belsey, Catherine. *Critical Practice.* London: Routledge, 1980.

Eagleton, Terry. *Literary Theory: An Introduction.* Minneapolis: University of Minnesota Press, 1983.

Rowe, John Carlos, ed. *Post-Nationalist American Studies.* Berkeley: University of California Press, 2000.

Said, Edward W. *The World, the Text, and the Critic.* Cambridge: Harvard University Press, 1983.

Shumway, David R. *Creating American Civilization: A Genealogy of American Literature as an Academic Discipline.* Minneapolis: University of Minnesota Press, 1994.

Part One

History and Literature in America

Chapter 1

Domesticating Virtue
Coquettes and Revolutionaries in Young America

Carroll Smith-Rosenberg

Introduction by Wai Chee Dimock

Is close reading an archaic skill, the province of literary connoisseurship? Is the study of history best conducted by way of measurable facts and numbers? And are literary analysis and historical analysis mutually exclusive, set apart by a disparity in scale—the former working with minute details, and the latter presiding over a big picture?

To all these questions, Carroll Smith-Rosenberg responds with an emphatic "No." Her memorable essay "Domesticating Virtue: Coquettes and Revolutionaries in Young America" is a sustained demonstration of why textual analysis still matters, and matters even in large-scale analyses. Smith-Rosenberg, a distinguished historian, is in one sense making an argument framed by the ongoing debates in her field. What makes her essay equally important to students of literature is the methodology she self-consciously proposes. Explicitly thanking the literary scholar Maureen Quilligan and her graduate students for having "taught [her] the fundamentals of close reading," Smith-Rosenberg shows that words are intricate, interlocking, and ever changing, that they are the most reliable signs of historical change, and that to analyze the semantic dynamism of words is to explore the past at its most dynamic.

Smith-Rosenberg begins with the premise that "the past" is broader and subtler than the archival material most often adduced to describe it: military victories, economic statistics, legislative actions. Such evidence, documented in black and white, apparently solid and indisputable, give us an overly distilled or crystallized account of the world. They filter out what remains messy and unsettled: the contrary structures of feeling revolving around any public event, the oscillations and divided allegiances lurking behind any solidified outcome. Such outcome has a deceptive unity and finality. History is rarely so neat and conclusive.

Not satisfied with the standard evidentiary domain, Smith-Rosenberg turns to an alternative archive: the popular novels of the early republic. To students of literature, of course, this is not a surprising thing to do. Smith-Rosenberg is making a familiar move, it seems. She is going to use this literary archive as supplementary evidence, to repeat arguments historians have already developed using nonliterary sources. This is precisely the move Smith-Rosenberg chooses *not* to make. For her, the literary archive is not a supplement but a corrective. Its job is to remind historians that they have blind spots, that other domains have something new to show. She is not convinced that history is governed by a unity that endlessly replicates itself: the same hegemonic structure, operating in the same way, leaving the same mark on every sphere of life. There is no such unity, Smith-Rosenberg argues. For the dynamics of historical processes are such as to translate every structural determinant into a multitude of entertainable articulations. The same economic statistics can have different meanings when they are subject to different descriptive languages, when they are put through different interpretive frames. Literature is one arena in which these meanings can fight out their differences. The fault lines of any culture are here dramatized and brought into the open.

Literature, in short, is not at all the same as sermons, advice manuals, or political tracts. These are univocal documents, and give us only a partisan account of the world. Literature, much more chaotic, is a superior form of evidence— more truthful and more comprehensive—for it registers what these other documents fail to. Here Smith-Rosenberg quotes Mikhail Bakhtin. The novel, Bakhtin says, is marked by its "heteroglossia," its hospitality to competing social dialects, competing belief systems, at odds with one another, but often coming out of the mouths of the same characters. Any speaker might yoke together several incompatible dialects. And any word might have simultaneous membership in several conflicting speech communities. In this way, the novel as a genre is always quarreling with itself: a quarrel woven into its very linguistic fabric, woven into every word, every sentence, every speaking voice. Lack of harmony is its starting point.

In the early republic, this lack of harmony was played out in the conflicting meanings of one particular word, "virtue." A keyword in the lexicon of classical republicanism, "virtue" initially referred to the civic responsibility of the male citizen, his dedication to the common good. Virtue, in this classical sense, had its place within a constellation of terms foundational to the republic. It was linked directly to "liberty" and "independence"—attributes of the landed gentry holding inherited property, free to exercise political judgment because they were not financially encumbered. By the 1780s, however, the rise of economic and political laissez-faire had produced a new middle class, amassing its wealth not from hereditary estates but from trade. This new class had a very different understanding of "liberty" and "independence." To it, these attributes were to be traced not to the landed gentry (now seen as idle and profligate), but to the industry and enterprise of commerce. Given this semantic realignment, the word "virtue" also came to have a second (and increasingly ascendant) meaning. Its embodiment was no longer the male citizen. Instead, it was now linked to the chastity of the domestic woman, economically unproductive, politically disenfranchised, but whose sexual propriety was nonetheless crucial as a symbolic marker of the new middle class.

The competing meanings of the word "virtue" thus throw into relief the two competing ideologies of the early republic. Semantic history, in this sense, is political history. Smith-Rosenberg analyzes both meanings in one particular work, Hannah Foster's *The Coquette; or the History of Eliza Wharton*. As the title of the novel suggests, its heroine is woefully lacking in "virtue" in the new sense of that word. She is otherwise a new woman, however, a practitioner of "liberty" and "independence," though unfortunately not in the newly approved commercial sphere. In this vexing combination, Eliza exemplifies and perverts the semantic transition from classical republicanism to economic laissez-faire. She renders unmistakable the fault lines at the heart of a metamorphosing culture. These fault lines are what interest Carroll Smith-Rosenberg as a historian. To study them, she needs the help of close reading.

———

PASSION CORRUPTING VIRTUE, libertines destroying happiness, independence misused, seduction, betrayal and death.

This is a summary not of the torrid plots of afternoon soap operas or harlequin romances, but rather of the themes that obsessed America's first novelists, in the years following the American Revolution. Written

From Elaine Scarry, ed., *Literature and the Body: Essays on Populations and Persons: Selected Papers from the English Institute*, pp. 160–175, 177–184. Copyright © 1988. Reprinted with permission of The Johns Hopkins University Press.

as our national identity and modern class structure first took shape, America's earliest best-sellers—*Charlotte Temple, The Coquette, Ormond*—were filled with scenes of fortune-hunting rakes and army officers, of young girls in flight from patriarchal homes, of unwed mothers and dying prostitutes.[1] Since popular fiction both reflects and shapes the world that reads it, the new American nation and the new middle class were formed at least in part by these lurid tales.

Historians, however, have rarely examined them. Melodramatic romances seemed to say little about the critical events of the early national period: the emergence of a capitalist class structure, the evolution of class identities, the ideological battle between classical republicanism and the rhetoric of economic and political laissez-faire.[2] Nor have historians been alone in their compartmentalized vision. The political debates of the new nation held little interest for literary scholars exploring the origins of the American novel.[3] But does only the coincidence of chronology connect these two genres? Or can we hear behind fantastical plots about virtue endangered and independence abused echoes of another quite different discourse, that of republican political theory? The vocabulary found in both genres is remarkably similar. In both corruption undermines "independence"; the vicious, nonproductive elegance of the aristocracy threatens "virtue"; reason and restraint serve the common good while passion promotes self-interest and civic disorder. Do the novels of the middle class and the political rhetoric of the middle class address the same social and political dilemmas?

To answer that question requires a radical repositioning of the novel of seduction and of republican political rhetoric. We must learn to read both as central components of the ideology and discourses of the emergent middle class. Sexual and domestic, political and economic discourses wove in and out of one another as that radically new and protean class sought to construct an identity inclusive enough to encompass its divergent, often warring, components. Repositioning the political and the sexual, we will reread the body. No longer will it appear simply as a repository of the erotic and the reproductive, a psychic entity confined to social margins and domestic space. As a physical text written and read within a political context, it assumes new dimensions. A representation of the civic individual, associated with themes of autonomy or aggression, it becomes a legitimate figure in the public arena. To reread the body in this way forces a second critical recognition—that the body's physical integrity constitutes as significant a material vehicle for symbolic representation as the body's evocative sensuality. After all, feminists have long argued that who controls the body is as important a question to ask as what excites the body—and that the first question must be understood in political, not erotic, terms.[4]

Let me rephrase this argument in the analytic language of the historian. Republican ideology cannot be studied in isolation from an analysis of middle-class discourse and identity formation, any more than middle-class discourse and identity can be understood isolated from the ways gender and sexuality were conceptualized and constructed—or gender and sexuality isolated from class and ideology. We cannot fully understand the construction of a new sexual and domestic female in America between the 1780s and the 1830s unless we view it against the constantly changing construction of the male citizen—from the opening shots of the American Revolution, until he emerged as both "the common political man" and "the self-made economic man" of Jacksonian America. The political body is always gendered just as the gendering of the body is always political—and relational.[5] The genders exist in conceptual opposition and in intimate social interaction. Whig theorists and republican mothers belonged to the same class, read in front of the same fires, often from the same texts.[6] The fundamental contradictions that characterize the developing civic and class ideologies of these years can be more fully understood if we examine them as shared texts which middle-class women and men understood and used in subtly different ways.

But we must beware of flipping backward through our texts. Too often we have read the class identities and the sexual attitudes of the Enlightenment conditioned by Victorian texts, permitting the dark hues of the later period to color our perceptions of the more ebullient and explorative eighteenth century. Sexual and class identities were more hesitant and ambivalent in the years when both were just taking form. The rigidities of the later period—and its new potentials for subversion and revolt—cannot be projected backward. To understand the women and men of the new class and the new nation we must, rather, trace the way they formed their ideologies out of the heritage of earlier eighteenth-century discourses and in interaction with the material practices of their own time. Affected by radical reworkings of those material practices—the rise of commercial economy and the commercial city, technological innovation, political revolution—they perceived those reworkings with minds conditioned by conceptual systems and values formed in interaction with older material and discursive practices. This heritage of words simultaneously blinded and directed them. As J. G. A. Pocock suggests, "men cannot do what they have no means of saying they have done and what they do must in part be what they can say and conceive that it is."[7] To read the texts and discourses of the new class our focus must simultaneously bridge material reality and its representation, link the past, as embedded in language and literary forms, with the present, caught at that moment when language intersects the material to produce perception.

We must also link the voices of the varied speakers—and the silences of the listeners. M. M. Bakhtin argues that a cacophony of social dialects representing different classes, ethnicities, generations, professions—and, I would add, genders—characterizes every heterogeneous society, a cacophony reproduced differently within the consciousness of each individual speaker in that society.[8] Power runs through this cacophony. The language of the economically and politically dominant will struggle to deny the legitimacy of more marginal social discourses, yet influences flow in both directions. Nor will the marginal ever be silenced. Rather, different social groups and subgroups will continually challenge each other's perceptions, conceptual systems, even the literal meanings of their words. Especially during periods of radical social change, this constant flow of conflicting meanings assumes an almost electrical urgency, like flashes of light refracting through a prism.[9] In this way, language represents social experience.

To elucidate the discordance inherent in the discourses of the new nation and the new class, to trace the complex and inharmonious interaction of the new gender, class, and political identities, let us examine the process by which the new capitalism complicated classical republicanism's linking of "virtue," "independence," "liberty," and "happiness." Such an examination is complicated by the fact that both American middle-class identity and ideology and republican political discourse in England and America were extremely protean entities. Throughout the eighteenth century, new speakers and new ideological dialects repeatedly transformed classical republicanism. Merchants in London and Philadelphia created the dialect of commercial republicanism; the artisans of London and New York constructed the dialogue of radical republicanism; women across a broad social and economic spectrum rewrote these varied male texts. By the century's end, the lexicon of republicanism had fragmented.[10]

To illustrate this point let us examine the transformation of the twin pillars of republican ideology, "virtue" and "independence."[11] Classical republicanism had identified the virtuous citizen as the free man who valued his liberty above all and who devoted himself to serving the common good. His ability to do both depended on an economic independence rooted in unalienated and unalienable property—literally, in the gentry's real estates secured by entail and primogeniture. Classical republicanism counterpoised the "virtuous" landed gentry to the "corrupt" new men of paper and place—the new capitalism's stock jobbers, government bureaucrats, and army officers. These men, the gentry argued, lived in a passionate and venal world driven by fantasy and credit, obsessed with stocks, speculation, and debt. Lacking landed independence, their interests, votes and pens were easily bought.

The man of trade occupied a more ambivalent position within classical-republican discourse. The value of the gentry's land, the source of the gentry's political independence, depended on trade, and hence on the actions of traders and on events occurring in London and in ports around the world. Their independence thus circumscribed by men and processes beyond their control or ken, the gentry responded with nervous suspicion. Trade, they wrote each other, was productive, linked to England's and their own prosperity. But trade also "introduces luxury . . . and extinguishes virtue." It depended on credit which hung upon opinion and the passions of hope and fear. It was cathected with desire. It might seduce independent men away from the simple ways of their fathers. It could entrap them in an endless web of debt and ruin.[12]

Creatures of trade and credit, middle-class men defended against this association of themselves with the corrupt world of fantasy and passion by redefining both "virtue" and "independence." In the commercial-republican lexicon, "independence" was rooted in productive labor and self-reliance. Talent, frugality, and application epitomized the new "virtue" and warded off the indulgences of luxury and indebtedness which the gentry had accused trade of eliciting. Traders were productive members of society, they argued. But were the gentry? Indeed, the new middle class began to take the offensive by reversing the symbols of corruption, proposing that the status of the gentry, like that of the aristocracy (the figure of corruption all republicans defined themselves against) depended on land inherited irrespective of talent or industry, and that the gentry, in common with the aristocracy, occupied political places secured not by productive labor but by family privilege. Challenges to patriarchy followed challenges to landed wealth, though the new bourgeois men spoke for the independence of sons far more than for the rights of wives and daughters. They also altered the meaning of "liberty." To the gentry it had meant the citizen's right to be actively involved in making and executing decisions in the public realm. The new commercial men, like Locke, saw liberty, rooted in the social contract, as the free man's right to secure his private property from the incursions of a potentially dangerous state. Inverting the gentry's understanding, they now claimed liberty as all men's right, not one class's privilege.[13]

The ways the men of the new middle class constructed the middle-class woman further complicated their inheritance of the political assumptions of the British gentry, not only because middle-class women occupied an ambiguous place within the economy and ideology of their class but, more importantly, because the middle-class men's construction of gender repeatedly contradicted the middle-class men's transformation of the male republican discourse.

To illustrate this point let me return to the word "virtue." Classical republicanism masculinized and gentrified virtue, rooting it in military service and landholding. In constructing their new class identity, middle-class men fused a republican understanding of civic virtue with more private and moral understandings garnered from evangelical religious texts.[14] In doing so they began to associate the virtue of their class not only with the frugality of middle-class men but also with the sexual propriety of middle-class women. Elite men within the new middle class, urban merchants and their professional coterie, then further complicated the sexually proper woman's relation to virtue by requiring her to embody their class in a second and equally significant way. The elite woman's personal elegance, in clothing and in speech, and her familiarity with things cultural were to represent middle-class men's own economic security and cultural superiority to all other classes. Yet their construction of the elegant woman as the sign of class warred with their earlier association of class with virtuous male frugality, and so a fundamental flaw emerged in middle-class men's symbolic representation of their class.

Shifting definitions of "independence," the material underpinning of both the gentry's and the middle class's understanding of "virtue," further compromised the middle-class woman's symbolic qualifications. Classical republicanism had rooted virtue in the independence created by unalienable land, and thus denied women access to civic virtue.

Commercial men had transposed the gentry's landed independence into the independence of productive industry. This shift in the grounding of independence occurred at the very moment when economic change and bourgeois ideology deprived the middle-class woman, and married women of all classes, of the opportunity to labor productively and to support themselves independently. Having required the bourgeois woman to be both elegant and nonproductive, how could the bourgeois man ever trust her virtue or rest securely in the symbols of his class?

These ideological ambiguities and contradictions only multiplied as middle-class men displaced onto middle-class women criticisms the gentry had leveled against them. As the gentry had accused middle-class men of venality and extravagance, so middle-class men, depicting themselves, as we have seen, as hardworking and frugal, harangued middle-class women for alleged extravagances in dress and household management. More seriously, the gentry had denied that commercial men, living in the fantastical, passionate, and unreal world of paper money, stocks, and credit, could achieve civic virtue. How significant, then, that throughout the eighteenth and nineteenth centuries middle-class men endlessly accused bourgeois women of being untrustworthy and incapable of virtue because they lived in another fantastical, passionate, and unreal world of paper—the world of the novel and the romance?[15]

The proliferation of popular literature, the explosive second paper revolution, gave both middle-class women and men ample opportunity to explore, defend, and re-form these contradictions and displacements. Although bourgeois men had inscribed a male text of class onto bourgeois women, bourgeois women did not always read that text as their men intended. Rather, bourgeois women, increasingly empowered by the printing press and the emergence of a commercial market for popular literature, began to produce their own texts of civic and class identity, texts that differed significantly from male inscriptions.

The novel is a particularly useful genre for historians in search of this discursive interchange. Not only was and is the novel considered a particularly female genre (romantic, fantastical, domestic, sexual, often written by women), more than most other literary and professional genres, but it also captures those dynamic moments of social change when disparate groups, battling for hegemony, form and reform language. "The novelistic word," Bakhtin tells us, "registers with extreme subtlety the nicest shifts and oscillations of the social atmosphere. . . . Each character's speech possesses its own belief system. . . . It . . . also refract[s] authorial intentions and consequently . . . constitute[s] a second language for the author."[16] The diversity of characters, the novel's reliance upon conflict and change for the development of plot and character, permit both the overt and covert expression of contradictions and conflicts inherent in the ideologies and discourses of the times. The evocative nature of the novel intensifies its ability to enact social conflict. While the hegemonic genres of a culture—sermons, for example, advice books, even political rhetoric—warn against danger and seek to repress ambiguities, the novel (and this was particularly true of the eighteenth-century novel of seduction) plays upon dangerous desires. Its melodramatic trials of a woman's virtue call forth its readers' repressed desires, permitting those desires to be vicariously enjoyed and as vicariously punished. While ultimately affirming the permissible, it makes us familiar with the forbidden. It is the novel, therefore, that most fully represents the conflicts and contradications of its time.

To explore this aspect of the novel, let us examine America's first bestseller, Hannah Foster's *The Coquette; or the History of Eliza Wharton. A Novel Founded on Fact. By a Lady of Massachusetts*, originally published in 1797 and repeatedly republished through the 1870s.[17] At first reading, *The Coquette* appears a melodramatic representation of the values of commercial republicanism. Eliza Wharton, a young and virtuous woman, has just ventured into the eighteenth-century marriage market. The daughter of a respected minister who, dependent on a salary, has left her little capital inheritance, Eliza plays the role of a venture capitalist. As such, she confronts the same dilemmas a young merchant faces in the confusing economic markets of the late eighteenth century: how to credit financial and moral worth in a world of words and fancy; whether to trust traditional community wisdom or, depending on her own judgment, to risk all for possible great gains. It is in the language of commercial metaphor that Foster has Eliza present herself to us and evaluate her chances. "Fortune," Eliza tells her friend and confidante, Lucy Freeman, "has not been very liberal of her gifts to me; but I presume on a large stock in the bank of friendship, which, united with health and innocence, give me some pleasing anticipation of future felicity." Freeman responds in kind: "I shall be extremely anxious to hear the process and progress of this business" (9, 27).

The plot revolves around the choice Eliza must make between two suitors. One, the Reverend Mr. Boyer, as a minister, represents simultaneously the authoritative voice of social norms and the hard-working, honest, professional middle class. Offering Eliza a life of respectable dignity and service to the community, he is rational, honorable, and prudent. His words harmonize with communal wisdom. The second suitor, Major Sanford, is a rake, corrupt and deceitful. He assumes the airs of the very wealthy and the distinction of a military title—both highly suspect within either classical or commercial-republican ideology. Worse yet, having wasted his fortune, he pretends to a station he has no right to claim. (This is symbolized by his mortgaged estate. An encumbered estate is an anathema to all forms of republicanism, a paper mortgage masking the reality of an empty purse.) He refuses honest employment as beneath the dignity of a "gentleman and a man of pleasure," preferring to prostitute himself to a marriage of convenience. With double deceit, he holds out to Eliza the temptations of a gay life and marriage although he cannot afford the one and does not intend the other. He compounds his sins by encouraging her resistance to the constraints of domesticity. Asserting her independence, Eliza sets out on her own to evaluate the worth of these two men. Swayed by fancy and ambition, scornful of her family's advice, Eliza judges wrongly and falls.

Read as a celebration of the values of commercial republicanism, this is just the novel we would expect to find written in the New England of the 1790s. But such a reading is too simple. *The Coquette* painstakingly and persistently complicates what should be clear-cut. First, Eliza is not a heroine like Pamela or Clarissa, virtuous to the core. Rather, as Cathy Davidson argues in her fine study of early American literature, *The Revolution and the Word,* Eliza fuses talent and virtues with serious moral failings. Even more remarkably, her failings and her fall endear her to her friends within the novel and to her readers outside. Second, the novel persistently leads the reader to resist the prudent marriage and to root for the rake. Third, the moral spokeswomen of the novel end by warning the heroine that male ministerial texts can be as misleading and dangerous as women's romances and novels. Finally, *The Coquette* is not simply a fiction, but, as Davidson details, a rewriting of an earlier, male-authored historical text, the popular reporting of the scandalous death of Elizabeth Whitman (xi).

Elizabeth Whitman, a respected daughter of New England's professional middle class, related to Jonathan Edwards, cousin of Aaron Burr, daughter of a highly respected Hartford minister, herself a frequently published poet and friend of the Hartford Wits, died, alone, under an assumed name in a Massachusetts inn, having given birth to an illegitimate child. Newspapers and sermons thundered against her criminal sexuality as they speculated about the name of her seducer. The men's reading of the event emphasized women's social and sexual vulnerability: woman's passion, uncontrollable when enflamed by novel and romance reading, easily overcame women's fragile hold on virtue (xi).

Hannah Foster's *Coquette* offers us a different narrative. Eliza Wharton's downfall, Foster tells us, was not lust but the desire for independence coupled with the wish to rise socially. As such she represented those within the emergent middle class, who, rejecting traditional norms, anxiously embraced individualism, risk, and the new capitalism.

To be appreciated fully, *The Coquette* must be read as a gendered misprisioning of the political and economic discourses of its time. Just as the capitalist revolution problematizes "independence" and "virtue" as understood within classical republicanism, so *The Coquette* underscores the ways concepts of female "independence" and "individualism" further complicated the republican lexicon. The book's opening sentence alerts the reader to the significance of this issue. "An unusual sensation possesses my breast," Eliza writes her friend, Freeman, "a sensation which I once thought could never pervade it on any occasion whatever. It is *pleasure,* pleasure, my dear Lucy, on leaving my paternal roof. Could you have believed that the darling child of an indulgent and dearly-beloved mother would feel a gleam of joy at leaving her? But it is so" (5). Two events, Eliza continues, have freed her: the death of her father and the death of the man her father had chosen as her husband, another minister, whom she did not love. While both patriarchal figures lived, Eliza had exhibited behavior appropriate to her class and gender. "Both nature and education had instilled into my mind an implicit obedience to the will and desires of my parents. To them, of course, I sacrificed my fancy in the affair, determined that my reason should concur with theirs, and on that to risk my future happiness" (5).

To read these statements in a political context, let us start by juxtaposing Eliza's comment, "determined that my reason should concur with theirs, and on that to risk my future happiness," to one drawn from that primer of American republican rhetoric, the Declaration of Independence. Here we find "certain unalienable rights" listed, "among these, life, liberty and the pursuit of happiness." *The Coquette* begins by telling us that the heroine, as a virtuous daughter, has resigned her *liberty* of choice and her pursuit of *happiness* in deference to parental wishes; she has agreed, that is, to link happiness to the sacrifice, not the assertion, of liberty. This pious sacrifice is then contrasted to the pleasure she now reports experiencing at resuming her lost independence, pleasure, a word that she twice repeats, and that Hannah Foster italicizes. Circumstances reversing her position, Eliza now associates liberty with pleasure—and with her ability to pursue happiness on her own.

The Declaration of Independence tells us that liberty and the pursuit of happiness are inalienable rights. Numerous other republican texts warn Americans that to relinquish them will endanger virtue. But the Declaration also insists that a passion for liberty be balanced by prudence. "Prudence, indeed, will dictate that Governments long established should not be changed for light and transient causes." But Eliza's very first sentence signals a subtle shift away from the hegemonical Declaration of Independence, a shift that challenges the traditional relation among pleasure, happiness, and prudence. Eliza has called pleasure an "unusual" emotion, especially when associated with independence and liberty. To most eighteenth-century republicans, it was both an unusual and a dangerous emotion. Popular versions of moral philosophy, especially that most common to Puritan New England, pitted pleasure against both happiness and prudence.[18] For them, "happiness" signified contentment with one's place in life, "the attainment of what is considered good."[19] It was subservient to, indeed rooted in, social norms. "Pleasure," in contrast, implied delight in the sensations; it hinted at passion—an association reinforced when Eliza represents her pleasure in a physical, indeed, a sensual vocabulary. Pleasure, invoked by her newfound independence, she tells Freeman, "possesses my breast." It illuminates her with "a gleam of joy." When independence is absent in this text, so is sensuality. In acquiescing to her parent's will, Eliza tells Freeman, she had "sacrificed my fancy." "My heart" was not "engaged." "I never felt the passion of love." Eliza, in short, has invested her female independence and liberty of choice with desire. And with an equally dangerous emotion—individualism. Pleasure, especially in Eliza's usage, presumes individuals capable of fancying and privileging their own desires, of acting independent of society's approval in order to secure them. Eliza significantly ends her letter by underscoring this note of individualism. "This letter," she confesses to Lucy, "is all an Egotism" (5–6). What a significant beginning for a novel written in the shadow of the American Revolution!

Throughout the novel, Eliza Wharton will insist that pleasure can legitimately be wedded to a desire for independence and liberty, that marriage without such a "wedding" will destroy happiness.[20] Her family and friends will tell her virtue and happiness are tied to prudence and a socially appropriate marriage, that pleasure and fancy will endanger both. Throughout, Eliza will insist on her right as an independent woman to pursue happiness guided by her own standards.

•   •   •

Here, then, is the dilemma Foster presents. Independence endangers at the same time as it gives pleasure; domestic restraints destroy pleasure and liberty at the same time as they guarantee virtue and economic security. At all the key points in the novel two critical disjunctures appear. The imagination and the passions threaten to distort perception; virtue, independence, liberty, and happiness are divided against themselves. Eliza would like to unite all. Her virtuous advisers tell her this is no longer possible. Take the correspondence between Eliza and Freeman in which Eliza contrasts social independence (which she depicts in corporeal and fanciful terms) to marriage and public service (which she associates with the loss of economic independence, social liberty—and pleasure). "My sanguine imagination paints, in alluring colors, the charms of youth and freedom, regulated by virtue and innocence," Eliza writes Freeman, "Of these I wish to partake." She tells of her fears of the stuffy minister who wants to carry her off to the wilderness of New Hampshire. "I recoil at the thought of immediately forming a connection which must confine me to the duties of domestic life, and make me dependent for happiness, perhaps, too, for subsistence, upon a class of people [the minister's parishioners] who will claim the right to scrutinize every part of my conduct, and, by censuring those foibles which I am conscious of not having prudence to avoid, may render me completely miserable." She then asserts her right to make her own decision. "You must either quit the subject, or leave me to the exercise of my free will" (29–30). Lucy Freeman, whose role in the novel is to express republican ideals, snaps back. Eliza's words and fancy have obscured Eliza's perceptions of reality.

Freeman's heated response underscores the opposition between pleasure and happiness, women and liberty, female independence and female virtue. "You are indeed very tenacious of your freedom, as you call it; but that is a play on words. A man of Mr. Boyer's honor and sense will never abridge any privileges which virtue can claim" (30–31). Indeed, liberty or "freedom" for women is so inconceivable to Freeman that it exists only "as a play on words." She replaces "freedom" with female "virtue" which can only claim privileges from a posture of dependence. And privilege, other republican texts tell us, is dangerous, tied to corruption, as in the unearned privileges of birth, which commercial republicanism scorns.[21]

If women's relation to liberty and freedom underscores the complexities and uncertainties of those words, women's relation to economic independence does the same. Indeed *The Coquette* quite pointedly spells out the ways women's relation to independence limits their right to liberty—and predetermines the boundaries of their happiness. The same characters that tell Eliza that her independence/freedom is a play on words, Freeman, Richman, and the Reverend Mr. Boyer, warn her that middle-class women lack the financial resources to support an independent social role. (Eliza stretches the limits of her mother's income when visiting Freeman in Boston and must compromise her independence by accepting presents [73].) Freeman and Richman warn her not to overstep her class in her ambition to make a fashionable show. A minister is just the right husband for her. "His situation in life," the prudent Freeman advises, "is . . . as elevated as you have a right to claim. Forgive my plainness, Eliza. . . . I know your ambition is to make a distinguished figure in the first class of polished society, to shine in the gay circle of fashionable amusements, and to bear off the palm amidst the votaries of pleasure" (27).

It is Eliza's twin desires for the pleasures of social independence and social eminence that attract her to the rake, Major Sanford. When Mr. Boyer finally rejects Eliza, it is not her loss of chastity that motivates the minister, but her independence coupled with her extravagance in dress and her desire to rise above her father's social station. And, significantly, it is at this point that Boyer enters into a debate about the contested meanings of the word "virtue," defining it as far more than sexual propriety. In a letter to his friend and colleague, the Reverend Mr. T. Selby, Boyer writes, "I would not be understood to impeach Miss Wharton's virtue; I mean her chastity. Virtue in the common acceptation of the term, as applied to the sex, is confined to that particular, you know. But in my view, this is of little importance, where all other virtues are wanting!" (78).

Boyer's denunciation of Eliza's assertion of social independence unsupported by economic independence is the turning point in the novel. Once the minister has rejected her as an appropriate wife for his class, no other man proposes. Eliza's passion for liberty and social independence has reached imprudent limits. It has propelled her into the classless state of the spinster, with only marginal rights to the economic resources of any man. Her independence has cost her what it at first promised: pleasure, happiness, free access to the world outside the home. It will ultimately cost her her sexual virtue as well. Though warned against the rake by friends and family, she insists on judging him by her own criteria and falls.

* * *

Eliza has already fallen victim, not to Sanford—he is secondary—but to the authoritative male discourse of her age. She has relinquished her quest to fuse independence and pleasure; she now accepts her community's definition of virtue. But such a definition, because it denies independence to women, brings neither happiness nor pleasure. "I frequent neither . . . the company [nor] the amusements of the town," she tells Julia. "Having incurred so much censure by the indulgence of a gay disposition, I am now trying what a recluse and solitary mode of life will produce. . . . I look around for happiness, and find it not. The world is to me a desart [sic]. And when I have recourse to books, . . . if novels, they exhibit scenes of pleasure which I have no prospect of realizing!" (135). Pallor, depression, an "emaciated form!" replace Eliza's gay independence (140). Only then, having lost independence, pleasure, and happiness, does Eliza relinquish her virtue as well.

Cathy Davidson reads Hannah Foster's Eliza Wharton as Everywoman who, during years marked by political and economic revolution, lusted for independence. She sees The Coquette as a subversive novel which encourages the reader, against her reason, to applaud Eliza's desires and mourn her death.[22] I embrace Davidson's reading but suggest an additional layering. Eliza Wharton is Every*man* as well as Everywoman. Her career underscores the way economic change has transformed the independence of classical republicanism, making it highly individualized and economically risky. No longer securing social order, independence, tied to liberty and freedom, endangers the individual and society. Foster dramatizes the new impotence of family and community against the autonomy of youth and the power of the individual. Familial and community spokesmen have become spokeswomen, the feminized Greek chorus of Richman, Freeman, and Eliza's widowed mother, who, at the end, can only mouth hollow platitudes as Eliza is seduced in her mother's parlor and then disappears into the night.[23]

Reading in this way we see that Foster has in fact rewritten woman's place within the male texts of nationalism and class. Middle-class men had made middle-class women their alter egos, bearers of criticisms the gentry had directed against middle-class men and against the paper revolution. Middle-class women, not middle-class men, were thus depicted as incapable of civic virtue. Not only does Foster's text suggest that men, not women, are incapable of true virtue, but she also makes Eliza the ego, not the alter ego, of the new nation and the new class. It is Eliza, not Boyer or Sanford, who takes on the challenges the new capitalism thrusts upon the new American republicans. It is she, not they, who assumes tragic proportions. It is in her language that the dilemmas of her age are debated. The principal question of *The Coquette* is the principal question of the new nation and the new class: how can independence and individual happiness be made compatible with social order? In the end, Foster gives no answer. We are left to hypothesize that, in the late 1790s, Americans had yet to resolve the fundamental inconsistencies between their new capitalist and individualistic economy and the civic humanism they had inherited from their Augustan ancestors. Yet the subversive tone that runs through *The Coquette* suggests that old paradigms are about to crack open, that the next generation of writers will represent Elizas who do not have to die.

The middle-class construction of gender frustrated this anticipation. Everyman—whether he appears as "the Deerslayer" in Cooper's canonical text, as "the common man" in Jacksonian political rhetoric, as "the self-made man" in laissez-faire economic theory, as Davy Crockett in the scatalogical comic almanacs—a generation later has broken the old paradigms of civic humanism and fused independence and individualism. But not Everywoman. The freedom Foster subversively permits Eliza will recede in the face of the cult of true womanhood's growing hegemony, and a hundred years later Lily in *The House of Mirth*, Edith in *The Awakening* will end, ironically, like Eliza—indeed, like ideal Revolutionary heroes—by giving their lives for their freedom.[24]

NOTES

1. Over seventy novels by American authors were published between the 1790s and 1821 when James Fenimore Cooper's canonical novel, *The Spy*, became a best-seller, an event traditionally thought to initiate the American novel. During these same years, English novels circulated widely in America as well. *Charlotte Temple*, the first best-selling novel in America, was first published in 1791 and republished continuously and in large editions in America throughout the nineteenth century. Indeed, 104 separate American editions have been traced. See, for example, Susanna Rowson, *Charlotte: A Tale of Truth by Mrs. Rowson*, 2d ed. (Philadelphia: printed for M. Carey, 1794). Rowson considered herself a British citizen at the time she wrote *Charlotte Temple*. Hannah W. Foster, the author of *The Coquette*, came from old New England stock and was married to a New England minister at the time she wrote the novel, which first appeared in 1797 and was repeatedly republished into the 1870s. Page citations to *The Coquette* are to the most recent edition, edited with an introduction by Cathy N. Davidson (New York: Oxford University Press, 1986), and are given parenthetically in the text. Charles Brockden Brown, a Philadelphia and New York merchant, was another prolific, widely published, and influential American author. His first American book, *Alcuin*, appeared in 1798. Six novels quickly followed, beginning with *Wieland* in 1798 and concluding with *Jane Talbot* in 1801. *Ormond* was first published in 1799; Ernest Marchand has edited and provided an introduction to a modern edition (New York and London: Hafner, 1937). For a brilliant analysis of the early American novel see Cathy Davidson, *Revolution and the Word: The Rise of the Novel in America* (New York: Oxford University Press, 1986). For an older survey see Lillie Deming Loshe, *The Early American Novel* (New York: F. Unger, 1958).

2. For classic studies of the revolutionary period which do not cite literary texts, see, for example: Gordon Wood, *The Creation of the American Republic, 1776–1787* (Chapel Hill: University of North Carolina Press, 1969); J. G. A. Pocock, *The Machiavellian Moment: Florentine Political Thought and the Atlantic Republican Tradition* (Princeton: Princeton University Press, 1975); Bernard Bailyn, *Ideological Origins of the American Revolution* (Cambridge: Harvard University Press, 1967); Jackson Turner Main, *The Social Structure of Revolutionary America* (Princeton: Princeton University Press, 1965); and Gary Nash, *The Urban Crucible: The Northern Seaports and the Origins of the American Revolution* (Cambridge: Harvard University Press, 1986). Richard Bushman is an exception to this list. See, for example, his essay "American High Style and Vernacular Cultures," in Jack P. Greene and J. R. Pole, *Colonial British America* (Baltimore: Johns Hopkins University Press, 1984).

3. Two important exceptions to this general rule among literary studies are:

Emory Elliott, *Revolutionary Writers: Literature and Authority in the New Republic, 1725–1810* (New York: Oxford University Press, 1982), and Davidson, *Revolution.*

4. I have long been indebted to the work of Mary Douglas and Victor Turner in my reading of the physical body as a representation of the social body. Mary Douglas, *Purity and Danger: An Analysis of Concepts of Pollution and Taboo* (London: Routledge & Kegan Paul, 1964), and *Natural Symbols: Explorations in Cosmology* (New York: Vintage Books, 1970); Victor Turner, *Dramas, Fields and Metaphors: Symbol and Action in Human Society* (Ithaca, N.Y.: Cornell University Press, 1974), and *The Ritual Process: Structure and Anti-Structure* (Ithaca, N.Y.: Cornell University Press, 1969).

5. I am particularly indebted to Elaine Scarry for suggestions leading to this phraseology.

6. Davidson argues that subscription lists of early American publishers and printers as well as other items in early books indicate that women and men read many of the same books (Davidson, *Revolution,* esp. chaps. 3 and 4). Linda Kerber has been particularly influential in terms of underscoring the use republican male theorists and social commentators made of the mother's role in the new republic. See her *Women of the Republic: Intellect and Ideology in Revolutionary America* (Chapel Hill: University of North Carolina Press, 1980) and "The Republican Ideology of the Revolutionary Generation," *American Quarterly* 37 (Fall 1985):474–95.

7. J. G. A. Pocock, "Virtue and Commerce in the Eighteenth Century," *Journal of Interdisciplinary History* 3 (Summer 1972):122, cited by Joyce Appleby, "Republicanism and Ideology," *American Quarterly* 37 (Fall 1985):466. Indeed, I find one of John Pocock's most interesting contributions to the theoretical armamentarium of the historian to be his insistence that we conceive of and perceive our world using concepts and rhetoric inherited from past eras. This vision is fundamental to my own analytical approach in this essay.

8. See especially M. M. Bakhtin's arguments in "Epic and Novel" and "Discourse and the Novel," in *Dialogic Imagination,* ed. Michael Holquist, trans. Caryl Emerson and Michael Holquist (Austin: University of Texas Press, 1981).

9. See, for example, Bakhtin's comment: "Any concrete discourse (utterance) finds the object at which it was directed already . . . overlain . . . by the light of alien words that have already been spoken about it . . . entangled, shot through with shared thoughts, points of view, alien value judgments and accents. The word directed toward its object, enters a dialogically agitated and tension-filled environment of alien words, value judgments and accents, weaves in and out of complex relationships, merges with some, recoils from others, intersects with yet a third group" (Bakhtin, *Dialogic Imagination,* 276).

10. Few issues are as hotly debated among early national historians as the

nature and sources of American republican political rhetoric. Two schools op-
pose each other. The older, led by Bailyn (*Ideological Origins*), Wood (*Creation
of the American Republic*), and Pocock (*Machiavellian Moment*), argues that
American republican ideology is deeply rooted in the early eighteenth-century
British gentry's transformations of earlier forms of civic humanism, though all
emphasize that economic change altered Americans' usage of the gentry's older
rhetorical devices. Joyce Appleby (*Capitalism and a New Social Order: The
Republican Vision of the 1790s* [New York: New York University Press, 1984]
and "Republicanism and Ideology"), Linda Kerber ("The Republican Ideology
of the Revolutionary Generation"), Drew R. McCoy (*The Elusive Republic:
Political Economy in Jeffersonian America* [Chapel Hill: University of North
Carolina Press, 1980]), and Isaac Kramnick ("Republican Revisionism Revisited," *American Historical Review* 87 [1982]:629–64) offer significant modifications to the Bailyn-Wood-Pocock thesis, stressing the disruptive influence of
economic change. They argue that Americans used republican political terms in
ways significantly different from the way in which the British gentry did earlier
in the century. These new scholars stress the more individualistic and overtly
capitalistic perspective of American theorists, as well as underscoring the influence of John Locke and Adam Smith on American republican thinkers. For a
recent summary of the controversy see the special issue of the *American Quarterly* 37 (Fall 1985), edited by Joyce Appleby.

11. Isaac Kramnick in "Republican Revisionism Revisited" is particularly
interested in the way the meanings the British gentry and American republicans
assigned words changed. I find his essay most suggestive.

12. Charles Davenant, *The Political and Commercial Works of Dr. Charles
D'Avenant*, ed. Sir Charles Whetworth, 6 vols. (London, 1771), cited by Pocock,
Machiavellian Moment, 443. For a lengthy discussion of the gentry's ambivalent
attitudes toward trade see Pocock, *Machiavellian Moment*, chap. 13, esp. 441–
50. See also Wood, *Creation of the American Republic*. I wish to thank Toby
Ditz for insisting on the ambivalence and contradictions that characterized the
gentry's vision of trade and of the trader.

13. Kramnick, "Republican Revisionism Revisited."

14. For the influence of evangelicalism upon American republican thought
see Ruth Block, *Visionary Republic: Millennial Themes in American Thought,
1756–80* (Cambridge: Cambridge University Press, 1985), and "The Gendered
Meaning of Virtue in Revolutionary America," unpublished paper, Organization
of American Historians, 1987 convention.

15. This is a central theme in fiction and in advice and sermon literature.

16. Bakhtin, *Diologic Imagination*, 300. See also Davidson, *Revolution*, 13
and 44.

17. Davidson has edited the most recent scholarly edition of *The Coquette*.

Her introduction to this edition, as well as chapter 6 in *Revolution,* offers a highly suggestive analysis of the subversive nature of *The Coquette* as a female novel. Davidson is less interested in the relation between *The Coquette* and republican political ideology than she is in Hannah Foster's use of *The Coquette* to underscore the contradictions inherent in middle-class men's construction of the female role. Thus Davidson uses *The Coquette* to expand our understanding of women's experiences during the early national period. See, especially, "Introduction," *Coquette* (xi–xx). In this present essay, I am more interested in using the new middle-class discourse on gender to throw light upon the complexities and contradictions inherent in American republican ideology. Yet while they differ so in focus, I see our approaches as compatible, not contradictory.

18. See, for example, Clyde A. Holbrook, *The Ethics of Jonathan Edwards; Morality and Aesthetics* (Ann Arbor: University of Michigan Press, 1973). For British usage, see Edward A. Bloom and Lillian Bloom, *Joseph Addison's Sociable Animal in the Market Place, on the Hustings, in the Pulpit* (Providence: Brown University Press, 1971).

19. *The Compact Edition of the Oxford English Dictionary* (Oxford and New York: Oxford University Press, 1971).

20. The comments in the Declaration of Independence concerning the purpose of a just government can also be read in relation to Eliza's concerns about the government of marriage and the family. The Declaration follows its initial sentence that states that life, liberty and the pursuit of happiness are inalienable rights with its definition of a just government. "That to secure these rights, Governments are instituted among Men, deriving their just powers from the consent of the governed,—That whenever any Form of Government becomes destructive of these ends, it is the Right of the People to alter or to abolish it, and to institute new Government, laying its foundation on such principles and organizing its powers in such form, as to them shall seem most likely to effect their Safety and Happiness." Only then does the Declaration proceed to a discussion of prudence (referred to above). A subversive reading of *The Coquette* (and of the Declaration) might suggest the question: if marriage and the family do not promote the liberty and happiness of women, do women have a right to alter or abolish them?

21. Kramnick, "Republican Revisionism Revisited."

22. Davidson, *Revolution,* 144–50.

23. Davidson points to Foster's construction of an impotent maternal figure in Mrs. Wharton. *Revolution,* 148–49.

24. James Fenimore Cooper, *The Deerslayer* (New York: New American Library, 1963). For an analysis of the Davy Crockett popular literature see Carroll Smith-Rosenberg, "Davy Crockett as Trickster: Pornography, Liminality, and Symbolic Inversion in Victorian America," in Smith-Rosenberg, *Disor-*

derly Conduct (New York: Knopf, 1985), 79–89. Edith Wharton, *House of Mirth* (New York: Scribners, 1976), and Kate Chopin, *The Awakening and Other Stories,* ed. Nina Baym (New York: Random House, 1981). Linda Kerber in *Women of the Republic* has already drawn attention to parallels between *The Coquette* and *The House of Mirth.*

Chapter 2

Vanishing Americans
Gender, Empire, and New Historicism

Lora Romero

Introduction by Ramón Saldívar

I hope that in the 1990s institutional circumstances will allow intellectuals
writing on minority cultures to create an alternative rhetoric of accreditation,
one which they can put to use in transforming the educational system and
making it more responsive to the needs of ethnic communities.

—Lora Romero

Lora Romero's great strengths in the areas of classical American studies, the
American Renaissance, the antebellum period broadly, and American modernism
allow her to forge connections between canonic and contestational literary
traditions. Her book *Home Fronts: Nineteenth Century Domesticity and Its Critics in
the Antebellum United States* (1997) is a study of classic American male novelists
and less frequently considered popular women writers of the antebellum era.
The book argues that nineteenth-century domestic ideology was a complex
cultural discourse that provided its contemporary users with an array of languages, gestures, and speech genres that could be manipulated in relation to a
variety of social concerns and political positions and a range of rhetorical and
interpretive contexts.

Romero worked at the forefront of American literary methodologies: she
drew upon the methods, insights, and vocabularies of critical feminism to study
the formation of gender identity, New Historicism to understand the relationship
between discourse and structures of power, and deconstruction to analyze the
workings of contemporary systems of rhetoric and thought. In the case of the
article reprinted here, this methodology leads Romero to demonstrate the fallacy

of Michel Foucault's "narrative of modernization"—which takes for granted the "massive destruction of populations designated as 'other' "—and the necessity of excising this premise to produce a more radical critique of the relationship between race and gender in the American nineteenth century. Though Romero interrogates the role that Foucault has played in New Historicism, she does not suggest abandoning historicism altogether as a critical method. To the contrary, Romero's work offers an elegant example of the way literary scholarship and its interpretive frameworks must respect the elastic dynamism of an earlier histori- cal period and its cultural products while responding to them with intellectual integrity and analytic rigor.

Romero's scholarship is concerned with cultural politics and the status of women and minorities in American culture generally. In one of her most search- ing early essays, " 'When Something Goes Queer': Familiarity, Formalism, and Minority Intellectuals in the 1980s,"[1] Romero discusses the role of "ethnic intel- lectuals" in American institutions of higher learning. The epigraph above is from that essay. In that work, Romero inquires into what makes something worthy of study, teaching, talking, and writing. Why should we study literature and culture? In answering the question, this comparative piece situates "minority" intellectuals within the discourse of "difference," but with a difference: to show that in their appropriation of critical theory, minority intellectuals are creating a peculiar, and fruitful, hybrid of cultural and political theory. Romero attempts to understand the relation between a scholar's community of origin and the community of learning she inhabits. And she attempts to understand the links between one's professional and political commitments. These are characteristics that will recur throughout Romero's published work.

A utopian streak in Romero's work compels her to ask readers to consider the type of culture and society they inhabit and to compare it to the type of culture and society that they might yet construct. Romero's scholarship embraces this implied vision of an uncharted world, as it addresses both the canonical authors of the American Renaissance and the "minority" and women authors who challenge the canon. Writing at a moment when the proper place of non- canonical literature in the curriculum was far from certain, Romero took the courageous stand of refusing to see ethnic, gendered, and racialized writings as uniquely separate from the broader context of American cultural patterns. Such a position vigorously contends the necessity of incorporating a critique of Amer- ican exceptionalism within the canon of U.S. literature itself, an argument tied to the political aim of national society cognizant of the pluralism already present within its borders. As a consequence, Romero's work was sometimes criticized from both sides of the canonical divide, for not desiring canonical purity on the one hand or defending cultural nationalist exceptionalism on the other. Romero's scholarship thus splendidly exemplifies why the ethical dimension of social life is practically unavoidable in the classroom.

In the work of Lora Romero, we have scholarship that represents the elaboration and interrogation of the field of ethnic and feminist literary studies as essential aspects of American literature. "Vanishing Americans" combines the methods of an exacting close reading of James Fenimore Cooper's *The Last of the Mohicans: A Narrative of 1757* (1826) with a brilliant feminist and New Historical analysis of contemporary nineteenth-century American texts on "mental cultivation and mental health." Using antebellum texts describing the mental well-being, proper social adjustment, child rearing, and education of children as the basis of her analysis, Romero moves to discussions of nineteenth-century formations of human sexuality and female education and their relationship to the imaginary modes by which political formations arose in nineteenth-century America. The informed interpretation of this historical context enables Romero, in turn, to uncover in Cooper a racialism rooted in presumptions of gendered difference that she contends has remained largely unquestioned to this day.

The essay is an intricate analysis of the relationships between formations of political power and methods of defining and regulating the body in early modern American society. Drawing on Foucault's theories of sexuality and gender formation, Romero explains in her reading of *The Last of the Mohicans* how political power and conceptions of the body discursively and socially linked theories of hygiene, social reform, women's work, and cultural production in the American late eighteenth and early nineteenth centuries. In linking ideologies of women's social roles, masculine reactions to those roles, and the construction of national imperial policy, Romero argues that the threat of women's power, invisible though it may be as exercised in the daily domestic routine of the home, nonetheless produces the very real, felt need on the part of American men for the unconstrained possibilities of the frontier, precisely in order to elude women's presence. This in turn makes imperative the removal of Indians from their homelands.

The logic of this argumentative sequence is stunning: coercive gender ideologies created by men for the safe regulation of the domestic sphere compel men to escape those same coercions, and in doing so to extend the borders of the continental nation, thus creating an empire that requires the removal or, failing that, the extermination of native peoples. The ideology surrounding the domestic sphere exists, according to Romero, precisely to sanction the work of nation building and to justify the disappearance of races that were in the way of the advance of civilization. For Romero, processes of gender formation and empire building are thus inseparably linked.

Romero concludes her essay by fashioning a provocative framework to argue that neither the poststructuralist upheaval nor the emergence of feminist critiques in the 1970s and 1980s have substantially altered the traditional narrative that makes domestication and normalization the chief ends of women's work. Even the immense contributions of the New Historicism to our understanding of the relationships between the articulation of a historical imagination and the construction of political institutions are subject to critical scrutiny on these grounds: these powerful twentieth-century methodological tools continue to exhibit the same imperialist nostalgia occasioned in the nineteenth century by the destruction of other cultures through the process of modernization. In the end, Romero questions whether the tools we commonly employ for understanding the modern American domestic sphere are not, in fact, products of the same process that distributed power in such a glaringly unequal manner.

NOTES

1. Lora Romero, " 'When Something Goes Queer': Familiarity, Formalism, and Minority Intellectuals in the 1980s," *Yale Journal of Criticism* (1993) 6(1):121–42.

———————

CULTURAL HISTORIANS HAVE identified James Fenimore Cooper's *The Last of the Mohicans* as one of approximately forty novels published in the U.S. between 1824 and 1834 that together suggest the existence of a virtual "cult of the Vanishing American" in the antebellum period. Requisite to membership in this cult was a belief that the rapid decrease in the native population noted by many Jacksonian-era observers was both spontaneous and ineluctable.[1] Cooper would seem to betray his indoctrination in the cult of the vanishing American when he states in the introduction to the 1831 edition of his novel that it was "the seemingly

inevitable fate of all [native tribes]" to "disappear before the advances
. . . of civilisation [just] as the verdure of their native forests falls before
the nipping frost."[2] The elegiac mode here performs the historical
sleight-of-hand crucial to the topos of the doomed aboriginal: it represents the disappearance of the native as not just natural but as having
already happened.[3]

In the novel itself, of course, Cooper's Indians "vanish" in somewhat
more spectacular fashion than the introductory invocation of forest and
frost leads us to anticipate. However pacific the introduction's simile, in
the narrative proper individual representatives of the *doomed* race expire
in utterly sensational ways. Indeed, the frequency with which Cooper's
Indians plunge to their death from great heights is positively dumb-
founding.

The most memorable instance of this is the villainous Magua's spectacular demise at the end of the novel. Evading pursuit by Cooper's
white hero Hawk-eye, Magua attempts to leap from the brow of a
mountain to an adjacent precipice, but he falls "short of his mark" and
finds himself dangling from a "giddy height," clinging desperately to a
shrub growing from the side of the precipice. Bent on destroying his
enemy, Hawk-eye fires. The wounded Magua's hold loosens, and "his
dark person [is] seen cutting the air with its head downwards, for a
fleeting instant . . . in its rapid flight to destruction" (p. 338).

To claim that Cooper earlier *foreshadows* Magua's Miltonic fall
would grossly understate the case. Indeed, the fall of dark persons from
on high is a virtual *theme* in *The Last of the Mohicans*. Similar rapid
flights to destruction abound, for example, in an early confrontation
between whites and enemy Indians that takes place in the vertiginous
topography of a huge cavern. One Indian plunges "into [a] deep and
yawning abyss" (p. 69). A second hurls "headlong among the clefts of
[an] island" (p. 70). A third tumbles down an "irrecoverable precipice"
(p. 71), while yet another drops "like lead" into the "foaming waters"
below (p. 75).

Mere sensationalism does not quite account for Cooper's fascination
with the precipitous dark person. The figure sometimes surfaces in relatively banal forms—for example, when the noble savage Uncas at one
point darts "through the air" and leaps upon Magua, "driving him many
yards . . . headlong and prostrate" (p. 113), or later when, in his fatal
attempt to save Cora Munro's life, Uncas leaps between her and Magua
in an act of what Cooper calls "headlong precipitation" (p. 336). And

perhaps the most banal reiteration of the figure occurs when the novelist describes a Huron, tomahawk in his hand and malice in his heart, rushing at Uncas. A quick-witted white man sticks out his foot to trip the "eager savage" as he passes, and the Huron is "precipitated . . . headlong" to the ground (p. 238). Etymologically considered ("precipitation" is from *praeceps* or "headlong"), the phrase is as peculiarly reiterative as the headlong aboriginal it describes.

I would like to suggest that the redundancy of both phrase and figure in Cooper's novel signals that text's participation in and instantiation of a larger antebellum cultural discourse in which the ethnographic and pedagogic overlap. Cooper at one point refers to an enemy Huron who is about to plunge down a precipice as a "prodigy" (p. 69). An educational treatise written by a doctor and appearing six years after *The Last of the Mohicans* discusses the phenomenon of precocity and provides a compelling if unlikely analogue to Cooper's precipitous native. In his *Remarks on the Influence of Mental Cultivation and Mental Excitement Upon Health*, Dr. Amariah Brigham records the case of a white prodigy, one William M., born in Philadelphia on the Fourth of July, 1820. While still a toddler, William M. astonished those around him with his musical talents, his conversational skills, and his lofty moral sentiments.

According to Brigham, "the heads of great thinkers . . . are wonderfully large." At birth William M.'s head "was of ordinary size," but "very soon, after an attack of dropsy of the brain, it began to grow inordinately." Indeed, by the time the child learned to walk, his head had grown so large that "he was apt to fall, especially forwards, from readily losing his equilibrium." This tendency proved to be more than a minor annoyance. At eight years of age he suffered a precipitous demise — a death both untimely and literally headlong. Losing his balance one day, he fell headfirst against a door, bruised his forehead, "became very sick, and died the next evening." William M.'s fatal loss of equilibrium evinces the thesis advanced in this section of Brigham's treatise, namely, that "mental precocity is generally a symptom of disease; and hence those who exhibit it very frequently, die young." A "passion for books" and other mental excitements may, in the doctor's opinion, presage early death.[4]

The ethnographic subtext of Brigham's thesis (and hence the treatise's relevance to Cooper's novel) becomes more legible when William M.'s story is juxtaposed against Margaret Fuller's discussion of equilibrium and race in her account of a journey into Indian territory in *A Summer on the Lakes* (1844). In fact, the case of William M. reads like a curiously materialist interpretation of what Fuller calls "civilized man['s] larger mind." Fuller sees the difference between "civilized" and "savage" as in part a matter of proportions, a difference of relative development of mind and body. Civilized man "is constantly breaking bounds, in proportion as the mental gets the better of the mere instinctive existence." In the process, however, "he loses in harmony of being what he gains in height and extension; the civilized man is a larger mind but a more imperfect nature than the savage." What Fuller calls "civilized man['s] larger *mind*," Brigham translates into civilized man's larger *head*—but even Fuller's analysis has a materialist component. She asserts that Indian tribes subjugated by whites cease to bear physical resemblance to members of their race as yet uncontaminated by civilization. Unlike other natives, members of conquered tribes, she writes, are "no longer strong, tall, or finely proportioned."[5]

Whereas Fuller imagines that physical degeneration in the form of disproportion is desirable because it fosters spiritual development, Brigham believes in "the necessity of giving more attention to the health and growth of the body, and less to the cultivation of the mind . . . than is now given." But Brigham's concern extends beyond individual bodies and their well-being. Educational treatises published in the U.S. in the antebellum period slide easily from the individual to the race. Brigham's preface declares, "The people of the United States ought to become the most vigorous and powerful race of human beings, both in mind and body, that the world has ever known."[6] William M.'s significant birthplace (Philadelphia) and birthdate (the Fourth of July) render him the local instance of an alleged racial defiance of Brigham's imperialist imperative.

The same entanglement of child-rearing and empire-building surfaces in the work of Catharine Beecher—whose popular advice to housewives and whose former position as head of the prestigious Hartford Female Seminary guaranteed her pedagogy both domestic and institutional influence.[7] Like Brigham, Beecher worried that Anglo-American children were "becoming less and less healthful and good-looking" and that they were every year producing children even "more puny and degenerate" than themselves. Beecher contrasts puny Anglo-Americans with the robust ancient Greeks, who, she asserts, were of a stock so vigorous that they "conquered nearly the whole world."[8] This last comment suggests the way in which early nineteenth-century educational treatises—characteristically if not constitutionally—traverse the discursive registers of home and empire. The figure of the prodigy, one may conclude, organizes into a single discursive economy two distinct cultural arenas expressed through binarisms of feminine and masculine, private and public, suburbia and frontier, sentiment and adventure.[9] Expressing these binarisms in somewhat different terms, I would claim that the prodigy illuminates the affiliations of the micro- and the macro-political.

Michel Foucault supplies a model for uncovering the connections between micro- and macro-politics when (in anticipating objections to his characterization of modern government as "power organized around the management of life rather than the menace of death")[10] he concedes that the modernity of the genocidal might seem to suggest that the life-destroying power of the sovereign not only survived his decapitation but actually *escalated* in the nineteenth and twentieth centuries. Conceiving of modern power as the power to administer life rather than the power to inflict death would seem to require ignoring the genocidal animus which has characterized Western interaction with both Jews and people of color in the modern era. By emphasizing production, Foucauldian theory would seem unable to account for the racial holocausts that have punctuated the modern era and hence would seem necessarily to marginalize (if not to erase altogether) an important part of the history of Jews and the Third World.

Yet, even if race remains a largely undeveloped category of analysis in the history it traces, still *The History of Sexuality* does theorize interracial conflict as an inevitable component of modernity. Foucault asserts that precisely inasmuch as power legitimates and incarnates itself through "the right of the social body to ensure, maintain, or develop its life," racial holocaust becomes "vital" to its expression. Arguing for the simultaneity of productive technologies that promote the well-being of the individual and deductive technologies that ensure the well-being of the race, he writes that in eighteenth- and nineteenth-century Europe "precocious sexuality was presented . . . as an epidemic menace that risked compromising not only the future health of adults but the future of the entire society and species."[11] Modifying Foucault's analysis slightly, I will be locating antebellum representations of the prodigy—a less explicitly sexualized relative of the precocious child—on the discursive axis of two distinctive forms of power in modern Western societies.

Foucault's remarks on genocide unsettle the thumbnail literary history proposed earlier in *The History of Sexuality*. There Foucault proposes that the rise of the micro-political corresponds roughly with the displacement of narratives of adventure by narratives of sentiment: "we have passed from a pleasure to be recounted . . . centering on the heroic . . . narration of 'trials' of bravery . . . to a literature ordered according to the infinite task of extracting [truth] from the depths of oneself."[12] Perhaps one consequence of this statement is that Foucauldian criticism has concentrated on domestic, realist, and sentimental fictions to the neglect of adventure fictions (which, because they so often unfold on borders between "civilized" and "savage," frequently engage questions of the survival of races). Foucauldian New Historicist critics writing about the nineteenth century—particularly, Richard Brodhead, Nancy Armstrong, and D. A. Miller—have constructed the home and its narratives as, in Miller's words, the domain of an "extralegal series of 'micropowers' " and hence the proper sphere for Foucauldian inquiry.[13] But if we take seriously Foucault's comments about the involution of micro- and macro-powers around questions of race, then we would expect to uncover not the superannuation of heroism by sentiment but rather their simultaneity and co-implication. The ease with which educational treatises like Beecher's and Brigham's oscillate from the individual to the race suggests the pertinence of Foucauldian analysis to race relations. Similarly, analysis of the figure of the precipitous aboriginal whose precocity signals his *inevitable* demise in *The Last of the Mohicans* suggests that this type of analysis is as relevant to imperial fictions as it is to domestic ones.

Such a reading of the relation between home and frontier, however, suggests more than the need for simple expansion of the domain of New Historicism. I would like to use this reading as an occasion to interrogate the politics of Foucauldian analysis itself. Uncovering the interaction between micro- and macro-political concerns raises some questions about the gender and racial politics of the Foucauldian "shift" from which New Historicist criticism on the nineteenth century proceeds. A shift from an economy of punishment to one of discipline is not just passively evidenced but rather *actively deployed* in early nineteenth-century U.S. representations of the prodigy. It is not simply that antebellum texts like *The Last of the Mohicans* either prefigure or preempt contemporary theoretical and critical developments (although I *would* claim that New Historicism of the Foucauldian variety has in its discussion of power recapitulated more than it has analyzed an important component of nineteenth-century discourse). More importantly, I would argue that a reading of antebellum texts demonstrates that narratives of the shift from punishment to discipline (like the one Foucauldian New Historicism has given us) have, historically, operated to the detriment of both white middle-class women and people of color. Whatever its politics within its own cultural setting, Foucauldian knowledge does not encounter a political vacuum when it enters contemporary U.S. critical discourse. Instead it meets with a history extending back to the antebellum period in which intellectuals have deployed narratives of a shift in the nature of power toward politically suspicious ends. For this reason contemporary intellectuals in the U.S. whose work has been influenced by Foucault (myself included) need to historicize their own discourse by reconstructing its genealogy and inquiring into the rhetorical work performed by the Foucauldian shift that supplies their work with its hard historical foundations.

Just as Brigham encodes in William M.'s brief life the ethnographic logic supporting an account of the decline of Anglo-Americans, compacted within Cooper's precipitous aboriginal is a logic ensuring the ideological transformation of Native Americans into Vanishing Americans. Despite the spectacular nature of their individual deaths, Cooper's natives, every bit as much as his introductory reference to the "verdure . . . fall[ing] before the nipping frost," expunge imperialist conflict from the Jacksonian cultural memory. They do so by foregrounding issues of proportion and equilibrium so crucial to antebellum accounts of the *disappearance* of races.

Cooper incorporates the racial other as an earlier and now irretrievably lost version of the self. Perhaps this is part of the reason why our culture has come to regard *The Last of the Mohicans* and other nineteenth-century Anglo-American frontier fictions as "children's literature." Just as Freud in his essay on "The Sexual Aberrations" collapses the "primitive" or "archaic" and the infantile,[14] Cooper conflates racial difference and temporal distance on an evolutionary continuum of human history. In other words, it is as though for him aboriginals represent a *phase* that the human race goes through but which it must inevitably *get over*. Regardless of whether the ethno-pedagogic text celebrates equilibrium (in the case of Cooper and Brigham) or disequilibrium (in the case of Fuller), in equating the savage and the juvenile it starts by assuming that certain Americans must vanish.

Cooper's concern with proportion registers his debt to ethno-pedagogic thinking. The novel's white characters marvel over the "perfection of form which abounds among the uncorrupted natives" (p. 53), and the narrator himself praises what he calls Uncas' "beautiful proportions" (p. 275). Uncas is "an unblemished specimen of the noblest proportions of man" and resembles "some precious relic of the Grecian chisel" (p. 53). In the Western tradition the ancient Greeks had long represented the ideal of physical beauty, but in the antebellum U.S. their beautiful proportions had become the *sine qua non* of a call for educational reform. Beecher, for example, launches her critique of the U.S. educational system with the observation that the Greeks "were remarkable, not only for their wisdom and strength, but for their great beauty, so that the statues they made to resemble their own men and women have, ever since, been regarded as the most perfect forms of human beauty." "Perfect forms" here conveys roughly what "beautiful proportions" connotes in Cooper: a balance of intellectual and physical culture —hence Beecher's interest in the Greek educational system as a model for contemporary times. According to her, the Greeks' perfection of form derived from the fact that "[t]hey had two kinds of schools—the one to train the minds, and the other to train the bodies of their children."[15]

Whatever nostalgia Cooper expresses for savage equilibrium in his description of Uncas, he imagines that civilization necessarily spells the end of archaic proportions. Hence Cooper contrasts Uncas' "beautiful proportions" with the white man David Gamut's "rare proportions" (p. 17). Gamut, writes the novelist, possesses "all the bones and joints of other men, without any of their proportions." While Cooper reassures us that Gamut is not actually physically "deformed," his description of Gamut does little to assuage his reader's anxiety on that score: "His head was large; his shoulders narrow; his arms long and dangling; while his hands were small, if not delicate. His legs and thighs were thin nearly to emaciation, but of extraordinary length; and his knees would have been considered tremendous, had they not been outdone by the broader foundations [i.e., his feet] on which this false superstructure of blended human orders, was so profanely reared" (p. 16).

Gamut's peculiar proportions are just one sign that he is the vehicle by which civilization is carried into the wilderness. Around him also accrue linked images of language, femininity, and power. Referring to Gamut's annoying habit of bursting into song whenever the proximity of enemy Indians demands absolute silence (Gamut is a psalmodist by profession), Hawk-eye laments the fact that, as he puts it, although the "Lord never intended that the man should place all his endeavours in his throat," Gamut had "fallen into the hands of some silly woman, when he should have been gathering his education under a blue sky, and among the beauties of the forest" (p. 224).

While perhaps Cooper, like Hawk-eye, believes that God never intended that *man* privilege language at the expense of the development of the body, both seem to believe that the Supreme Being intended that *woman* do so. This is suggested by Cooper's habitual association of feminine control over education in the settlements with both the proliferation of words and with precipitous behavior. For example, as darkness begins to settle on his party's search for clues to the whereabouts of the captive Munro sisters, Hawk-eye advises his companions to abandon the trail until morning. "[I]n the morning," he insists, "we shall be fresh, and ready to undertake our work like men, and not like babbling women, or eager boys" (p. 189).

•   •   •

Cooper's Rousseauvian subtext emerges when one of his noble savages asserts that "Men speak not twice" (p. 314). Real men do not need words because they have physical strength. Women and precocious sons, however, require verbal prosthetics to get what they want. Furthermore, for Cooper words represent a whole economy of power marked as feminine. Thus, after declaring himself a warrior not a reader, Hawk-eye asserts that he, unlike Gamut, is no "whimpering boy, at the apron string of one of your old gals" (p. 117). Free of books, Hawk-eye liberates himself from the power that nineteenth-century domesticity gave to women—liberates himself from what Leslie Fiedler calls the "gentle tyranny of home and woman."[16] Hence when Gamut demands that Hawk-eye buttress one of his numerous philosophical speculations with some authoritative textual prop, the enraged scout demands: "[W]hat have such as I, who am a warrior of the wilderness . . . to do with books! I never read but in one [that is, the book of nature], and the words that are written there are too simple and too plain to need much schooling" (p. 117). I would argue that the fiction of the "plainness" of the book of nature in this passage supports another fiction: that of the legibility of paternal power imagined as simple physical force. Cooper attempts to differentiate between knowledge gained from experience on the trail and "bookish knowledge" (p. 189) in order to create the fiction of power relations "plain" as nature itself.

Both the disregard for books and the association of them with the newly-empowered antebellum woman are staples of the period. Although *the book* is usually associated with the reign of the father, in the antebellum period *books* seem to be associated with the reign of the mother. The pervasiveness of this association is suggested by Thoreau's chapter on "Reading" in *Walden*. There the author expresses his disgust not just over the *quality* of popular books but also over their *quantity*. Embedded within Thoreau's anxiety about multiplicity lies an anxiety about the mother's assumption of the educational duties formerly administered by the father—or so Thoreau's confusion of mechanical production and female sexual reproduction leads one to suspect.

Thoreau confuses the printing press with the womb when he derides the "modern cheap and fertile press." Machine-like literary mothers produce not only insubstantial volumes (like the popular series called "Little Reading," which the author came across one day in his local library); they also produce insubstantial people. Thoreau characterizes the readers of "Little Reading" as themselves little, like the "modern puny and degenerate race" described by Beecher. They are "pygmies and manikins" and "a race of tit-men." Thoreau distinguishes this modern race from the archaic, athletic, and robust race of men nurtured by literary fathers before the age of mechanical reproduction. According to "Reading," in a heroic age long past it "require[d] a training such as the athletes underwent" to read literature. Whereas the modern press is "fertile," "the heroic writers of antiquity" produced works which were "solitary."[17]

Thoreau's opposition of the feminine, the diminutive, and the multiple against the masculine, the massive, and the singular services a Rousseauvian distinction between power conceived of as a physical force and power conceived of as verbal and sentimental manipulation. The *solidity* of the paternal book in "Reading" symbolizes the visibility of power relations under the patriarch, and the robustness of the (male) reader of the (male) classics denotes his ability both to see and to fight whatever threatens his autonomy. Hence Thoreau writes that, even if read in translation (in what he calls "our *mother* tongue") the massive "heroic books" are written in a language alien to the modern reader. They "will always be in a language dead to degenerate times," and therefore they require their readers to seek "laboriously . . . the meaning of each word and line." The laboriousness of the reading preserves the autonomy of the subject. The classics speak in a "*father* tongue, a reserved and select expression" that does not compromise volition because, rather than lulling the reader to sleep, it demands that he "devote [his] most alert and wakeful hours" to reading. By contrast, we learn our "mother tongue . . . unconsciously" and hence read popular books like sleepwalkers. In "Reading" the smallness of books written by women suggests not just their trivial contents, but also the microscopic scale of maternal power. Thoreau's comment that readers of little books are "machines" anticipates the Foucauldian anxiety over a power whose invisibility (accomplished through domestication, decentering, and proliferation) only augments its efficiency.[18]

Although Thoreau's chapter reads like an attempt to disempower the domestic woman, the same disparaging association of mass-production and female generativity made by Thoreau surfaces even in the texts apparently most instrumental in instituting the reign of the mother. Domestic ideology's demonic double, what Michael Paul Rogin dubs "momism,"[19] is if anything even more evident in the work of Hannah More, the British author generally credited with the founding of domestic ideology. Her influential treatise on female education was reprinted in numerous editions in the U.S. between 1800 and 1826 and helped determine the shape of domesticity in this country as well as in Britain.

In *Strictures on the Modern System of Female Education*, More, like Thoreau, expresses anxiety about the quantity of "little books" on the market. "Real" knowledge and piety, she writes, have suffered from "that profusion of little, amusing, sentimental books with which the youthful library overflows."[20] After questioning the pedagogical value of multiplying the number of books students read, More is overcome by a proto-Malthusian vision of the uncontrollably generative popular press. She writes: "Who are those ever multiplying authors, that with unparalleled fecundity are overstocking the world with their quick-succeeding progeny? They are the novel-writers; the easiness of whose productions is at once the cause of their own fruitfulness, and of the almost infinitely numerous race of imitators, to whom they give birth." More's nightmare vision collapses the mechanical production increasingly characterizing the book industry with female sexual reproduction. Mass-production of children (the creation of a "race of imitators") is the evil twin of domestic ideology's attempt to standardize child-rearing practices. The hys-

teria over the abundance of books in the antebellum period both represents and creates an anxiety over the violation of the independence of
the subject by disciplinary methods directed at the interior rather than
at the body. An anxiety over the decorporealization of power compels
the advice offered time and again in educational treatises in the early
nineteenth century: more emphasis should be placed upon the cultivation
of the juvenile body and less upon the development of the juvenile mind.
The excessively cerebral Anglo-Saxon in More's text stands on the verge
of disappearing as power disappears. The Anglo-Saxon race, she writes,
is threatened with the same "quick succession of slavery, effeminacy, . . .
vice, . . . and degeneracy" that overtook the inhabitants of ancient
Rome.[21]

For Cooper, to read in the book of nature is to be educated through
the paternal apprenticeship system rather than the maternal representational system. Cooper suggests this when at one point in the narrative
Chingachgook and Hawk-eye lose Magua's trail. Uncas, who has long
since uncovered the proper path, nevertheless assumes a "calm and
dignified demeanour" suggestive of "dependen[ce] on the sagacity and
intelligence of the seniors of the party" (p. 213). Savage society, in
Cooper as in Rousseau, does not produce prodigies. According to the
novelist, when members of Indian tribes convene to confer on matters
important to the whole community, "there is never to be found any
impatient aspirant after premature distinction, standing ready to move
his auditors to some hasty, and, perhaps, injudicious discussion, in order
that his own reputation may be the gainer. An act of so much precipitancy and presumption, would seal the downfall of precocious intellect
for ever. It rested solely with the oldest and most experienced of the men
to lay the subject of the conference before the people" (p. 292). Indian
society then offers a highly visible version of power. According to the
narrator, the power of the Indian leader is the power of physical force:
"the authority of an Indian chief [is] so little conventional, that it [is]
oftener maintained by physical superiority, than by any moral supremacy he might possess" (p. 92).

If basing power on physical superiority prevents aboriginal precocity,
it also makes the patriarch's control over the tribe tenuous. Even Cooper's most noble savages seem barely restrained by the father. Uncas'
"dignified and calm demeanor" disappears at a moment's notice. As
soon as Chingachgook solicits his help, Uncas bounds "forward like a
deer" and directs his elders to the proper trail (p. 213). The young

Mohican's sudden shift from rock-like self-restraint to frenetic activity is one that characterizes natives whether represented individually or in groups. Such fluctuations in Indian demeanor suggest what Cooper imagines as the fundamental exteriority to the self of power legitimated by physical superiority. Despite its patriarchal nature, Indian government permits radical independence because, like the authority exercised by Foucault's sovereign, that restraint is imagined to be of a strictly corporeal nature.

Fiedler's "gentle tyranny," on the other hand, would subvert radical native independence and undermine native proportions. This is in fact what happens to Uncas. Aware at some level of Uncas' admiration of her, Cora gains an "intuitive consciousness of her power" over the young Mohican (p. 79). Like the ethnologists of his day, Cooper believed Indians experienced no romantic passion.[22] Hence he calls Uncas' enamored ministrations to Cora both a "departure from the dignity of his manhood" and an "utter innovation on . . . Indian customs" (p. 56). His love "elevate[s] him far above the intelligence, and advance[s] him . . . centuries before the practices of his nation" (p. 115).

It seems that Cooper imagines that Cora's gentle tyranny "seal[s] the downfall" of Uncas' "precocious intellect." Falling under Cora's power, educated without his knowledge, Uncas dies a racial prodigy. Hawk-eye notes the Mohican's uncharacteristic precipitancy during their search for the captive Munro sisters. He chastises Uncas for suddenly becoming "as impatient as a man in the settlements" (p. 185). The noble savage turned eager savage repeatedly puts himself at risk in pursuing the captive Cora Munro: "In vain Hawk-eye called to him to respect the covers; the young Mohican braved the dangerous fire of his enemies, and soon compelled them to a flight as swift as his own headlong speed" (p. 334).

Significantly, it is this precocious development under woman's invisible tutelage that makes Uncas the *last* of the Mohicans. At the end of the novel, he stands upon a ledge overlooking Magua who is threatening Cora with a tomahawk. The impassioned Mohican leaps "frantically, from a fearful height" and falls between Magua and his intended victim, but only to fall victim himself to his enemy's tomahawk (p. 337). Cooper reports Magua's headlong death at Hawk-eye's hands on the very next page of the novel and the language of precipitancy, the reiteration of the image of the headlong Indian, encourages us to confuse the two red men. Invoking the antebellum figure of the prodigy, Cooper's text replaces

Hawk-eye's rifle with the middle-class woman's apron strings.[23] It translates firepower into mother power.

The Last of the Mohicans deflects attention from the macropolitical realm represented in the text by the army (for which Hawk-eye is a scout), and upon women falls the responsibility for the *disappearance* of the native. But the prodigy's presence does more than deflect. The threat that woman's invisible power poses to the male subject produces the need for some space (the frontier) to elude her miasmic influence and hence makes imperative the macro-political controls effecting Indian removal from contiguous territories. In other words Cooper's "discovery" of the discipline deployed against his white men legitimates the technologies of punishment deployed against his red men.

Antebellum discourse, I have argued, uses images of the modern proliferation of words as a sign that feminine words have replaced masculine muscle as the basis of authority. Momist imagery of the loss of autonomy resulting from this feminization of power expresses nostalgia for a form of power whose lack of psychic consequences guarantees that it does not compromise the autonomy of the male subject. Yet neither this subject nor this form of power ever existed. Because it is administered and experienced by human agents, even "simple" brute force must have psychic consequences and must produce subjectivities particular to it.

The myth of simple brute force in antebellum discourse generates what Renato Rosaldo calls "imperialist nostalgia." "When the so-called civilizing process destablizes forms of life," writes Rosaldo, "the agents of change experience transformations of other cultures as if they were personal losses."[24] Developing Rosaldo's point, Amy Kaplan suggests that such nostalgia makes aggression against Third World peoples the logical consequence of anti-feminism directed against First World women because in it "the empire figures as the site where you can be all that you can no longer be at home—a 'real live man'—where you can recover the autonomy denied by social forces of modernization, often aligned in this way of thinking with feminization."[25]

Following Rosaldo and Kaplan, I would argue that in our own time scholarship on the alleged feminization of society itself participates in the imperialist nostalgia of the discourse it analyzes. Traditionally, momist texts like Cooper's were seen as evidence of a historical "feminization of American culture" in which expanded female leisure and literacy permitted Hawthorne's "scribbling women" to usurp the cultural offices once occupied by less prolific but more profound male authors.[26] More recently, New Historicist criticism of the Foucauldian variety has encouraged us to regard the feminization of culture as a symptom of a larger feminization of power. Yet, the novelty of New Historicism does not reside in its emphasis on power. Earlier cultural analysis also equated feminization with normalization. Richard Brodhead's recent characterization of the modern ideal of maternal love as a power whose "silken threads are harder to burst than the iron chains of authority" employed by "old-style paternal discipline" recalls Fiedler's analysis of the rise of a "gentle tyranny of home and woman" in the nineteenth century.[27] D. A. Miller's revelation of a nineteenth-century "field of power relations" masquerading as a "domesticating pedagogy" harkens back to Ann Douglas' discussion of the "manifold possibilities" offered by Victorian maternal influence for "devious social control."[28] Nancy Armstrong's assertion that domestic ideology provided the "logic" that permitted women to enter the world of work through social services and thereby extended "subtle techniques of domestic surveillance beyond the middle-class home and into the lives of those much lower down on the economic ladder" mirrors Christopher Lasch's claim that the "rise of the 'helping professions' " allowed "society in the guise of a 'nurturing mother' [to invade] the family, the stronghold of . . . private rights."[29]

Neither the poststructuralist upheaval that divides the cultural analysis of the 1960s and 1970s from that of the 1980s nor the feminist critiques to which these analyses have been subjected have altered the basic narrative: normalization is still women's work. What is even more startling is that this narrative appears to date back to antebellum times. Yet, the failure of New Historicists to articulate a genuinely novel reading of the nineteenth century troubles me far less than their apparent obliviousness to the rhetorical content of what they present as historical facts.[30] Even if exposing the rhetorical work of Foucauldian history does not *in and of itself* undermine the facticity of New Historicist claims (all facts require human interpreters and so all truth is necessarily rhetorical), still its practitioners cannot possibly hope to direct their own rhetoric toward progressive ends without first inquiring into the gender and race politics perpetuated by their use of Foucauldian knowledge.[31]

New Historicists' dependence upon Foucault's narrative of modernization would seem to account for their apparent obliviousness to the way in which they have been engaged in the retelling of a politically suspect nineteenth-century narrative of modernization. Despite the emphasis I have put on it, Foucault's assertion that the West's commitment to managing the life of its own population also entails a commitment to massive destruction of populations designated as "other" is parenthetical to the history outlined in the first volume of *The History of Sexuality*. Whereas his brief comments on modern racial holocausts suggest the simultaneity of deductive and productive manifestations of power, Foucault's larger historical narrative (as represented by both *The History of Sexuality* and *Discipline and Punish*) is founded upon a temporal distinction between them such that the deductive (punishment) represents the pre-modern and the productive (discipline), the modern form of power. Hence Foucault's own narrative is subject to the same critique to which I have subjected antebellum narratives of modernization. Inasmuch as he defines modernity as the decorporealization of power, he participates in the construction of an utterly mythic time in which authority represented simple physical superiority. Foucault's temporalization of the difference between discipline and punishment suggests that even contemporary images of modernity collaborate in the production of the imperialist nostalgia I have been describing.

NOTES

1. Brian W. Dippie, *The Vanishing American: White Attitudes and U.S. Indian Policy* (Middletown, Conn.: Wesleyan Univ. Press, 1982), p. 2. Dippie borrows the phrase from G. Harrison Orians, *The Cult of the Vanishing American A Century View* (Toledo, Ohio: H. J. Chittenden, 1934).

My own essay grows out of talks I gave in 1988 at the University of California at Los Angeles, Northwestern University, Princeton University, the University of Rochester, and at the annual meeting of the American Studies Association in Miami Beach, Florida. The current version is based on talks delivered at the University of Texas, Austin, in 1989 and at a conference sponsored by The Center for the Critical Analysis of Contemporary Culture at Rutgers University in 1990. I wish to thank Ann Cvetkovich, Walter Michaels, Jeff Nunokawa, Michael Rogin, Eric Sundquist, and Lynn Wardley—each of whom offered indispensible advice on one of the multitude of earlier drafts of this essay.

2. *The Last of the Mohicans: A Narrative of 1757* (Albany, N.Y.: State Univ. of New York Press, 1983), pp. 6–7. Hereafter quotations will be taken from this edition and cited parenthetically in the text.

3. In fact, the rise of the cult of the Vanishing American corresponds roughly

with the rise of the U.S. government's policy of Indian Removal, a massive military campaign of systematic dispossession and effective extermination begun in the late 1820s. According to Francis Paul Prucha in *The Great Father: The United States Government and the American Indians* (Lincoln: Univ. of Nebraska Press, 1984), "the military phase of Indian relations" would not end until the early 1880s (p. 560). Thus we see just how much effort went into effecting the "inevitable."

4. *Remarks on the Influence of Mental Cultivation and Mental Excitement Upon Health*, 2nd ed. (Boston: Marsh, Capen & Lyon, 1833; rpt. New York: Arno, 1973), pp. 49, 42, 36, 45.

5. *Summer on the Lakes, in 1843* (Boston: Charles C. Little and James Brown; New York: Charles S. Francis, 1844), pp. 221, 182.

6. Brigham, pp. vii, viii.

7. For a relevant discussion of the intersecting rhetoric of domesticity and imperialism see Amy Kaplan, "Romancing the Empire: The Embodiment of American Masculinity in the Popular Historical Novel of the 1890s," *American Literary History*, 2 (1990), 659–90.

8. *Letters to the People on Health and Happiness* (New York: Harper & Row, 1855), pp. 8, 10, 8.

9. The criticism on the Leatherstocking tales has played a crucial role in establishing for us a sense of ideological distance between the frontier and the home. Since D. H. Lawrence's famous analysis of Cooper's Leatherstocking series appeared in 1923, Cooper criticism has taken as one of its perennial themes the anti-feminine (if not outright misogynist) sensibility compelling Natty Bumppo's flight from the civilized society of women into the savage society of the red man. See, for example, Lawrence's *Studies in Classic American Literature* (Garden City, N.Y.: Doubleday, 1951) and Leslie A. Fiedler's *Love and Death in the American Novel* (New York: Meridian, 1960).

10. *The History of Sexuality, Volume I: An Introduction,* trans. Robert Hurley (New York: Vintage, 1980), p. 147.

11. Foucault, pp. 136–37, 146.

12. *Ibid.*, p. 59.

13. *The Novel and the Police* (Berkeley and Los Angeles: Univ. of California Press, 1988), p. viii.

14. Freud writes, "In inverted types, a predominance of archaic constitutions and primitive psychical mechanisms is regularly to be found." See "The Sexual Aberrations" in *Three Essays on the Theory of Sexuality,* trans. and revised by James Strachey (New York: Basic Books, 1962), p. 12n. My belief in the relevance of the Freudian developmental narrative to genocidal thinking grows out of discussions with Jeff Nunokawa about his work on the figure of the doomed male homosexual in British Victorian literature.

15. Beecher, p. 8.

16. Fiedler, p. 189.

17. *Walden* in *Walden and Civil Disobedience,* ed. Owen Thomas (New York: Norton, 1966), pp. 72, 68.

18. Thoreau, pp. 67 (my italics), 68 (my italics), 70, 68, 71.

19. "Momism" is Rogin's term for a "demonic version of domestic ideology" that expresses anxiety over the "maternal power generated by domesticity." Whereas Rogin discusses momism as a twentieth-century response to the revival of the domestic ideal in the 1950s, I am suggesting that domesticity and its demonic double arose simultaneously in the antebellum period. See Michael Paul Rogin, "Kiss Me Deadly: Communism, Motherhood, and Cold War Movies," *Representations,* No. 6 (1984), 6–7.

20. *Strictures on the Modern System of Female Education,* 3rd American ed. (Boston: Joseph Bumstead, 1802), p. 97. My argument here has been influenced by Mark Seltzer's analysis of the deployment of gender in literary naturalism in his "The Naturalist Machine" in *Sex, Politics, and Science in the Nineteenth-Century Novel,* ed. Ruth Bernard Yeazell (Baltimore: Johns Hopkins Univ. Press, 1986), 116–47.

21. More, pp. 104, 48.

22. In *White Over Black: American Attitudes Toward the Negro, 1550–1812* (Chapel Hill: Univ. of North Carolina Press, 1968), Winthrop D. Jordan notes that early U.S. ethnographers frequently represented the Native American as "deficient in ardor and virility" (p. 162). Cooper's contemporary Lewis Henry Morgan claimed that "the passion of love was entirely unknown among" the Iroquois. See Morgan's *League of the Iroquois* (1851; rpt. New York: Corinth, 1962), p. 322.

23. My identification of Cora with the middle-class woman is complicated by the fact that, even though she has been raised white, she is in fact mulatta—the product of the British imperialist effort in the West Indies. It might be more accurate to say that Cora represents the Third World woman through whose agency the colonial power exerts its influence. In Frantz Fanon's analysis of "the colonialist program" in Algeria, "it was the woman who was given the historic mission of shaking up the Algerian man." One could argue that Cora performs a similar function for Uncas. Fanon's analysis appears in *A Dying Colonialism* (New York: Grove, 1965), p. 39, and is quoted in Kaplan, 673.

24. Renato Rosaldo, "Imperialist Nostalgia," in *Culture and Truth: The Remaking of Social Analysis* (Boston: Beacon Press, 1989), p. 70.

25. Kaplan, p. 664.

26. The classic statement of this position is, of course, Ann Douglas' *The Feminization of American Culture* (New York: Avon, 1977). For a more developed critique of claims for the feminization of U.S. culture in this period, see my essay "Domesticity and Fiction" in *The Columbia History of the American Novel,* ed. Emory Elliott (New York: Columbia Univ. Press, 1991).

27. "Sparing the Rod: Discipline and Fiction in Antebellum America," *Representations*, No. 21 (1988), 87. Actually, this characterization of maternal love appears in an antebellum publication entitled *Mother's Magazine,* which Brodhead quotes; however, it is clear in context that Brodhead regards the quote as an accurate description of maternal authority.

28. Miller, p. 10; Douglas, p. 81.

29. *Desire and Domestic Fiction: A Political History of the Novel* (New York: Oxford Univ. Press, 1987), p. 93; Christopher Lasch, *Haven in a Heartless World: The Family Besieged* (New York: Basic Books, 1977), p. 18.

30. I admit that "obliviousness" is probably too strong a word to use in Armstrong's case. On p. 26 of the introduction to her book she manifests a good deal of self-consciousness about the gender politics of her own claims, even if she seems not to recognize the way in which they implicate her in the historical discourse she analyzes.

31. Previous feminist critiques of New Historicism include Judith Lowder Newton, "History as Usual?: Feminism and the 'New Historicism,' " in *The New Historicism,* ed. H. Aram Veeser (New York: Routledge, 1989), pp. 152–67 and Carolyn Porter, "Are We Being Historical Yet?" *South Atlantic Quarterly,* 87 (1988), 743–86. For reasons I explain in my article "Bio-Political Resistance in Domestic Ideology and *Uncle Tom's Cabin*" (*American Literary History,* 1 [1989], 715–34), I do not endorse the view shared by Newton and Porter that by subscribing to theory that (in Newton's words) "den[ies] the possibility of change and agency" (p. 118) New Historicism disallows the possibility of political resistance.

Chapter 3

Seeing Sentiment
Photography, Race, and the Innocent Eye

Laura Wexler

Introduction by Werner Sollors

In 1946, Richard Wright selected Gertrude Stein's "Melanctha" for the book with the wonderful title *I Wish I Had Written That*. It would also be an appropriate title for the present collection, which is based on some critics' responses to the editors' request to present exemplary, innovative, and interdisciplinary essays in the field of American literary studies. In choosing an essay that lives up to an interdisciplinary American Studies tradition, I was drawn to the work of a scholar who examines and advances the concept of "sentimentalism" in American literary history, focuses centrally on photography, and simultaneously employs, with excellent results, the often maligned "race-class-and-gender" approach to its subject.

Laura Wexler brings to this topic a long-standing and sophisticated engagement with photography. An essay in *Prospects* of 1988 was devoted to the photographer Frances Benjamin Johnson and her work on black and Indian students at the Hampton Institute; and Wexler's reading of the images included questions bearing on the relationship with literature (the no-longer-canonical Whittier, for example, who appears in one of the photographs), with ethnic representation from an external vantage point (showing students who seem "uniformly eager, virtuous, energetic, and receptive"), and the somewhat contradictory "matter of gender" (in one of Johnson's self-portraits as an un-"ladylike" artist, smoking and revealing her legs and her petticoat).

Another, and perhaps the most famous, of Wexler's essays, "Tender Violence: Literary Eavesdropping, Domestic Fiction, and Educational reform" (1992) maps and negotiates the famous Ann Douglas/Jane Tompkins dispute about the nature of nineteenth-century sentimentalism (was it the pathway to debased and uncritical mass consumer culture or the source of women's power and agency?). Setting a new standard for studies of sentimentalism, Wexler points out that both Douglas and Tompkins stayed within Victorian notions of a white, middle-class, Christian, native-born readership. She, instead, proposes to interpret the "expansive, imperial project of sentimentalism" as meaning the "externalized aggression" toward different classes and races who could not easily participate in the culture of domestic ideals except as its objects. One of Wexler's examples of this sentimental dilemma is Zitkala-Sa (portrayed in a famous photograph by Gertrude Käsebier). Wexler convincingly reads Zitkala-Sa's autobiographical writings as a response to the way in which the Indian school the Dakota Sioux woman attended enforced her conformity to American sentimental culture. "Sentimental 'power' struck its victims differently from its middle-class audience," Wexler concludes.

It is from a background of such concerns—reading photographs and literary texts together and worrying about the often conflicting categories of race, class, and gender—that Wexler turned to "Seeing Sentiment: Photography, Race, and the Innocent Eye." The 1997 essay, the main part of which is reprinted below, emerged in the context of a collection on psychoanalysis, race, and feminism; and its preamble (not reprinted here) makes these links explicit.

Wexler begins "Seeing Sentiment" with a brief reflection on the term ekphrasis (the Greek word for putting words to an image) and offers a close reading of a photograph that has become quite familiar to Americanists and general audiences interested in American slavery. Perhaps it has become so familiar as an illustration that it has not really been analyzed as an image. It has variously been called "a nursemaid and her charge" or "former slave with white child." Wexler's detailed iconographic reading of the photograph raises questions that lead her, as a good cultural studies detective, to the specific historical contexts of the image. Who was the photographer and what was his project? Who was the child? How did the photograph of the unnamed "nursemaid" compare with pictures of the photographer's wife? Was this photograph a "mirror" and part of a "democratic medium"? Or was it an ideological tool for the perpetuation of inequalities? How did servants tend to appear in other nineteenth-century family portraits? How did photographs of slaves relate to contemporary proslavery and "mammy" poems?

In addressing and answering such questions, Wexler leaves no stone unturned. She places the image both in the Christian tradition of portraying the Madonna and child and in the context of Orlando Patterson's understanding of slavery as "social death." She incorporates the history and theory of photography, the genre of the family photograph, and the specifics that are known about the photographer and his family. She unearths a mammy poem written by a family friend of the photographer, lets poem and image interact with each other, and suggests that the nursemaid comes to represent earthly care while her (absent) mistress stands for eternal love. She contemplates the infamous slave daguerreotypes that were made for ethnological purposes only to look more closely at her central photograph, observing this time that there is fabric draped around the nursemaid's shoulder, "as if she were a chair," so as to make a better backdrop for the baby's head.

Wexler's rich contextualization will impress archivally oriented readers; and she also forces cultural studies practitioners to reflect on their own blind spots. While the research behind this essay is extensive, the concentrated focus on the image at hand never dissolves the photograph into previously known generalities. Inspired by a wide range of theoretical sources, Wexler does not simply "apply" any preexisting theoretical model to her reading of American photography and literature but instead develops these models dialectically from the materials. She subjects these materials to a very careful examination that combines close reading (derived from literary training) and attention to detail and nuance with a keen sense of historical contexts, aesthetic possibilities, and social constraints. And she confronts the difficulty of reading a photograph and struggling for a meaning that does not come, as Alan Trachtenberg put it, "intact and whole." Readers of Laura Wexler's "Seeing Sentiment" begin to feel as if they were looking at a familiar photograph, *really* looking at it, for the first time.

———————————————

Our white sisters
radical friends
love to own pictures of us
sitting at a factory machine
wielding a machete
in our bright bandanas
holding brown yellow black red
   children
reading books from literacy campaigns
holding machine guns bayonets bombs
   knives

Our white sisters
radical friends
should think
again.
—Jo Carrillo,
   And When You Leave, Take
   Your Pictures with You

THE GREEKS had a word, *ekphrasis,* that we don't have, which designated an art that we also don't have—the virtuoso skill of putting words to images. Writing a while ago in the *New York Times,* John Updike reported his joy on discovering this word, for it named what had long been an insistent but faintly embarrassing passion of his and made it seem legitimate. Similarly, Bryan Wolf recently came out in the *Yale Journal of Criticism* as a "closet ekphrastic . . . [hurling] caution and nicety of distinction to the winds . . . and [arguing] both for the rhetoricity of all art and the ideological work performed by all rhetoric."[1] But ecstatic ekphrastics hardly ever turn to photographs. Not one of the readings legitimated by Greek paternity in Updike's book of essays on art, *Just Looking,* is of a photograph, for instance, even though Updike devotes the entire lead essay to the Museum of Modern Art (MoMA) ("What MoMA Done Tole Me") and the MoMA he remembers haunting for an unforgettable twenty months between August 1955 and April 1957 housed at that time what was arguably one of the most important collections and display spaces of photographs in the country.[2]

Serge Guilbaut and Christopher Phillips have pretty well demonstrated that, through its cooperation with the government and its curatorship of the photography collection at that time, MoMA turned itself into one of the country's most productive bastions of cold war ideological politics.[3] Perhaps it is too much to have expected John Updike to have noticed any of this, even though he was there during the very months that the *Family of Man* exhibition was installed in MoMA and was drawing enormous crowds of visitors; it subsequently toured Europe, Asia, and Latin America, traveling for over two years. The *Family of Man* exhibition was an anthology of images edited to show the universality of daily human life all over the world, a universality that purportedly revolves around utterly dehistoricized, utterly naturalized experiential categories such as "birth," "death," "work," "knowledge," and "play." Supported by quotations from "primitive" proverbs or verses from the Bible, the message of this spectacle, sent by the American government all over the world, was that we are all one family.[4]

But Updike's neglect of these photographs while attending to the more prestigious realm of high art painting suggests more than a personal lapse. It represents a critical tendency that is not Updike's alone, and it suggests the need of inventing another term, *anekphrasis,* coined from its opposite. Photographic *anekphrasis* would describe an active and selective refusal to read photography—its graphic labor, its social spaces—even while, at the same time, one is busy textualizing and contextualizing all other kinds of cultural documents.[5]

Photographic anekphrasis is not innocuous. The comparative dearth of critical attention to the social productions of the photographic image is a class- and race-based form of cultural domination. It represses the antidemocratic potential of photography and distorts the history of the significance of race and gender in the construction of the visual field. The dynamic meanings of cultural forms produced and marketed since the mid-nineteenth century simply cannot be fully adduced without concurrent attention to the way in which those cultural forms have used photography to naturalize and enforce their message. One might even go so far as to say that photographic anekphrasis itself is an institutionalized form of racism and sexism, insofar as photography has always been deeply involved in constituting the discourse of the same.

Cultural theory is not guilty of photographic anekphrasis overall. Indeed, feminism has sustained a major critical engagement with the photographic image. No one has ever attributed more social power to photography than the antipornography movement. In addition, crucial questions about the commodification of representations of women's bodies in advertising; the cultural enforcement of women's positioning as representation, as image; and the reconstruction of a basis for female spectatorship that moves out from under the dominion of the "male gaze"—all have had their most serious considerations within feminist analysis of photography and film. Yet even within this significant enlargement of the critical gaze, feminist interpretation has often made it seem as if issues of gender and sexuality can be separated analytically from those of race and class.[6] While the feminist movement has been brilliantly effective in forcing discussion of the domination and objectification of women by men, it has been relatively silent about the internal dynamics of objectification within its own ranks, woman over woman, and about the ways in which women themselves have gained and lost from the race- and class-based power differentials among men. Second-wave U.S. feminism allowed the image of the middle-class white woman to circulate as the signifier of the category "woman." The third wave has made an effort to claim the gaze of "third world women." But gender distribution is not the same thing as race distinction. The notion that they are parallel inequalities and that an analysis of the sexism of photographic practice will automatically yield a model for thinking about race as a category of difference is one of feminism's *anekphrases*. Thus, although feminism sees photographs, it has become a question, frankly, of just what is it that feminism sees.

Antebellum sentimentality in the United States was a theory of gender. It held that differences among the domestic lives of peoples were natural, rather than historical, divisions, and that a new education in white domesticity was necessary for nondominant peoples to rise in the scale of evolution toward a greater capacity for self-government through the acquisition of greater self-control. That is in good part why twentieth-century white feminist criticism has been able to retrieve so successfully the sentimental writings of the "Other" American Renaissance.[7] *Both* forms of cultural critique—domestic ideology in the nineteenth century and feminist theory in the twentieth—largely bracket the history of the racialized female gaze in an unarticulated insistence on the specificity of gender.

However, sentimentality left another record of these operations—in photographs. Through them it is possible to see around the edges of its masquerade as nature and into the dynamic of its production of difference. After the abolition of slavery and throughout the post–Civil War period, photography was part of the master narrative that created and cemented new cultural and political inequalities of race and class by manipulating the sign "woman" as an indicator of "civilization." Seeing sentiment in domestic photographs is one way of exposing the internal dynamics within which the subsequent imperial exchange of signs went forward.

We do not know the name of the Cooks' nursemaid or even exactly when George Cook took her photograph, which has been variously dated as circa 1865, and 1868.[8] The photograph is a paper image made from a glass negative, a technology that would support any of these dates. Joan Severa's analysis of the nursemaid's clothing, offered in *Dressed for the Photographer,* which reprinted the photograph in 1995, likewise supports either of these dates.[9] The negative is currently housed within the George Cook archive at the Valentine Museum in Richmond, Virginia, among the rest of Cook's family and business papers and memorabilia.[10]

That it was a domestic image displayed within the house, not simply any image of a domestic, is the supposition I have chosen. But it is at least within the realm of possibility, although it seems unlikely, that it was a carte de visite like the one Sojourner Truth ordered made of herself to mark (and financially support) her life in freedom.[11] Or, it could also have been a personal photograph like the one Harriet Jacobs had made of herself, as a way of "owning herself," after her escape to the North from slavery.[12]

The fact that the Cook archive contains at least two more images of women identified as "nursemaids" with family babies argues against the nursemaid's control over her own representation, however. Quite the contrary, it suggests that it was Cook who thought to make the image and wanted to keep it as a personal record of the domestic nature of his home, even if, at the same time, he gave a copy of this record to the "nursemaid" herself. The fact that this is a sentimental image of the nursemaid's labor and not of her own family also works against the idea that the young woman chose it in freedom to represent her own domestic life. Neither Sojourner Truth nor Harriet Jacobs, for instance, two black women concerned to establish the visible demeanor of emancipation, picture freedom as having anything to do with white infant "charges."

I take the "Nursemaid and Her Charge" to be a rhetorical figure in a white ambition that sought to establish the relative social weight of black and white domesticity in the immediate post-emancipation years. When we pair the nursemaid with a contemporary photograph that George Cook made of his own wife, an image that I will also analyze, we can begin to see how all three figures—"nursemaid," "baby," and "mother"—play interdigitated roles in Cook's manipulation of what Roland Barthes called the "empire of signs." They are actual people who have been photographed, but they are also symbolic constructions that produced the highly political meaning of post–Civil War white domesticity.

In "Nursemaid and Her Charge," the young woman sits for the camera in a good striped dress with a white collar. A small, simple broach is pinned exactly at the meeting place of the two starched white points of the collar, which rise up slightly from the surface of her dress. Formally, with its quiet precision, its simplification of background space, its tonal balance, its graphic playfulness, and its flat, tight framing of the figure, this image reflects the long tradition of plain-style American portraiture that unites the primitive folk art practices of the early itinerant portrait-ists like Ammi Phillips and Erastus Salisbury Field with the vernacular masterpiece daguerrcotypes made by J. S. Plumbe and by Southworth and Hawes.

Iconographically, this image also relates to a long symbolic tradition in Western art of portraying the Madonna and Child. This tradition is a tribute to the highest achievement that womanhood can attain in Christian culture and a paean to the actual woman who occupies that mythical role. As Julia Kristeva writes in "Motherhood According to Bellini," "craftsmen of Western art have revealed better than anyone else the artist's debt to the maternal body and/or motherhood's entry into symbolic existence."

·   ·   ·

As in this photograph, the painted Madonna is often rendered in vivid detail. Also as in this photograph, the attentive "truthlikeness" to the materiality of the figure being depicted often blends into some other unidentifiable expression, one that is "unrepresentable" or disengaged. Painted Madonnas are often holding the baby Jesus but looking away. In this averted gaze, Kristeva notes, "the maternal body slips away from the discursive hold" to become "a sacred beyond."[13]

It used to be only artists' models or wealthy, aristocratic women who could see themselves painted in this role, but the discovery of photography in the nineteenth century allowed millions of ordinary mothers to have images of themselves made in that virginal and compelling guise. On the strength of its formal and symbolic characteristics alone this photograph belongs in the procession of religiously influenced American art. And like the Catholic paintings of the Madonna that, as Lynn Wardley has argued, the Protestant Harriet Beecher Stowe urged her readers to hang upon the walls of their homes to signal the sisterhood of spirit and the communal reservoir of art that nurtured faith no matter of what denomination, this photograph formally considered would be an upholder of the canons of domestic sentiment.[14]

However, "a nursemaid and her charge" (as this photograph is entitled in *We Are Your Sisters,* edited by Dorothy Sterling) or "former slave with white child" (as it is captioned in *Labor of Love, Labor of Sorrow,* by Jacqueline Jones) is not an image of the vaunted female icon of Christian humanism, nor is it an example of popular folk art; merely to repeat such a formal, iconographic analysis would be deeply misleading. In fact, this image ironizes both the self-absorption that Kristeva refer-

Figure 1. Nursemaid and her charge. Photograph courtesy of The Valentine Museum, Richmond, Virginia.

ences in Western religious painting and the unexamined populism of the vernacular approach to the photographic image. For this image was made in Richmond, Virginia, circa 1865, by a skilled, white studio photographer named George Cook of his own family's "nursemaid," or "former slave" for his own family's consumption. It is a highly material picture of a maternal body whose role as "sacred beyond" has been removed.

George Cook was a northerner who settled in the South just before the Civil War. He is widely known for his pictures of military officers on both the Union and the Confederate sides. After the war he continued to photograph, maintaining a thriving studio business in Richmond. According to Norman Yetman, the one historian who has written even briefly about the political conditions under which the picture was made, the young woman depicted is almost certainly a slave or only just recently freed.[15] Since the baby on her lap appears white and she is black, most viewers would assume that it is not her baby at all, but another woman's child. And, in fact, the baby is Heustis Cook, the son of the photographer, who himself grew up to be a photographer.

"Heustis Cook," notes Yetman, "was one of the first of the 'field' photographers who packed his buggy with cameras, glass plates, plate holders, collodion, silver nitrate, plus his tent or 'darkroom' and all his developing supplies and took photography to the back roads."[16] The father and son's collection of pictures of the former slave population of Virginia, South Carolina, North Carolina, and Washington, D.C., is now in the Valentine Museum in Richmond, Virginia. A substantial portfolio of their images was reproduced in *Voices from Slavery,* edited by Norman Yetman, in 1970.

This particular Madonna is therefore a weirdly skewed rendition of the Christian story. Like Mary, she holds a baby who is virtually, perhaps even literally, her master. But this baby is not the baby that God the Father gave her to bear. That baby, if it exists, is elsewhere. Despite her youth and beauty, this woman cannot be simply another mother who commemorates the ecstatic moment of typological juncture, the swelling pride of womanhood fulfilled, since as a slave or former slave she has been at the same time human chattel and, to adopt Orlando Patterson's pungent figure from *Slavery and Social Death,* a social corpse.

Motherhood may be what the Madonna genre marks as woman's

great accomplishment, but sitting for the white man's camera as the white woman sat, in the pose that the white woman held, holding, in fact, the white woman's baby within the iconographical space and actual society that claimed for white women an exclusive right to occupancy, the slave or domestic servant brings into existence not her own family's precious keepsake, but a monument of doubleness and double entendre. Rather than bonding figure to type, as in the painting tradition, the photograph displays instead the innumerable barriers and memories that stand in the way of that apotheosis. The "unrepresentable" that Kristeva invokes is not some abstract sacred principle, but the maternal material-ity of the figure of a young black woman. Working for someone else's transcendence, she is not allowed to signify her own.

In the earliest years of its existence, photography was laminated to sentimental functions along with domestic novels, domestic advice man-uals, educational reform propaganda, and abolitionist agitation. While the middle-class home became the port of entry for sentimental fictions of all sorts, the hall table and the parlor were accumulating photographs at an impressive rate. Like domestic novels, the resulting accumulation of images helped to make, not merely to mirror, the home. Photography was another mode of domestic representation. It worked by staging affect or imaging relation—literally *seeing sentiment* as a way of organ-izing family life. Wrote one white settler of his new home in Montana,

> Our cabin measured 16 × 20 feet in the clear. The logs were chinked and painted with clay. The roof was of poles covered with hay and sodded; we filled in the crevices with loose dirt, fondly hoping that it wouldn't leak. The floor was of earth, beaten hard and smooth. . . . A box cupboard held our stock of dishes and cooking materials. Beside it stood the churn. The flour barrel was converted into a "center-table" whereon reposed the family Bible and photograph album with their white lace covers.[17]

Or, as Nathaniel Hawthorne observed in his notebooks, when his wife Sophia rearranged the parlor and put a table with books and pictures at its center, their new house in Lenox became a home.

Valorization of the visual image of the middle-class white woman as the signifier of the category "woman," which makes other social rela-tionships invisible, was also taking shape in the early nineteenth century. Sentimental ideologues of womanhood explicitly turned to drawn or painted images to mark the social divisions advanced by the middle class and to make them seem to be rooted in something actual. Photography, invented in 1839, was an even better technique than drawing or painting for making images of "nature," and photography was therefore conscripted for the myth-making cause.[18] The idea was, if you could take pictures of something, it must exist. To the middle-class nineteenth-century viewer, a photograph was not only a "mirror" of nature, but, unlike other mirrors, it had a "memory" too. Photography inscribed, therefore, a very powerful image of the "Real."

But what this idea disguised is the fact that photographs have meaning only as elements of a set. Photographic meaning is a system of relations that are established not *in* but *between* images. As Patricia Holland, Jo Spence, and Simon Watney explain, photography is ideological in that it is a "set of relations established between signs, between images—a way of narrating experience in such a way that specific social interests and inequalities are thought about, discussed and perpetuated."[19] Or, in the formulation of Griselda Pollock, to interpret images of women it is necessary to develop "a notion of woman as a signifier in an ideological discourse in which one can identify the meanings that are attached to woman in different images and how the meanings are constructed in relation to other signifiers in that discourse."[20] Early-nineteenth-century, bourgeois domestic photography, then, became as productive and constitutive a force as it did because it related images of women to one another and to other cultural practices through a hierarchizing narrative of social signs. Thus, photographic sentiment helped to create the hierarchies of domesticity that, ostensibly, it only recorded.

•   •   •

The figure of the nursemaid was a material and ideological weapon that could be used against, as well as for, women of both the laboring and the governing classes. As a job category, for instance, it pressured black families to accept instruction in servitude and the "domestic arts" as progressive education for their daughters, who were taught that the "hoeing, picking, mining, washing, and ironing that black southerners had done as slaves for centuries" were now "ideas and skills of 'self-help' and 'self-sufficiency.' "[21] As a marker of class for white families, it was a litmus test of domestic propriety whose manipulative and misogynistic value was not lost on such an educator as Booker T. Washington.

In a fund raising speech in 1907, he presented a white audience with the following thought:

> In the average white family of the South, you will find that the white child spends a large proportion of his life in the arms or in the company of a negro woman or of a negro girl. During the years when that child is most impressionable, when he is at a point where impressions are perhaps most lasting, that child is in the company of the black woman or the black girl. My friends it is mighty important, in my opinion, for the civilization, for the happiness, for the health of the Southern white people that that colored nurse shall be intelligent, that she shall be clean, that she shall be morally fit to come in contact with that pure and innocent child.[22]

As Glenda Gilmore has pointed out, black women of course understood that these "images of the immoral black woman and the barbaric black home" were "grist for the white supremacy mill," and many worked to break the "direct link between the fabricated discourse on black barbarity and the industrial education movement."[23]

Seldom, however, do any of these black nursemaids have the prominent visible place within the records of a white family that is seen in the Cook collection. Cook's "Nursemaid and Her Charge" is distinctive for being, as Severa observes, exceptionally focused on the nursemaid herself:

> Baby Heustis Cook, shown here with his nurse, was the son of Richmond photographer George Cook, who took this record portrait of his baby son and his son's nurse. Heustis himself grew up to become a noted photographer of Southern life.
>
> But the attractive and neatly dressed nurse is the focus of attention in this photograph. Her bold, black-and-white-striped dress, with its directional treatment in the yoke bands, is of a most current fashion for morning dress. The small round puff at the top of the sleeve is a stylish addition that has no basis in pure function; it is cut on the bias and perfectly set in. The sleeve below it is perhaps somewhat looser than the fashion, which is generally shown as very snug below such puffs. This adaptation, however, undoubtedly made lifting and caring for a baby easier. The bodice of the dress is gathered into a waist so neat and small that it is obviously fitted over a proper corset. Snow white linen is worn at the throat, as is a cameo brooch. Her hair is done smoothly in a net in a simple manner followed by most women for everyday.
>
> The attire and grooming of this highly visible servant reflects the pride

of the Cook family in its home and position in the community; house servants appeared as extensions of the family's means and taste. As the child's nurse, this woman would ideally stay with him, in the background, all the years of his growing up and remain with the family to care for any future children.[24]

In this particular instance, George Cook himself was a professional photographer, which made the acquisition of such a family nursemaid picture especially easy. But making the nursemaid so much the focus of attention, in her exemplary clothing and her vivid figuration, raises crucial questions about the intention of the image. It suggests that Cook might have had in mind something more specific than the usual discursive "charge" to naturalize the mammy relationship. He wished, instead, to dwell on it, as did Heustis later.

·   ·   ·

By and large, the sentimentality in all the Cooks' postslavery images appears on the surface to be well intentioned toward black people. Aside from some egregious counterexamples, such as the figure of the banjo player, they are, at least apparently, nonstereotyped and generous toward the personalities and human worth of their sitters.[25] The majority of the photographs in the set clearly present the former slaves to be people of dignity, with few or no visible debilitating marks of slavery. In the Cooks' images, in fact, the former slaves appear as bona fide members of the universal "family of man." Such images could easily have had a place in Steichen's famous exhibition.

This impression of an absence of wounding mystifies the historical relation between the photographic gaze of the Cooks and the former slave population of Richmond and the surrounding area upon whom they trained it. We can sketch at least some of its ominous associations by quoting briefly from the poetry of Benjamin Batchelder Valentine, a close family friend of the Cooks, in whose Richmond mansion, now turned into a museum, the Cook family archive is located.

In Valentine's book, *Ole Marster and Other Verses,* published posthumously in 1921, Valentine makes a sustained apology for slavery and the social order it supported. In a poem entitled "The Race Question," written, as is most of his poetry, in a black dialect voice, Valentine argues, for instance, that slave labor was more beneficial to the southern black population than free labor:

When I wuz young de color'd folks
  Wuz 'low'd ter lay de bricks;
Dey climbed de scaffolds, toted hods,
  An' made de mortar mix.

Dey'd handle hammers, saws an' planes,
  An' any tools dey'd choose
It wan' no folks 'cep' niggers den
  What use' ter half-sole shoes.

In dem dyar times 'twas nigger backs
  Whar gave de scythes de swing;
'Twuz big, black, shiny nigger arms
  Whar made de anvils ring.

An' settin' on de wooden horse
  Wid staves betwix' dey laigs,
Wid drawin' knives an' hic'ry poles
  De niggers hooped de kaigs.

You couldn' fin' no barber shop
  Dat we-all folks wan' dyar
De little ones er-shinin' shoes,
  The big ones cuttin' hyar.

Wid high up gem-man names print' on
  De mugs er-settin' roun';
Er heap o' niggers made dey piles
  Frum shaves an' breshin' down.

But 'tain' so now, nor dat it aint,
  De white-folks cuts us out;
Dey jumps right in an' gits de wuk
  'Fo' we knows what dey's bout.

Dey 'trac's de trade—dem out-land folks
  Dem 'Talians, Dutch, an' Greeks,
Aldo' 'tain' none whar understands
  De 'spressions whar dey speaks.

Dey shaves an' shampoos all day long,
  Dey never, stops
Dey don' pick banjers for dey fr'en's,
  An' cake-walk in de shops.

De Orishman is wuss er all
  Jes' time er nigger nod,

He step right up an' shev' him down
    An' grab er hol' his hod.

An' den de Unions layin' bricks,
    Dey hollers out ter Mike
"Ef dat dyar nigger gits dat hod,
    We-all is gwine ter strike."

Den ev'y body on de job
    Er-j'inin' in de fray,
Jes' tells de niggers, up an' down,
    Ter go 'long out de way.

De bosses don' cyar nothin' 'tall;
    Dey say we's mighty slow;
Dey kinder laugh an' los it's time
    De nigger got ter go.

An' ef we turns den ter de farms,
    Whar we had ought ter been,
We dyar gwine find some big machines
    Fer us ter buck erg'in.

Dey's took an' drove out all de scythes
    I'clar, it is er crime
Ter reap, wid one dem whirlin' things,
    De whole crop at er time.

I know we's gittin' mighty larned—
    Folks say we's making has'e;
Dyar's heap o'sass an' argyment
    'Bout "Progress er de Race."

I 'lows we' settin' up de tree—
    De nigger's on er boom—
But I wan' know whar 'bouts is I
    Gwine git some elbow room.

Er-stydy'n' bout one question, Suh,
    Nigh bu'sts my brain 'jints loose,
"Is niggers now er-cotchin' holt,
    Er is day off de roos'?"[26]

In the opinion of Mary Newton Stanard, a friend of Valentine's who wrote the introduction to *Ole Marster and Other Verses,* Valentine was

Figure 2. Banjo player. Photograph courtesy of the Valentine Museum, Richmond, Virginia.

entirely correct in his analysis of what African Americans had lost by gaining their freedom. She wrote,

> Southern negroes brought up by 'Ole Marster' and 'Ole Mistis,' and even descendants of these dear, dark folk who inherited their character, manners, speech and devotion to 'we all's white folks' are rapidly becoming mere tradition, and with them is passing from the American scene something vital, something precious.[27]

Valentine, in Stanard's opinion one of the "white people who were associated with them in a relation unique then and impossible now, whom they loved and served and who loved and served them," was one of the rare whites who "possessed a supreme gift for interpreting" the speech of the black population. She was relieved that "through his work they will live always." Stanard knew directly of the power of this interpretive gift, for Valentine used to give performances in which he impersonated the "faithful colored folk" in dialect verse in his "old and storied Richmond mansion, whose rooms were filled with books and treasures of artistic and sentimental value."[28] To attend a performance of these poems, remembered Stanard, was "an unforgettable experience":

> Under the quaint humor which bubbled on their surface flowed a deep current whose echo could be heard in his mellow, lilting voice, for all its contagious chuckles, and which could be glimpsed in his expressive eyes for all their merry twinkling—showing that with fine imagination, with sympathy amounting to genius, he felt at once the picturesque traits of his subjects which shallower interpreters are prone to caricature and their mental and spiritual processes. Whether or not the philosophy which was a marked characteristic of these simple souls was an original development or was imbibed from their "white folks" and passed on in intensified form to their "white folks" children, is impossible to say, but as seen in the work of "Ben Valentine" it is as typical of the interpreter as of the interpreted. Each portrait in the gallery which his negro verse comprises is sketched with unerring touch from some point of vantage peculiar to itself, and the whole thus presents, as nearly complete as could be within the bounds so circumscribed, a visualization of a vanishing race.[29]

It seems, therefore, that the poems published in *Ole Marster and Other Verses* are the texts of the blackface performance pieces that Valentine used to present. It is likely that the Cook family also attended Benjamin Valentine's dialect performances in Richmond. Certainly they would have known of them. Part of the interest that the father and son shared in "taking photography to the back roads" was probably to present a parallel in photography to the kind of preservation of a "vanishing race" that, according to Stanard, their friend Ben Valentine was so successfully producing in dramatic verse.

In this context the "Banjo player" is not merely an egregious image but actually menacing. As Valentine's poem "The Race Question" establishes, the purpose of the effort to visualize the ex-slaves was to turn back the clock, to force Reconstruction to deconstruct, to argue that slavery was not only harmless but that it was better for the "simple souls" than the system of free labor, with its immigrant competition and labor agitation, that followed. The "Banjo player" is a figure from that supposed happy past.

Like the figure of the banjo player, the "significant figure of the Mammy," writes Catherine Clinton in *The Plantation Mistress,* "as a familiar denizen of the Big House is not merely a stereotype, but in fact a figment of the combined romantic imaginations of the contemporary Southern ideologue and the modern Southern historian."[30] Clinton found that although there were some female slaves who "served as the 'right hand' of plantation mistresses," records show that there were only very few. The Mammy is a *post*slavery invention. "Not until after Emancipation did black women run white households or occupy in any significant number the special positions accorded to them in folklore and fiction. The Mammy was created by white southerners to redeem the relationship between black women and white men within slave society in response to the antislavery attack from the North during the antebellum era, and to embellish it with nostalgia in the postbellum period."[31] In other words, the invention of the Mammy (as a sort of super nursemaid) was a political ploy of white supremacy. Her image, seen in this context, announces the reassertion of white patriarchy.

Not only that, but it was also a clear rhetorical threat. As journalist Edward A. Pollard, another of Cook and Valentine's contemporaries in Richmond and an ardent Southern nationalist, wrote in *The Lost Cause,* the true social status of the Negro was dictated by the "fact" of "the permanent, natural inferiority of the Negro," which the white man had to control.[32] The ostensible need for white men to control the supposedly "'sauage'-like behavior" of this "inferior" population was offered as an excuse for deadly violence against that population. As Sandra Gunning has explained in *Race, Rape, and Lynching,* "the interracial male struggle over the terrain of the public would always be figured finally within the terms of the domestic—the privatized expression of the nation's political anxieties. White Americans' conflation of the public and the private as the twin targets of black designs meant that the figure of the black as beast threatened to become a totalizing symbol of a race war many felt was already in progress."[33] Whatever their original humanistic intent toward the "hidden witness" in their midst, therefore, "permanent, natural" images made of black people framed in terms of white sentimental domesticity—such as the Cook photographs—functioned as attempts to exhibit the superior evolution of the white family and its household. When Cook photographed his private nursemaid in the early 1860s, he was demonstrating his public role as an upper-class white man in Richmond. This *included* the superlative display of the nursemaid.

I would hold, in fact, that this trajectory of white supremacy in Richmond is why the Cook photographs, including that of the nursemaid, bear no visible relation to the hardly distant violence of slavery but only allude directly to the impressive dignity possessed by their subjects. Such respectful and innocuous images would have been much more useful than deliberately damaging images to support the claim of white domestic virtue that circulated throughout the south during the Reconstruction era. The need was to establish that slavery *did* the violence.

But the photograph that George Cook made of his nursemaid also punctures this reverie.[34] It is distinct from the rest of his "portrait gallery" because of its exceptionally intimate and focused vision of its cross-racial subject. The baby, like the domesticity, is his.

The chief contradiction that the Cook photograph of "a nursemaid and her charge" poses for critical consideration of a structure of sentimentality like that of the Cooks, is that however it might function rhetorically in public, such a use of photography *within* the private zone of the family could run directly afoul of a basic sentimental principle: keeping maternity and labor separate within one's own household. The idea was clearly articulated by Stowe, Warner, Gilman, and others, that the images of women that are to be accumulated for the domestic circle— women whose physical presence, by being photographed, was in fact to be rendered permanently and intimately familiar to the family—should be images of women of sensibility in its white, middle-class incarnation. For the white, middle-class household, photographs, like paintings, are a way of instructing children. "Pictures hung against the wall, and statuary lodged safely on brackets speak constantly to childish eyes, but are out of reach of childish fingers," wrote Harriet Beecher Stowe, who also advised:

> They are not like china and crystal, liable to be used and abused by servants; they do not wear out; they are not consumed by moths. The beauty once there is always there; though the mother be ill and in her chamber, she has no fears that she shall find it wrecked and shattered. And this style of beauty, inexpensive as it is, is a means of cultivation. No child is ever stimulated to draw or to read by an Axminster carpet or a carved center-table; but a room surrounded with photographs and pictures and fine casts suggests a thousand inquiries, stimulates the little eye and hand.[35]

The people in such photographs do not have to be kin. As the mid-nineteenth-century cult of collecting celebrity images in cabinet photographs and cartes de visite demonstrates, they could be strangers, just so long as they were an uplifting influence. Middle-class sensibility was the possession and mark of the moral being of such a person. Images like these, as Stowe put it, were all extensions of the moral function of the middle-class mother. They represented the "affective life of property" that Gillian Brown describes as "sentimental possession."[36]

A photograph such as that of the Cooks' nursemaid, one that actually focuses on a servant or a slave, could destabilize the comforting economy of this vision, just as it destabilized the relation of figure to type in the Madonna. Certainly such an image needed to be displayed very carefully when it was used for domestic consumption. Photographing the black nursemaid does not threaten the hegemony of white domestic sentiment, but it can "raise a thousand inquiries," questions that one might not want the "little eye and hand" to uncover. Therefore, unlike the white mother, the black nursemaid must not come to possess an inward sensibility by the re-creation of her image as an object of "depth" in the romantic vein. Nor can she accrue any authentic recognition of the value of her maternal labor. Instead, as Clinton writes, "[The mammy] image reduced black women to an animal-like state of exploitation. Mammies were to be milked, warm bodies to serve white needs—an image with its own sexual subtext. The Mammy does not, by any means, validate the 'closeness' of the races."[37]

I do think there is an additional layer of meaning encoded in the Cook image of the "Nursemaid and Her Charge" although I have not been able to establish it on any historical grounds. Nevertheless, it seems appropriate to say that nursemaids nurse babies, that in order to nurse a baby one must have recently borne a baby oneself, and that therefore the presence of Heustis Cook in the image may erase the presence of the nursemaid's own baby, who remains invisible. What the social relationships were that surrounded that baby, if it existed, are impossible to tell.[38] Nonetheless, the reproductive body of the nursemaid is very much part of the figure's construction.

What we do know is that in spending time and money on the nursemaid photograph, in accumulating and preserving her image in the mode of a member of the family, Cook was still not displaying her as a woman, a mother, a person. It was her job to "enhance by contrast," as Harryette Mullen has put it, the maternal power of her mistress.

In the one instance that I have located of a formal photographic portrait that Cook made of his wife, the ideological framing and mise en scène of the figure does indeed contrast with the portrait of the nursemaid. Much about the portrait of Mrs. Cook is similar to that of the nursemaid. She is dressed in a similar style to that of her slave or servant, with again a brooch pinned at the meeting place of the two halves of the white collar of her dress. The two young women even seem to be about the same age. But unlike the nursemaid, Mrs. Cook as an individual is the sole focus of the camera. She is not holding her child. She wears as if by simple right a wreath of flowers in her hair, symbols of freshness and natural innocence that have not been provided to the nursemaid. The nursemaid, by contrast, wears a uniform.

The portrait of Mrs. Cook bears the mark of patriarchal protection, in that it casts her in an ethereal light like that described by Kristeva. The photographer has lingered on the luminosity of her eyes, on the gentle smile that plays about her lips, and on the way that the braid in her hair picks up light like a halo, wanting to record them. Her figure is different from the figure of the nursemaid in that the image of the slave or servant does not offer any of these supplementary signifiers that register innocent and fragile womanhood, thus placing her within the bounds of southern patriarchal male protection.

At the same time, the photograph of the nursemaid and her charge engages in the threat by which the boundary of the white woman's innocent gaze was policed. It openly displaces the white mother by handing her baby to the black nursemaid but dissembles its threat by celebrating the sentimental framework of the white woman's motherhood. The adulatory portrait of Cook's wife reflects the conciliatory aspect of the honorific image. The shadow archive of women who could not be included is referenced in the photograph of the nursemaid and her charge, which seeks to discipline the white woman by reminding her of the "protective barriers, ideological and institutional, around the form of the white mother, whose progeny were heirs to the economic, social, and political interests in the maintenance of the slave systems," as Hazel Carby puts it, by raising the specter of black motherhood, which lacked these protections.[39]

The figure of Mrs. Cook is also different from the other family figures who appear on the porch in the group portrait, of whom Mrs. Cook was presumably one. The scale of its close-up focus magnifies the impression of a delicate individuality and distinction. In particular, Mrs. Cook's eyes, though lively and focused, are averted slightly from the camera, in a relaxed indirection that signifies that she has no need to protect herself: the operator of the camera, who is her husband, has her best interests at heart. Whereas even if the nursemaid also looks away, there is a vigilance of self-regard in her gaze not invited but *demanded* of those in her position who cannot depend on such protection by law. Read in the context of the crisis of white supremacy in Richmond in the 1860s, the innocent averted gaze of his wife is perhaps one of the clearest signs Cook can make with his camera of the white man's ability to keep the Old South alive in his family life. The potential violence of this determination is registered in the tense, self-conscious look in the nursemaid's eye.

In another of Ben Valentine's poems, entitled "Mammy's Charge," the figure of the nursemaid is counterposed to that of the mother in such a way that every considerable virtue the nursemaid evinces is literally "outshone" by the fact that the mother has died, gone to heaven, and become a star. In this poem, a little girl's mother has died and a grieving "Mammy" has been given the assignment of keeping the child occupied during the day of the funeral. "Mammy" holds her up before the window, and eventually the child falls asleep in her arms.

> My heart is mos' broke, Judy, an' my haid is achin' bad,
> Dis is de sor'ful's evening honey, dat I is ever had.
>> Dey knowed I love dat dear sweet Chile, an' now her Mummer's daid
>> Dey could trus' her ole black mammy fer ter treat her good, dey said.

So dey lef' me in de nursery fer ter keep de chile up dyar,
But I still culd heah de service, an' de preacher read de pra'r;
  De chile too kotch de singing an' de tears I had ter hide,
  When, in play she kep' on 'peatin', "O Lord, wid me abide."

When de fune'al it wuz over, an' de hearse wuz driv' away
I try might'ly fer ter 'muse her, an' ter keep her dyar at play,
  But she 'sist on asking questions like, "What is my Farver gone?
  I wants ter see my Mummer; will she stay 'way frum me long?"

I cyar' her ter de winder, an' she look' out in de street,
'Tel she got so tired waiting dat she went right fas' asleep;
  But I set dyar in de twilight an' I hel' de little dear,
  'Tel de street wuz onty darkness, an' de stars bein ter 'pear.

Den one star come out, Judy, what I never sees befo',
An' I look at it so studdy dat de tears wuz 'bleege ter flow;
  Den I tu'n an' see my darlin', in her sleep, begin ter smile;
  An de new star seem' a-shinin' right down upon de chile.[40]

Despite the tender warmth and sympathy extant in "Mammy's" heart, it is clear that benediction comes only from the white mother, who is, not coincidentally, "up above." If my comparisons of the photographs are apt, this sort of enhancement by contrast should also illuminate Cook's portrait of the nursemaid. It was evidently her part in the family to represent the best of earthly care, while her mistress allegorized eternal love. It is relevant that this is also not an unfamiliar role for white women, who, in sentimental structures, show their truest strength when dead.

The trouble is, photographing the nursemaid so splendidly—even if only to reflect the family's social position—also threatens to alter the balance of power between these "facts" of sentiment and hidden others. It threatens to give the nursemaid a social currency that she should not have. Therefore, it seems apparent that although the photograph imbues the figure of the nursemaid with the outward signs of feminine sensibility—the baby, the Madonna-like pose, the domestic reference, indeed almost all of the chief technologies of gender—these signs are used as a caul, to disguise rather than to convey human relation.

For the young woman portrayed within this extension of domestic representation, being rendered with visible sentiment just makes her social personhood more invisible than ever. The portrait is, in Hortense Spiller's words, a "violent jamming, two things enforced together in the same instance, a merciless, unchosen result of the coupling of one into an alien culture that yet withholds its patronym."[41] As a nursemaid, she might really teach the baby; but as an image, she must have less meaning than a piece of furniture.

This reification is also apparent in the subsequent treatment of the Cook nursemaid image. Putting her in their photograph seems to have been almost like hiding her in plain sight. The Cook family themselves could not have bothered to read the complicated body language and facial expression of the nursemaid in the photograph in their midst; or reading it, they could not have lent it even the remotest capacity to signify. Otherwise, the photograph, coded as a sentimental family memento of her faithful devotion, must have acquired a more problematic meaning than its history as a cherished keepsake of the family would allow. Arguably, it is as much an image of the violation of her social personhood as are the more infamous Zealey daguerreotypes of Delia, Renty, and Jack; and it is as eloquent a record of the social relations that grew out of slavery.[42]

The photograph of the teenaged, bare-breasted Delia was given by a South Carolina slaveholder to Professor Louis Agassiz of Harvard University to help him to "study anatomical details of 'the African race' " in order to "prove" his theory of that blacks were a distinct species,' separately created. Harryette Mullen writes of Delia,

> History preserves only the picture of her body, photographed as a 'scientific' exhibit. Prefiguring the critique of bourgeois power/knowledge monopolized by privileged white males, represented by private tutors who serve the slaveholding elite in Williams' *Dessa Rose,* Morrison's *Beloved,* and Johnson's *Oxherding Tales,* are the historical encounters of slave women with white men of science: Dr. James Norcum ("Dr Flint" in Jacobs's narrative), who instructed his slave that she had been 'made for his use'; Dr. Strain, who desired visual proof of Sojourner Truth's sex, viewing the self-empowered black woman as a freak; and Professor Louis Agassiz, who conceived a project in which the illusory immediacy of the subjugated image would provide seemingly irrefutable proof of African inferiority through a photographic display of black bodies, a project in which racial and sexual differences were to be read as perceptible evidence of inferiority.[43]

For Mullen, Agassiz's "coercive recording of her barebreasted image leaves her silent, underscoring Delia's materiality as 'property,' and 'exhibit,' as scientific evidence,' a unit of data within a master discourse controlled by white men, bent on denying her subjectivity. . . . [But] the lowered lids shade what is otherwise a direct outward gaze without the least suggestion of embarrassment. Stripped naked, her objectified body functions as a veil for her soul, her subjectivity retreating before the gaze of scientific objectivity materialized by the camera."[44]

Similarly, what is at stake for me, in the photograph of the "Nursemaid and Her Charge" is that there seems to be something in her body language that "escapes or at least challenges the subjugating gaze that holds her body captive." The compelling visual pattern of the striped dress is uncannily like a subliminal message to the viewer to "read between the lines." If the white cloth at the bottom of the frame, which a viewer easily could have processed at first as a single, vague entity, were earlier interpreted entirely as the infant's dress, it will now resolve itself assertively into two distinct shapes—the apron that designates a servant/slave as well as the clothing of the child. The cloth across the young woman's left shoulder, which might have been something any mother or nanny would use in a multitude of ways to protect and shelter and swaddle the baby and herself, comes to appear as much a curtain separating the two as it does the implement of any ritual of care or bonding.

As one looks more closely, it even becomes apparent that the cloth covers unnaturally and entirely her left arm and hand; in fact, that it has been arranged or flung upon her much as if she were a chair or some other piece of upholstery, so as to set off the baby's head against a dark solid surface that corrects for the photographically busy background of the eloquent striped dress. Evidently it was very important that the baby's individuality come through sharply in this portrait; and for this purpose, the woman is merely the setting, the not quite perfect background that needs to be improved. But her body language suggests that she comprehends this expediency and that she resents it, for she makes no effort to hold or cradle the baby, but merely suffers him to be balanced upright and exhibited to the camera as he waves his arm in the crook of her exaggeratedly extended elbow.[45]

Not only the Cooks refused to read this photograph. Although the "Nursemaid and Her Charge" has three times recently been reprinted in widely read books on African American history, including feminist books, it has never yet drawn a critical glance beyond Norman Yetman's general assessment that her image, like all the images in the Cook collection, is "sensitive . . . honest . . . [and] forthright," and that "a quality exists in each of them that marks them as an interesting composition and a work of art in their own right."[46]

Furthermore, each time it has been reprinted, the photograph has been rendered outside of the particular political context of its production in Richmond in the 1860s. What does this continuing disregard of the figure of the "Nursemaid and Her Charge" tell us about the allegiances of our critical institutions that have, since slavery, continued to govern the interpretation of the photographic gaze? Does seeing nineteenth-century middle-class "sentiment," that critical turn that has been so vitally important for the establishment of a feminist standpoint in literary criticism, actually function as a mechanism of displacement in and by photography, ensuring that other sentiments will not be seen?

.   .   .

NOTES

1. Wolf, "Confessions of a Closet Ekphrastic," 185.

2. Updike, *Just Looking.*

3. See Guilbaut, *How New York Stole the Idea of Modern Art*; and C. Phillips, "Judgment Seat of Photography," 14–47. See also Steichen, *Family of Man*; Allan Sekula, "The Traffic in Photographs," in *Photography Against the Grain*; and Roland Barthes's classic deconstruction of the exhibition, "The Great Family of Man."

4. Marianne Hirsch cautions against adopting the facile assumption that the ideological effect of the *Family of Man* was either puerile or reactionary in the postwar period. See her thoughtful essay "Reframing the Family Romance," in Hirsch, *Family Frames*, 41–77.

5. Alan Trachtenberg has been the chief and most persuasive advocate for reading the historical evidence of photographs. In his most recent book, *Reading American Photographs: Images as History, Mathew Brady to Walker Evans*, Trachtenberg argues a social constructionist position for photographs as documents of American cultural history: "Just as the meaning of the past is the prerogative of the present to invent and choose, the meaning of an image does not come intact and whole. Indeed, what empowers an image to represent history is not just what it shows but the struggle for meaning we undergo before it, a struggle analogous to the historian's effort to shape an intelligible and usable past" (xvii). The politically nuanced attention that Trachtenberg is advocating as "readings" should not be confused with formalism.

6. An excellent discussion of the pitfalls of a merely additive conceptualization of oppression may be found in Spelman, "Theories of Race and Gender: The Erasure of Black Women." See also Spelman, *Inessential Woman.*

7. See Tompkins, *Sensational Designs.* See also Reynolds, *Beneath the American Renaissance.*

8. Dorothy Sterling dates the image "circa 1865." Sterling, *We Are Your Sisters,* 359. Jacqueline Jones dates it 1865 but locates it, incorrectly, in Charleston, South Carolina. Jones, *Labor of Love, Labor of Sorrow,* 122. Joan Severa dates it more precisely, as "July, 1868." Severa, *Dressed for the Photographer,* 281. Norman Yetman does not date the image but places it within a portfolio of images of "Former Slaves" photographed "during the period from about 1861 to 1935 in Virginia, South Carolina, North Carolina, and Washington, D.C." Yetman, *Voices from Slavery,* portfolio of images following p. 338.

9. Severa, *Dressed for the Photographer,* 281.

10. The Cook photographs I am analyzing in this chapter may all be found in the George Cook Collection of the Valentine Museum in Richmond, Virginia. Although the "Nursemaid and Her Charge" has been reprinted, there are still hundreds of unpublished images by George and Heustis Cook extant in the archives.

11. Painter, *Sojourner Truth,* 185–99.

12. Jacobs, *Incidents in the Life of a Slave Girl,* cover and frontispiece.

13. Kristeva, "Motherhood according to Bellini," 241, 237.

14. See discussion in Wardley, "Relic, Fetish, Femmage," 216–17.

15. Yetman, *Voices from Slavery,* portfolio of images following p. 338.

16. Ibid.

17. Dickson, *Covered Wagon Days,* 191–92.

18. The locus classicus on this role of photography in the process of mythologization (and still one of the best discussions of this process) is Barthes, "Myth Today."

19. Holland, Spence, and Watney, *Photography/Politics: Two,* 2.

20. Pollock, "What's Wrong with 'Images of Women'?" 26.

21. Anderson, *Education of Blacks in the South,* 55.

22. Booker T. Washington, "Address before the Faculty and Members of the Theological Department of Vanderbilt University and Ministers of Nashville," March 29, 1907, quoted in ibid.

23. Gilmore, *Gender and Jim Crow,* 153, 138.

24. Severa, *Dressed for the Photographer,* 281.

25. For a provocative account of the complex social significations of the banjo player figure, see Lott, *Love and Theft.*

26. Valentine, *Ole Marster,* 60–63.

27. Mary Newton Stanard, "Foreword," in Valentine, *Ole Marster,* 9.

28. Ibid.

29. Ibid., 10–11.

30. Clinton, *Plantation Mistress*, 201.

31. Ibid., 201–2.

32. Edward A. Pollard, *The Lost Cause*, quoted in Fredrickson, *Black Image in the White Mind*, 187.

33. Gunning, *Race, Rape, and Lynching*, 21.

34. I am using the term "puncture" here in accordance with Roland Barthes's account of the "punctum" in *Camera Lucida*. I differ from Barthes, however, in that the puncture he seeks is a purely private sensation, whereas my notion of the punctum includes as well the registration of ideological rupture, like puncturing a balloon that has kept one from seeing where one really is. For a helpful way to extend the Barthean dichotomy of "studium" and "punctum" in this direction, see Hall, "The Rediscovery of 'Ideology.' "

35. Harriet Beecher Stowe, *Household Papers and Stories* (Boston: Houghton Mifflin, 1896), quoted in Wardley, "Relic, Fetish, Femmage," 216.

36. Brown, *Domestic Individualism*, 60.

37. Clinton, *Plantation Mistress*, 202.

38. Gabrielle Foreman first pointed out to me the possible link between a nursemaid, nursing, and the invisible presence of a child of her own.

39. Carby, *Reconstructing Womanhood*, 31.

40. Valentine, "Mammy's Charge," in *Ole Marster*, 56–57.

41. This citation is based on the October 1992 version of a paper entitled " 'All the Things You Could Be by Now If Sigmund Freud's Wife Was Your Mother': Psychoanalysis and Race," presented by Hortense Spillers at the conference "Psychoanalysis in African American Contexts: Feminist Reconfigurations," held at the University of California, Santa Cruz. In the significantly revised version of Spillers's paper published in 1997 in Abel, Christian, and Moglen, *Female Subjects in Black and White*, some of these words have disappeared.

42. Alan Trachtenberg published several of these photographs in *Reading American Photographs*, 55, along with an extensive discussion. They are also published in Banta and Hinsley, *From Site to Sight*, 56; Goldberg, *Power of Photography*, 64–65; and Moutoussamy-Ashe, *Viewfinders*, 5. In response to the "Hidden Witness" exhibition at the J. Paul Getty Museum in 1995, Carrie Mae Weems made an installation titled "From Here I Saw What Happened and I Cried," which powerfully reframes them. See Larsen, "Between Worlds." I thank Cheryl Finley for bringing this to my attention.

43. See Mullen, "Gender and the Subjugated Body," 223.

44. Ibid., 227.

45. This reading of resistance accords with Barbara Christian's assertion that the mammy figure in slave narratives, "unlike the white southern image of

mammy," is "cunning, prone to poisoning her master, and not at all content with her lot." Christian, *Black Feminist Criticism, 5*. See also Harris, *From Mammies to Militants,* and Collins, "Mammies, Patriarchs, and Other Controlling Images," in *Black Feminist Thought,* 4–90. But I want to add a cautionary note to the idea that resistance to the master discourse may be legible in the body language and discursive signs of the photograph. As both Carla Kaplan and Franny Nudelman have recently argued, the assignation by a would-be "emancipatory reader" of a language of resistance to individuals who are placed in situations of domination and oppression is a complex wish, and such an assignation, when it is merely projection, may be a subtle form of "othering." See Kaplan, "Narrative Contracts and Emancipatory Readers," and Nudelman, "Harriet Jacobs and the Sentimental Politics of Female Suffering." Yet, to refuse to read such a language is also to objectify.

46. Yetman, *Voices from Slavery,* introduction to "A Photo Essay of Former Slaves," following p. 338.

Works Cited

Anderson, James D. *The Education of Blacks in the South, 1860–1988.* Chapel Hill: University of North Carolina Press, 1988.

Banta, Melissa, and Curtis M. Hinsley, eds. *From Site to Sight: Anthropology, Photography, and the Power of Imagery.* Cambridge: Harvard University Press, 1986.

Barthes, Roland. *Camera Lucida: Reflections on Photography.* Translated by Richard Howard. New York: Hill and Wang, 1981.

———. "The Great Family of Man." In *Mythologies,* 100–102. Translated by Annette Lavers. New York: Hill and Wang, 1957.

———. "Myth Today." In *Mythologies,* 105–109. Translated by Annette Lavers. New York: Hill and Wang, 1957.

Brown, Gillian. *Domestic Individualism: Imagining Self in Nineteenth-Century America.* Berkeley: University of California Press, 1990.

Carby, Hazel. *Reconstructing Womanhood: The Emergence of the Afro-American Woman Novelist.* New York: Oxford University Press, 1987.

Christian, Barbara. *Black Feminist Criticism: Perspectives on Black Women Writers.* New York: Pergamon, 1985.

Clinton, Catherine. *The Plantation Mistress: Women's World in the Old South.* New York: Pantheon, 1982.

Collins, Patricia Hill. *Black Feminist Thought: Knowledge, Consciousness, and the Politics of Empowerment.* Boston: Unwin Hayman, 1990.

Dickson, Arthur Jerome. *Covered Wagon Days: A Journey across the Plains in the Sixties, and Pioneer Days in the Northwest; from the Private Journals of Albert Jerome Dickson.* Cleveland: Arthur H. Clark Co., 1929.

Fredrickson, George. *Black Image in the White Mind: The Debate on Afro-American Character and Destiny, 1817–1914.* Hanover, N.H.: University Press of New England, 1987.

Gilmore, Glenda Elizabeth. *Gender and Jim Crow: Women and the Politics of White Supremacy in North Carolina, 1896–1920.* Chapel Hill: University of North Carolina Press, 1996.

Goldberg, Vicki. *The Power of Photography: How Photographs Changed Our Lives.* New York: Abbeville, 1991.

Guilbaut, Serge. *How New York Stole the Idea of Modern Art: Abstract Expressionism, Freedom, and the Cold War.* Chicago: University of Chicago Press, 1983.

Gunning, Sandra. *Race, Rape, and Lynching: The Red Record of American Literature.* New York: Oxford University Press, 1996.

Hall, Stuart. "The Rediscovery of 'Ideology': Return of the Repressed in Media Studies." In *Culture, Society and the Media,* edited by T. B. Michael Gurevitch, Tony Bennett, James Curran, and Janet Woollacott, 56–90. London: Routledge, 1982.

Harris, Trudier. *From Mammies to Militants: Domestics in Black American Literature.* Philadelphia: Temple University Press, 1982.

Hirsch, Marianne. *Family Frames: Photography, Narrative and Postmemory.* Cambridge: Harvard University Press, 1997.

Holland, Patricia, Jo Spence, and Simon Watney, eds., *Photography/Politics: Two.* London: Comedia, 1986.

Jacobs, Harriet. *Incidents in the Life of a Slave Girl, Written by Herself.* Edited by Jean Fagan Yellin. Cambridge: Harvard University Press, 1987.

Jones, Jacqueline. *Labor of Love, Labor of Sorrow: Black Women, Work, and the Family from Slavery to the Present.* New York: Basic, 1987.

Kaplan, Carla. "Narrative Contracts and Emancipatory Readers." *Yale Journal of Criticism* 6 (Spring 1993): 93–119.

Kristeva, Julia. "Motherhood according to Bellini." In *Desire in Language,* edited by Leon S. Roudiez. New York: Columbia University Press, 1980.

Larsen, Ernest. "Between Worlds." *Art in America* (May 1999): 122–29.

Lott, Eric. *Love and Theft: Blackface Minstrelsy and the American Working Class.* New York: Oxford University Press, 1993.

Moutoussamy-Ashe, Jean. *Viewfinders: Black Women Photographers.* New York: Dodd, Mead, 1986.

Mullen, Harryette. "Gender and the Subjugated Body: Readings of Race, Subjectivity, and Difference in the Construction of Slave Narratives." Ph.D. diss., University of California, Santa Cruz, 1990.

Nudelman, Franny. "Harriet Jacobs and the Sentimental Politics of Female Suffering." *ELH: A Journal of English Literary History* 59, no. 4 (Winter 1992): 939–64.

Painter, Nell Irvin. *Soujourner Truth: A Life, a Symbol.* New York: W. W. Norton, 1996.

Phillips, Christopher. "The Judgement Seat of Photography." In *The Context of Meaning,* edited by R. Bolton. Cambridge: MIT Press, 1989.

Pollock, Griselda. "What's Wrong with 'Images of Women'?" *Screen Education* 24 (1977): 25–33.

Reynolds, David. *Beneath the American Renaissance: The Subversive Imagination in the Age of Emerson and Melville.* New York: Alfred A. Knopf, 1988.

Sekula, Allan. *Photography against the Grain: Essays and Photo Works, 1975–1983.* Halifax: Press of the Nova Scotia College of Art and Design, 1984.

Severa, Joan L. *Dressed for the Photographer: Ordinary Americans and Fashion, 1840–1900.* Kent, Ohio: Kent State University Press, 1995.

Spelman, Elizabeth V. "Theories of Race and Gender: The Erasure of Black Women." *Quest* 5, no. 4 (1982): 36–62.

———. *Inessential Woman: Problems of Exclusion in Feminist Thought.* Boston: Beacon, 1988.

Spillers, Hortense. " 'All the Things You Could Be by Now If Sigmund Freud's Wife Was Your Mother': Psychoanalysis and Race." In *Female Subjects in Black and White: Race, Psychoanalysis, Feminism,* edited by E. Abel, B. Christian, and H. Moglen. Berkeley: University of California Press, 1997.

Steichen, Edward. *Family of Man.* New York: Museum of Modern Art, 1955.

Sterling, Dorothy, ed. *We Are Your Sisters: Black Women in the Nineteenth Century.* New York: W. W. Norton, 1984.

Tompkins, Jane. *Sensational Designs: The Cultural Work of American Fiction, 1790–1860.* New York: Oxford University Press, 1985.

Trachtenberg, Alan. *Reading American Photographs: Images as History, Mathew Brady to Walker Evans.* New York: Hill and Wang, 1989.

Updike, John. *Just Looking: Essays on Art.* New York: Alfred A. Knopf, 1989.

Valentine, Benjamin Batchelder. *Ole Marster and Other Verses.* Richmond: Whittet and Shepperson, 1921.

Wardley, Lynn. "Relic, Fetish, Femmage: The Aesthetics of Sentiment in the Work of Stowe." In *The Culture of Sentiment: Race, Gender, and Sentimentality in the Nineteenth Century,* edited by Shirley Samuels. New York: Oxford University Press, 1992.

Wolf, Bryan. "Confessions of a Closet Ekphrastic." *Yale Journal of Criticism* 3 (Spring 1990): 181–203.

Yetman, Norman. *Voices from Slavery.* New York: Holt, Reinhart, and Winston, 1970.

Chapter 4

The Queen of America Goes to Washington City

Harriet Jacobs, Frances Harper, Anita Hill

Lauren Berlant

Introduction by Marilee Lindemann

Is it fair to compare an autobiographical narrative of 1861, a novel of 1892, and testimony given before the U.S. Senate in 1991—and to top off the comparison with a few words on a once popular TV sitcom? That is precisely what Lauren Berlant undertakes in her bold analysis of the racial and sexual politics of the public sphere in America, "The Queen of America Goes to Washington City: Harriet Jacobs, Frances Harper, Anita Hill." It is audacious to move across history and genre in the way Berlant does here, for one runs the dual risk of being ahistorical and of seeming to compare apples with oranges. The risk is worth taking, though, for it enables Berlant to elucidate what she describes as the "structural echoes and political continuities" that characterize these diverse social and literary texts, all of which offer examples of women—and mostly African American women—going public with experiences of sexual violation in order to call the nation to account for "the continued and linked virulence of racism, misogyny, heterosexism, economic privilege, and politics in America." Each woman may have lost her individual battle to protect her sexual dignity and failed to realize her political desires (Anita Hill's charges of sexual harassment did not, for example, prevent Clarence Thomas from gaining confirmation to the Supreme Court), but their testimonies stand as powerful acts of critique and resistance that radically reimagine relations between politics and the body in America.

In this essay, as in most of her work, Berlant views texts as actors and agents that have designs upon the world, seeking in these cases to effect change, to intervene in situations of crisis and injustice. Thus, it is appropriate that she concludes her analysis with discussion of a show called *Designing Women*. For her, texts are never innocent, neutral, or merely reflective of some reality that exists apart from literature or other communications media. They are social fields marked by the power relations and the ideological contradictions of the culture in which they were produced. The theoretical apparatus that undergirds her project is dense and multifaceted. She draws from a wide-ranging body of work in critical and social theory, including feminism, queer studies, Marxist cultural theory, and studies of nationality. She brings all that material to bear upon her interest in the practices and rhetorics—the "technologies," as she calls it—of citizenship: How is it that people living in the United States come to think of themselves as "Americans"? How do they learn to be competent citizens? What are the fantasies, images, and narratives of citizenship circulating in the culture, both now and in the past, and how do race, sex, gender, and class figure into them? What happens when individuals who, legally or otherwise, lie outside the horizons of proper citizenship offer up counter fantasies that compete with and critique the dominant, official view? How do images of the body get caught up in discourses of proper and improper citizenship and in the contradiction between America's commitment to the equality of abstract persons and the reality of inequalities between groups of actual people?

In "The Queen of America," Berlant's three primary examples—Harriet Jacobs's *Incidents in the Life of a Slave Girl* (1861), Frances E. W. Harper's *Iola Leroy* (1892), and Hill's Senate testimony—are deployed to generate a "genealogy" of sex and sexual harassment in America that focuses specifically on African American women because they have served as a kind of sexual underclass whose coercion has been vital to sustaining the coherence of a nation erotically and politically dominated by white men. The term "genealogy" is important to understanding the methodology of the essay, for it is an indication of Berlant's debt to Friedrich Nietzsche and Michel Foucault, both of whom looked to the past as a way of illuminating the present. Thus, for example, Foucault offers his analysis of the modern penal system, *Discipline and Punish,* as both a genealogy and "a history of the present"—for example, an account of current conditions that explains how they came into being, how they emerged out of the past. Similarly, one could say that Berlant's real interest in "The Queen of America" is to explain Anita Hill by excavating earlier examples of African American women "who have sought to make the nation listen to them." She focuses, therefore, on the "rhetorical gestures that rhyme" among her three texts rather than on the differences among them, though she is careful to acknowledge that each is situated in and responds to a different "national emergency." A more conventional historical discussion of the two nineteenth-century examples would have devoted more attention to the social and literary conditions under which they were produced and initially received.[1]

Part of what makes Berlant's essay so stimulating is the critic's fascination with queenly, larger-than-life figures who emerge in her analysis as embodiments of the possibility of "Diva Citizenship," her term for "a revitalized national identity" that would allow for "corporeal dignity" and open up space for new forms of political activity. This concept arises out of the powerful strain of utopianism that animates Berlant's study of American culture and marks her critical practice as a form of deeply committed cultural work. Near the end of the essay, she speaks movingly of her passionate sense of identification with Anita Hill and of her own fantasies of addressing the nation directly, an identification that implicitly links Hill's testimony and Berlant's criticism, suggesting that each is an example of a "failed pedagogy" that might nonetheless create new horizons of citizenship.

Berlant is clearly drawn to the allure of the diva as a powerful and compelling individual, and she celebrates the diva's "queenly gestures and impulses toward freedom" as examples of how subordinated peoples sustain a sense of agency, insurgency, and optimism in the face of multiple, persistent assaults upon their dignity. She also recognizes, however, the limits of Diva Citizenship, for the diva with her forceful individuality tends to operate in a splendid but politically defeating isolation. (So, too, one might say, does the literary critic, no matter how much she might wish her scholarship to be socially relevant. The critic may also be a "designing woman," but the audience for her designs is likely to be local rather than national, and modest in size.) The Diva Citizen may momentarily captivate the world, but she is unable to transform it. That large-scale, long-term work, Berlant implies, will have to be a collective, collaborative project performed upon several levels of U.S. culture and society. Even the savviest diva girl—whether citizen, critic, or citizen-critic—couldn't do it all by or for herself.

NOTES

1. For just such a discussion of Jacobs and Harper, see Hazel Carby's *Reconstructing Womanhood: The Emergence of the Afro-American Woman Novelist* (New York: Oxford University Press, 1987).

FOR MANY READERS OF HARRIET JACOBS, the political uncanniness of Anita Hill has been a somber and illuminating experience. These two "cases" intersect at several points: at the experience of being sexually violated by powerful men in their places of work; at the experience of feeling shame and physical pain from living with humiliation; at the use of "going public" to refuse their reduction to sexual meaning, even after the "fact" of such reduction; at being African American women whose most organized community of support treated gender as the sign and structure of all subordinations to rank in America, such that other considerations—of race, class, and political ideology—became both tacit and insubordinate. In these cases, and in their public reception, claims for justice against racism and claims for justice against both patriarchal and heterosexual privileges were made to compete with each other: this competition among harmed collectivities remains one of the major spectator sports of the American public sphere. It says volumes about the continued and linked virulence of racism, misogyny, hetero-sexism, economic privilege, and politics in America.

In addition to what we might call these strangely non-anachronistic structural echoes and political continuities, the cases of Hill and Jacobs expose the unsettled and unsettling relations of sexuality and American citizenship—two complexly related sites of subjectivity, sensation, af-fect, law, and agency. The following are excerpts from Frances Harper's 1892 novel *Iola Leroy*, Jacobs's narrative, and Hill's testimony. Al-though interpretive norms of production, consumption, and style differ among these texts, each author went public in the most national medium available to her. For this and other reasons, the rhetorical gestures that rhyme among these passages provide material for linking the politics of sex and the public sphere in America to the history of nationality itself, now read as a domain of sensation and sensationalism, and of a yet unrealized potential for fashioning "the poetry of the future" from the domains where citizens register citizenship, along with other feelings:[1]

[Iola Leroy:] "I was sold from State to State as an article of merchandise. I had outrages heaped on me which might well crimson the cheek of honest womanhood with shame, but I never fell into the clutches of an

From *American Literature*, 65:3 (September 1993). Copyright © 1993, Duke University Press. Reprinted with permission.

owner for whom I did not feel the utmost loathing and intensest horror."
. . . [Dr. Gresham:] "But, Iola, you must not blame all for what a few have
done." [Iola:] "A few have done? Did not the whole nation consent to our
abasement?" (Frances E. W. Harper, *Iola Leroy* [1892])[2]

I have not written my experiences in order to attract attention to myself;
on the contrary, it would have been more pleasant to me to have been
silent about my own history. Neither do I care to excite sympathy for my
own sufferings. But I do earnestly desire to arouse the women of the North
to a realizing sense of the condition of two millions of women at the
South, still in bondage, suffering what I suffered, and most of them far
worse. . . . [My] bill of sale is on record, and future generations will learn
from it that women were articles of traffic in New York, late in the
nineteenth century of the Christian religion. It may hereafter prove a useful
document to antiquaries, who are seeking to measure the progress of
civilization in the United States. (Harriet A. Jacobs, *Incidents in the Life
of a Slave Girl* [1861])[3]

It is only after a great deal of agonizing consideration, and sleepless—
number of—great number of sleepless nights, that I am able to talk of
these unpleasant matters to anyone but my close friends. . . . As I've said
before, these last few days have been very trying and very hard for me and
it hasn't just been the last few days this week.

It has actually been over a month now that I have been under the strain
of this issue. Telling the world is the most difficult experience of my life,
but it is very close to having to live through the experience that occasioned
this meeting. . . .

The only personal benefit that I have received from this experience is
that I have had an opportunity to serve my country. I was raised to do
what is right and can now explain to my students first hand that despite
the high costs that may be involved, it is worth having the truth emerge.
(Anita Hill, *New York Times*, 12 October 1991; 15 October 1991)[4]

On the Subject of Personal Testimony and the Pedagogy of Failed Teaching

When Anita Hill, Harriet Jacobs, and Frances Harper's Iola Leroy speak
in public about the national scandal of their private shame, they bring
incommensurate fields of identity into explosive conjunction. Speaking
as private subjects about sexual activities that transpired within the

politically charged spaces of everyday life, their testimony remains itself personal, specifically about them, their sensations and subjectivity. We hear about "my experiences," "my own suffering," "unpleasant matters"; we hear of desires to return to silence, and of longings to be relieved of the drive to consign this material to public life, which requires the speaker to re-experience on her body what her rhetoric describes. But since their speech turns "incidents" of sexuality into opportunities for reconstructing what counts as national data—that is, since these sexual autobiographies all aim to attain the status of a *finding,* an official expert narrative about national protocols—the authors must make themselves representative and must make the specific sensational details of their violation exemplary of collective life. It is always the autobiographer's task to negotiate her specificity into a spectacular interiority worthy of public notice. But the minority subject who circulates in a majoritarian public sphere occupies a specific contradiction: insofar as she is exemplary, she has distinguished herself from the collective stereotype; and, at the same time, she is also read as a kind of foreign national, an exotic representative of her alien "people" who reports to the dominant culture about collective life in the crevices of national existence. This warp in the circulation of identity is central to the public history of African American women, for whom coerced sexualization has been a constitutive relay between national experience and particular bodies.

Hence the specifically juridical inflection of "personal testimony." This hybrid form demarcates a collectively experienced set of strains and contradictions in the meaning of sexual knowledge in America: sexual knowledge derives from private experiences on the body and yet operates as a register for systemic relations of power; sexual knowledge stands for a kind of political counterintelligence, a challenge to the norms of credibility, rationality, and expertise that generally organize political culture; and yet, as an archive of injury and of private sensation, sexual knowledge can have the paradoxical effect of *delegitimating* the very experts who can represent it as a form of experience. As the opening passages show, these three women produced vital public testimony about the conditions of sexuality and citizenship in America. Their representations of how nationality became embodied and intimate to them involve fantasies of what America is, where it is, and how it reaches individuals. This requires them to develop a national pedagogy of failed teaching: emerging from the pseudo-private spaces where many kinds of power are condensed into personal relations, they detail how they were forced to deploy persuasion to fight for sexual dignity, and how they lost that fight. They take their individual losses as exemplary of larger ones, in particular the failure of the law and the nation to protect the sexual dignity of women from the hybrid body of patriarchal official and sexual privilege. They insist on representing the continuous shifting of perspectives that constitutes the incommensurate experience of power where national and sexual affect meet. They resist, in sum, further submission to a national sexuality that blurs the line between the disembodied entitlements of liberal citizenship and the places where bodies experience the sensation of being dominated. For all these verbs of resistance, the women represent their deployment of publicity as an act made under duress, an act thus representing and performing unfreedom in America. These three narrators represent their previous rhetorical failures to secure sexual jurisdiction over their bodies, challenging America to take up politically what the strongest individualities could not achieve.

Anita Hill is the most recent in a tradition of American women who have sought to make the nation listen to them, to transform the horizons and the terms of authority that mark both personal and national life in America by speaking about sexuality as the fundamental and fundamentally repressed horizon of national identity, legitimacy, and affective experience. That these are African American women reflects the specific sexual malignity black women have been forced to experience in public as a form of white pleasure and a register of white power in America. In this sense the imagination of sexual privacy these women express is a privacy they have never experienced, except as a space of impossibility. Anita Hill situated her own testimony not as a counter to the sexual economy of white erotics but in the professional discourse of an abused worker. Therefore, in Hill's testimony, two histories of corporeal identity converge. In both domains of experience, before sexual harassment became illegal, it was a widespread social practice protected by law. Invented as a technical legal category when middle-class white women started experiencing everyday violations of sexual dignity in the workplace, it has provided a way to link the banality and ordinariness of female sexualization to other hard-won protections against worker exploitation and personal injury.[5] It has also contributed to vital theoretical and policy reconsiderations of what constitutes the conditions of "consent" in the public sphere, a space which is no longer considered "free," even under the aegis of national-democratic protections.

What would it mean to write a genealogy of sexual harassment in which not an individual but a nation was considered the agent of unjust sexual power? Such an account of these complaints would provide an incisive critique of the modes of erotic and political dominance that have marked gender, race, and citizenship in America. It would register the sexual specificity of African American women's experience of white culture; it would link experiences of violated sexual privacy to the doctrine of abstract national "personhood," making America accountable for the private sexual transgressions of its privileged men and radically transforming the history of the "public" and the "private" in America; it would show how vital the existence of official sexual underclasses has been to producing national symbolic and political coherence; finally, and more happily, it would provide an archive of tactics that have made it possible to reoccupy both the sexual body and America by turning the constraints of privacy into information about national identity. I take the texts which I have quoted—Harriet Jacobs's slave narrative *Incidents in the Life of a Slave Girl,* Frances E. W. Harper's novel *Iola Leroy,* and the testimony of Anita Hill—as my sensorium of citizenship. The women in these texts each determine, under what they perceive to be the pressure or the necessity of history, to behave as native informants to an imperial power, that is, to mime the privileges of citizenship in the context of a particular national emergency. These national emergencies are, in chronological order, slavery, reconstruction, and the nomination of Clarence Thomas to the Supreme Court. They respond to these emergencies, these experiences of national sexuality, by producing what might be read as a counterpornography of citizenship. For the next two sections I will locate the history of gesture and sense that characterizes this genre in readings of the nineteenth-century texts, and then shift historical perspective to Anita Hill in section four. Senators without pants, lawyers without scruples, and a national fantasy of corporeal dignity will characterize this story.

A Meditation on National Fantasy, in which Women Make No Difference

These texts provide evidence that American citizenship has been profoundly organized around the distribution and coding of sensations. Two distinct moments in the nineteenth-century texts crystalize the conditions and fantasies of power motivating this affective domination, and so represent the negative space of political existence for American women in the last century. It may not appear that the sexual and affective encounters I will describe are indeed national, for they take place intimately between persons, in what look like private domains. The women's enslavement within the sensational regime of a privileged heterosexuality leads, by many different paths, to their transposition of these acts into the context of nationality. Even if sexual relations directly forced on these women mark individuals as corrupted by power, the women's narratives refuse to affirm the private horizon of personal entitlement as the cause of their suffering. America becomes explicitly, in this context, accountable for the sexual exploitation it authorizes in the guise of the white male citizen's domestic and erotic privilege.

Incidents in the Life of a Slave Girl registers many moments of intense corporeal stress, but one particular transitional gesture measures precisely on Harriet Jacobs's body the politics of her situation: hers is a hybrid experience of intimacy and alienation of a kind fundamental to African American women's experience of national sexuality under slavery. A mulatta, she was thought by some whites to be beautiful, a condition (as she says) that doubles the afflictions of race. She writes that the smallest female slave child will learn that "If God has bestowed beauty upon her, it will prove her greatest curse. That which commands admiration in the white woman only hastens the degradation of the female slave" (28). Racial logic gave America a fantasy image of its own personal underclass, with European-style beauty in the slave population justifying by nature a specific kind of exploitation by whites, who could mask their corporeal domination of all slaves in fantasies of masculine sexual entrapment by the slave women's availability and allure. For dark-skinned "black" women this form of exploitation involved rape and forced reproduction. These conditions applied to mulatta women too, but the lightness of these women also provided material for white men's parodic and perverse fantasies of masking domination as love and conjugal decorum.[6] Theatrically, they set up a parallel universe of sexual and racial domestic bliss and heterosexual entitlement: this involved dressing up the beautiful mulatta and playing white-lady-of-the-house with her, building her a little house that parodied the big one, giving her the kinds of things that white married ladies received, only in this instance without the protections of law. Jacobs herself was constantly threatened with this fancy life, if only she would consent to it.

This relation of privilege, which brought together sexual fantasy and

the law, disguised enslavement as a kind of courtship, and as caricature
was entirely a production of the intentions and whims of the master.
Harriet Jacobs was involved in an especially intricate and perverse game
of mulatta sexual guerilla theater. One of *her* moves in this game was to
become sexually involved with a white man other than her owner, Dr.
Flint. (This man's *nom de théatre* is "Mr. Sands," but his real name was
Samuel Tredwell Sawyer and he was a United States Congressman, a
status to which I will return in the next section.) Jacobs reports that Mr.
Sands seemed especially sympathetic to her plight and that of their two
children, and when he is introduced in the narrative's first half he seems
to represent the promise of a humane relation between the sexes in the
South—despite the fractures of race and in contrast to the sexual and
rhetorical repertoire of violences with which Dr. Flint tortures Jacobs
and her family. But the bulk of *Incidents* finds Jacobs in constant psychic
torture about Sands himself. Her anxiety about whether he will remember her when she is gone, and remember his promises to free their
children, makes her risk life and limb several times to seek him out.

•   •   •

No longer believing that Sands is a man of his word, Jacobs at length
decides to escape—not at first from the South, but from Dr. Flint,
following an intricately twisted path through the swamps, the hollow
kitchen floors, and the other covert spaces of safety semi-secured by the
slave community.[7] This spatial improvisation for survival culminates in
a move to her grandmother's attic, where she spends seven years of so-
called freedom, the price of which was lifelong nervous and muscular
disruptions of her body. On the last day of her transition from enslavement, which was also the end of her freedom of movement, Jacobs's
final act was to walk the public streets of her home town (Edenton,
North Carolina) in disguise, one that required perverse elaborations of
the already twisted epidermal schema of slavery. In her traveling clothes
she does not assume white "lady's" apparel but hides her body in men's
"sailor's clothes" and mimes the anonymity of a tourist, someone who
is passing through; second, in this last appearance in her native town she
appears in blackface, her skin darkened with charcoal. A juridically
black woman whose experience of slavery as a mulatta parodies the
sexual and domestic inscription of whiteness moves away from slavery
by recrossing the bar of race and assuming the corporeal shroud of
masculinity. This engagement with the visible body fashions her as ab-

solutely invisible on the street. Moving toward escape, she passes "several people whom [she] knew," but they do not recognize her. Then "the father of my children came so near that I brushed against his arm; but he had no idea who it was" (113).

When Mr. Sands does not recognize Jacobs, though he sees her and touches her body, it becomes prophetically clear how specific his interest in her was. He desired a mulatta, a woman who signifies white but provides white men a different access to sexuality. Dressed as a man, she is invisible to him. With a black face, she is invisible to him, no longer an incitement to his desire. Touching him she thinks about other kinds of intimacy they have had—she calls him the father of their children— but in a certain sense her body registers what is numb to his *because* he is privileged. He has the right to forget and to not feel, while sensation and its memory are all she owns. This is the feeling of what we might call the slave's two bodies: sensual and public on the one hand; vulnerable, invisible, forgettable on the other.

· · ·

If Jacobs experiences as a fact of life the political meaninglessness of her own sensations, Harper represents the process whereby Iola is disenfranchised of her sensations. In the following passage Iola discovers that she is a slave, politically meaningful but, like Jacobs, sensually irrelevant. Harper meticulously narrates Iola's sustained resistance to the theft of her senses by the corporeal fantasies of the slave system.[8] This resistance is a privilege Iola possesses because of the peculiar logic of racial identity in America, which draws legal lines that disregard the data of subjectivity when determining the identity of "race." Iola is a mulatta raised in isolated ignorance of her mother's racial history. Her mother Marie was a Creole slave of Eugene Leroy's, manumitted and educated by him before their marriage. Against Marie's wishes, the father insists that the children grow up in ignorance of their racial complexity, the "cross" in their blood. He does this to preserve their self-esteem, which is founded on racial unselfconsciousness and a sense of innate freedom (84). When the father dies, an unscrupulous cousin tampers with Marie's manumission papers and convinces a judge to negate them. He then sends a lawyer to trick Iola into returning South and thus to slavery. Her transition between lexicons, laws, privileges, and races takes place, appropriately, as a transition from dreaming to waking. She rides on the train with the lawyer who will transport her "home" to the slave system, but she is as yet unknowing, dreaming of her previous domestic felicity:

> In her dreams she was at home, encircled in the warm clasp of her father's arms, feeling her mother's kisses lingering on her lips, and hearing the joyous greetings of the servants and Mammy Liza's glad welcome as she folded her to her heart. From this dream of bliss she was awakened by a burning kiss pressed on her lips, and a strong arm encircling her. Gazing around and taking in the whole situation, she sprang from her seat, her eyes flashing with rage and scorn, her face flushed to the roots of her hair, her voice shaken with excitement, and every nerve trembling with angry emotion. (103)

When, like the Prince in a debauched *Sleeping Beauty*, the lawyer kisses Iola, he awakens her and all of her senses to a new embodiment. At first Iola dreams of life in the white family, with its regulated sexualities and the pleasure of its physical routine. Feeling her father's arms, kissing her mother, hearing the servants, snuggling with mammy: these are the idealized domestic sensations of white feminine plantation privilege, which provides a sensual system that is safe and seems natural. This is why Iola does not understand the lawyer's violation of her body. Since he already sees her as public property, authorized by a national slave system, he feels free to act without her prior knowledge, while she still feels protected by white sexual gentility. Thus the irony of her flashing-eyed, pulsating response: to Iola this is the response of legitimate self-protectiveness, but to the lawyer the passion of her resistance actually increases her value on the slave market. Her seduction and submission to the master's sexuality would reflect the victory of his economic power, which is a given. Her sensations make no sense to the slave system; therefore they are no longer credible. Her relation to them makes no difference. This is the most powerful index of powerlessness under the law of the nation.

Slavery, Citizenship, and Utopia: Some Questions about America

I have described the political space where nothing follows from the experience of private sensation as a founding condition of slave subjectivity, a supernumary nervous system here inscribed specifically and sexually on the bodies and minds of slave women. We see, in the narratives of Jacobs and Iola Leroy, that the process of interpellating this affective regime was ongoing, and that no rhetoric could protect them from what seemed most perverse about it, the permission it seemed to give slave owners to create sexual fantasies, narratives, masquerades of domesticity within which they could pretend *not* to dominate women, or to mediate their domination with displays of expenditure and chivalry.

But if this blurring of the lines between domination and play, between rhetorical and physical contact, and between political and sexual license always worked to reinforce the entitled relation to sensation and power the master culture enjoyed, both *Incidents* and *Iola Leroy* tactically blur another line—between personal and national tyranny. In the last section I described the incommensurate experiences of intimacy under slavery. Here I want to focus on how these intimate encounters with power structure Jacobs's and Harper's handling of the abstract problem of *nationality* as it is experienced—not as an idea, but as a force in social life, in experiences that mark the everyday. For Jacobs, writing before Emancipation, the nation as a category of experience is an archive of painful anecdotes, bitter feelings, and precise measurements of civic failure. She derives no strength from thinking about the possibilities of imagined community: hers is an anti-utopian discourse of amelioration. In contrast, Harper writes after the war and enfranchisement. These conditions for a postdiasporic national fantasy provide the structure for her re-imagination of social value and civic decorum in a radically reconstructed America. The felt need to transform painful sexual encounters into a politics of nationality drove both of these women to revise radically the lexicon and the narratives by which the nation appears as a horizon both of dread and of fantasy.

Jacobs's *Incidents* was written for and distributed by white abolitionists whose purpose was to demonstrate not just how scandalous slavery was but how central sexuality was in regulating the life of the slave. Yet the reign of the master was not secured simply through the corporeal logics of patriarchy and racism. Jacobs shows a variety of other ways her body was erotically dominated in slavery—control over movement and sexuality, over time and space, over information and capital, and over the details of personal history that govern familial identity—and links these scandals up to a powerful critique of America, of the promises for democracy and personal mastery it offers to and withholds from the powerless.

Jacobs's particular point of entry to nationality was reproductive. The slave mother was the "country" into which the slave child was born, a realm unto herself whose foundational rules constituted a parody of the birthright properties of national citizenship. Jacobs repeatedly recites the phrase "follow the condition of the mother," framed in quotation marks, to demonstrate her only positive representation in the law, a representation that has no entitlement, a parodically American mantra as fundamental as another phrase about following she had no right to use, "life, liberty, and the pursuit of happiness."

But the technicalities of freedom were not enough to satisfy Jacobs that America had the potential to fulfill its stated mission to be a Christian country. To gain free, unencumbered motherhood would be to experience the inversion of the sexual slavery she has undergone as a condition of her noncitizenship: at the end of the text, her freedom legally secured, she considers herself still unfree in the absence of a secure domestic space for her children.[9] But if Jacobs's relation to citizenship in the abstract is bitter and despairing, her most painful nationally authorized contact was intimate, a relation of frustrating ironic proximity.

I have characterized her sexual and reproductive relation with Mr. Sands, the United States Congressman Samuel Tredwell Sawyer. A truly sentimental fiction would no doubt reveal something generous about Congressman Sawyer, about a distinguished political career that might have included, somehow, traces of the influence Jacobs had on Sawyer's consciousness, revealed in a commitment to securing legal consensus on the humanity of slaves; and it would be simply trivial to note that issues of the *Congressional Globe* from 1838 reveal him in another universe of political consciousness, entirely undistinguished (he seems concerned with laws regulating duelling). More important, *Incidents* establishes that his rise to national office directly correlated with his increasing disregard for his promises to emancipate their children and her brother, both of whom he had bought from Flint in isolated acts of real empathy for Jacobs. Like many liberal tyrants, Sawyer so believes that his relative personal integrity and good intentions place him above moral culpability that he has no need to act morally within the law. Indeed, the law is the bar to empathy.

•   •   •

The Congressman whose sexual pleasure and sense of self-worth have been secured by the institution of slavery is corrupted by his proximity to national power. Yet Jacobs speaks the language of power, while Sawyer speaks the language of personal ethics; she looks to political solutions, while his privilege under the law makes its specific constraints irrelevant to him. Under these conditions Jacobs concludes three things about the politics of national sexuality. One is borne out by the performative history of her own book: "If the secret memoirs of many members of Congress should be published, curious details [about the sexual immorality of official men] would be unfolded" (142). The second she discovers as she returns from a trip to England where she has found political, sexual, racial, and spiritual peace and regeneration: "We had a tedious winter passage, and from the distance spectres seemed to rise up on the shores of the United States. It is a sad feeling to be afraid of one's native country" (186). Third, and finally, having established America as a negative space, a massive space of darkness, ghosts, shame, and barbarism, Jacobs sees no possibility that political solutions will ameliorate the memory and the ongoing pain of African American existence—as long as law marks a border between abstract and practical ethics. By the end of *Incidents* national discourse itself has become a mode of memorial rhetoric, an archive of dead promises.

I have identified thus two kinds of experience of the national for Jacobs: the actual pain of its practical betrayals through the many conscriptions of her body that I am associating with national sexuality and a psychic rage at America for not even trying to live up to the conditions of citizenship it promises in law and in spirit. After emancipation, in 1892 when Frances Harper is writing *Iola Leroy,* speaking at suffrage conferences, at the National Congress of Negro Women, and at the Columbian Exposition, she imagines that citizenship might provide a model of identity that ameliorates the experience of corporeal mortification that has sustained American racisms and misogyny.[10] Harper argues that "more than the changing of institutions we need the development of a national conscience, and the upbuilding of national character," but she imagines this project of reconstruction more subtly and more radically than this kind of nationalistic rhetoric might suggest.[11] She refuses the lure of believing that the discourse of disembodied democratic citizenship applies to black Americans: she says, "You white women speak here of rights. I speak of wrongs. I, as a colored woman, have had in this country an education which has made me feel as if I were in the situation of Ishmael, my hand against every man, and every man's hand against me."[12] But Jacobs's solution to the enigma of social life under racism and misogyny—to privatize social relations—was not the only solution to this violent touching of hands. In contrast to Jacobs's narrative, Harper's *Iola Leroy* seizes the scene of citizenship from white America and rebuilds it, in the classic sense, imagining a liberal public sphere located within the black community.[13] More than a critical irritant to the white "people," the text subverts the racially dominant national polity by rendering it irrelevant to the fulfillment of its own national imaginary. Harper's civic and Christian black American nationality depends not only on eliding the horizon of white pseudo-democracy; she also imagines that African American nationalism will provide a model of dignity and justice that white American citizens will be obliged to follow.

A double movement of negation and theorization transforms the condition of citizenship as the novel imagines it. Harper's critical tactic banishes white Americans from the utopian political imaginary activity of this text. The initial loss of white status is performed, however, not as an effect of African American rage but rather as an act of white political rationality. A general in the Northern Army, encountering the tragedy of Iola's specific history and the detritus of the war, disavows his own identification as an American: he thinks, "Could it be possible that this young and beautiful girl had been a chattel, with no power to protect herself from the highest insults that lawless brutality could inflict upon innocent and defenseless womanhood? Could he ever again glory in his American citizenship, when any white man, no matter how coarse, cruel, or brutal, could buy or sell her for the basest purposes? Was it not true that the cause of a hapless people had become entangled with the lightnings of heaven, and dragged down retribution upon the land?" (39). This repudiation envelops national, racial, and gendered self-disenfranchisement, and clears the way for a postpatriarchal, postracist, Christian commonwealth. Its ethical aura hovers over the novel's postwar narrative as well: Iola's experience of racism and misogyny in the metropolitan and commercial spaces of the North induces more pronouncements by whites about the unworthiness of white people to lead America in official and everyday life, since it is white national culture that has transformed the country from a space of enlightenment to a place of what she calls shadows and foreshadowing.

Such political self-impeachments by whites make it possible for Harper to reinvent a truly African American-centered *American* citizenship. In this sense, race in *Iola Leroy* is not solely a negative disciplinary category of national culture but becomes an archive of speech and life activities recast as a political arsenal. The originary form for African American insurgent community building derives from the subversive vernacular practices of slave life—from, as the first chapter title suggests, "The Mystery of Market Speech and Prayer Meetings." The narrative opens in the marketplace, where the slaves are shown to use an allegorical language to communicate and to gossip illegally about the progress of freedom during the Civil War. Just as the white masters travel, "talking politics in . . . State and National capitals" (7), slaves converse about the freshness of butter, eggs, and fish: but these ordinary words turn out to contain covert communication from the battlefield (7–8). In addition to exploiting the commercial space, the slave community performs its political identity at prayer meetings, where more illegal communication about the war and everyday life under slavery also transpires in allegory and secrecy.

The internal communications and interpretations of the community become public and instrumental in a different way after the war, when the place where the community met to pray to God and for freedom is transformed into a site where families dispersed by slavery might recombine: "They had come to break bread with each other, relate their experiences, and tell of their hopes of heaven. In that meeting were remnants of broken families—mothers who had been separated from their children before the war, husbands who had not met their wives for years" (179). These stories demonstrating kinship locate it not, however, in memories of shared lives or blood genealogies but rather in common memories of the violence of familial separation and dispersal. Under the conditions of legal impersonality which had governed slave personhood, the repetition of personal narratives of loss is the only currency of identity the slaves can exchange. The collective tactic here after slavery is to circulate self-descriptions in the hope that they will be repeated as gossip and heard by relatives, who will then come to the next convention and recite their own autobiographies in the hope that the rumor was true, that their story had an echo in someone else's life.

The collective storytelling about the diasporic forces of slavery is reinvented after the migration north, in salons where what Harper calls *conversazione* take place. Habermas and Landes have described the central role of the salon in building a public sphere.[14] Its function was to make the public sphere performatively democratic: more permeable by women and the ethnic and class subjects who had been left out of aristocratic privilege and who learn there to construct a personal and collective identity through the oral sharing of a diversity of written ideas. Harper explains at great length how conventions and *conversazione* transformed what counted as "personal" testimony in the black community: the chapter "Friends in Council," for example, details papers and contentious conversations about them entitled "Negro Emigration," "Patriotism," "Education of Mothers," and "Moral Progress of the Race," and a poem written by Harper herself entitled "Rallying Cry." All of these speeches and the conversations about them focus on uplifting the race and rethinking history; and the conditions of uplifting require imagining a just America, an America where neither race nor sexuality exists as a mode of domination. As Iola's friend, Miss Delaney, says, "I want my pupils to do all in their power to make this country worthy of their deepest devotion and loftiest patriotism" (251). Finally, after these face-to-face communities of African Americans seeking to transform their enslaved identities into powerful cultural and political coalitions are established, a literary tradition becomes possible: Iola herself is asked to serve the race by writing the story of her life that is this novel. Harper, in the afterword to the novel, imagines a new African American literature, "glowing with the fervor of the tropics and enriched by the luxuriance of the Orient." This revisionary aesthetic will, in her view, fill the African American "quota of good citizenship" and thus "add to the solution of our unsolved American problem" (282). In sum, the transmission of personal narrative, inscribed into the interiority of a community, becomes a vehicle for social transformation in *Iola Leroy,* recombining into a multicultural, though not multiracial, public sphere of collective knowledge. In so reconstructing through mass-circulated literature the meaning of collective personhood, and in so insisting on a "quota system" of good citizenship based not on racial assimilation but on a national ethics, the African American community Harper imagines solves the problem of America for itself.

Diva Citizenship

When you are born into a national symbolic order that explicitly marks your person as illegitimate, far beyond the horizon of proper citizenship, and when your body also becomes a site of privileged fantasy property and of sexual contact that the law explicitly proscribes but privately entitles, you inhabit the mulatta's genealogy, a genealogy of national experience. The national body is ambiguous because its norms of privilege require a universalizing logic of disembodiment, while its local, corporeal practices are simultaneously informed by that legal privilege and—when considered personal, if not private—are protected by the law's general proximity. The African American women of this narrative understood that only a perversely "un-American" but nationally addressed text written from the history of a national subculture could shock white citizens into knowing how compromised citizenship has been as a category of experience and fantasy, not least for the chastised American classes.

This question of sexual harassment is thus not just a "woman's" question. A charged repertoire of private domination and erotic theatricality was licensed by American law and custom to encounter the African American women of whom I have written here, and many others, whose locations in hierarchies of racism, homophobia, and misogyny will require precisely and passionately written counter-histories. In twentieth-century America, anyone coded as "low," embodied, or subculturally "specific" continues to experience, with banal regularity, the corporeal sensation of nationality as a sensation over which she/he has no control. This, in the broadest sense, is sexual harassment. These texts break the sanitizing silences of sexual privacy in order to create national publics trained to think, and thus to think differently, about the corporeal conditions of citizenship. One of these conditions was the evacuation of erotic or sexual or even sensational life itself as a possible ground of personal dignity for African American women in America. As the rational, anti-passional logic of *Incidents* and *Iola Leroy* shows, the desire to become national seems to call for a *release* from sensuality— this is the cost, indeed the promise, of citizenship.

But the possibility of a revitalized national identity flickers in traces of peculiar identification within these texts. I call this possibility Diva Citizenship, but can only describe, at this point, the imaginable conditions of its emergence as an unrealized form of political activity. Diva

Citizenship has a genealogy too, a dynastic, dignified, and pleasuring one. It courses through a variety of media forms and public spheres—from the Old Testament through CNN, through the works of bell hooks, Donna Haraway, Wayne Koestenbaum, and others.[15] For Haraway, cyborg citizenship replaces the "public/private" distinction as a paradigm for political subjectivity; hooks similarly derives the potential politics of the "third world diva girl" from the everyday forms of assertive and contesting speech she absorbed among "Southern black folk." These forms of speech are lived as breaches of class decorum between and among white, Third World, and African American feminists who discipline the ways women take, hold, use, respect, or demonize public authority: hooks sees the transgression of these decorums as central to liberation politics. For Koestenbaum, the Diva's public merging of "ordinariness touched by sublimity" has already been crucial to the emergence of a "collective gay subcultural imagination," where the public grandiosity of survival, the bitter banality of negotiating everyday life, generates subversive gossip about icons that actually works to create counterculture. "Where there is fever," he writes, "the need for police arises." Crossing police barricades and the civilizing standards of public life, Diva Citizenship takes on as a national project redefining the scale, the volume, and the erotics of "what you can [sincerely] do for your country."

One strategy of slave literature has been its royalist strain.[16] In *Iola Leroy*, Harper locates the promise of Diva Citizenship in the Biblical story of Queen Esther. Marie, Iola Leroy's mother, makes an abolitionist speech, executing a performance of refracting ironies. Marie speaks as a Creole slave woman to a free white audience on the day she graduates from the "finishing" school that will enable her to pass as the white wife of Albert Leroy: "Like Esther pleading for the lives of her people in the Oriental courts of a despotic king, she stood before the audience, pleading for those whose lips were sealed, but whose condition appealed to the mercy and justice of the Nation" (75). The analogies between Marie and Esther are myriad: forced to pass as a Persian in the court of Ahasuerus, the King and her husband, Esther speaks as a Jew to save her people from genocide. She mobilizes her contradictions to unsettle the representational and political machinery of a dominant culture that desires her. It is not only in the gesture of special pleading that Marie absorbs Esther, but in the analogy between the mulatta woman and the assimilated Jew. Esther's capacity to pass likewise not only made her erotic masquerade the default activity of her everyday embodiment but also gave her sexual access to power—which she used not in a prevaricating way but under the pressure of a diasporic ethics. Purim, Queen Esther's holiday, is offered as a day of masquerade, revelry, and rage at tyranny—although as a story additionally about a wronged Queen (Vashti) and a holocaust, its status as an origin tale of domestic and imperial violence cannot be glossed over.[17] But Queen Esther stands in Harper's text as another foreign national separated at birth from the privileges of nationality, and also as a slave to masterly fantasies of sexual hierarchy and sensational excess who learned to countertheatricalize her identity and to wield it against injustice.

Jacobs's contribution to this monarchical fantasy politics deploys the Queen not as a figure of tactical self-distortion and instrumental sexual intimacy but as a figure of superior power who remakes the relations between politics and the body in America. She represents the "state of civilization in the late nineteenth century of the United States" by showing a variety of indirect and noncoherent ways the nation came into deliberate contact with slaves—through scandalous and petty torture. In turn, Jacobs shows how the slaves misrecognize, in potentially and sometimes strategically radical ways, what constitutes the nation. This passage takes place in an extraordinary chapter titled "What Slaves Are Taught to Think of the North." Jacobs describes at great rageful length the relation between the sexual brutality of masters to slaves and their lies, what she calls "the pains" masters take to construct false scenarios about "the hard kind of freedom" that awaited freed or escaped slaves in the North. She argues that these slaves, so demoralized by the impossibility of imagining political freedom, become actively complicit in the local scene of sexual savagery—actually sneaking "out of the way to give their masters free access to their wives and daughters" (44)—because sexuality is the only exchange value the slaves pseudo-possess. Jacobs takes the example of these relations of misrecognition and affective distortion and turns them back on the nation:

> One woman begged me to get a newspaper and read it over. She said her husband told her that the black people had sent word to the queen of 'Merica that they were all slaves; that she didn't believe it, and went to Washington city to see the president about it. They quarreled; she drew her sword upon him, and swore that he should help her to make them all free.
>
> That poor ignorant woman thought that America was governed by a

Queen, to whom the President was subordinate. I wish the President was
subordinate to Queen Justice. (45)

Let us suppose it were true that the Queen of America came down to
Washington and put the knife to the President's throat. Her strategy
would be to refute his privilege, and that of citizens like him, to be above
the sensational constraints of citizenship. The Queen of America edu-
cates him about his own body's boundaries with a cold tip of steel, and
he emancipates the slaves. But Jacobs, never one to give the nation credit
for even potentially recognizing its excesses, closes this anecdote not
advocating violence on this individual President but subversively trans-
ferring the horizon of national identity to its illiterate citizens. She does
this in order to counter what Donna Haraway has called "the informat-
ics of domination":[18] using the misrecognitions of everyday life as the
base of her national archive, Jacobs shows how national consciousness
truly cuts a path through gossip, deliberate lies of the masters, the
national press, the President of the United States who lives in Washington, the Queen of America who is dislocated from any specific capital,
and the Queen of Justice who rules, perhaps in a universe parallel to
that of the other Queen, and who has no national boundaries. In so
creating this genealogy, this flow chart of power whose boundaries expand with every sentence written about America, Jacobs dislocates the
nation from its intelligible forms. She opens up a space in which the
national politics of corporeal identity becomes displayed on the monarchical body, and thus interferes with the fantasy norms of democratic
abstraction; in so doing, she creates an American history so riddled with
the misrecognitions of mass nationality that it is unthinkable in its typical form, as a narrative about sovereign subjects and their rational
political representation. For no American president could be subordinate
to any Queen—of America or of Justice. Bracketing that horizon of
possibility, it becomes imperative to take up the scandalous promise of
Jacobs's strategy, which is to exploit a fantasy of cutting across the space
that doesn't exist, where abstract and corporeal citizenship come into
contact not on the minoritized body but on *the body of the nation*.

It is this phantasmatic body that the Anita Hill/Clarence Thomas
hearings brought to us in the delusional week before the vote. It was
alluded to in the corporeality of Thomas himself: in his alleged exploitation of personal collegiality in federal workspaces; in the racist fantasies that he evoked to account for his victimization by Hill and on the

Hill; in the aura of the minority stereotype black authority represents as a "token" on the Supreme Court. The national body is signified in Hill's own body as well, which displayed all of the decorums of bourgeois national polity while transgressing the veil between official and private behavior that grounds the erotic power of the state. Finally, the body of the nation was configured in the images of senators sitting in judgment and in the experts they brought in to testify to the law and to issues of "character" and "appearance."[19]

What I want to focus on is a displaced mediation of the national embodiment Hill and Thomas produced, in a television sitcom about the activities of a white and female-owned Southern business; the episode of *Designing Women* entitled "The Strange Case of Clarence and Anita" that aired shortly after the vote. In many ways, this episode reproduces the legitimacy of masculine speech over feminine embodiment in the political public sphere, most notably by contrasting news clips of speaking powerful men to clips that represent Hill only in tableau moments of demure silence before the Senate Judiciary Committee. Thus in one light the show's stifling of Hill reproduces a version of the imperial fantasy Gayatri Chakravorty Spivak describes, in which white women "heroically" save brown women from brown *and* white men. But while Hill herself demonstrated respect for national decorums and conservative ideologies of authority, her *case* substantially disrupted norms of embodiment of the national space and, indeed, revealed and produced disturbances in what counts as the national space itself.[20]

In this episode, the characters share private opinions about Thomas and Hill, along with painful personal memories of sexual harassment; but under the pressure of historical circumstance, the ordinary space of intimacy they share comes into contact with a media frenzy: tee shirts they buy at the mall that say "He did it" or "She lied" turn their bodies into billboards, which they flash angrily at each other; opinion polls that register the micro-fluctuations of "public sentiment" generate conversation about linguistic bias and motivate assertions of their own superiority to the numerically represented "people"; CNN, reinstated as the source of national identity, transforms the undifferentiated stream of opinions from all over the country into national data as "official" as that emanating from Washington itself; the television set focuses the collective gaze, such that domestic and public spheres become merged, as do news and entertainment (the character Julia Sugarbaker, for example, suggests that Thomas belongs not on the Supreme Court, but in the National Repertory Theatre); and, in the climactic moment, a local television reporter tapes an interview with Suzanne Sugarbaker, a Thomas supporter, and Mary Jo Shively, a self-described "feminist," right in their living room. What's striking about the condensation of these media forms and forms of embodied political intimacy is how close so many different and overlapping American publics become—and in the context not of a soap opera but of a situation comedy that refuses, this time, to contain the "situation" within the frame of its half-hour. Judge Thomas and Professor Hill turn into "Clarence" and "Anita" in this situation, like TV neighbors having a domestic row; and the diverse, incorrect, passionate, and cynical range of opinions that flow in the room take on the status of personal and political gossip. Not just gossip about judges or senators without pants but about the intimate details of national identity.

At one point Mary Jo explodes in rage at Senator John Danforth's claim, shown on CNN, that Anita Hill suffered from a delusional disease in which she confused her own desire for power with the power of Thomas's sexual desire. Hearing Danforth's pleasure in this pop-psych diagnosis rouses Mary Jo to call his office in Washington. But she is frustrated in this desire because the line is busy. I myself wanted to call Washington during Hill's testimony or to testify in any way to my own banal/expert knowledge of the nonconsensual erotics of power we code as "harassment." The desire for contact sometimes took the phantasmatic form of a private letter to a senator, or one to a newspaper, sometimes a phone encounter, sometimes a fantasy that a reporter from the national news or "Nightline" would accost me randomly on the street and that my impromptu eloquence would instantly transport me to the televisual realm of a Robert Bork, where my voice and body would be loud, personal, national, and valorized.

In my view this ache to be an American diva was not about persuasion. It derived from a desire to enter a senator's body and to dominate it through an orifice he was incapable of fully closing, an ear or an eye. This intimate fantasy communication aimed to provoke sensations in him for which he was unprepared, those in that perverse space between empathy and pornography that Karen Sánchez-Eppler has isolated as constitutive of white Americans' interest in slaves, slave narratives, and other testimonials of the oppressed.[21] And in so appealing to a senator's authority over the terms in which I experience my (theoretically impossible) sexualized national being, I imagined making him so full and so sick with knowledge of what he has never experienced officially that he would lose, perhaps gratefully, his sensual innocence about—not the power of his own sexuality—but the sexuality of his own power, and . . .

This is where my fantasy of swearing out a female complaint would falter, stop knowing itself and what it wanted. The desire to go public, to exploit the dispersed media of national life, became my way of approximating the power of official nationality to dominate bodies—a motive which, in a relation of overidentification, I and many others had mapped onto Hill's majestic and courageous citizenship. It also suggested to me that the fantasy of addressing the nation directly, of violating the citizen's proper silence about the sensations of citizenship, is a fantasy that many Americans live.[22]

The horizon of critical possibility lies, however, not in orchestrating mass culture and mass nationality through the pseudo-immediacy of "electronic town halls," currently offered as a solution to the problem of recovering representational politics as a kind of collective decision making in the United States. Diva Citizenship reminds us that the legal tender of contemporary politics is no longer calibrated according to a gold standard of immediacy, authenticity, and rationality; the bodily distortions and sensual intimacy of national media degrade representations of political agency and therefore bleed into a space of surprise where political experiments in re-imagining agency and critical practice itself can be located, perhaps among the kinds of queenly gestures and impulses toward freedom I have recorded here.

To close: the final narrative image of *Designing Women,* which merges a radical embodied female citizenship with the aura of the star system. Annie Potts, who plays Mary Jo Shively, wears Bette Davis drag. Dixie Carter, who plays Julia Sugarbaker, masquerades as Joan Crawford. Having come directly from a dress rehearsal of a local theatrical adaptation of *What Ever Happened to Baby Jane?* they sit on the couch, exhausted. They are not exhausted from the rehearsal, but from the rage they have expended on what they call this "day of [national] infamy." Meanwhile, their friends slow dance the night away, like pre-adolescents at a slumber party. Bette asks Joan to dance with her. They get up and look at each other. "Who should lead?" asks Bette Davis. "Well, Bette," says Joan Crawford, "considering who we are, I think we both should." And who are they? As Joan says to Bette in an earlier moment, "two of the toughest talking big-shouldered broads ever to live in this country."

NOTES

Special thanks to Gordon Hutner, Miriam Hansen, and audiences at Rutgers, the University of North Carolina, Chicago State, and the MLA for insightful and impassioned critical responses.

1. The word "experience" is important in the texts I am addressing and in the one I am writing here, and requires some explication. The category "experience" is not meant to refer to self-evident autobiographical data over which the experiencing person has control: the experience of being dominated, for example, is subjective, and therefore incompatible descriptions of it might engender legitimate contestation. But I take experience here more fundamentally to be something produced in the moment when an activity becomes framed as an event, such that the subject enters the empire of quotation marks, anecdote, self-reflection, memory. More than a category of authenticity, "experience" in this context refers to something someone "has," in aggregate moments of self-estrangement. Jacobs, Harper, and Hill are aware of the unreliability of experience as data both in their own perceptions and in their drive to produce convincing evidence to buttress their arguments for social change or informed consciousness. For a strong summary of the current historicist argument over the evidentiary use of experience, see Joan W. Scott, "The Evidence of Experience," *Critical Inquiry* 17 (Summer 1991): 773–97; and, more critically, Mas'ud Zavarzadeh and Donald Morton, "Theory Pedagogy Politics: The Crisis of 'The Subject' in the Humanities," in their collection *Theory/Pedagogy/Politics: Texts for Change* (Urbana: Univ. of Illinois Press, 1991), 1–32; and Chris Weedon, "Post-Structuralist Feminist Practice," in the same volume, 47–63. The phrase "the poetry of the future" comes, famously, from Karl Marx, *The 18th Brumaire of Napoleon Bonaparte.*

2. Frances E. W. Harper, *Iola Leroy; or, Shadows Uplifted* (1892; rpt., College Park, Md.: McGrath, 1969), 115–16. All further references will be contained in the text.

3. Harriet A. Jacobs, *Incidents in the Life of a Slave Girl: Written by Herself* (edited by Lydia Maria Child), ed. Jean Fagan Yellin (Cambridge: Harvard Univ. Press, 1987).

4. Anita Hill, *New York Times,* 12 October 1991, sec. 1; 15 October 1991, sec. 1.

5. For the myriad transformations in legal theory and practical juridical norms regulating what counts as "injury" and "harm" to women, see *At the Boundaries of Law: Feminism and Legal Theory,* ed. Martha Albertson Fineman and Nancy Sweet Thomadsen (New York: Routledge, 1991); and *Feminist Legal Theory: Readings in Law and Gender,* ed. Katharine T. Bartlett and Roseanne Kennedy (Boulder: Westview, 1991).

6. There is a large outstanding bibliography on this subject. It includes Hazel

Carby, *Reconstructing Womanhood* (New York: Oxford Univ. Press, 1987); P. Gabrielle Foreman; "The Spoken and the Silenced in *Incidents in the Life of a Slave Girl* and *Our Nig*," *Callaloo* 13 (Spring 1990): 313–24; Jane Gaines, "White Privilege and Looking Relations: Race and Gender in Feminist Film Theory," *Screen* 8 (Autumn 1988): 12–27; Hortense J. Spillers, "Notes on an Alternative Model—Neither/Nor," in *The Difference Within: Feminism and Critical Theory*, ed. Elizabeth Meese and Alice Parker (Philadelphia: John Benjamins, 1989), 165–87 and "Mama's Baby, Papa's Maybe: An American Grammar Book," *Diacritics* 17 (Summer 1987): 65–81.

7. See Valerie Smith, " 'Loopholes of Retreat': Architecture and Ideology in Harriet Jacobs's *Incidents in the Life of a Slave Girl*," in *Reading Black, Reading Feminist*, ed. Henry Louis Gates Jr. (New York: Meridian, 1990), 212–26.

8. I adapt this notion of "theft" from Harryette Mullen's work on orality and writing in *Incidents in the Life of a Slave Girl*. See "Runaway Tongue: Resistant Orality in *Uncle Tom's Cabin, Our Nig, Incidents in the Life of a Slave Girl*, and *Beloved*," in *The Culture of Sentiment: Race, Gender, and Sentimentality in Nineteenth-Century America*, ed. Shirley Samuels (New York: Oxford Univ. Press, 1992), 244–64.

9. On the counternational politics of gender and kinship in *Incidents*, see Spillers, "Mama's Baby, Papa's Maybe."

10. To place *Iola Leroy* in the context of Harper's complex political activities, see Carby, *Reconstructing Womanhood*, 63–94. Carby's chapter on Harper emphasizes the race/gender axis of her concerns, and provides crucial support to my thinking about nationality. See also Frances Smith Foster's Introduction to Frances Ellen Watkins Harper, *A Brighter Coming Day: A Frances Ellen Watkins Harper Reader* (New York: Feminist Press, 1990), 3–40.

11. Frances Ellen Watkins Harper, "Duty to Dependent Races," in *Black Women in Nineteenth-Century American Life: Their Words, Their Thoughts, Their Feelings*, ed. Bert James Loewenberg and Ruth Bogin (1891; rpt., University Park: Pennsylvania State Univ. Press, 1976), 245.

12. Harper, *A Brighter Coming Day*, 218.

13. The argument that nationality can overcome the fractures of race operates throughout Harper's speeches and poems as well. Perhaps the most condensed and eloquent of these was delivered at the Columbian Exposition. See "Woman's Political Future," in *The World's Congress of Representative Women*, ed. May Wright Sewall (Chicago: Rand, McNally, 1894), 433–38.

14. Jürgen Habermas, *The Structural Transformation of the Public Sphere: An Inquiry into a Category of Bourgeois Society*, trans. Thomas Burger (Cambridge: Harvard Univ. Press, 1989), 31–43; Joan B. Landes, *Women and the Public Sphere in the Age of the French Revolution* (Ithaca: Cornell Univ. Press, 1988), 22–31.

15. Donna Haraway, "A Manifesto for Cyborgs," in *Simians, Cyborgs, and*

Women: The Reinvention of Nature (New York: Routledge, 1991), 162; bell hooks, "Third World Diva Girls," in *Yearning: Race, Gender, and Cultural Politics* (Boston: South End, 1990), 89–102; Wayne Koestenbaum, "The Codes of Diva Conflict," chap. 3 of *The Queen's Throat: Opera, Homosexuality, and the Mystery of Desire* (New York: Poseidon, 1993). See also Laura Kipnis, "'(Male) Desire and (Female) Disgust: Reading *Hustler*," in *Cultural Studies*, ed. Lawrence Grossberg, Cary Nelson, and Paula Treichler (New York: Routledge, 1992), 373–91; Miriam Hansen, "The Return of Babylon: Rudolph Valentino and Female Spectatorship (1921–1926)," part 3 of *Babel and Babylon: Spectatorship in American Silent Film* (Cambridge: Harvard Univ. Press, 1991); Andrew Ross, *No Respect* (New York: Routledge, 1989); Carole-Anne Tyler, "Boys Will Be Girls: The Politics of Gay Drag," in *Inside/Out: Lesbian Theories, Gay Theories* (New York: Routledge, 1991), 32–71; and Patricia J. Williams, "A Rare Case Study of Muleheadedness and Men," in Toni Morrison, *Race-ing Justice, En-gendering Power: Essays on Anita Hill, Clarence Thomas, and the Construction of Social Reality* (New York: Pantheon, 1992) 159–71.

16. Barry Weller, "The Royal Slave and the Prestige of Origins," *Kenyon Review* 14 (Summer 1992): 65–78.

17. I focus here on the analogy Harper seems to make between Esther's complicated ethnic masquerade and Marie's racial one, and on the conditions for political speech that ensued. The *Book of Esther* as a whole tells a far more complex story. On the one hand, it might have provided Harper, and us, with a less patriarchalized model of feminine power: Queen Vashti, whose refusal to display her royal beauty to a banquet of drunken courtiers provoked Elizabeth Cady Stanton's *The Woman's Bible* to name her "the first woman recorded whose self-respect and courage enabled her to act contrary to the will of her husband . . . [in] the first exhibition of individual sovereignty of woman on record . . . true to the Divine aspirations of her nature" (86–88). On the other hand, the *Book of Esther* is a story about holocausts, a Jewish one averted and a Macedonian one revengefully executed by the Jews themselves (Elizabeth Cady Stanton and the Revising Committee, *The Woman's Bible* [1898; rpt., Seattle: Coalition Task Force on Women and Religion, 1974]).

18. Haraway, 161.

19. See especially Waneema Lubiano, "Black Ladies, Welfare Queens, and State Minstrels: Ideological War by Narrative Means," in Morrison, 321–63.

20. The original sentence, describing the mentality of "imperialist subject-production," is "White men are saving brown women from brown men" (Gayatri Chakravorty Spivak, "Can the Subaltern Speak?" in *Marxism and the Interpretation of Culture* [Urbana: Univ. of Illinois Press, 1988], 296).

21. Karen Sánchez-Eppler, "Bodily Bonds: The Intersecting Rhetorics of Feminism and Abolition," *Representations* 24 (Fall 1988): 28–59.

22. The fantasy of diminishing the scale of America to make the nation a

place one might encounter has a long history in American letters. See Lauren Berlant, *The Anatomy of National Fantasy: Hawthorne, Utopia, and Everyday Life* (Chicago: Univ. of Chicago Press, 1991); Jody Berland, "Angels Dancing: Cultural Technologies and the Production of Space," in Grossberg, Nelson, and Treichler, 39–55; and John Caughie, "Playing at Being American," *Logics of Television: Essays in Cultural Criticism,* ed. Patricia Mellencamp (Bloomington: Indiana Univ. Press, 1990), 44–58.

Part Two

Reading "Culture"

Chapter 5

Mass Culture/Popular Culture
Notes for a Humanist's Primer

Roy Harvey Pearce

Introduction by Frances Smith Foster

In 1961, Roy Harvey Pearce won the Chap-Book Award of the Poetry Society of America for *The Continuity of American Poetry,* the "first full-length and comprehensive study of the tradition of American poetry." This "ambitious undertaking" was, in his words, "a study in *cultural* history" (emphasis added). The next year, Pearce published "Mass Culture/Popular Culture: Notes for a Humanist's Primer," a manifesto that more succinctly articulated the theory implicit in his earlier book. In this essay he confesses that his project is nothing less than the transformation of the study of literature from what he called "the reductionism of positivistically inclined historiography and the formalism of *explication de texte,* each pursued as an end in itself" to a larger, more inclusive, and more intrusive work of cultural redefinition and social reconstruction.

To understand better and more accurately appreciate the innovative qualities of "Mass Culture/Popular Culture," one must recall the prevailing literary practices, definitions of culture, and construction of the USAmerican society during the 1960s. Formalism, especially the New Critical approach that examined texts as organic wholes, was still the standard literary method for college courses in American literature. Students studied and professors pontificated on "the best thoughts of the best minds"—virtually all of which apparently came from Anglo-American males.

Yet when "Mass Culture/Popular Culture" appeared, the Beatles were boring holes in college dormitory doors; folk songs and sermons from the Southern-based Civil Rights Movement (sometimes in the voices of Joan Baez, Pete Seeger, the Kingston Trio, and Peter, Paul, and Mary) informed the politics and poetics of countless students. Undergraduates quoted the sayings of Chairman Mao and the writings of Frantz Fanon, the letters of Martin Luther King, Jr., and the novels of Chinua Achebe almost as much as, if not more than, those of James Joyce, T. S. Eliot, and William Faulkner. USAmerican campuses were literal battlegrounds as increasingly larger groups of students and would-be students, at least those who were not too "Beat" or too "Hip," struggled to scale the walls of higher education's Ivory Tower, and when they met resistance were ready to burn the "Mother" down. In short, the previously privileged and the disadvantaged of all colors and contours were not content to sit quietly in the rear of the classroom and silently learn to appreciate Jefferson, James and Twain, Pound and Hemingway. Daughters of millionaires, sons of senators, middle-class Midwesterners, migrant workers, political refugees, African Americans, Hispanics, Native and Asian Americans were demanding representation and relevance from their professors and those who paid their professors' salaries.

In the face of these pressures, Pearce proposed transforming, rather than abandoning, literary studies by directing new attention to the relationship between literature and culture. Literature, he wrote, was a "living thing" that helped those in the present to know the values of the past, and through that knowledge to understand better the present and its potential for the "personal and collective future." Exegesis was not an end in itself but an essential tool to enable readers to develop a "lively sense of the possibilities for belief and commitment." The emphasis of "Mass Culture/Popular Culture" upon cultural diversity (folk, mass, popular, and elite) acknowledged the class bias of canonical literature and the aesthetics upon which they had achieved that status, even as it declared that mass culture was "easy play" and thus lower than the "higher forms" that exploited or fully engaged the "reality-principles" of real humanists. Though the sexism and Eurocentrism of the essay might occasionally rankle our twenty-first-century sensibilities, "Mass Culture/Popular Culture" was among the first essays of its age to argue that the goal of the cultural revolutionaries storming and infiltrating the halls of academe ought not to be understood as "out with the old and in with the other." Instead, Pearce urges enlightened humanists to realize that culture is constructed differently by people of various ethnicities, sexualities, and historical positions and to recognize that new technologies and other ways of knowing could be incorporated into the humanities if humanists understood and tolerated those differences. This attention to and conception of culture has since become a methodological starting point for American literary studies.

In "Mass Culture/Popular Culture," Pearce's writing makes the medium at least a part of the message. His tone of reason and logic begins with the first word: "Thinking." He asserts his membership in the fraternity of scholars by referring to "we." He often qualifies his more dramatic accusations or assertions with words such as "perhaps," assertions that his essay is really "notes," and assurances that he does "not mean to exclude the middle—the myriad essays, books, meditations, editorials on mass culture," but merely to recognize them as being a bit premature, simplistic, or misleading. The philosophical tone predominates in part because of the long, elaborate, or circumlocutory sentences. An air of conservatism (not entirely feigned) comes from asides such as "alas" and "unfortunately" that assure readers that despite his radical reinterpretation of literary criticism priorities and his blunt admission that "elite" more appropriately reveals the class issues that "high" hides, Pearce's humanist's goal is "to insure that there always will be the possibility for the transcending; in short, that mass culture has a viable relationship with *elite* culture."

At the same time, he offers cunning complications and heretical interpretations made more potent by sound that betrays sense. Here, too, the form of Pearce's prose reinforces the content of his argument. The almost nineteenth-century style of the Latinate and ornate sentences is again and again interrupted by the staccato, journalistic sectioning into ten parts. The headlines in capital letters that introduce the power points of his presentation depart from the gentlemanly transitions favored in other scholarly essays. And, perhaps most tellingly, Pearce employs examples from rock and roll and the blues, from James Baldwin's essays, and from mimeographed copies of commencement speeches, thereby elevating recording artists, African American writers, and college deans to equal status with Whitman and Emerson, and expanding the range of scholarly resources to include architectural histories and television scripts.

"Mass Culture/Popular Culture: Notes for a Humanist's Primer" is an excellent example of the early USAmerican formulations of cultural studies theory. In the strange way of the sixties, it complements and coincides with other cultural theorists such as Leroi Jones,[1] Claudio Guillén,[2] and Jerome Rothenberg and George Quasha.[3] When we read this essay today, particularly with an awareness of its historical context, many of us are surprised at its prescience and its relevance to our continued search for adequate and appropriate methodologies for studying literary and cultural forms.

NOTES

1. Jones is known today as Amiri Baraka, but during the period of his *Home: Social Essays* (New York: William Morrow, 1966) and *The System of Dante's Hell* (New York: Grove Press, 1965) to which I allude here, he was publishing as Leroi Jones.

2. Guillén's *Literature as System: Essays toward the Theory of Literary History* (Prince-

ton: Princeton University Press, 1971) understands itself as being part of theoretical innovations across disciplines such as linguistics and anthropology.

3. In *America a Prophecy: A New Reading of American Poetry from Pre-Columbian Times to the Present* (New York: Vintage Books, 1974), editors Rothenberg and Quasha posit USAmerican poetry as powerful through the "hidden unity" of Native American poetry, Shaker sacred writings, African American blues, Edgar Allen Poe, Emily Dickinson, Gertrude Stein, H. D., and others.

———— ▬▬▬ ————

> ". . . limits
> are what any of us
> are inside of."
> —Charles Olson, *The Maximus Poems, 5*

THINKING ABOUT MASS CULTURE these days, we seem increasingly to want to take a second or third or fourth step before we have taken the first. Or so I think a careful study of our essays and studies shows. Perhaps we fear that that first step is a step backward. And so it is—into ourselves. For once we admit something so overwhelmingly simple as the fact that we must live together in our community, we shall be obliged to inquire into what Edward Sapir long ago taught us to call the genuineness or spuriousness of our culture: that which gives our community such wholeness as it has. We say that our culture, any culture, is genuine to the degree that it allows full play to our sense of the dignity of man, spurious to the degree that it narrows or distorts or inhibits that sense. Hence we can do no less than begin at the beginning, within ourselves in our community, however narrow, distorted, or inhibited we may be. But it has been ever thus in the humanistic studies.

I mean to suggest in these notes that in the beginning and at the end the study of mass culture is the business—in our time a necessary condition—of the humanistic studies. So far we have not been able to envisage the end clearly because we have not sufficiently considered the beginning. I do not mean to exclude the middle—the myriad essays, books, meditations, editorials on mass culture. I mean only to get them into focus, to set them over against the image of man in which they must be conceived if they are to have any validity whatsoever. I am sure that most of those who have given us the essays, books, etc. have proceeded out of their faith in man. But on most humanists the net effect of their work, since it is so often programmatic and artificially particularized, has been to confuse the issue by simplifying it. To be sure, the simplification is often merely strategic, or "heuristic." Yet as often the stratagem has involved losing sight, if only temporarily, of him on whose behalf the issue has been raised, in whose image the issue must be conceived.

For the humanist the overwhelming consideration here derives from his vocation as teacher. In our world, humanists, whatever their special fields, are almost invariably teachers. The humanist's subject-matter indeed is his students; in the field of his special expertise, he is concerned with object-matter. In his meetings with his students, the humanist must inevitably put to the test the image of man as his special knowledge of his special field empowers him to. I mean by humanist, then, the worker in the humanistic studies, who, whatever else he is, is a teacher and must accordingly face the fact day-to-day that his students, his audiences in general, have had their lives and sensibilities markedly formed by mass culture. This is an aspect—unhappily, a necessary condition—of their life-styles. I suspect that it usually turns out that the humanist soon enough discovers that his life and sensibility have been so shaped too. He need not have any particular "professional" interest in mass culture, but he needs to learn how to think about it, how to interpret the burgeoning "professional" interest in it, as it bears on his role in the teacher-student relationship.

The central fact is quite simple: We do *not* live, alas, in a world we never made. Maybe we did not *really* make it; but it is ours, and it is pointless to conceive of ourselves in another world. As this world is ours we are this world's. As we have taken the good things it has given us, as we have perforce had to take the bad things which have inevitably come with the good things, so we must pay for them. Drive as hard a bargain as we can, we must, nonetheless, pay for them: pay by knowing them and living with the knowledge. Let us freely admit that on the whole mass culture is one of the "bad" things. But let us drive ourselves to go all the way in knowing it—to ask what it is, how it has developed, what it can *do* to us, what it can do *for* us.

By now these questions have all been pretty satisfactorily answered.

And I shall give the answers in summary fashion, and then consider a question which the received answers make inevitable: what are we to do with what we know—than to act? I shall not be able to answer this last question satisfactorily, of course; I know of no one who has. But I am impressed by the fact that he who asks that question inevitably is asking a question about himself *in* his culture. Indeed, it is the implications of that word "in" which give rise to these notes.

1. WHAT IS MASS CULTURE? The products of the imagination and intellect—at some stage mass-produced, of course—which are intended to image life's possibilities for men whose lives are for the most part dominated by such rationalized and technified modes of behavior and governance as have increasingly ensured (and also endangered) the continuity of society since the Renaissance. The song suits the singer; and its creation and production are set by the same pattern which sets his character. Neither song nor singer is marked by much of that *human* impulse, as we like to think of it, to rise above one's cultural matrix, comprehend it, and so become a better, fuller, more comprehensive person. The song, confirming the singer in what he is, seems then inevitably to exploit his anxieties, disable him, and make it all the more difficult for him to conceive of any way of life but his own. So that his life style, insofar as the songs he sings are involved, will become all the more rigid, all the less flexible, and he the less able to conceive of the genuinely new in life's possibilities.

2. HOW HAS MASS CULTURE DEVELOPED? The answer, of course, is implicit in my brief definition. The necessary condition of mass culture is technology, as this is the necessary condition of mass man. The outcome of the technification of society is what Marx called "alienation," meaning thereby to indicate the fact that, as mass production techniques take over, the worker loses a sense of genuine participation in the product of his work. At its worst, mass culture is thus "alienated" culture: a contradiction in terms, really. Our songs are not made for us as persons, but as members of a group, *consumers* all, our functions dominated by whatever the group must get done in order to keep up with the demands for production which we let our technology set for us. According to this way of thinking, he who makes our songs (or writes our stories, or produces our TV programs, or whatever) can do so only if he lets himself be alienated from that which he produces. The apparatus whereby the songs get from writers to audience is such as to demand of the writer that he produce not for persons, but for groups, masses,

crowds. The faceless middlemen who form the intervening invariables between writer and audience know what the audience wants, and therefore what the writer must produce. But they know in reality only what the audience has previously consumed (which they have previously supplied), and so the point of the least common denominator is soon reached. It is incorrect, then, because irrelevant, to say that today's mass culture is simply analogous to yesterday's—this century's to the eighteenth century's, or the nineteenth century's. For, so far, the level of mass culture has descended, precisely as the role of technology in making it available has ascended.

3. WHAT CAN IT DO TO US? WHAT COULD IT DO FOR US? To ask this question in such an alternative fashion is to catch a glimpse of a ray of hope—which comes from the candle which the lords of the media have not yet been able to extinguish. What mass culture can do *to* us is sufficiently evident in what I have said already—and in the nature of the things which bombard us day by day. To reinforce what I have said, let me quote the words of one of the writers of the most successful rock-and-roll songs of our day: "Basically, these songs are a means of escape from reality. We write lyrics deliberately vague. The songs are egocentric and dreamy. Lots of basic blues ideas wouldn't work as rock-and-roll ideas because the blues are too real, too earthy. You have to make them dreamlike and very moral. That's why you're rarely going to hear even a plain, *happy* rock-and-roll song, because happiness is a real emotion." (*Esquire* [*sic! sic! sic!*], March, 1961, p. 71.)

• • •

In short, the world of this song-writer is the one of official Hollywood, whose productions—according to the language of a 1960 release of the Motion Picture Producers Association—are based on the notion that "drama . . . almost always deals with the unusual, the unique and the departure from normal human experience." The "normal" is not to be enhanced, our sense of it deepened; it is uninteresting. The consonance of normality and individuality (i.e., uniqueness) presumably has been proven (by market analysis?) to be the stuff that humanistic-type daydreams are made on. The screen-writer, like the song-writer, is supposed to live in a world in which alienation from reality is the rule—in which through some anti-miraculous genetic transformation, men are born lobotomized. Or should be.

But of course they are not. And the nature of mass society induces in them—which is to say in us—a whole complex of anxieties (beyond tranquilizing) over the establishment and preservation of their (which is to say our) identities as what Whitman called in more hopeful days "simple, separate persons." The anxieties seem to be the necessary product of our lives in a mass society, the psychological form of that alienation which technology is a prime agent in bringing about. And here, I should say, mass culture can do something *for* us; and does, if not often enough. Its products can be composed so as to take into account our anxieties, our concern to establish and confirm our positive identities, even as we enjoy (as we should) all the material goods that technology gives us—and have the increased leisure to enjoy them. It can engage us in our spare time in such a way as to let us enjoy the realities, even the trivial realities, of our lives—not necessarily going deep, or seeking to enhance or enrich or transform our sense of reality; just letting us coast along, storing up energy for those moments when we can look deeply into reality and allow ourselves to be guided by poets, storytellers, philosophers, intellectuals, what Melville called "thought-divers." Mass culture can be *fun*—easy play, as against the harder ritualized play of higher forms of culture, with our sensibilities loosened and relaxed, our reality-principles neither exploited nor fully and drivingly engaged. And it can be *serious,* as we contemplate in general terms matters of import to the lives of our spirits. In either case, it can be charged with "real emotions." It could be, and it must be. (When it is, as I shall suggest later, it perhaps had better be called "popular" culture.)

•   •   •

The humanist, of course, grounds his vocation in a commitment to the idea that men are alike above all in their capacity to be different, "en masse" (to use Whitman's words again) to the degree that they can realize that they are "simple and separate," "normal" to the degree that they can be "unique." (He knows too that in our culture he most likely would be unable to be indignant about mass culture if he were not the recipient of a mass education.) That is to say, simply enough, he would understand mass culture, so to transcend it. But he would, or should, admit that even he cannot transcend it all the time—perhaps even most of the time. What he wants is to insure that there always will be the possibility for the transcending; in short, that mass culture has a viable relationship with *elite* culture.

I emphasize: *elite* culture. Let us not be irresponsible, or cowardly, and call it *high* culture. Let us not conceal from ourselves the fact that, like mass culture, it must always involve the problem of social status, measured some way or another. For "elitism" carries responsibilities which mere "height" does not. In cultivating his responsibilities—a measure of *his* dignity—the humanist will perforce cultivate his elitism, and so do what he can to work toward the production of not mass but *popular* culture.

I suggest that when mass culture is healthy, when a good part of its health derives from the fact that it has a viable relation with elite culture, it is, or could be, *popular* culture; and that it might well counter, or at least slow down, the forces of depersonalization and alienation which threaten us. I shall suggest that one of the necessary conditions of an authentic community is a *popular* culture—an authentic people's culture.

In the nature of modern life such a culture—popular or elite—must be accessible to all; and although it is likely that the great number of men will for the most part be capable of only popular culture and that there will be the usual minority whose capabilities direct them for the most part to elite culture, nonetheless the general rule will be that even that minority will (simply because men are not highpowered enough to live with elite culture alone) find itself increasingly involved with popular culture. As humanists, we work in the hope that most men will be of that minority. And one of our tasks, whether professionally or as an aspect of our day-to-day lives, is to see to it that there is kept going that viable relationship whereby we are assured of a popular, not a mass, culture. The possibility of the withering away of popular culture seems to me to be so distant right now—granting the fix we are in—as not to be worth speculating about. I am a short-range utopian, I suppose: characteristically a mere humanist.

I defined *mass culture* toward the beginning of these notes. Let me venture some related definitions. I mean to give some criteria for the various modes, or levels, of culture and to suggest their socio-cultural origins and implications:

1. A FOLK CULTURE is one whose homogeneity is inclusive, and is such that close, almost anonymous identifications are possible by the terms set by the quality of its homogeneity. It is non-urban, usually village, pre-literate, minimally technological. Its artistic products, what-

ever their range of complexity in technique, tend to be thematically simple (i.e. non-complex—reflecting the assurance in person-to-person relations of both artist and him toward whom the artist directs his work). In fact, the artist is only minimally, if at all, differentiated as artist. His work, thus, is directed at a whole community, to the vitality of whose being all of its members are felt genuinely to contribute. The artist is *merely* one of those members.

2. AN ELITE CULTURE is one whose homogeneity is exclusive, and is such that identifications within the terms set by that homogeneity must perforce be particular and individualistic—some of its well-endowed members being set apart from the ordinary run of their fellows. The artist is thus one specialist among many, even though the intended import of his art is nothing if not general. For the elite exists because, in the mass of society above or beyond which its members must place themselves in order to be themselves, identifications are not, as it were, automatically guaranteed; identifications are not an assured aspect of intra-group understanding. Rationalization, bureaucratization, and the like preclude this, and the artist must adapt to the fact. An elite culture's artistic products are contrived so that, through their technique—indeed, *only* through their technique—their necessarily difficult and complex themes may be perceived. The themes are necessarily difficult and complex because they derive from the artist's elite understanding of complexities of socio-cultural and "spiritual" behavior which the very nature of mass society (without which there would be no occasion for an elite) somehow conceals from the vast majority of its members. Even literacy and all that it promises is under the aegis of rationalization and bureaucratization. Technical (in the sense of "technique") expertise, self-consciously cultivated, becomes a necessary means of assuring that the artist's special insights cannot be in any way reduced to those of the mass of the members of his society. Any member of the society who wants to gain those insights must himself somehow join the elite—or, rather, that segment of the elite whose insights (and roles) he aspires to. Technical expertise, thus, becomes a means whereby the artist (and likewise those to whom he would speak) can differentiate his special product from that of all others, even from that of other artists. It is his lead which humanists follow when they ask what is entailed by their commitment to the idea that men are most valuable when they would realize their likeness in terms of their differences. I should guess that

these observations apply, with some shifting of terms, to all members of the "intelligentsia."

3. POPULAR CULTURE represents the attempt, under the increasingly stratified, non-homogeneous (but increasingly homogenized) conditions of modern society, to achieve something like a folk culture to parallel and perhaps interact with the elite culture to which such conditions, in their very nature, give rise. It is increasingly produced for a mass, not a public. (A "public" has a character; a mass is denied one.) The producers of such culture (who may well nominally be members of the elite) assume and accept (what else can they do?) the social and technological arrangements which an elite culture, particularly in modern times, must surmount; moreover, they *may* assume that those arrangements are such (or can be made such) as to create a satisfactory substitute for the totally permeating, conventionally stylized person-to-person communication which makes for a folk culture and for the marginal, unconventionally stylized communication which makes for an elite culture. Thus the problem for him who would participate in the creation of a popular culture is to make the technology of mass production (of books or whatever) subsidiary to the techniques of individual composition and production: to compose and produce in such a way as to reach the reader whom mass production makes possible, meantime not diluting or weakening the product while it moves between writer and reader. The problem is to design a work of "popular" art which has built into it safeguards against that further dilution-on-the-way; or which, as is more likely, somehow anticipates those dilutions and the nature and qualifications of the reader for whom they are to be made—anticipates them in such a way as to guarantee the preservation of such integrity as the artist, accepting fully the conditions under which he writes, has put into his work in the first place. Such dilutions—which above all characterize popular culture—must be made on behalf of the popular reader, with his nature and his needs in mind, not on behalf of the technological apparatus whereby the work will reach him. It may still be possible to distinguish between "public" and "mass." It is one of the ironies of modern life that only an "elite" is in a position to do so—to stem the drift of the "public" toward the "mass."

We must remember that in times long past when our society was dominated by a political elite, the members of such an elite not only conceived of themselves as but actually were members of a cultural elite—not only patrons of art and artists but genuine "consumers" of their work. Domination passed in turn to an economic and then—in relatively recent times—to a power elite. For members of the economic and power elites, to rule society came less and less to entail seriously encouraging and cultivating its arts. For a member of the economic elite—say, a nineteenth-century entrepreneur—the arts were to be cultivated by sheer accumulation of art objects; the artist was supported, but out of a sense of a dimly remembered obligation, inherited from the era of political elitism. The outcome of this situation, ironically enough, was the development of the fellowship and foundation system in our society. More recently, members of the power elite have had even less to do with the arts. The role of the cultural elite has become free-floating, assumed in turn by, say, an academic intelligentsia and a non-academic (or anti-academic) avant-garde, who between themselves have divided the role of a member of the cultural elite into that of the critic and artist. They quarrel constantly—not seeing clearly that neither is in a position to do his job successfully without the other; that they can be effective only if they are allied. Thus in our own time, when we do have such an alliance, it is under the constant tension of a pull from the one side by the sort of artist who boasts that the only thing he has to defend is his ignorance and on the other by the sort of critic who doesn't dare admit that he is ignorant of anything. But the alliance can be strong, especially when it occurs in the academy—the one thing artists and critics being able to agree upon being the fact that members of a cultural elite are nothing if not teachers, humanists all. Now, I am suggesting by this little disquisition on elitism that it is a primary task of those who live in this alliance to dedicate themselves to the cause of a genuinely popular culture. Indeed, anyone who is dedicated to the cause of a genuinely elite culture shirks his duty if he does not also dedicate himself to the cause of a genuinely popular culture.

Disengagement is possible only in theory; and we have had a good deal of that—essays, for all the sharpness and acuity of their particular critiques, wherein, between generous mouthfuls, the writer disclaims a taste for the cultural fruits of our mass society. Indeed, it would be interesting to study the by now wearisome, because irrelevant, argument typical of such essays: in which, out of an unhappiness we can only share, the writer is driven to claim that modern life is a game of Russian roulette which he will not play. (We might call this his conspicuous assumption.) Meanwhile, back at his ranch, he shoots sitting ducks, mass produced. He has succumbed to the greatest temptation for the humanist in times of crisis: marginality. For the humanist, if he be true to his vocation, must will himself to be at the center of his world, in the heart of the man in whose image it must be shaped. The American humanist, in point of fact, can best understand the problem of mass culture and so participate in its solution, because his is the society in which mass culture has taken deepest root. He is at once its most characteristic beneficiary and its inevitable victim. Its history is his, writ large—as is its life.

Although the rise of mass culture is surely a worldwide phenomenon, Europeans are fond of equating it with "Americanization," a nasty term. In reality, it is a corollary of technology, as I have remarked; and it just happens that our culture was more amenable to rapid technification, and all it implies for social, economic, and artistic matters, than were other so-called tradition-rooted cultures. So we get blamed a little unfairly. Yet we must admit that ours is the place and the occasion where the problem of mass culture can be remarked most clearly.

· · ·

One of the great hopes in post–Revolutionary American culture was for an authentic people's poetry. This is an aspect of the quest for a national literature which has been the object of much recent literary-historical study. Everything seemed to favor the rise of such a poetry: a new land, a new government, freed from its ties with Europe; a new social system, as it was felt; enough land to guarantee good fortune to all; an intention to educate all. The Jeffersonian hope for a natural aristocracy soon came to be a hope for a universal, leveling aristocracy. There were conservative doubts, to be sure. But they were at most cautionary. By the 1840's this could be said—and it is only one such statement among many:

> . . . the national literature could only be enriched if American "scholars" would abandon their "lone reveries" and "scholastic asceticism" and rather seek their inspiration in the "thronged mart" and "peopled city," in the "really living, moving, toiling and sweating, joying and sorrowing people around them." . . . "To obtain an elevated national literature, it is not necessary to look to great men, or to call for distinguished scholars; but to appeal to the mass. . . ." When genuinely "*American* authors ap-

pear . . . They will form a most numerous class, or rather be so *numerous as not to form a class;*" . . . they will utter "the best thoughts of us all." (B. T. Spencer, *The Quest for Nationality* [Syracuse, 1957], p. 113.)

It all looked so easy; and it is precisely because it looked so easy that the history of popular culture in the United States is the great paradigm case for the history of popular culture in Western European civilization. The statement [by B. T. Spencer] I have quoted is a reconstruction from a group of essays by Orestes Brownson, who was then in his radical, transcendental phase. It is matched, as I have said, by many others— usually by radicals and liberals in politics, the most famous exemplars being statements by Whitman, beginning with the preface to the 1855 *Leaves of Grass*. It is worth recalling these words from "Democratic Vistas":

> The word of the modern . . . is the word Culture.
>   We find ourselves abruptly in close quarters with the enemy. This word culture, or what it has come to represent, involves, by contrast, our whole theme, and has been, indeed, the spur, urging us to engagement. Certain questions arise. As now taught, accepted and carried out, are not the processes of culture rapidly creating a class of supercilious infidels, who believe in nothing? Shall a man lose himself in countless masses of adjustments, and be so shaped with reference to this, that, and the other, that the simply good and healthy and brave parts of him are reduced and clipp'd away, like the bordering of a box in a garden?

Ironically enough, we might well apply Whitman's words to the danger of mass culture in our times, although he was attacking elite culture in his time. In any case, we must be still urged to engagement on both fronts.

For what actually happened? We have that curious phenomenon of a group of poets, almost all of them radical or liberal in their politics, discovering gradually that to make authentic poems they had somehow to disengage themselves from their politics, or transcend them; at best, they hoped through their poems to transform excessively political (and therefore partial) men into whole men. I think of Emerson and even Whitman himself. But note that Poe too felt himself to be a liberal, sometimes a radical. And, beyond poets, note that both Hawthorne and Melville were good liberals, at the same time as they were writing the stories and novels which put them out of the reach of the very popular audience with whom they shared their liberalism. In all, they became to some extent "private" artists. As their correspondence and journals tell us, they had to, in order to survive as artists. The humanity which they wished to put into their poems and stories could not be trimmed to fit the political beliefs which, as men living and acting in society, they were quite willing to make the best of.

Yet during the period of Emerson and his peers—radicals and liberals whose art was not consonant with their politics—during this time, a people's poetry, an authentic popular poetry did rise: along with a vulgar imitation of it, in the scribblings of Mrs. Sigourney and her kind. The "authentic" popular poetry was Longfellow's, Lowell's, Holmes', and Whittier's. The first three were conservatives all the way. (Lowell wavered a good deal, however, but he was a notable trimmer.) And Whittier was in a way, after his earlier abolitionist phase, curiously a-political. The first three of these men were academics, Boston aristocrats; the fourth, Whittier, became their patriarch, the man whom they admired most. It was these men who constituted the Fireside Poets, the Schoolroom Poets. Their poetry assured their readers that life was not an empty dream, that all was real and earnest, that the natural world was as it was to give men lessons-by-analogy, that their Snow-Bound reveries were means of getting perspective on the actualities of their day-to-day life. They reminded their readers regularly that their origins were in virtual folk-cultures—small communities in which inter-personal relations were stable and assured; they idealized such origins. And these poets were popular in an even more modern sense. They sold well; they were all deeply aware of the fiscal problems of the market for popular books; they took their publishers' advice as to what would and would not sell; they let their publishers mediate between themselves and their readers. But note, withal: they meant to "minister" to their readers' needs. They brought elite culture (in their translations from European literature in particular) to their readers. And they struck out against those other popular writers who would exploit their readers' needs. Their record is one, whatever we can say against them, of patriarchal responsibility. They seem to have been born graybearded, hanging in portraits over the ordinary man's fireside: *lares* and *penates* for readers who would be frightened of sublimer gods.

But in their success and the way it was achieved lay the undoing of their kind of poetry after their own time. The rest of the story takes us into our time: with, above all, the publisher and his staff constantly searching for the least common denominator at which books can be sold, now not advising the writer but telling him what to do, what to write. The publisher is himself a victim of the technological demands (the get-out figure, it is called) of the market. Moreover, there are the magazines which exist primarily as advertising organs and which require, occasionally, poetic squibs to fill out their columns. In this case, publisher and editor are selling to advertising men, who gauge the market, then instruct editor and publisher on what is needed, and so on down the line to the writer—separated by an iron curtain of economic, technological, and even psychological factors from his reader. So that the Longfellows of our time have shifted from Evangelines to paperbacks, TV scripts, and magazine pieces; or perhaps the Longfellows of our time have either taken shelter in the academy (where misery finds company) or have joined up with the publishing apparatus, having given up hope of licking it.

My example out of the nineteenth century is perhaps too simple. But, as I have said, I think that it can be a paradigm case for our thinking about the problem of a popular as against a mass culture—the crucial concept in developing the one as against the other being that of "responsibility." We must not forget how difficult it was for the "serious" writer who, producing genuinely popular work, wanted to do more.

The American situation was characteristically more extreme than the British—where a Dickens, for example, could manage to use the vehicles of popular art to carry stories which, upon examination in depth, turn out often to have been elite art of the most demanding kind. Indeed, we must recall that the novel as a genre came into being as an essentially popular form; and that its greatest practitioners were often able to do what Dickens did. And to our own day the novel remains the only form in which literary art seems at once to be popular and elitist. Only *seems*. For in the later nineteenth century, it too was increasingly refined into the "difficult" form it is at its best today—such refinement being the writer's way of avoiding being homogenized by the demands of the mass market and its entrepreneurs. And the popular novelist, instead of transforming the popular into the elitist, now superimposes elitist conceptions of fiction onto an essentially popular form and makes for that special version of mass culture, the middlebrow.

· · ·

But now I begin to run into the problem of classification, gradation, and the like. And I shall not go on. I want to point out, indeed, that in matters of this kind, we are too prone to classify, pigeonhole, file away, and so say we have done our duty. This is, I think, one of the easier ways of becoming morally indignant. And I am proposing a more difficult way—that of confrontation and evaluation, the humanist's first step.

Thus I think that a good deal of the contemporary debate about mass (or popular) culture is beside the point. Opponents in the debate have accepted—too soon I think—somewhat simplified versions of the historical situation which has made for mass culture and then gone on to show how the products of mass culture demonstrate the horror or the glory of the historical situation.

If history evidences progress, mass culture must somehow be a "good" thing: if it evidences regress, mass culture must somehow be a "bad" thing. To show that it is good, you point out how many good LPs, good paperbacks, good prints are selling and you bring up the fact of our museums-without-walls. To show that it is bad, you point out how much trash we are exposed to, how the purchase of good LPs and the like may be simply marks of longing for status; and you bring up the fact that in the museum-without-walls the great painting, cut down to its viewer's size, may function merely as a decorative plaque, part of the wallpaper. And of course, both sides of the debate are right insofar as their evidence is concerned. Strangely enough, they often interpret a given piece of evidence identically and then proceed to evaluate it in diametrically opposed fashions—according to their progressive or regressive theories of history. The debaters (they are lined up neatly in the Rosenberg-White 1957 *Mass Culture* volume and the Spring 1960 issue of *Daedalus*) are not really quarreling with each other; they are quarreling with history—with the fact that they, like the rest of us, have been born into this world. The net result is the fact that nearly everyone is now his own mass medium; that writing about mass culture has become a form of mass culture; and that whereas we may well be satisfied by a given writer's account of the intrinsic nature and quality of a given item of mass culture, we may well be dissatisfied with his account of the implication of that nature and quality for our quite concrete and specific existential problem: what is mass culture to us and what are we to mass culture? The problem, I suggest, is one of attaining a perspective that will not allow us to escape the fact that, like it or not, we have to *live* with mass culture. We must take our history straight. Which is to say, take ourselves in our history straight.

How, in the midst of the mass of mass culture, bowed down by its weight, seeing the hopes for a popular culture increasingly frustrated, how are we to know, judge, and discriminate? How are we to establish the means whereby such knowledge, judgment, and discrimination might not only preserve and inculcate the idea of a popular culture, but advance it?

My suggestions are humanistic, therefore academic. They consist essentially in learning how to think of mass as against popular culture, then—and only then—to act as one can. In these notes I am concerned to set down some necessary conditions of the act.

1. HISTORICALLY. I have meant in my little tale of Fireside Poetry and in my comments on a too simple idea of progress (or regress) to indicate how such thinking might proceed. Such thinking, I am sure, will clarify our notion of the role of the maker of mass (and/or popular) culture and the special mode of responsibility he should assume. We will observe, I think, that even at its best popular culture is a peculiarly historistic thing—by which I mean to say that it is not intended to survive the lifetime of its immediate audience, or the phase-of-sensibility of its immediate audience. It gets used up, consumed, but it need not thereby be poisonous. Too, we will observe, of course, that in the nature of the increasing technification of the media, in the development of the mass media themselves, the possibility of such responsibility becomes increasingly difficult of realization. Careful, objective historical studies— sympathetic where sympathy is deserved—will at least sharpen and deepen our sense of the qualitative criteria of popular (as against mass) culture.

2. SOCIOLOGICALLY. (I use the term in the sense of what Wright Mills calls "the sociological imagination"—which "enables its possessor to understand the larger historical scene in terms of its meaning for the inner life and the external career of a variety of individuals." For Mills "history" is essentially contemporary history—the way we categorize and comprehend our lives now, our experience, in our milieu as a somehow coherent complex of lived-through events.) The problem here is to

isolate for study the relation of mass culture as produced and consumed (horrible words!) to the socio-political structure and function of our society. What is it, we ask, to be a mass-consumer? And inevitably our gaze is drawn hypnotically to the young—for whom the mass media have not only transformed a life style but have created one. Their character is one which is in great part fixed by the fact that everything—information, material goods, means of having fun, even the monuments of elite culture—seems to be available with the minimum effort on their part. They grow up very fast—having in high school worked through all the "activities" which used to be in the purview of college. They are trained to be consumers—their only consumer's guide the radio-TV segments which give the show a reason for going on. Their world view is fatefully conditioned by the idea of automation and of simultaneity of communication. Everything seems to happen, perhaps does happen, at once—yet the happenings are fragmented and the center will not hold. Perhaps there *is* no center, just a homogenized whole. Young people, as Paul Goodman says, grow up "absurd." Their need is to *fill* all the free time they have, not to *use* it; and their need is confirmed and deepened by the cultural fare they are offered. They become mistrustful of information as such, of words, of gestures, of ideas: all of which imply a central cultural style which they cannot sense. Unhappily, the more "insightful" among them are cynical, or at best disenchanted, about the possibility of a popular, as opposed to a mass, culture—about a popular, as opposed to a mass, education. They are so cynical that they don't bother to confront squarely the fact that their world has been transformed once and for all, irreversibly, into one in which the mass media, automation, and the like have freed them from some of the discontents of work. Surely their obligation is also to live in the world, even in that part of it we would teach them to earn the right to despise; they can't earn the right to despise it by disaffiliating from it. One way of living in the world, so even this sociological critique would seem to demonstrate, is to learn to think intelligently and critically about mass culture and to learn to differentiate it from popular culture.

3. FORMALLY. The problem here is one for the "critic," and involves his usual compulsion to see the relation of form to content. He studies an item of popular culture. Is this a daydream, he asks, or a nightmare? Is it held in proper check, psychically contained, by its form? Is it related to reality? Or does the form serve only to make it a substitute for reality? (Here, of course, "reality" is the first term of Freud's "reality-

principle": what is, in the nature of man and his world, humanly possible of achievement.) What portion of reality does it deal with and how? What are the characteristics of its medium and what problems do these characteristics pose for the popular artist who would to his reality principle be true? What is the conception of human nature upon which the operation of the medium is postulated? And then follows a question as to the relation of particular forms as used in mass (or popular) culture and their use in elite culture: the question, of course, of what is called *kitsch*. Critics have more and more observed how the objects of elite art are imitated in mass culture, and in the imitating drained of their integral value and import. Corollary to this is the fact that objects of folk art too have been imitated thus—from folklore to fakelore, as the saying goes. Certainly, it is true that only the inauthentic—mass culture at its most vicious—is produced when an object of mass culture is offered as an easily earned surrogate for an object of elite or of folk culture. But I am not convinced entirely that the intelligent borrowing of forms and motifs from elite and folk art is necessarily vicious. After all, the wonderful popular songs of the seventeenth century take much of their strength from the folk songs which inspire them; and this is true in our own time too. There is clearly a descending line from the performance of a Mississippi chain gang to that of The Weavers to that of The Kingston Trio. Yet the performance of the latter still is not necessarily offered as a substitute for the performance of the former, but, as it were, only as an introduction to it. And there might well be an *ascending* line. From rock-and-roll to Washboard Sam and the country blues—who knows? The point is that the possibility of moving from a popular to a folk form is not foreclosed. In its not being foreclosed—this is perhaps the proper relation of popular art to folk art; and I should think something comparable holds for the relation of popular art to elite art: *My Fair Lady* to *Pygmalion*; advertising layout to Mondrian; Paddy Chayefsky to Chekov; Ted Williams to Nick Adams. When the possibility of moving from a popular to a folk or elite form is foreclosed, when there is no vital relation between the one and the other, then we have mass art for the mass consumer—not popular art for the popular auditor or reader or singer or whistler or whatever.

•   •   •

Popular culture, considered formally, must be "standardized," so that through technology it can be made readily available to the popular audience. But, within the limits of its audience's sensibility, it can be made adjustable—so as to let members of the audience relax, refresh themselves, and simply enjoy the fact that what they have in common is the fact that they are different: their humanity half-engaged. And I should say that it is the corollary function of elite art to urge its audience to commitment, meditation in depth, so to contemplate the fact—so "real" as to be beyond enjoyment—that what makes its members different is what they have in common: their humanity *fully* engaged. Mass culture, of course, is humanity *dis*engaged, atrophying—form exhausting content, content eating cancerously at form. It is predicated upon the existence of a world in which our central problem—holding together our images of the world we have and the one we ought to have—is as irrelevant as are those of us who would think about it. We intellectuals don't understand the mass audience, so proclaims Dr. Frank Stanton of CBS—and I am here paraphrasing some words of his published in the mass-culture issue of *Daedalus*. We are given part of CBS's time: so we should let the masses enjoy themselves. What Dr. Stanton doesn't understand is that willy-nilly we are part of the mass audience too. Only, being intellectuals, we know the difference between a mass and a public, a crowd and community, between aspirin and that stuff Dr. Stanton's clients would overcharge us for—the overcharge being our ticket of admission to Madison Avenue produced entertainments whose aim is to convince us that it is worthwhile being overcharged: proof positive of the value of the American way of life; brain-tinting out of the laboratories of Helena Rubinstein. Happily, there are a few (not many, but a few) self-parodists in the mass arts who know, or seem to know, the difference too—for example, he who creates Pogo; he who publishes *Mad*; and he who recorded a couple of years ago chipmunk voices which are like Fabian's and Frankie Avalon's—only more so.

·   ·   ·

So far we are losing the battle, because so far, we have in our panic not been quite able to conceive what it would be like to win it. Were we to be possessed of a truly popular culture as well as a truly elite culture, the condition of our lives would be such as to force us frankly to admit that popular culture played a significant part in our lives—as, in point of fact, it already does. In the unattainable utopia for which we must work (because if we are honest with ourselves, there is nothing else to do), the terms *popular* and *elite* would refer to books and music and pictures which differed in value not as regards the segment of the population which comprehended them but as regards the degree of comprehension which they demanded: *full* and *middle* culture we might call them; and have to add a third term, *minimal* culture. All segments of the population would have free access to all levels. In the nature of things, there would be more devotees to the last two than to the first; nonetheless it is most likely that a man devoted to full culture would give himself to middle and minimal culture too, and so strengthen them and the viable relationship, without foreclosure, which should exist among them. And it would happen, I suppose, that just because a man was capable of comprehending full culture, he would comprise part of an elite dedicated to serving his culture as a whole. From the *power* elite to the *cultural* elite; from *full power* as a mode of governance to *full culture*. For full culture would entail full responsibility, the fullest sense of humanity and community.

But, saying all this, the humanist is properly wary of his own speculations—lest they blind him to the facts of life. Yet he *must* speculate, in order that he may the more sharply look about him and see and assess and work to amend such facts. For he can't but know that the problem of popular as against mass culture is embedded in our task of salvaging our world. Which is to say, of salvaging ourselves. Mass culture most often is not only sub-culture but anti-culture. It destroys culture, our means of working out a relationship between what we are and what we ought to be, and so would destroy us, and deliver us packaged— to whom? That is the true horror. For the lords of the media and their minions are not satanic or dictatorial or consummately villainous. Indeed, they would destroy themselves along with us—and all without really knowing what they are doing. In our brave new world we have reached the stage where we can destroy and package ourselves to no purpose whatsoever. For there would be neither sender nor receiver: just that glittering package. Mass culture truly bores from within, bores us to death, bores us in the name of entertaining us, bores us into the state where we don't know that we are being bored, where boredom becomes normalcy. Meanwhile, The Package awaits.

I conclude these notes with some words, published in the mass-culture issue of *Daedalus,* which put well the desperate hope (what else is open to us?) in which we must speak about such matters. They are not mine, but the novelist James Baldwin's:

> Perhaps life is not the black, unutterably beautiful, mysterious and lonely thing the creative artist tends to think of it as being; but it is certainly not the sunlit playpen in which so many Americans lose first their identities and then their minds.
>
> I feel very strongly, though, that this amorphous people are in desperate search for something which will help them reestablish their connection with themselves and with one another. This can only begin to happen as the truth begins to be told. We are in the middle of an immense metamorphosis here, a metamorphosis which will, it is devoutly to be hoped, rob us of our myths and give us our history, which will destroy our attitudes and give us back our personalities. The mass culture, in the meantime, can only reflect our chaos: and perhaps we had better remember that this chaos contains life—and a great transforming energy.

I can add to this only my conviction that the life and the energy are such—as are we whose life and energy they are—as still to make it possible for us to have a popular, not a mass, culture: one which will let us live our history and store up the energy for those high occasions when we try to confront and understand it; one which will give us a casual sense of our personal ties and prepare us for those critical occasions when we try to know them fully and freely. (And, Bomb or no Bomb, we are possible for the foreseeable future, if only because it is *we* who foresee it.) Such a culture is possible so long as we are possible. If we are to survive our metamorphosis, such a culture—at least working in the living hope of such a culture—is imperative.

Chapter 6

Dancing for Eels at Catherine Market

W. T. Lhamon, Jr.

Introduction by Christopher J. Looby

Race, racial identity, racialization, race-crossing, and race-mixing: these rubrics have been central, quite properly, to much recent research and writing in American literary studies. What has been more central, after all, to American culture than the experience of racial conflict, contact, and occasional compact? The great virtue of W. T. Lhamon, Jr.'s work is that it brings to these matters not predetermined critical attitudes but an unjaundiced curiosity and hope. What it also brings: deep and intellectually searching archival research, a lively eye and ear for unexpected subtleties and surprising inflections, and an engaging writerly style that respects the norms of academic research (look at those footnotes) but equally honors the intricacies of vernacular culture, the refinements of popular expression, and the bottomless, confounding mischief of low cultural forms. Lhamon is willing to make bold historical connections across vast stretches of time—for instance, between the gestural innovations of anonymous black marketplace performers in the early nineteenth century and the recent stylizations of Michael Jackson. But he is also willing to tease out patiently the rich meanings of small details in debased texts like the song "De New York Nigger" (for example, the vertiginous semantic flux of words like "sally," "missy," and "houru"). This is, after all, to fulfill the classical requirements of textual interpretation: to read the part with and against the whole, and vice versa, deftly closing the hermeneutic circle.

"Dancing for Eels at Catherine Market," from the first chapter of *Raising Cain,* analyzes in turn visual culture (the illustrated covers of song sheets; an anonymous 1820 folk drawing; a playbill and a lithographic illustration that appear to derive from that folk drawing; and an 1822 oil painting by John Searle of elites in attendance at the Park Theatre), musical culture (streetcorner improv, early American opera, touring minstrel groups, popular song), literary culture (Fanny Kemble, Charles Dickens, Harriet Beecher Stowe and her stage adapters, Herman Melville), stage drama (bowery b'hoy skits, blackface revues, Thomas Holcroft's *The Road to Ruin*), journalism (De Voe's *The Market Book,* which provides his epigraphs; James Watson Webb's *Morning Courier and New York Enquirer;* Arthur Tappan's *Journal of Commerce;* the *Working Man's Advocate*), and dance (the gestural motif of turning about and wheeling that is canonical to this genealogy of dance-making and performing). Coordinated with brief or sustained analyses of such performances and texts are claims about the pressures that demographic trends, immigration patterns, political events, abolitionist and other reform movements, riots and mobs and plots, evangelical efforts, economic transformations, class alliances and antagonisms, and material spatial developments in the city exerted on all these different modes of expression. Perhaps the better way to say this would be to say that expressive culture feels—and innovatively responds to—such social and historical impingements.

While this is a tour de force of methodological integration, it also involves, quite importantly, ongoing reflection about its own methods and motives. Much of this self-reflection takes a metaphoric form: the author remembers and reimagines himself walking through the spaces in lower Manhattan where the performances he is rediscovering first took place. Now covered over with roads, bridges, and new buildings, undercut by subways, his attempt to see the Catherine Market as it once existed is a figure for his attempt to reinterpret early blackface performance afresh despite a history of prejudicial preinterpretation that has bequeathed to us a reflexive suspicion and distrust of—and even righteous contempt for—blackface forms. The combination of virtuoso primary research and high methodological self-consciousness creates what is, to my mind, a powerfully persuasive argument. (Lhamon's forthcoming edited collection of hitherto unknown minstrel plays—discovered serendipitously in, of all places, the British Library—will place a big chunk of his evidentiary archive before other scholars and readers.)

Like the best arguments, however, it is one that allows for its own contestability and acknowledges its own partiality. Because it is not simply stating the obvious and rehearsing liberal pieties (in fact, it may be making claims that are surprisingly counterintuitive and saying things that at first glance might seem implausible), it recognizes other viewpoints and welcomes debate. It is itself a rejoinder in an ongoing collective discussion and expects rejoinders in turn. In a well-known essay, Fredric Jameson once wrote that all mass cultural texts necessarily contain a utopian moment: people generally want a better world, and the expressive forms and performances that speak to them most powerfully (measured by their mass popularity) must, on that assumption, speak—in however baffled, indirect, distorted, deformed, cagey, deniable, deluded, coded, insinuating, or evasive a fashion—to their high hopes and cherished dreams.[1] What Lhamon —in certain very distinctive ways but also in line with some of the work of other recent scholars of blackface—has done is to set aside liberal posturing and pious condemnation and find (guided by candid desire and frank hope) the utopian moment(s) secreted in some unlikely cultural places. He has done this not by overestimating the receptive agency of audiences who are presumed to read "against the grain" of texts that are assumed to be always corrupt (although the place of the audience in his account is ever an active and productive one). Rather, he attributes to cultural producers qualities of wit, guile, and intelligence that we might choose to honor if only we can keep up with them. Others have frequently shown how blackface minstrelsy has been often abominably racist. Lhamon shows the surprising "way[s] mintrelsy saps racism from within," the way a song like "De New York Nigger" in fact "criticizes the racism of its own minstrel form."

NOTES

1. Fredric Jameson, "Reification and Utopia in Mass Culture," *Social Text* 1 (1979): 130–48.

After the Jersey negroes had disposed of their masters' produce at the "Bear Market," which sometimes was early done, and then the advantage of a late tide, they would "shin it" for the Catherine Market to enter the lists with the Long Islanders, and in the end, an equal division of the proceeds took place. The success which attended them brought our city negroes down there, who, after a time, even exceeded them both, and if money was not to be had "they would dance for a bunch of eels or fish."
—Thomas F. De Voe, *The Market Book*

WE WANT TO DANCE, too. Let's shin it for the Catherine Market ourselves. Let's enter the lists with the Long Islanders. Shucking our constraints, let's admit their old, low, and large ambition is also ours. Success attended them, De Voe says, and it has since attended others. Fascination adheres in these gestures, their contest, and their coining. To coin those gestures was to produce currency for exchange. As this currency accumulated interest, it was codified and it persisted. The gestures gathered momentum. When we can see their momentum, we can see their economy: the conditions of their cultural transmission. It is pretty to think that we might all share "in the end, an equal division of the proceeds." We all want those eels.[1]

Catherine Market was a short sail in breezy weather, or a moderate row on still days, across the East River from the truck farms of Long Island. The skiffs from Long Island came from towns just on the other side, from Williamsburgh and Brooklyn, and tied up at Catherine Slip. At its edge was Catherine Market, which joined the Slip to Catherine Street, and thence to the rest of the city via the Five Points, which was six blocks up to Chatham Square and two over. From Chatham Square and the Five Points, the Bowery went uptown, Pearl Street downtown, Worth and Canal Streets across town one way and Division the other. Maps today still give us "Catherine Slip" at the wide spot where the market was.

Today, Catherine Slip seems to bisect the territory between the Brooklyn and Manhattan bridges that have put it in parentheses. The more recent subway tunnels further bracket the market a little way along in each direction, north toward Corlears Hook, south toward the Battery. In its day Catherine Slip handled most of the traffic that all those conduits came to replace. The bridges and tunnels made massive arteries to replace the delicately negotiating capillary action of Catherine Market, the Five Points, and its tributary veins.

Catherine Market was the spot where the goods of Long Island slipped in and out of the isle of Manhattan when the river was both a boundary and a conveyance. Catherine Market, like all traditional markets, paradoxically smudged that borderline and also reinforced it. The market's presence as the membrane of the city emphasized its border, but managed its permeability, too. The culture in and of the market did the same, as we shall see: the culture of Catherine Market drew boundaries and managed their crossings.

At Catherine Slip the pedestrian and the riparian overlapped, like a skiff pulled across a shoreline, and those men who flourished in both realms had a special cachet. That's an initial reason why the slaves who planted and grubbed the potatoes, then rowed them across the water, then called their sales in the market were paid to dance there. Jersey, Williamsburgh, Brooklyn, and "our own" Negroes, said Thomas De Voe, danced out their regional affiliation and their identity. This overlap is first among several that are important in these early commercial performances of an independent Atlantic popular culture.

From its earliest instances, probably in the eighteenth century, this dancing for eels at Catherine Market addressed the issue of overlap. It appealed to several audiences who were finding different values in the dance at the same time. It was a yoking across perceived differences at least as much as it was a closing out or a separation. When they tied their hair in tea-lead, combed it out to imitate and mock the long wigs then in fashion, or wound their foreheads in eelskins, the dancers played out charismatic singularities that were to be made available to others. After all, appeal and exchange was what display in a market was about. And from the outset this dancing was supported, applauded, and desired by others.

Fascinated whites and blacks congregated to pay for that style and copy it. These marks of grace and difference they appreciated and wanted to absorb. They wanted to overlay this black cachet on their own identities—even *as* their own identities. And they did. Anyone today can see that the cultures of the Atlantic world are in good measure joinings and mergers that follow from such fascinations as occurred at Catherine Market. The dancing for eels was a performance of eclecticism that modeled later performance in the Atlantic world.

This early support of blacks dancing for eels is a sure instance of a public becoming patron to a specific style. In doing so it risks slippage from *patron* to *patronize*, nurture to condescension. So much depends on the slippery difference between the two. The crudest mistake we can make, however, is to assume that the connection between public and performance is unalloyed—either simple patrons or simple patronization. In blackface performance, both attitudes converge at once, kinetic in each other.

The overlays of rural and riparian, seafaring and metropolitan cultures indicated a willingness to merge and make combinatory that is associated with markets and bazaars. Roger Abrahams has studied market performance up and down the Americas. He describes marketplaces as edgy areas, contact zones between cultures on the outskirts of towns or up against their walls. In markets, people wink at various civic constraints so that exchange may take place. In order to sell goods, creole language develops and extravagant gestures thrive. "For trade to occur," he has written, "frontiers have to be established that can be crossed, or zones created in which different peoples may come together with impunity. These sanctuaries are fire free zones, places in which difference itself, especially stylistic difference, is transvalued. In such environs, what other peoples make and perform becomes positively attractive."[2]

I begin my study of the Atlantic blackface lore cycle in Catherine Market because I want to insist, with Abrahams, on the mingled behavior that "fire free zones" encouraged in the traditional market. At Catherine Market and other early spots for the performances of American culture there was an eagerness to combine, share, join, draw from opposites, play on opposition. An enthusiasm for the underlying possibilities in difference continually reappears in this popular-folk culture of the Atlantic diaspora. People in the market at Catherine Slip articulated these possibilities early. The market at Catherine Slip was a relay in the conduction of that culture, a relay that stamped what it passed on.

These overlaps of difference so attractive in the market will later be pointed at formally by the blackface mask. The mask is itself an excellent signifier of overlap as a principle. We wear the mask, said blackface performers, a good century before Paul Laurence Dunbar enlisted the phrase for his poem.

We wear the mask, said Bob Rowley. Belonging to the Long Island farmer William Bennett, Bob Rowley was one of the favorites among the men dancing for eels at Catherine Market. When Rowley performed he overlaid his slave name with a performance name: "Bobolink Bob." The name was catchy in its alliteration but, more significantly, it pointed at his overlapping identity. The Bobolink *(Dolichonyx oryzivorus)* is a field bird, a new world passerine, rarely vagrant in Europe, whose male's brown underparts and face change to black while it breeds in spring. Joining himself to these attributes, Bobolink Bob crossed close rural observations with the requirements of market performance. He was a proto-blackface performer for a new North Atlantic culture. One wants very much to have heard Bobolink Bob's whistle. I will show that this whistle is one of the most talismanic aspects of blackface performance, retained and referenced even as late as Al Jolson's performance in *The Jazz Singer* (1927).[3]

Today Catherine Slip and the spot of its former market are surrounded by some of New York's earliest public housing: Knickerbocker Village to the east and the Governor Smith Houses to the west. China Town supplants the European and African ethnic mixture that in the late eighteenth and early nineteenth centuries populated the Five Points and Chatham Square. During the waves of Atlantic immigration that rolled up the East River throughout the nineteenth century, this area gradually became the "Jewtown" that would bring forth Irving Berlin and a large portion of Tin Pan Alley.[4] But the culture that came out of it had Catherine Market and the gestures of the Slip working through it no matter what the overlay.

The East River Drive hugging the shoreline stops pedestrian movement. Out on the river, Circle Liners, tugs, and barges press against the current. One hears the dull traffic on the bridges and highways, the white noise of the city's churning. But at Catherine Slip, now, the human touches of enterprise and exchange sound distant. The structures of the present baffle what went on here. Standing in the midst of these physical overlays it is hard to imagine how the capillary connections of Catherine Slip were commercially significant in its formative moment, around 1820. More important to imagine is how at Catherine Market cultural work was performed that proved important well beyond the city.

Gestures gathered into dance contests. Habits of response clustered observers into publics providing patronage. Conventions of praise and blame arched around the performances in the lists of Catherine Market. All these stimuli and responses arranged themselves in patterns like iron filings around a magnet. Their apparently mutable and delicate tracings—so easy to turn away from or scatter on the surface—conform to enduring force fields deeper than we have realized. Beneath these surface clues, patterns organize relations among citizens not only in the United States but also throughout the Atlantic world. This persisting template held for Catherine Market, as for its nearly neighboring theatres—the Bowery and the Chatham. It survived transatlantic crossing and held sway both south and north of the Thames. It held for the traveling minstrel show in metropolitan and frontier venues. It survived, even showed the way for, silent and talking films. It was popular on TV in the fifties and even now organizes much of MTV.[5]

We will have to push back the fortress façades of Knickerbocker Village, forget the autos, erase the limited-access highways, bring down the bridges, and fill up the subways if we wish to recall Catherine Market as it was and enter the lists with the Long Islanders. There is also a further structure muffling the actuality of Catherine Market that we must sidestep.

We must work against inherited abstractions that have distorted or erased those who danced for eels at Catherine Market. People have tried to tell stories that made sense, and did damage, according to their needs. The first chroniclers of blackface performance accepted its declared premises. These first historians said blackface was about happy Negroes. Minstrelsy told of black people's genius for contentment, they said; it told of their supposedly simple southern ways. Theirs was organic harmony on the Plantation; the hands were in the fields; Ol' Massa and Missus were deservedly well-loved in the big house. From Fanny Kemble's fancied discovery in 1838 of "Jim Crow—the veritable James" to Charles Dickens's *American Notes* in 1842 and Robert Nevin writing in the *Atlantic Monthly* in 1867 right up through Brander Matthews in *Scribner's Magazine* in 1915 and even Constance Rourke's pathbreaking *American Humor* in 1931, historians of several sorts repeatedly validated the southern authenticity of blackface performance.[6]

Then Hans Nathan's study of Dan Emmett in 1962 and particularly Robert Toll's history of minstrelsy in 1974 reversed many of the earlier understandings of the form. The racism in minstrelsy appalled Toll and the form's subsequent critics. The newly conventional embarrassment at white racism popularized in the fifties and sixties had so determined public responses that simply underlining the stereotypes in minstrelsy served as a satisfactory analytic maneuver for this new wave of scholarship. Current historians have extended Toll's noticing that the minstrel show was neither about authentic black life nor about an authentic South. Alexander Saxton, David Roediger, and Eric Lott have more recently argued that blackface performance was a fantasy of northern white performers, largely from middle-class homes, who knew little or nothing of black life.[7]

Although I have lived in the same culture that shaped the attitudes of this more recent group of critics, the story I will tell is rather different.

One does not approve the abhorrent racism in most minstrelsy by emphasizing its presence, then moving on to discuss the form's other—even its counter—aspects. I analyze the multiple aspects in blackface performance because it was not a fixed thing, but slippery in its uses and effects. Indeed, this late in the cycle, it seems most important to notice how blackface performance can work also and simultaneously *against* racial stereotyping. The way minstrelsy saps racism from within has almost never been mentioned. Its anti-racist dimensions—occasionally abolitionist but usually supplemental to both abolitionist and anti-abolitionist doctrine—are remaining secrets among the phenomena of blackface performance.

Raising Cain is about this resistance to racism, for sure, but also about a wider recalcitrance. I want to bring out the broad interracial refusal of middle-class channeling that working men and women of all hues mounted using the corrupt tools bequeathed them by the marketplaces and other locations where they could make spectacles of themselves. Their refusal was not set in amber. It pulsed and warped over time. It was human—vibrant, confused, always mixed. Many of the workers in minstrelsy, most often early but also late, took the racism that was the given of their days and raised it against its original wielders. People work with what they have. What they have is mixed and messy. To think otherwise is the real fantasy in this business.

Much might be said regarding the shifting accounts of minstrelsy that obscure its complex cultural work. Historians have covered over what performers were doing as much as the altered physical structure of Catherine Market has obscured the early activities danced out on its ground. Commentators' shifting analyses say as much or more about the needs of successive eras as about minstrelsy. Nevertheless, the vernacular tradition—right up through Michael Jackson (who emblemizes the conflicted nature of blackface performance)—keeps alive insouciant practices whose party I, for one, am little loath to join. The patterns in these disdained actions persist down all the years of their exclusion from respect.

I, too, am doubtless misusing, therefore abusing, the legacy of blackface performance. What might I say in my defense? Only what is compelling in the stories I tell. What distinguishes my approach from those who have told their stories before me? I am not surprised to find culture corrupt and its measures mixed. Minstrelsy is often racist, growing more complex and more codified as time went on. So much is true of human action by all peoples. Minstrelsy usually misrepresents women, as have most men and women throughout history. In its development, minstrelsy bellied up to power; show me a movement that has not. When I speak about the achievements of blackface performance, I hardly condone its denigration of blacks or its misogyny. I condemn them. What I want most to account for, however, is the way blackface actions have often contradicted what was expected of them. Like the teeming, recoiling eels which early figured it, the conundrums of blackface performance have certainly flopped out of, and knocked over, all the buckets into which people poured them.

•   •   •

Blackface action is usually slashing back at the pretensions and politesse of authority more than at blackness. Certainly in these earliest instances of white fascination with black performance there was little laughing at blacks, alone or even primarily. Instead, there was laughter in the face of the gallows and violence, the gibbet of public remark, and preaching censure. Particularly at Catherine Market, there was dancing among the memory of the chains. The spectacular discipline left its traces on workers who were both enslaved and pressed, whipped and waged. What is mistaken is the suggestion that poor whites had no significant contact with black culture in nineteenth-century New York City.

The same year as the plague that occurred in the surrounding streets, a stallholder at the market composed a remarkable folk drawing: "Dancing for Eels *1820* Catharine Market" (Figure 3). The subjects are pressed among several layers of surveillance. In the left middle of the space are the three black performers—a dancer, a drummer, a second dancer who is watching and clapping for his colleague. To their left and our right is a threesome of tightly engaged white watchers, leaning intently into the dance. In front of the dancers is the artist, for whom each group performs in its way, certainly all in the center of the drawing are aware of being watched. Behind the dancers and their appreciative white threesome are an integrated crowd of onlookers. Notice how our view peers out from inside a stall. This drawing shelters the point of view of its maker: the roof covers the peeking artist, not the dancers nor the crowd watching beyond, who are exposed in the plain air.

This drawing is a hieroglyph suggesting many stories. The two most basic are of the market dance and of the comfort the artist draws in watching it—and they may prove inseparable. The dancer is clearly the

DANCING FOR EELS, 1820 CATHARINE MARKET.

Figure 3. Folk drawing of "Dancing for Eels, 1820 Catharine Market."

focus of the drawing, but I start my discussion of its meaning by noticing the roof that segments off the watcher's comfort. These rudimentary boards provide a top for the drawer's stall. They mark out his space in the crowded market just as boards underlie the space for the dancers. As the dancer performs on his boards, the stallholder cries his wares under his. Furthermore, the roof lines are part of the linearity ruling the space in this folk drawing. All the human elements counteract that wooden straightness of buildings and masts. These boards segment planes for performance. Pressing in on the players, the vertical boards indicate the divisions that will most change during the development of this scene over the next quarter-century, as the butcher's crew incorporates the dancer and his crowd. Their gestures will be staged together inside theatres and inserted into Atlantic consciousness. The roof protected the artist; it thus distinguished the roofed stallholders from the unprotected dancers. The roof above the privileged watcher also marked a rudimentary destination for the black dancer: a cover to come under.

The drawing shows activities *taking place* in an elaborately ruled-off Catherine Market. Fluid activity jigs across a boarded structure, composing a poignant contest of formal elements. Dancers and stallholders try with their uneven powers to own the space they cohabit. The dancer's turning solicitations to the attending public are one sort of drawing in. What does he need from them beyond their porgies and eels? He needs their legitimation. When viewers gather to watch his gestures they warrant his position. His dancing lays claim to the place and his public attests his hold. At the same virtual time, the butcher is drawing the space from under his cover. He acts out a similar taking of place. The butcher is partly competing, partly wanting to join. These two performances, dancing and drawing, occupy one plane, pressed between shingle and roof. An incorporation of the participants into a shared event is going on here. Each is freely choosing to join the contest and draw in others. In the passage I quoted at the beginning of this chapter, De Voe called this eager joining a shinning "to enter the lists." In actions like this dancing for eels, and the drawing of that dance as responsive counterpoint, each participant tries to take the place with the differentiated others in it.

Further difficulties follow from these conflicts. These participants engage in mutual activities; but they are not wholly congenial; they occupy places that are unequal; and they use uneven power to do it. Some are sheltered, some shingled. Aggression, passivity, and types of power (ownership, charisma) are rapidly showing their hands—but nothing is swapping any faster than the paradoxes and pleasures of the cultural transmission which these overlays figure. Taking the other's place, willy-nilly also means taking the other. Whether that is desired, as I think it usually is in blackface, or despised and feared, as others have emphasized, the incorporation means that blackness (or whiteness) comes along. It comes along like a burr beneath a saddle.

So far as curators know, this small (10 1/4 × 12 inches) folk drawing, this world of watching in colored India ink on draftsman's tracing cloth, has been exhibited just twice. The first time was in 1969, at the Downtown Gallery in New York, in an exhibit of American Folk Art. The second and last was for six days at Sotheby's, November 1973, when it sold as part of a large folk art collection. Its image was reproduced in a catalogue for the sale. Thus this folk drawing has remained in recent times for all practical purposes out of view. It has certainly remained unenlisted in the study of blackface performance or black dance. Nevertheless, before it was closeted as a work of art, early in the nineteenth century this drawing did determinative cultural work as a robust market drawing. Once it was considered art, its work was inhibited. Nothing new about that. But I am reenlisting it. I try to read its signals again as its contemporaries did, in order to regain a sense of this first American popular culture from its own angle.

•   •   •

I don't like de house; I wish it was bigger,
'Cause dey neber, hab rom to let in de nigga.
I wind it up now.
                                        —"De New York Nigger"

At this moment for young workers in the markets and trades, in service domestic and commercial, as the 1820s grade into the Jacksonian 1830s, matters are winding up ever more tightly in New York. Unattached youths crowd the boarding houses. The system of learning a trade by apprenticing oneself to an artisan is breaking down as managed employment is incorporating more and more skilled work. This puts the squeeze on artisanal shops, and their owners are increasingly feeling edgy. By the simplest definition, artisans are middle class, for they own their means of production, and they understand that their interests lie with the merchants and an established order. But this alignment is tenser now because production modes are changing decisively. Artisans lose independence if they throw in with the big merchants, and their knowhow separates them from the young workers, sailors, most free or enslaved blacks, immigrant Europeans. The working class suffers another of its splits. Its potentially stablest members, its artisans, separate from it, and one sign of this separation is that artisans disproportionately engage in urban riots.[8]

In the 1820s and 1830s everyone is looking askance, trying to figure out where they stand in relation to everyone else. Merchant managers like the Tappans are improvising the piecing-out system of production, particularly developed in lower Manhattan. Many coordinations are necessary for this piecing out. So many parts of so many products assembled in so many sweat shops move via so many cartings across town through so many separate agencies that owners must inculcate predictable uniformity, clockwork, and well-seated behavior. From their angle of view, such managers as the Tappans are not simply sticking busybody noses in the lives of others. Paradoxically, they are trying to bring home to the metropolis some of the cooperation that the plantations and ships in Atlantic trade had pioneered.[9]

But this is also the period when New York fills with heterogeneity unprecedented even in European urban life. The challenges of different cultures living cheek by jowl, as along Catherine and Chatham Streets and in the Five Points, winds up by several notches the mixing of behavioral cues, making everyone the more conscious of gestures as signs, and of cultural presentation in general. Youthful workers run on their own mad clocks, unsettled in their hormonal anarchy, their syncopated sleep rhythms, and their stimulant habits.

The Tappans thus enter this story about the fascination of blackface action because they attempted to lead the containment. They wanted to straiten the youth culture that was then defining itself to itself by turning around black song and dance. Among all the reasons for this fascination, not the least for these young workers was to confound and contradict the simple, romantic racism that the abolitionist conception of blacks was broadcasting. It follows, in such a positional analysis, that the Codfish group achieved much of *its* identity from disciplining these dizzy energies of dissipation and recalcitrance.

There are good reasons why cross-racial folk mimicry pushed into professional practice at particular moments, beginning in the 1820s. Blackface was a distinct and, at first, minor part of a much larger stirring of race issues in the Atlantic world. Tens of thousands of runaway slaves were pouring through border and northern cities. Many merchant abolitionists like the Tappans were accused of promoting "amalgamation." This perceived aggression by the abolitionist movement upset the liberal-conservative alliance for African colonization and culminated in such violence as the July 1834 riot in New York City, which began at the Chatham and had one of its ends burning out Lewis Tappan's Rose Street home. So, blackface was one among several factions articulating responses to race issues. Blackface performance was, however, a *distinct* faction.

Although it is newly conventional to say that blackface performance

contributed to white anger at blacks competing for jobs—that it constructed whiteness—in fact, this claim is methodologically weak. The
closer one looks at the police blotters, the more they reveal that the
people arrested at the riots were less often workers than artisans desperate to clarify their position in the economy. Also, the claim that
blackface performance—as opposed to simple disguise—contributed to
these riots is interpretively naive. The forms of blackface delineation are
so complex and multidimensional, performed by so many different actors in so many different situations, that they worked generally to confound political action. Therefore, I argue that blackface developed distinct responses to "amalgamation"—not by attacking but by enacting
miscegenation.

Blackface performers worked out ways to flash white skin beneath a
layer of burnt cork, stage the pastiche grammar of a creole dialect, and
recast traditional Irish melodies with fantasy images of fieldhand fun
shadowed by violence and dislocation. As fear and fascination grew
apace in different parts of the several newly urban audiences, so did
minstrel shows proliferate, all the while compacting and compounding
their motivating images. Their effects were as multiple, and as troubling,
as the pressures they were winding up to keep in play.

Blackface minstrelsy was a much more complex attempt to understand racial mixing and accommodate audiences to it than either abolitionist propaganda or the counter-riots of the artisanry. These wrangling
middle-class antagonists had specific intentions and policies to promote.
To boost their intentions both these parties needed to reduce images to
fundamental singularity and freeze matters there. Despite their internal
dissensions, the abolitionists were gifted at creating firm tableaus—"Am
I not a brother?" asked the kneeling slave that the Tappans were selling
during the 1830s printed in four poses "suitable, perhaps . . . as a purse
covering or lamp mat." Likewise, the artisan mobs in New York,
Charleston, Cincinnati, Boston, Philadelphia, and elsewhere were winding themselves up with similar images of simplified blacks, but more
grotesquely racist. Of all the parties to this argument who had access to
the stage or other media, only one group broadcast complex and contradictory images of blacks. Only one saw blacks as people with an implicit
intelligence evinced by explicit talent, irony, and capacious resistance.
This singular group was blackface performers and their publics, still in
their protean early phases during the 1830s.[10]

As befits the different and complex sources for their imagery, this first popular culture in the United States used blackface distinctively. In this popular culture, blackface was not a figment of illegal or sinful issues, as the merchant press or Christian pamphleteers understood it; not an arm either of abolitionist or proslavery propaganda; not a symbol of wretched animalism, as the Davy Crockett almanacs and earlier popular American imagery had conceived blackness. In this new popular culture, blackface was not the insipid blackness of romantic English abolitionist narratives, patronizing indigenous peoples in order to sustain imperial governance. Disempowered young workers applied blackface as a defiant measure of their own distance from those arguments among enfranchised interests. Youths in blackface were almost as estranged from the bourgeois inflections of the slavery quarrel as were the blacks whom they therefore chose to figure their dilemma and emphasize their distance. Blackface picked up steam exactly because it kept itself distinct from the arguments of the several ensconced groups and provoked their combined disdain.

In its early commercial stages, minstrelsy was one development young workers themselves could shape with their patronage, for what youths did not pay to see did not remain in the nightly posted theatre bills. Performers kept close tabs on their gate receipts and changed the skits and patter to keep the sales high. Sam Sanford (1821–1905), before going out on his own, was one of the early troupers with the Buckley Family Minstrels, who were subsequently incarnate as New Orleans Serenaders and then Ethiopian Serenaders. Sanford gives many instances in his unpublished autobiography of how closely he watched the gate receipts and played to the taste of the audience. His quintet appeared once in New Orleans at the same time as the Sable Harmonists, who had reached the city before them. Sanford describes their competition:

> The press gave us the preference and thus so dismayed the Sables, that they left in disgust starting up the river. I will here say the press did not do them justice for myself and old man Buckley both admitted they were our superiors in singing—but they had no Banjo or jig dances, this negro element we had. And it was the most relished part of the programme. Again, their end men could not display wit. But their choruses and songs were given in a pure operatic style, having operatic singers in the company, they done justice to all their singing. It would be presumed they were the best if number should have an advantage, they having eight, and our party five. *Yes* only *five* and we took the rag off the bush.[11]

Thus the minstrel show was the first among many later manifestations, nearly always allied with images of black culture, that allowed youths to resist merchant-defined external impostures and to express a distinctive style.

Abstracting themselves as blacks allowed the heterogeneous parts of the newly moiling young workers all access to the same identity tags. Irish, German, French, Welsh, and English recent immigrants, as well as American rustics, could all together identify in the 1830s with Jim Crow, Bone Squash, and Jumbo Jim, then in the forties with Tambo and Bones.[12] Disparate ethnic and class groups could not come together like this over theatrical images of English figures from whatever class. Nor could they identify with rural American types, like the Kentucky Rifleman, Davy Crockett, or the Yankee Peddler, certainly not with anything like the same paradoxical fit that they could feel with the raggedy black figure. All the extant figures which preceded Jim Crow carved out their space by representing power or position that opposed the positions of the new publics. Plucking a chord close to home in this heterogeneous cohort, the caroming jitters of the Jim Crow figure nixed the bluster of his western competitors. Precisely because middle-class aspirants disdained the black jitterbug in every region, the black figure appealed all across the Atlantic as an organizational emblem for workers and the unemployed. Hated everywhere, he could be championed everywhere alike.

In such early blackface acts as the entr'acte dances and the initial narrative skits, white working youths, many of them Irish immigrants like a portion of their audiences, were identifying with blacks as representations of all that the YMCAs and evangelical organizers were working to suppress. Whether their songs were inaccurate pictures of African-American culture is not the point. Until the cows come home, we might debate how well or ill minstrels copied black culture. But that is a fruitless task and always to be followed by such further imponderables as, What is authentic black culture? Is any authenticity there? What is "black"? Therefore, no matter how racist the resultant crude stereotypes became in blackface performance during the 1850s and afterward, one must neither miss nor forget the less obvious uses that proletariat youths were even then making of the material. They were flaunting their affection for these signs of akimbo insurrection against the conventions of control.

When the formal minstrel show developed after 1843, these youth publics were on the side of the spontaneous Tambo and Bones rather than that of the middlemen. The middleman's correct speech and elaborate attire represented protocols which the Tappans and other merchants hoped to inculcate. It was no accident that the middlemen, who came later to be called "interlocutor," began every show addressing the end-men with the exasperated dictum: "Gentlemen, be seated!" From beginning to end of each individual show, as well as over the extent of the entire blackface lore cycle, the minstrel show has displayed struggle over the seating of chaotic energy. Youths have projected themselves as blacks partly in order to rouse and engage just such commitments in their various fundamentalist opponents.

The expressive union between perceived black performance and young workers occurred when industrial capital was reaching dominance on both sides of the Atlantic. But neither this motley class nor its expressive union lasted through the 1850s. After that, the momentum of their coded images carried their original union disturbingly deep within blackface performance, but not in the narrative form that had emerged during the 1830s. This early blackface narrative drama unmistakably expressed fondness for black wit and gestures. But it did not last long in the cauldron of entrepreneurial pressure leading up to the Civil War. To sustain its sentiments, performers had to chop them up into the pastiche effects of the minstrel variety show. And this minstrel show survived seemingly to serve new interests. That is to say, the industrial economy of the Atlantic world and the microeconomy of minstrel theatre producers reversed the original Jim Crow engagement. As blackface minstrelsy gathered momentum in the 1850s and afterward, gathered stereotypes and gathered power, it expanded its public beyond the culture of rogue working youths. Entrepreneurial control absorbed and damped the implicit critique youths in blackface were making of upright mercantile style.

Merchants seemed to rein in insurgent expression, but what sort of success did they have? When the white minstrel's engagement with black charisma seemed to be contained, even turned inside out to derogate that charisma, the identification was still there in fact, but encoded. Apparently controlled and debased, it had a momentum of its own. Apparently deflected and defused, blackface was nevertheless raising Cain autonomously. It would be quite a while before any of this became apparent in history.

"Dancing for Eels *1820* Catharine Market" pictures the birth of a young, ragged, cross-racial culture nobody knew what to Do With. It was a force that surprised the old elites, the Knickerbockers and their equivalents in other cities, too. In some instances they were surprised into bitter retirement from the lists. Their places, however, would be taken by others. Rising elites would prove their mettle by entering the lists with those who danced for eels—not to dance, too, as we have agreed to do, but to tamp the dance and stifle the song, rechannel the manpower and housebreak its energy. It is not difficult to imagine that those two well-fed interlopers standing stiff as their sticks at the left side of the Browns' 1848 lithograph represent just these stifling elites. Arthur Tappan was one of those aspirant elites who thought he Knew What To Do.[13]

Arthur Tappan gave $5,000 for the purchase of modern steam presses when he helped found the American Tract Society. These merchant tractarians were willing to invest heavily to impose their Connecticut creeds on the surging populations of the Fourth, Sixth, Seventh, and Tenth Wards of New York City. The cultural lists were moving slowly toward the center of Manhattan from the edge. They all came together where Catherine Street met the bottom of the Bowery at the compound joint of Chatham and Division. Indeed, the tractarians and the youth culture were going to kick heels and lock heads wherever they went, edge or center of the city, edge or middle of the country.

Working for the clampdown, Lewis Tappan and colleagues handed out tracts. They "roamed the wharves of the East River; they entered the dingy stores and taverns of Five Points; they stopped in the counting-houses of Wall and State Streets. To each person they met they gave a tract, or, if rebuffed, perhaps a word of warning. By May, 1831, Lewis Tappan and the other distributors in the wards of the city had dispensed six million pages."[14]

At this point, too, the Tappans worked particularly to clamp every-thing down on Sunday, including the Sunday mails, saloons, whaling ships. This Sabbatarian impulse increased their conflict with the Catholic working class and with the Jacksonians. "Treating" to rounds of beer was a customary rite of democratic sovereignty. Bone Squash, one of the early blackface theatre's most popular workers on the lam, sings of this custom:

> And ebery Nigger dat I meet,
> I'll stop him in de street
> And I'll up wid a penny
> Head or tail for a treat.[15]

Bone literally sells his soul to a Yankee devil (modeled more than a bit on Arthur Tappan), in order to participate in this fondest rite of democratic brotherhood.

Sunday was often the one day free for this bonding. Therefore it was also a serious contradiction of democratic custom when Arthur Tappan founded the New York *Journal of Commerce,* in 1827, to rival the theatre and liquor advertising gazettes of the city. By the 1830s Arthur Tappan had become the scapegoat in the dispute between New York's clamped and their clampers. The *Working Man's Advocate* said that his name was "a running title to volumes of recorded sneers and sarcasms." Satirical poems on the streets mocked the American Tract Society by inserting its founder in street poems as "St. Arthur de Fanaticus" or "A. T. Burgundy" for the grape juice Arthur Tappan permitted at communion.[16]

This give-and-take went on for years. Increasing layers of codified anger piled on the black stereotypes of minstrelsy and the white stereotypes of the meddling clampdown. In the early blackface song "De New York Nigga," Arthur appears as "Massa Arfy Tappan." He is stepping out with Miss Dinah (as in Someone's in the Kitchen with Dinah):

> His Dinah walkin' wid Massa Arfy Tappan.
> Old Bobolition Glory, he live an' die in story,
> De black man's friend, wid de black man's houru.

It is a mistake to read, or to read off, even these most apparently vile songs in the minstrel songsters too quickly. This one sets up Tappan as Massa on an urban plantation, replete with sexual hierarchies. The punning on *houru* is complex enough to throw the point of view up for grabs. A "houri" implies a mixed-race person, specifically a white-skinned black-eyed person, a mulatta perhaps, or an actor in a mask. This wordplay indicates what I assess as a fairly typical self-consciousness about the performance.[17] The pun on *whore,* additionally, shows aggression about Dinah's betrayal of the speaker that is part of the larger song's stirring together of conflicting attitudes. The song provokes so much clashing that I present it whole to show its shocks at once:

> When de Nigger's done at night washing up de china,
> Den he sally out to go and see Miss Dinah,
> Wid his Sunday go-to-meetins segar in his mouth a
> He care for no white folk, neder should he ought to,

His missy say to him, I tell you what, Jim,
Tink you gwan now to cut and come agin.

He walk to de Park, an' he hear such mity music,
A white man he did say enuff to make him sick,
He turn round to see who make de observation
An de sassy whites laugh like de very nation,
Jim was in de fashion, so he got into a passion.
Cause de damn white trach was at him a laffin.

Jim cut ahead an tink he never mind 'em,
White folks got de manners—he tink he couldn't find 'em
He walk a little furder an tink he die a laffin,
To see his Dinah walkin' wid Massa Arfy Tappan.
Ole Bobolition Glory, he live an die in story,
De black man's friend wid de black man's houru.

He gwan to de Bowery to see Rice a actin,
He tink he act de brack man much better dan de white 'un,
Only listen now, a nigga in a operar,
Rice wid a ball an' brush tink much properer
He cut de pigeon wing, an' he do de handsome ting,
Wheel about and turn about, an' bring de money in.

De little house now, what is called de Olympic,
Wha massa Geo. Holland makes de people grin,
Ching a ring, Pompey Smash, an, ride upon a rail, sir,
De little house coin de cash, while de big ones all fail,
But I don't like de house; I wish it was bigger,
'Cause dey neber, hab rom to let in de nigga.

I wind it up now, I tink you say 'tis time, sir,
You got no reason, but got plenty ob rhyme, sir,
I'se gwan to go away, but first I leave behind me
What ebery brack man wish, in dis happy land of liberty;
Here's success to Rice, to Dixon, and to Lester,
May dey neber want a friend, nor a hoe-cake to bake, sir.

> Spoken.—Rice, Dixon, an' Lester, de proud supporters ob de
> brack drama, may dey neber want de encouragement de greatness
> ob de subject demands.[18]

This song was still current in the year of the Emancipation Proclamation. It had a performance cycle of a quarter-century, from before 1840 until some years after its 1863 publication. T. D. Rice had died in 1860, his performances had lost popularity since at least the mid-1850s, and he had been notoriously acting *Bone Squash Diavolo* (signified by the "ball and brush" reference) in the early 1830s, opposed by a Yankee Devil. When Arfy walks out with Dinah, he culminates a quarter-century's insinuation that those Codfish elite were all Yankee devils. They came at first for the soul of working youth. They returned for the working women.

My supposition here supplements the critique of blackface performance since the 1960s. It looks to me that the singer and his public are *identifying* with "De New York Nigger" at least as much as they are distinguishing themselves from him. The New York Nigger is us, Sir or Missy—says this song—may we Jims neber want a friend nor a hoecake to bake. In songs like "De New York Nigger" a popular culture is discovering for its public who they are, what alliances are possible for them, who is betraying them, and why.

This song only more clearly than many others is about its own packaging, playing on mixing and prostitution, and the eagerness in various groups to slide up and down social hierarchies leaving traces of their having been there. The main thrill and pain of the song is over the double-edged capacity to cut and come again. This is a masquerade capacity made possible by urban closeness, material sufficiency, symbolic surplus, and egalitarian excitement. Jim can cut out with his cigar jutting in front of him, leaving behind his mistress with her intimate wink of his coming again. She's used to his interruptions. When he sallies out, the military verb nicely balances a martial eruption through a gapped fortress with the contrary mincing embodied in its feminine tag. He can sally nightly to the theatre to see and be seen, but in the passage he runs a gauntlet of manners and abuse. "Jim" is already a come-again figure, the truncated return of Jim Crow, with the crow associations cut. That he used to claim he was fresh from frontier regions like Kentucky and Virginia is conveniently censored for this New York variant.

The fourth line of "De New York Nigger," constant in all the variants I have seen, is worth emphasizing: "He care for no white folk, neder should he ought to." These declarations of sympathy for Jim's black pride, and, more, the justness of this sympathy, are what the outraged critics of minstrelsy programmatically ignore in order to make the songs seem programmatically racist. In fact the song is as wholly on the side of Jim as it can be, given that it also laughs with his plight, which is the plight of the song and the plight of its public. Laughing in this song is laughing at one's own male plight, black or white.

The song repeatedly sympathizes with Jim's foiled attempts to find dignity commensurate to what the urban parade offers others. In one of its several sly rhetorical expansions, the song makes the "sassy whites" persecuting Jim's sartorial efforts expand so that they "laugh like de very nation" at him. This then is a double intensifier, laughing hard, yes, but also laughing in national unison, which has a political bite. But the image defuses itself, too, when challenged. That is, the political bite can also be denied by the simple intensified meaning—the singer might say he did not mean the whole nation was laughing, just that people were laughing hard, Whatsa matter, you don't understand street talk? So it feints and retreats, dodging. Maybe the singer just means that people will laugh at strutting youths of every hue. Jim and Dinah *are* every hue, whiteness beneath blackness in his case, blackness beneath whiteness in her case. Even the "missy" of the first stanza is ambiguous. She is probably a white woman, a middle-class employer. But the diminutive Jim uses for her is part of a common pun in these blackface songs on *mistress*. Public laughter at Jim humanizes his reaction in the next stanza when he sees Dinah also cutting out on him, as he implicitly cut out on his employer, "missy." Whether Dinah and Jim will come again, and with whom, is still an open question for these youths of New York, newly understanding themselves as distinctive, newly understanding themselves, too, as "niggers."

This identification of many ethnic groups under the banner of "De New York Nigger" is tainted through and through. It is a Gordian knot of acknowledged taintedness. Their identification displays their condition as that of the lowest and least powerful in the city in order to shock and confound the middle-class proprieties. They identify with blacks to bring themselves together and to explain to themselves how others disdain them. They do so in order to score blows against others of their class—"white trach"—who are cruel to blacks. But *white trash* is not a northern urban term; it is a southern black name for poor whites, which intensifies its usefulness as a marker of northern urban black/white affinity: we integrate, they segregate. Another reason to profess this low bond with other youths is to complain and gird themselves against female betrayal. Dinah is the butt in this song because she fancies rising sexually beyond their class.

Those are some of the tainted strands tied up in this song, but they are mild, and I believe are meant to seem mild, when they are understood in relation to the cable that is the song's real armature: the racist context which tangles its many strands and to which they allude. A specific master rhetoric contains this song even while it allows the actor to play out his resentments.

> O den I goes to New York,
> To put dem rite all dare;
> But find so many tick heads,
> I gib up in dispair
> Weel about, and turn about, And do jis so;
> Ebry time I weel about, I jump Jim Crow
> For dare be Webb he tick upon,
> De paper dat he sell;
> De Principal, wat he say good,
> I tink him worse as hel.
> —Jim Crow, "as sung by all the comic
> 　singers," Harvard Theatre Collection

James Watson Webb, on 3 August 1835, complained in his paper the *Morning Courier and New York Enquirer* that "The air in all our public conveyances is poisoned with the rank effluvia of . . . aromatic damsels, who . . . always challenge the favorite seats . . . dressed in silks obtained from the munificence of Arthur Tappan."[19] Webb wears on his sleeve, for all to see, the same possessives ("our" public spaces) that Henry Ward Beecher used to possess white working youths going to the theatre, that Thomas De Voe used to describe Manhattan Negroes dancing at Catherine Market. Webb feels aggrieved when anyone else sits in a seat he assumed was his prerogative. Here, then, in this aggression, is the master rhetoric, as published by the Tammany editor James Webb, whom Jim Crow thought "worse as hel."

　Both song and editorial were doubtless bandying images circulating orally at the time. While Webb's editorial clearly had the most immediate clout, nevertheless minstrel song had wiles enabling its destabilizing effects to last the longer and work the sneakier. That's what interests me about "De New York Nigger" and its taintedness. It does not picture Webb's power versus worker powerlessness; it does not show one discourse mastering another. Rather, it admits imbalance of power but displays the resourceful ways that vernacular culture marked out its position within the taint of this imbalance.

　Did Webb dictate terms to blackface performers? Probably. Certainly his heavy hand indexes the dominant racist reality. The class disdain and racism expressed in Webb's editorial remark drive the omnibuses in which all the "floating population" must move. Webb did not invent the terms, but he employs them forcefully. Workers with no access to presses or to boardrooms had to resort to minstrel songs and shingle boards to sing and dance their positions. It was that or float in the flow that Webb spewed. Carried nested in the poisons that elite politics broadcast, it is no wonder that songs like "De New York Nigger" are tainted. Their soiling is the condition of culture in the unsettled space of the early industrial world.

"De New York Nigger" is not free art. Its performers are not free agents in some never-never land of free self-activation. The song attests to a thoroughly nested cultural struggle. The imagery in such struggles is shared, but the power is not. The power remains unequally dispersed. This is not to say that the singer has no power. Rather, what power he has manifests itself in different ways than Webb's. Webb is upfront, so sure his prejudices reign that he need not hide them. The singer is forced to be downback: sneaky and two-faced, which is one possible definition of "blackface."

Webb's editorial and the song's recalcitrant disturbance of "his" imagery both struggle to control a mutually engaged energy. They share terms, but it is perfectly clear they do not share intentions, and they are not alone in this fight. There are additional parties—more bodies wrestling under the blanket. The Tappans fought this master rhetoric more directly than proletarian self-activation could. The Tappans bought physical space to preach their rhetoric, paid for presses to churn out tracts to disseminate it and a newspaper to second it. Gentlemen of property and standing like Webb and his Tammany rump had their own newspaper, the *Courier and Enquirer,* to broadcast their side. These vicious fights about who was controlling urban ideology revolved around questions of who would draw the limits of civilized behavior. That's what was really going on when Webb talked about "aromatic damsels" and the Tappans strove to keep free Negroes in New York rather than ship them, colonization-style, back to Liberia.

Here is Webb again, in an even more abusive and telling remark, directed once again specifically at the Tappans:

The egis of the law indignantly withdraws its shelter from them . . . when they debase the noble race from which we spring—that race which called civilization into existence, and from which have proceeded all the great, the brave, and good, that have ever lived—and place it in the same scale as the most stupid, ferocious and cowardly of the divisions into which the creator has divided mankind, then they place themselves beyond the pale of the law, for they violate every law divine and human.[20]

This middle-class struggle to locate the edge of the community as the "pale of the law" is what contaminates the world of "De New York Nigger." The reverse of the same token shows just how radical and threatening to that internecine bourgeois conflict a song such as this can be. These songs mock that struggle by determinedly crossing and recrossing, tirelessly tangling and looping that border line. Jim has imaginative access everywhere. But he has sovereign access nowhere: "dey neber, hab room to let in de nigga." In lines like this, we see declared that old Catherine Market spirit. Bobolink Bob and Jim Crow survive, nested in "De New York Nigger."

What is remarkable about this song, like much of minstrelsy behind it, like all lore with legs, is its *compaction*. It winds up so many references and conflicting attitudes in Jim that he proves unreadable, irresolvable, backing one agenda or ideology only if he is excerpted in fragments. He is a working-class flâneur strolling through swamps of disdain, and he knows it. Looking wryly on as the abolitionist leader walks off with his lover, Jim remains on the outside, scorned by whites whose manners are undiscoverable. He is a man with no home but a place to scrub other people's china. Arfy and Dinah surpass him. The opera house that represents him prohibits his entrance. But no one else in the world of the song shares his modicum of dignity: he tells plain truth. And plainly his audience is meant to feel the unfairness of his betrayal and exclusion. While the storied actors and pretenders of both genders enrich themselves at his expense, he retains his put-upon, Chaplinesque dignity. He still hopes that the black drama will have success, because that is the one place that his story can peep out, in its way, between the cracks, hoping there will be auditors to hear its codes.

Nevertheless, "De New York Nigger" criticizes the racism of its own minstrel form: the exclusions of some of the theatres, the laughing at blacks. This is one of the ways it shows its awareness of its own genealogy, to which it alludes in snatched phrases ("Ching A Ring Chaw" and "Pompey Smash," in stanza 5, are both early minstrel songs that themselves blend lines from a storehouse of minstrel-song couplets). That these references cohabit with the phrase "ride upon a rail" shows that the singer is aware of the broad connection between shivarees (charivari, Skimmington rides, rough music) and the social function of blackface performance as vernacular struggle. Much of the fullness of the song, as in other blackface actions behind it, develops from holding together this conflicted gene pool. A cynicism and a humor cut every which way unpredictably in this song, including at the end against itself—though it has more "reason" than it admits. And the doubleness of the spoken end is also a tough nut—"de greatness ob de subject" is undoubtable even within the self-mocking terms of the song, even without the Civil War, Reconstruction, the civil rights movements, and subsequent liberal empathy to validate it. The singer knows the seriousness but reasonably suspects that little people will always be paraded about even while they are barred from the very institutions that represent them. In actions like this song, the spirit of Catherine Market escaped the containers in which New York's elites, of all sorts, were trying to catch it.

"De New York Nigger" is a small skit which samples dance and vocal gestures from earlier performers. It replays the integrated fascination of the neighborhood as a distinct consciousness. It shows itself separate from and harassed by more powerful ideologies. It finds wiles within this unbalanced power to mount nightly sallies. We can think of "De New York Nigger" as dancing out the codes of Catherine Slip as the Chatham incorporated them. When it could, the Chatham gave hospitable space to the spirit of the dancers for eels; it was, after all, the closest of the theatres (whose productions have come down to us) to Catherine Market.

The struggles waged over the Chatham's stage instruct us about the importance of vernacular gesture and its persistence. The Chatham enclosed the rudimentary performance space that truck farmers, slaves, free blacks, butchers, sailors, carvers, navvies, and other roustabouts of every color, all exploring their conditional stages of freedom, and its lack, parceled out at Catherine Slip. But the Chatham housed a good bit more. Because it was giving venue to these gestures, it too became a contested space. As soon as it became a recognizable determinant of the popular mind, this dancing, this popular lore, became something to promote and to stifle. When these forms of popularity stepped on stage, and drew audiences, a wrangling consortium of politicians, editors, reformers, and religious tractarians began their oppositional moves. They were not subtle. They were direct.

An inventory was done of the goods at the Chatham when the Tappans leased it. Two of the musical items listed among the properties to be transferred were "Incle & Yarico Score & Parts" valued at $3.50 and "Padlock bound score" valued at $2.50. In July 1833 these and the rest of the music in the theatre were summarily taken to Franklin Square to be sold off "to the best advantage."[21] These staples of the Atlantic community's budding opposition to race slavery, sentimental division, were just more detritus to the earnest Tappans. But throw them away? No, sir. Sell them. Turn scores and lyrics to tracts. Opened in 1824, conventional theatre until May 1832, evangelical chapel for more than seven years, pressure cooker for the early classic minstrel shows in February 1843, Chanfrau's stage to present eel dances for the widening proletariat public from the spring of 1848, and the first Manhattan home to *Uncle Tom's Cabin* in 1852: the Chatham was a thorough example of the push come to shove between the many forces of propriety and the various arms of the western Atlantic's first proletarian youth culture.

Now the Chatham is gone. Knickerbocker Village squats at the site of Catherine Market. The whole city has grabbed the butchers' and the Codfish strategies of taking and occupying the territory. The East River with its Slip at the end of Catherine Street hardly seems a membrane of Atlantic culture any longer.

But the eels, those cultural eels for which we have danced: they lasted longer. They were coded in turning gestures. The eels have it.

NOTES

1. For this book about cultural cycles, it has helped me to remember that those who early noticed our gestural vocabulary kept their eyes cocked on quite real tides: "The farmers living in New Jersey and the neighboring counties, both on the North and East Rivers brought [their goods] also down in the same manner to the nearest waterside—unloaded into their skiffs; then, with the tide of ebb, easily rowed to the city direct to the various markets on the shores, where they usually disposed of their products in time to return with the flood tide." Thomas F. De Voe, *The Market Book,* vol. 1 (1862; New York: Burt Franklin, 1969), p. 137. Founded on the west side of lower Manhattan around 1771, Bear Market was an early market supplying Manhattan from Jersey's farms. Catherine Market, on the East River, was several along in a series of smaller markets that gradually were superseded as population density moved up, and sometimes back down, the eastern shore of Manhattan from the Battery to

178   W. T. LHAMON, JR.

Corlear's Hook and as it adjusted to the suppliers across the river in Brooklyn and Williamsburgh.

2. Roger Abrahams, "The Winking Gods of The Marketplace," paper circulated about 1986.

3. De Voe, *The Market Book*. A full-blown reference to bobolinks appears in classic minstrelsy, too. The song, cited in Sam Dennison, *Scandalize My Name: Black Imagery in American Popular Music* (New York: Garland, 1982), p. 81, is "Oh, Mr. Coon": "De white bird an de black bird settin' in de grass,/ Preachin' 'malgamation to de bobolinks dat pass;/To carry out de doctrine dey seem little loth,/When along cum de pigeon hawk and leby on 'em both." Even here, well down the pike of blackface becoming racist, the bobolinks are still the birds with which the audience identifies. They are birds that consciously play and stay in the middle, while the pigeon-hawk police lower their hard talons on the propagandists at both extremes.

4. Irving Berlin's family lived briefly on Monroe Street (which had been Bancker in the years Catherine Market was prominent), then at 330 Cherry Street. He performed first as a singing waiter at 12 Pell Street, Five Points, at "Nigger Mike's" saloon, also known as the Pelham owned by Mike Salter.

5. I outline the long cycle of minstrel performance in "Ebery Time I Wheel About I Jump Jim Crow: Cycles of Minstrel Transgression from Cool White to Vanilla Ice," in *Inside the Blackface Mask*, ed. Anna Bean James V. Hatch, and Brooks McNamara (Middletown, CT: Wesleyan University Press, 1996).

6. Frances Anne Kemble, *Journal of a Residence on a Georgian Plantation in 1838–1839*, ed. John A. Scott (Athens: University of Georgia Press, 1984), p. 131. Dickens wrote about William Henry Lane dancing as Juba at the Five Points in *American Notes* (1842; New York: Oxford University Press, 1987). Robert P. Nevin, "Stephen C. Foster and Negro Minstrelsy," *Atlantic Monthly* 20, no. 121 (1867). Brander Matthews, "The Rise and Fall of Negro Minstrelsy," *Scribner's* 57, no. 6 (1915). Constance Rourke, *American Humor: A Study of the American Character*, ed. W. T. Lhamon Jr. (1931; Tallahassee: Florida State University Press, 1985).

7. Hans Nathan, *Dan Emmett and the Rise of Early Negro Minstrelsy* (Norman: University of Oklahoma Press, 1962). Robert C. Toll, *Blacking Up: The Minstrel Show in Nineteenth-Century America* (New York: Oxford University Press, 1974). Alexander Saxton, in *The Rise and Fall of the White Republic: Class Politics and Mass Culture in Nineteenth-Century America* (London: Verso, 1990), extends pioneering work he did on minstrelsy and Jacksonian democracy in 1975. David R. Roediger, in *The Wages of Whiteness: Race and the Making of the American Working Class* (London: Verso, 1991), shows that antebellum white workers used the minstrel show to distinguish themselves from blacks. Eric Lott's *Love and Theft: Blackface Minstrelsy and the American Working Class* (New York: Oxford University Press, 1993) voices a newly sophisticated

understanding of minstrelsy, arguing that even as it showed white attraction toward black culture, the form helped whites control and steal what fascinated them.

8. Susan G. Davis, *Parades and Power: Street Theatre in Nineteenth-Century Philadelphia* (Philadelphia: Temple University Press, 1986); Linda K. Kerber, "Abolitionists and Amalgamators: The New York City Race Riots of 1834," *New York History* 48 (1967); above all Leonard L. Richards, *"Gentlemen of Property and Standing": Anti-Abolition Mobs in Jacksonian America* (New York: Oxford University Press, 1970) and Sean Wilentz, *Chants Democratic: New York City and the Rise of the American Working Class, 1788–1850* (New York: Oxford University Press, 1984).

9. Peter Linebaugh, "All the Atlantic Mountains Shook," *Labour/Le Travailleur* 10 (1982).

10. Bertram Wyatt-Brown, *Tappan and the Evangelical War against Slavery* Cleveland: Press of Case Western Reserve University, 1969), p. 155. The most generative work on the images of mob racism in the period that I know about is Phillip Lapsansky, "Graphic Discord: Abolitionist and Antiabolitionist Images," in *An Untrodden Path,* ed. Jean Fagin Yellin and John C. Van Horne (Ithaca: Cornell University Press, 1994).

11. Samuel S. Sanford, "Personal Reminiscences of Himself Together with the History of Minstrelsy from the Origan [*sic*] 1843 to 1893 with a sketch of all the celebrities of the Past and Present," holograph MS, Harry Ransom Humanities Research Center, University of Texas, pp. 24–25.

12. All these tags of identity—national, ethnic, class, regional—are too gross for intimate meaning. Once in a taxi in Bloomington, Indiana, I tried to strike up conversation with the cabbie. Are you from the Midwest, I asked him. No, he replied, I'm from right around here.

13. My phrasing here is from the opening of Thomas Pynchon's novel *V.* (New York: Lippincott, 1963), p. 10, about the 1950s. Pynchon reckoned the menace of popular culture was even then still Atlantic, conveyed to ports by a cross-racial community of sailors, and derived from their rogue surplus energy and symbolism: "East Main, a ghetto for Drunken Sailors nobody knew what to Do With, sprang on your nerves with all the abruptness of a normal night's dream turning to nightmare. Dog into wolf, light into twilight, emptiness into waiting presence." This is the underlying creed of *Raising Cain.*

14. Jane P. Tompkins, *Sensational Designs: The Cultural Work of American Fiction, 1790–1860* (New York: Oxford University Press, 1985), p. 53.

15. *Bone Squash Diavolo,* MS in Lord Chamberlain's Papers, British Library, scene 1. See my anthology *Jump Jim Crow: Plays, Lyrics, and Street Prose of the First Atlantic Popular Culture* (Cambridge: Harvard University Press, forthcoming).

16. Wyatt-Brown, *Tappan and the Evangelical War against Slavery,* pp. 54,

67. See also Lydia Maria Child's letter, 22 Aug. 1835, to Ellis Gray Loring: "A virulent little paper is buzzing about here, called the Anti-Abolitionist. Over it is a large wood cut, representing men and women, black and white, hugging and kissing each other; and on the table are decanters marked A.T.B.—which signifies Arthur Tappan's Burgundy." *Lydia Maria Child: Selected Letters, 1817–1880*, ed. Milton Meltzer and Patrica G. Holland, assoc. ed. Francine Krasno (Amherst: University of Massachusetts Press, 1982), p. 34.

17. The two versions of this song I am working from here are in *Jim Crow's Vagaries* (London, dated by the British Library as 1840), p. 9, and *De Susannah, and Thick Lip, Melodist* (New York, [1863]), p. 74. Eric Lott in *Love and Theft* also notices the self-consciousness in this song, calling it subtle, guilty, and unexpected. To me it seems rather the opposite—straightforward, guilt-free, and usual. One of the fundaments of early minstrelsy is that it shows no guilt about black oppression. Even when it is sympathetic to black suffering, its relationship to that suffering is not that of someone, or some class, feeling responsibility for that suffering. Blackface performers owned no slaves, minted no guineas, often could not vote, could make no Fugitive Slave Laws, set no demeaning wages. They did not even exclude black performers from the theatres where they performed. Theatre owners and others more powerful, the very people they were fighting, were responsible for those practices. I am not speaking of the large touring minstrel shows after the Civil War. I speak only of the early blackface performers, of the impulse at Catherine Market and in the Chatham and the early Bowery.

18. In the earlier, English, version, the house is the Franklin rather than the Olympic, and the comedian is John Sefton rather than Holland. "Lester" is probably a reference to a performer named Leicester, who performed at the Franklin.

19. Quoted in Wyatt-Brown, *Tappan and the Evangelical War against Slavery*, p. 151.

20. *Courier and Enquirer*, 11 July 1834, cited in Kerber, "Abolitionists and Amalgamators," p. 37.

21. *Inventory:* Holograph MS Thr. 391, Harvard Theatre Collection, pp. 47, 50. Charles Bickerstaff's *The Padlock* (1768) was an English comic opera with an early blackface character, Mungo. In London Bickerstaff played Mungo's role himself. In New York Lewis Hallam played the part famously from May 1769, all through that summer. This play was a very mixed bag, playing the suffering of blacks, and their whipping, for laughs, but at other moments indicating sympathy for slaves. Mungo's most famous song drips with pity:

> Dear Heart! what a terrible life am I led!
> A dog has better, that's shelter'd and fed;
> Night and day 'tis the same

My pain is dere game;
Me wish to de Lord me was dead.
Whate'er's to be done,
Poor Blacky must run;
Mungo here, Mungo dere,
Mungo every where.
Above or below,
Sirrah, come, sirrah, go;
Me wish to de Lord me was dead.

Quoted in S. Foster Damon, "The Negro in Early American Songsters," *Papers of the Bibliographical Society of America,* 28 (1934), p. 134.

Inkle and Yarico (1787) was George Colman Jr.'s opera on the century-old story of Yarico, a North American Indian maiden who fell in love with Inkle, who took her to Barbados and almost sold her into slavery. During Colman's handling of the story, Yarico darkened from Indian to Negro. After Inkle tries to betray his lover, but learns better from his servant's example and the outrage of the Governor of Barbados, the story ends in a double miscegenation, wealthy Englishman and his servant both marrying their dark lovers. This opera was performed in Boston in 1794 and in New York in 1796. See Lawrence Marsden Price, *Inkle and Yarico Album* (Berkeley: University of California Press, 1937). Price's concluding sentence on the story puts it as a lore cycle: "The slave-dealer and the master took on a more definite form and thus the legend grew as legends will, but what it gained in breadth it lost in depth and after a century of praise the name of Yarico was rarely heard again" (p. 138).

Chapter 7

AIDS, Homophobia, and Biomedical Discourse

An Epidemic of Signification

Paula A. Treichler

Introduction by Priscilla Wald

The contentiousness evident in English departments and professional meetings of late signals a discipline in flux. The demand for social relevance issued from a variety of directions since the 1960s has transformed the subject matter and methodologies that students encounter when they take "English classes." We have broadened both what it means to "read literature" and what constitutes "reading practices." Self-scrutiny—coming in a range of forms from manifestos and position papers to institutional analyses—has challenged scholars in the field to rethink what we do and how and why we do it. The clarity and compassion evident in Paula Treichler's *How to Have Theory in an Epidemic: Cultural Chronicles of AIDS* bears witness to the importance of those challenges. Taking what she calls "an epidemic of signification" produced by the AIDS epidemic as the subject of her book, Treichler at once demonstrates what it means to take a "literary approach" to a nonliterary work—in this case, both a disease and the many representations of that disease—and shows how such an approach yields insights that would not be available from other sources or approaches.

At this point it is not unusual to argue that the AIDS epidemic refers to a set of social, ethical, and political issues that extend beyond and are inseparable from the medical implications of the disease. But Treichler demonstrates exactly how the language and narratives used by those touched by the epidemic simultaneously register the larger social and cultural contexts of the disease and actually shape scientific perceptions and medical treatments. Everyone who speaks or even thinks about HIV and AIDS—from medical practitioners to patients and their communities, policy makers and activists, to the general public—does so from within cultural narratives that make the disease and its implications meaningful in a variety of ways. In her analysis of those processes, Treichler demonstrates both that language is not transparent and that there is still significant resistance to that claim. She is sensitive to the fact that human suffering can make abstract ideas about social and rhetorical construction seem frivolous and irrelevant. Yet her point is precisely to identify the danger in constructing an opposition between the actual disease and the terms through which it is apprehended. Human suffering remains central to her discussion; in fact, it motivates the inquiry and crystallizes the analysis. But Treichler reminds us that human suffering is not reducible to physical pain, and it is, therefore, inseparable from language and other forms of representation. We do not simply know the world through language; we construct it. Language constitutes physical as well as emotional experience.

That observation, of course, does not distinguish Treichler's analysis. Rather, her attention to the nuances and subtleties of its implications for understanding the AIDS epidemic—and human experience more broadly—makes *How to Have Theory in an Epidemic* an especially clear and forceful example of how and why literary critical methodologies yield important insights into a culture. Here I want to distinguish between Treichler's literary critical approach to disease and that of a medical ethicist. While the latter could certainly point to problems in, for instance, the way HIV testing might encroach upon individual liberties or the way the media depicts those who test positive, Treichler identifies the terms through which different groups (the medical profession, journalists, the public) understand and define the disease, and she shows how these terms literally affect the experience and even treatment of the disease itself. The future is an important concern for medical ethicists; they try to imagine the implications for the future of contemporary medical theories, discoveries, and treatments. A literary critical approach, which attends to the nuances of language usage and narrative frames, can identify cultural biases of which the speakers may be unaware and that can influence the direction of medical protocols. In other words, Treichler's methodology has important ramifications for medical (and other) ethicists.

Treichler offers more than an important analysis of the AIDS epidemic (although, of course, *How to Have Theory in an Epidemic* is certainly that). She demonstrates a paradigmatic application of a literary critical approach to the study of culture and shows how such an approach can serve the project of social justice.

The academy is currently undergoing a kind of intellectual meiosis in which the disciplines are recombining in response to the new knowledge and skills needed in a world in which globalization and unusually rapid technological growth have mandated new modes of inquiry. As the disciplines recombine, we must be open to the insights that such combinations of methodologies and fields of inquiry will yield. But we must also be careful not to lose the particular insights that the methodologies of current disciplines can offer. Treichler's work exemplifies the elegant and persuasive cultural inquiry that can emerge when a careful critic takes a contextualized literary critical approach to the analysis of social and cultural phenomena.

THE AIDS EPIDEMIC IS CULTURAL AND LINGUISTIC as well as biological and biomedical. To understand the epidemic's history, address its future, and learn its lessons, we must take this assertion seriously. Moreover, it is the careful examination of language and culture that enables us, as members of intersecting social constellations, to think carefully about ideas in the midst of a crisis: to use our intelligence and critical faculties to consider theoretical problems, develop policy, and articulate long-term social needs even as we acknowledge the urgency of the AIDS crisis and try to satisfy its relentless demand for immediate action. This book documents cultural and linguistic dimensions of the AIDS epidemic and examines the tension between theory and practice as it recurs in diverse arenas.

•   •   •

This enterprise focuses on a body of linguistic data and, through time, space, and multiple cultural venues, keeps this body in view. The evolution of the AIDS epidemic has coincided with a period of attention to language. Scientists commonly point out that AIDS arrived at the "right time"—that is, a time when basic scientific research in molecular biology, virology, and immunology could provide a foundation for an intensive research effort focused on AIDS. They point out that no other epidemic disease has been analyzed so quickly or had its cause so efficiently determined. At the same time, as the British critic and AIDS activist Simon Watney has often pointed out, investigation in the human sciences provides an equally crucial foundation for the understanding of AIDS. The apparatus of contemporary critical and cultural theory prepares us to analyze AIDS in relation to questions of language, representation, interpretation, narrative, ideology, social and intellectual difference, binary division, and contests for meaning. But the AIDS epidemic does not exist to demonstrate the value of contemporary theory. If anything, it puts theory stringently to the test, serving as a useful and often dramatic corrective for inadequate theoretical formulations. Of course, to my mind, *theory* is not the constellation of texts and thinkers demonized by William Bennett et al. Nor is it the creature disdained by other anti-intellectual traditions, including U.S. medicine, for whom *theory* is defined as that which is devoid of relevance for "practice" and real-life experience. At the end of the day, *theory* is another word for *intelligence,* that is, for a thoughtful and engaged dialectic between the brain, the body, and the world that the brain and the body inhabit.

My investigation of language in a medical and cultural crisis like AIDS is thus framed by a more profound question: What should be the role of theory in an epidemic? Of all the meanings and metaphors generated by the AIDS epidemic, AIDS as a war—a long, devastating, savage, costly, expensive, and continuing war—best helps us consider this question. When we try to account for the social and cultural impact, the economic toll, the multiplicity of understandings, and the unpredictable cultural upheavals and realignments that the AIDS crisis continues to generate, the major wars of our time offer a precedent as useful as plague, polio, and other more conventional comparisons. AIDS is a war whose participants have been in the trenches for years, surrounded daily by death and dying, yet only gradually has the rest of the population come to know that there is a war at all. To quote Simon Watney again, "for those of us living and working in the various constituencies most devastated by HIV it seems . . . as if the rest of the population were tourists, casually wandering through at the very height of a blitz of which they are totally unaware" (1994, 47).

The war metaphor also captures the dichotomy between theory and practice that marks the AIDS epidemic as well as U.S. cultural life more generally. The very mention of *theory, cultural construction,* or *discourse* may be exasperating or distressing to those face to face with the epidemic's enormity and overwhelming practical demands. Nowhere has this pressure for action been more poignant than in questions about treatment, an arena of the epidemic wholly informed by the sense of time passing and time lost. Martin Delaney, the AIDS treatment activist who founded Project Inform in San Francisco, participated in a forum on treatment options for people with HIV and AIDS at Columbia University in 1988; in a panel on AZT, Delaney argued that, however flawed or incomplete, results to date suggested AZT's benefits and that, in any case, it was a present the best hope. When other panelists urged caution and encouraged audience members to be skeptical of AZT's success, Delaney lost his patience with what he perceived as a quest for abstract truth: "This isn't an argument about how many angels can dance on the head of a pin. People's lives hang in the balance of this decision" (quoted in Douglas 1989, 33).

Yet theory is about "people's lives." As Stuart Hall (1992) has said, our inability to end this epidemic humbles us as intellectuals; at the same time, the epidemic demands our attention:

> AIDS is one of the questions which urgently brings before us our marginality as critical intellectuals in making real effects in the world. And yet it has often been represented for us in contradictory ways. Against the urgency of people dying in the streets, what in God's name is the point of cultural studies? What is the point of the study of representations, if there is no response to the question of what you say to someone who wants to know if they should take a drug and if that means they'll die two days later or a few months earlier? At that point, I think anybody who is into cultural studies seriously as an intellectual practice, must feel, on their pulse, its ephemerality, its insubstantiality, how little it registers, how little we've been able to change anything or get anybody to do anything. (pp. 284–85)

At the same time, Hall writes, AIDS

> is indeed a more complex and displaced question than just people dying out there. The question of AIDS is an extremely important terrain of struggle and contestation. In addition to the people we know who are dying, or have died, or will, there are the many people dying who are never spoken of. How could we say that the question of AIDS is not also a question of who gets represented and who does not? AIDS is the site at which the advance of sexual politics is being rolled back. It's a site at which not only people will die, but desire and pleasure will also die if

certain metaphors do not survive, or survive in the wrong way. Unless we operate in this tension, we don't know what cultural studies can do, can't, can never do, but also, what it has to do, what it alone has a privileged capacity to do. (p. 285)

This tension permeates the present book as it considers how the AIDS epidemic helps us understand the complex relation between language and reality, between meanings and definitions—and how those relations help us understand AIDS and develop interventions that are more culturally informed and socially responsible. Camus called the plague itself a kind of abstraction; "Still," he wrote, "when abstraction sets to killing you, you've got to get busy with it" ([1947] 1948, 81). But abstraction plays a central role in our ability to "get busy with it." To speak of AIDS as a linguistic construction that acquires meaning only in relation to networks of given signifying practices may seem politically and pragmatically dubious, like philosophizing in the middle of a war zone. But making sense of AIDS compels us to address questions of signification and representation. When we deduce from the facts that AIDS is an infectious, sexually transmitted disease syndrome caused by a virus, what is it that we are making sense of? *Infection, sexually transmitted, disease,* and *virus* are also linguistic constructs that generate meaning and simultaneously facilitate and constrain our ability to think and talk about material phenomena. Language is not a substitute for reality; it is one of the most significant ways we know reality, experience it, and articulate it; indeed, language plays a powerful role in producing experience and in certifying that experience as "authentic."

• • •

In multiple, fragmentary, and often contradictory ways, we struggle to achieve some sort of understanding of AIDS, a reality that is frightening, widely publicized, yet finally neither directly nor fully knowable. AIDS is no different in this respect from other linguistic constructions that, in the commonsense view of language, are thought to transmit preexisting ideas and represent real-world entities yet in fact do neither. The nature of the relation between language and reality is highly problematic, and *AIDS* is not merely an invented label, provided to us by science and scientific naming practices, for a clear-cut disease entity caused by a virus. Rather, the very nature of AIDS is constructed through language and in particular through the discourses of medicine and science; this construction is "true" or "real" only in certain specific ways—for example, insofar as it successfully guides research or facilitates clinical control over the illness.[1] The name *AIDS* in part *constructs* the disease and helps make it intelligible. We cannot therefore look "through" language to determine what AIDS "really" is. Rather, we must explore the site where such determinations *really* occur and intervene at the point where meaning is created: in language.

Of course, AIDS is a real disease syndrome, damaging and killing real human beings. Because of this, it is tempting—perhaps in some instances imperative—to view science and medicine as providing a discourse about AIDS closer to its "reality" than what we can provide ourselves. Yet, with its genuine potential for global devastation, the AIDS epidemic is simultaneously an epidemic of a transmissible lethal disease and an epidemic of meanings or signification. Both epidemics are equally crucial for us to understand, for, try as we may to treat AIDS as "an infectious disease" and nothing more, meanings continue to multiply wildly and at an extraordinary rate.[2] This epidemic of meanings is readily apparent in the chaotic assemblage of understandings of AIDS that by now exists.

• • •

AIDS and Homophobia: Constructing the Text of the Gay Male Body

Whatever else it may be, AIDS is a story, or multiple stories, and read to a surprising extent from a text that does not exist: the body of the male homosexual. People so want—need—to read this text that they have gone so far as to write it themselves. AIDS is a nexus where multiple meanings, stories, and discourses intersect and overlap, reinforce and subvert each other. Yet clearly this mysterious male homosexual text has figured centrally in generating what I call here an *epidemic of signification*. Of course, "the virus," with mysteries of its own, has been a crucial influence. But we may recall Camus's ([1947] 1948) novel: "the word 'plague' . . . conjured up in the doctor's mind not only what science chose to put into it, but a whole series of fantastic possibilities utterly out of keeping" (p. 37) with the bourgeois town of Oran, where the plague struck. How could a disease so extraordinary as *plague* happen in a place so ordinary and dull? Initially striking people perceived as alien and exotic by scientists, physicians, journalists, and much of the U.S. population, AIDS did not pose such a paradox. The "promiscuous" gay male body—early reports noted that AIDS "victims" reported having had as many as a thousand sexual partners—made clear that, even if AIDS turned out to be a sexually transmitted disease, it would not be a commonplace one. The connections between sex, death, and homosexuality made the AIDS story inevitably, as David Black (1986) notes, able to be read as "the story of a metaphor."[3]

Ironically, a major turning point in the U.S. consciousness came when Rock Hudson acknowledged that he was being treated for AIDS. Through an extraordinary conflation of texts, the Rock Hudson case dramatized the possibility that the disease could spread to the "general population."[4] In fact, this possibility had been evident for some time to anyone who wished to find it: as Jean Marx summarized the evidence in *Science* in 1984, "Sexual intercourse both of the heterosexual and homosexual varieties is a major pathway of transmission" (p. 147). But only in late 1986 (and somewhat reluctantly at that) did the CDC (1986b) expand on its original "4-H list" of high-risk categories: *homosexuals, hemophiliacs, heroin addicts,* and *Haitians* and the sexual partners of people within these groups. The original list, developed during 1981 and 1982, has structured evidence collection in the intervening years and contributed to the view that the major risk factor in acquiring AIDS is being a particular kind of person rather than doing particular things.[5] Ann Giudici Fettner, AIDS reporter for the *New York Native,* pointed out in 1985 that "the CDC admits that at least ten percent of AIDS sufferers are gay *and* use IV drugs. Yet they are automatically counted in the homosexual and bisexual men category, regardless of what might be known—or not known—about how they became infected" ("AIDS: What Is to Be Done?" 1985, 43). So the "gay" nature of AIDS was in part an artifact of the way data were collected and reported. Although, almost from the beginning, scientific papers have cited AIDS cases that appeared to fall outside the high-risk groups, it has been generally hypothesized that these cases, assigned to the categories of *unknown, unclassified,* or *other,* would ultimately turn out to be one of the four Hs.[6] This commitment to categories based on monolithic identity filters out information. Shaw (1986) argues that when women are asked in CDC protocols." Are you heterosexual?" "this loses the diversity of behaviors that may have a bearing on infection." Even now, with established evidence that transmission can be heterosexual (which begins with the letter *h* after all), scientific discourse continues to construct women as "inefficient" and "incompetent" transmitters of HIV ("the AIDS virus"), passive receptacles without the projectile capacity of a penis or a syringe—stolid, uninteresting barriers that impede the unrestrained passage of the virus from brother-to-brother.[7] Exceptions include prostitutes, whose discursive legacy—despite their long-standing professional knowledge and continued activism about AIDS—is to be seen as so contaminated that their bodies are virtual laboratory cultures for viral replication.[8] Other exceptions are *African women,* whose exotic bodies, sexual practices, or who knows what are seen to be so radically different from those of women in the United States that anything can happen in them.[9] The term *exotic,* sometimes used to describe a virus that appears to have originated "elsewhere" (but *elsewhere,* like *other,* is not a fixed category), is an important theme running through AIDS literature (Leibowitch 1985, 73). The fact that one of the more extensive and visually elegant analyses of AIDS appeared in the *National Geographic* (Jaret 1986) is perhaps further evidence of its life on an idealized "exotic" terrain.

After the first cases appeared in New York, Los Angeles, and Paris, the early hypotheses about AIDS were sociological, relating it directly to the supposed "gay male lifestyle." In February 1982, for example, it was thought that a particular supply of amylnitrate (poppers) might be contaminated. "The poppers fable," writes Jacques Leibowitch (1985), becomes

> a Grimm fairy tale when the first cases of AIDS-without-poppers are discovered among homosexuals absolutely repelled by the smell of the product and among heterosexuals unfamiliar with even the words *amylnitrate* or *poppers.* But, as will be habitual in the history of AIDS, rumors last longer than either common sense or the facts would warrant. The odor of AIDS-poppers will hover in the air a long time—long enough for dozens of mice in the Atlanta epidemiology labs to be kept in restricted cages on an obligatory sniffed diet of poppers eight to twelve hours a day for several months, until, nauseated but still healthy, without a trace of AIDS, the wretched rodents were released—provisionally—upon the announcement of a new hypothesis: *promiscuity.* (p. 5)

This new perspective generated numerous possibilities. One was that sperm itself could destroy the immune system. "God's plan for man," after all, "was for Adam and Eve and not Adam and Steve."[10] Women, the "natural" receptacles for male sperm, have evolved over the millennia so that their bodies can deal with these foreign invaders; men, not thus blessed by nature, become vulnerable to the "killer sperm" of other men. In the lay press, AIDS became known as the "toxic cock syndrome." While scientists and physicians tended initially to define AIDS as a gay sociological problem, gay men, for other reasons, also tended to reject the possibility that AIDS was a new contagious disease. Not only would this make them sexual lepers, but it also did not make sense: "How could a disease pick out gays? That had to be medical homophobia" (Black 1986, 40).[11] Important to note here is a profound ambivalence about the origins of illness. Does one prefer an illness that is caused by who one is and that can therefore perhaps be prevented, cured, or contained through "self-control"—or an illness that is caused by some external "disease" that has a respectable medical name and can be addressed strictly as a medical problem, beyond individual control? The townspeople of Oran in *The Plague* experience relief when the plague bacillus is identified: the odd happenings—the dying rats, the mysterious human illnesses—are caused by something that has originated elsewhere, something external, something "objective," something that medicine can name, even if not cure. The tension between self and not-self becomes important as we try to understand the particular role of viruses and origin stories in AIDS.

But this anticipates the next chapter in the AIDS story. Another favored possibility in the early 1980s (still not universally discarded, for it is plausible so long as cases among monogamous homebodies are ignored) is that sex is a "cofactor": no *single* infectious agent causes the disease; rather, someone who is sexually active with multiple partners is exposed to a kind of bacterial/viral tidal wave that can crush the immune system.[12] Gay men on the sexual "fast track" would be particularly susceptible because of the prevalence of specific practices that would maximize exposure to pathogenic microbes. What were considered potentially relevant data came to be routinely included in scientific papers and presentations, with the result that the terminology of these reports was increasingly scrutinized by gay activists:[13] examples from *Science* from June 1981 through December 1985 (collected in Kulstad 1986) include "homosexual and bisexual men who are extremely active sexually" (Marx 1983, in Kulstad 1986, 22), "admitted homosexuals" (Gelmann et al. 1983, in ibid., 40), "homosexual males with multiple partners" (Barré-Sinoussi et al. 1983, in ibid., 49), "homosexual men with multiple partners" (Essex et al. 1983, in ibid., 65), "highly sexually active homosexual men" (Richards et al. 1984, in ibid., 142), and "promiscuous" versus "nonpromiscuous" homosexual males (Gallo et al.

1984, in ibid., 160). Also documented (examples are again from the *Science* collection) are exotic travels or practices: "a Caucasian who had visited Haiti" (Gallo et al. 1983, in ibid., 47), "persons born in Haiti" (Jaffe et al. 1983, in ibid., 130), "a favorite vacation spot for U.S. homosexuals" (Marx 1983, in ibid., 73), rectal insemination (Richards et al. 1984, in ibid., 142–46), "bisexual men" (Jaffe et al. 1983, in ibid., 130), "increased frequency of use of nitrite inhalants" (Curran et al. 1985, in ibid., 611), and "receptive anal intercourse" (Curran et al., 1985; in ibid., 611).

Out of this dense discursive jungle came the "fragile anus" hypothesis (tested by Richards et al. [1984, in Kulstad 1986], who rectally inseminated laboratory rabbits) as well as the vision of "multiple partners." Even after sociological explanations for AIDS gave way to biomedical ones involving a transmissible virus, these various images of AIDS as a "gay disease" proved too alluring to abandon. It is easy to see both the scientific and the popular appeal of the fragile anus hypothesis: scientifically, it confines the public health dimensions of AIDS to an infected population in the millions—merely mind-boggling, that is—enabling us to stop short of the impossible, the unthinkable billions that widespread heterosexual transmission might infect. Another appeal of thinking of AIDS as a gay disease is that it protects not only the sexual practices of heterosexuality but also heterosexuality's ideological superiority. In the service of this hypothesis, both homophobia and sexism are folded imperturbably into the language of the scientific text. As I noted above, women are characterized in the scholarly literature as "inefficient" transmitters of AIDS; Leibowitch refers to the "refractory impermeability of the vaginal mucous membrane" (1985, 36). In the *Journal of the American Medical Association* (Redfield et al. 1985) a study of German prostitutes who seemed to demonstrate female-to-male transmission of AIDS was interpreted by some as representing "quasi-homosexual" transmission with successive male clients infecting each other via deposits of contaminated semen (quoted in Langone 1985, 49).

But the conception and the conclusion are inaccurate. It is not monogamy or abstention per se that protects one from AIDS infection but practices that prevent the virus from entering one's bloodstream. Some evidence suggests that prostitutes are at greater risk not because they have multiple sex partners but because they are likely to use intravenous drugs; indeed, they may protect themselves better "than the typical woman who is 'just going to a bar' or a woman who thinks of herself as not sexually active but who 'just happens to have this relationship.' They may be more aware than women who are involved in serial monogamy or those whose self-image is 'I'm not at risk so I'm not going to learn more about it' " (Shaw and Paleo 1987, 144). At this point, COYOTE and other organizations of prostitutes had been addressing the issue of AIDS for several years.[14]

Donald Mager (1986) discusses the proliferation among heterosexuals of visions about homosexuality and their status as fantasy:

> Institutions of privilege and power disenfranchise lesbians and gay men because of stereotypic negative categorizations of them—stereotypes which engage a societal fantasy of the illicit, the subversive, and the taboo, particularly due to assumptions of radical sex role parodies and inversions. This fantasy in turn becomes both the object of fear and of obsessed fascination, while its status as fantasy is never acknowledged, instead; the reality it pretends to signify becomes the justification of suppression both of the fantasy itself and of those actual persons who would seem to embody it. Homophobia as a critique of societal sexual fantasy, in turn, enforces its primary location as a gay discourse, separate and outside the site of the fantasy which is normative male heterosexuality.

Leibowitch (1985) comments as follows on AIDS, fantasy, and "the reality it pretends to signify": "When they come to write the history of AIDS, socio-ethnologists will have to decide whether the 'practitioners' of homosexuality or its heterosexual 'onlookers' have been the more spectacular in their extravagance. The homosexual 'life style' is so blatantly on display to the general public, so closely scrutinized, that it is likely we never will have been informed with such technicophantasmal complacency as to how 'other people' live their lives" (p. 3).

It was widely believed in the gay community that the connection of AIDS to homosexuality delayed and problematized virtually every aspect of the country's response to the crisis. That the response *was* delayed and problematic is the conclusion of various investigators (see, e.g., U.S. House 1984; Schwartz 1984; Office of Technology Assessment 1985; and Institute of Medicine and National Academy of Sciences 1986). Attempting to assess the degree to which prejudice, fear, or ignorance of homosexuality may have affected policy and research, Panem (1985, 24; 1988) concluded that homosexuality per se would not have deterred scientists from selecting interesting and rewarding research projects. But "the argument of ignorance appears to have more credibility." She quotes James Curran's 1984 judgment that policy, funding, and communication were all delayed because only people in New York and California had any real sense of crisis or comprehension of the gay male community. "Scientists avoid issues that relate to sex," he said, "and there is not much understanding of homosexuality." This was an understatement: according to Curran, many eminent scientists during this period rejected the possibility that AIDS was an infectious disease because they had no idea how a man could transmit an infectious agent to another man. Other instances of ignorance are reported by Patton (1985a, 1985b) and Black (1986). Physician and scientist Joseph Sonnabend (1985) attributes this ignorance to the sequestered ivory towers that many AIDS investigators (particularly those who do straight laboratory research as opposed to clinical work) inhabit and argues instead that AIDS needs to be studied in its cultural totality. Gay male sexual practices should not be dismissed out of hand because they seem "unnatural" to the straight (in both senses) scientist: "The rectum is a sexual organ, and it deserves the respect that a penis gets and a vagina gets. Anal intercourse is a central sexual activity, and it should be supported, it should be celebrated." An Institute of Medicine/National Academy of Sciences panel studying the AIDS crisis in 1986 cited an urgent need for accurate and *current* information about sex and sexual practices in the United States, noting that no comprehensive research had been carried out since Kinsey's studies in the 1940s; they recommended, as well, social science research on a range of social behaviors relevant to the transmission and control of AIDS.

It has been argued that the perceived *gayness* of AIDS was ultimately a crucial political factor in obtaining funding. Dennis Altman (1986) observes that the principle of providing adequate funding for AIDS research was institutionalized within the federal appropriations process as a result of the 1984 congressional hearings chaired by Representatives Henry Waxman and Theodore Weiss, members of Congress representing large and visible gay communities: "Here one sees the effect of the mobilization and organization of gays . . . ; it is salutary to imagine the tardiness of the response had IV users and Haitians been the only victims of AIDS, had Republicans controlled the House of Representatives as well as the Senate (and hence chaired the relevant oversight and appropriations committees) or, indeed, had AIDS struck ten years earlier, before the existence of an organized gay movement, openly gay professionals who could testify before the relevant committees and openly gay congressional staff" (pp. 116–17).

But these social and political issues were becoming, for many, essentially irrelevant. The hypothesis that AIDS was caused by an infectious agent, favored by some scientists, was strengthened when the syndrome began to be identified in a diversity of populations and found to cause apparently identical damage to the underlying immune system. By May 1984, a viral etiology for AIDS had been generally accepted. The real question became precisely what kind of viral agent this could be, and how the epidemic could now be re-read.

• • •

Reconstructing the AIDS Text: Rewriting the Body

• • •

Repeated hints that the male body is sexually potent and adventurous suggest that homophobia in biomedical discourse may play out as a literal "fear of the same." The text constructed around the gay male body—the epidemic of signification so evident in the conceptions cited above and elsewhere in this essay—is driven in part by the need for constant flight from sites of potential identity and thus the successive construction of new oppositions that will barricade self from not-self. The homophobic meanings associated with AIDS continue to be layered into existing discourse: analysis demonstrates ways in which the AIDS virus is linguistically identified with those it strikes: The penis is "fragile," the urethra is "fragile," the virus is "fragile." The African woman's body is "exotic," the virus is "exotic." The virus "penetrates" its victims; a carrier of death, it wears an "innocent" disguise. AIDS is "caused" by homosexuals; AIDS is "caused" by a virus. Homosexuality exists on a border between male and female, the virus between life and nonlife. This cross-cannibalization of language is not surprising. What greater relief than to find a final refuge from the specter of gay sexuality where the language that has obsessively accumulated around the body can attach to its substitute: the virus. This is a signifier that can be embraced forever.

The question is how to disrupt and renegotiate the powerful cultural narratives surrounding AIDS. Homophobia is inscribed within other discourses at a high level, and it is at a high level that these narratives must be interrupted and challenged. Why? The following scenario for Armageddon (believed by some, desired by many) makes clear why: AIDS will remain confined to the original high-risk groups (primarily gay males and IV drug users) because of their specific practices (like anal intercourse and sharing needles). At the Paris International AIDS Conference in June 1986, the ultimate spread of the disease was posed in terms of "containment" and "saturation." "Only" gay males and drug addicts will get infected—the virus will use them up and then have nowhere to go—the "general population" (which is also in epidemiological parlance a "virgin" population) will remain untouched. Even if this view is correct (which seems doubtful, given growing evidence of transmission through plain old everyday heterosexual intercourse) and the virus stops spreading once it has "saturated" the high-risk population, we would still be talking about a significant number of U.S. citizens: 2.5 million gay men, 7 million additional men who have at some time in the last ten years engaged in same-sex activity, 750,000 habitual intravenous drug users, 750,000 occasional drug users, 10,000 hemophiliacs already infected, the sex partners of these people, and the children of infected women— in other words, a total of more than 10 million people (the figures are from the June 1986 Paris conference). And "saturation" is currently considered a *best*-case scenario by the public health authorities.[15]

The fact is that any separation of not-self ("AIDS victims") from self (the "general population") is no longer possible. The U.S. surgeon general's and National Academy's reports make clear that "that security blanket has now been stripped away" ("Science and the Citizen" 1987, 58). Yet the familiar signifying practices that exercise control over meaning continue. The *Scientific American* column goes on to note fears that the one-to-one African ratio of females with AIDS to males may foreshadow U.S. statistics: "Experts point out, however, that such factors as the prevalence of other venereal diseases that cause genital sores, the use of unsterilized needles in clinics and the lack of blood-screening tests may explain the different epidemiology of AIDS in Africa" ("Science and the Citizen" 1987, 59). Thus, the African data are reinterpreted to reinstate the us/them dichotomy and project a rosier scenario for "us." (Well, maybe it improves on comic Richard Belzer's narrative: "A monkey in Africa bites some guy on the ass, and *he* balls a guy in Haiti, and now we're all gonna fuckin' die. THANKS A LOT!"[16]

Meanwhile, on the home front, monogamy is coming back into its own along with abstention, the safest sex of all. The virus itself—by whatever name—has come to represent the moment of truth for the sexual revolution: as though God has once again sent his only beloved son to save us from our high-risk behavior. Who would have thought that he would take the form of a virus: a viral Terminator ready to die for our sins.[17]

The contestations pioneered by the gay community over the last decade offer models for resistance. As old-fashioned morality increasingly infects the twentieth-century scenario, whether masquerading as "preventive health" or spiritual transformation, a new sampler can be stitched to hang on the bedroom wall: BETTER WED THAN DEAD. "It's just like the fifties," complains a gay man in San Francisco. "People are getting married again for all the wrong reasons" (quoted in FitzGerald 1986). One disruption of this narrative occurs in the San Francisco *A.I.D.S. Show* (Adair and Epstein 1986): "I *like* sex," a young man reminisces nostalgically; "I like to get drunk and smoke grass . . . and sleep with strangers: Call me old-fashioned, but that's what I like!" A gay pastor tells FitzGerald that the new morality threatens the gay community with pre-Stonewall repression: "If I had to go back to life in the closet again, I'm not sure I would not rather be dead." For Michel Foucault, the "tragedy" of AIDS was not intrinsically its lethal character but that a group that has risked so much—gays—is looking to standard authorities—doctors, the church—for guidance in a time of crisis. "How can I be scared of AIDS when I could die in a car?" Foucault asked a year or so before he died. "If sex with a boy gives me pleasure . . ." (Horvitz 1985, 80). And he adds: "Don't cry for me if I die."[18]

In AIDS, where meanings are overwhelming in their sheer volume and often explicitly linked to extreme political agendas, we do not know whose meanings will become "the official story." We need an epidemiolog of signification—a comprehensive mapping and analysis of these multiple meanings—to form the basis for official definition that will in turn constitute the policies, regulations, rules, and practices that will govern our behavior for some time to come. As we have seen, these may rest on "facts," which in turn may rest on the deeply entrenched cultural narratives that I have been describing. For this reason, what AIDS signifies must be democratically determined: we cannot afford to let scientists or any other group of experts dismiss our meanings as "misconceptions" and our alternative views as noise that interferes with the pure processes of scientific inquiry. Rather, we must insist that many voices contribute to the construction of official definitions—and specifically certain voices that need urgently to be heard. Although the signification process for AIDS is by now very broad—just about everyone, seemingly, has offered a reading of what AIDS means—one excluded group continues to be users of illegal intravenous drugs. Caught between the "first wave" (gay white men) and the "second wave" (heterosexuals), drug users at high risk for AIDS remain silent and invisible (Barrett 1985; Joseph 1986). One public health official recently challenged the rush to educate heterosexuals about their risk when what is needed (and has been from the beginning) is "a massive effort directed at intravenous-drug abusers and their sex partners. This means treatment for a disease—chemical dependence on drugs. We have to prevent and treat one disease, drug addiction, to prevent another, AIDS" (Joseph 1986).[19]

If AIDS's dual life as both a material and a linguistic entity is important, the emphasis on *dual* is crucial. Symbolic and social reconceptualizations of AIDS are necessary but not sufficient to address the massive social questions that AIDS raises. The recognition that AIDS is heterosexually as well as homosexually transmitted certainly represents progress, but it does not interrupt fantasy. It is fantasy, for example, to believe that "safer sex" will protect us from AIDS; it may save us from becoming infected with the virus—New York City has instituted Singles Night at the Blood Bank, where people can meet and share their seropositivity status before they even exchange names. But AIDS is to be a fundamental force of twentieth-century life, and no barrier in the world can make us "safe" from its complex material realities. Malnutrition, poverty, and hunger are unacceptable, in our own country and in the rest of the world; the need for universal health care is urgent. Ultimately, we cannot distinguish self from not-self: "plague is life," and each of us has the plague within us; "no one, no one on earth is free from it" (Camus [1947] 1948, 229).

The discursive structures I have discussed in this essay are familiar to those of us in "the human sciences." We have learned that there is a disjunction between historical subjects and constructed scientific objects. There is still debate about whether, or to what extent, scientific discourse can be privileged—and relied on to transcend contradiction. My own view is unequivocal: it cannot be privileged in this way. Of course, where AIDS is concerned, science can usefully perform its interpretive part: we can learn to live—indeed *must* learn to live—as though there are such things as viruses. The virus—a constructed scientific object—is also a historical subject, a "human immunodeficiency virus," a real source of illness and death that can be passed from one person to another under certain conditions that we can apparently—individually and collectively—influence. The trick is to learn to live with this disjunction, and it is a lesson we must learn. Dr. Rieux, the physician-narrator of Camus's novel, acknowledges that, by dealing medically with the plague, he is allowing himself the luxury of "living in a world of abstractions." But not indefinitely, for, "when abstraction sets to killing you, you've got to get busy with it" (Camus [1947] 1948, 81).

But getting busy with it may require us to relinquish some luxuries of our own: the luxury of accepting without reflection the "findings" that science seems effortlessly able to provide us, the luxury of avoiding vigilance, the luxury of hoping that it will all go away. Rather, we need to use what science gives us in ways that are selective, self-conscious, and pragmatic ("as though" they were true). We need to understand that AIDS is and will remain a provisional and deeply problematic signifier. Above all, we need to resist, at all costs, the luxury of listening to the thousands of language tapes playing in our heads, laden with prior discourse, that tell us with compelling certainty and dizzying contradiction what AIDS "really" means.

NOTES

1. Discussing the validity of their interpretation of everyday life in a science laboratory, Latour and Woolgar claim, similarly, that the "value and status of any text (construction, fact, claim, story, this account) depend on more than its supposedly 'inherent' qualities. . . . [T]he degree of accuracy (or fiction) of an account depends on what is subsequently made of the story, not on the story itself" ([1979] 1986, 284).

2. The term *signification,* derived from the linguistic work of Ferdinand de Saussure ([1916] 1986), calls attention to the way in which a language (or any other "signifying system") organizes rather than labels experience (or the world). Linking signifiers (phonetic segments or, more loosely, words) and signifieds (concepts, meanings) in ways that come to seem "natural" to us, language creates the illusion of "transparency," as though we could look through it to "facts" and "realities" that are unproblematic. Many scientists and physicians, even those sensitive to the complexities of AIDS, believe that "the facts" (or "science" or "reason") will resolve contradiction and supplant speculation; they express impatience with social interpretations that they perceive as superfluous or incorrect. Even Leibowitch writes that, with the discovery of the virus, AIDS loses its "metaphysical resonances" and becomes "now no more than one infectious disease among many" (1985, xiv). The position of this essay is that signification processes are not the handmaidens of "the facts"; rather, "the facts" themselves arise out of the signifying practices of biomedical discourse.

3. Black: "I realized . . . that any account of AIDS was not just a medical
story and not just a story about the gay community, but also a story about the
straight community's reaction to the disease. More than that: it's a story about
how the straight community has used and is using AIDS as a mask for its feelings
about gayness. It is a story about the ramifications of a metaphor" (1986, 30).
AIDS is typically characterized as a "story," but whose? For AIDS as a story of
scientific progress, see Relman (1985, 1), Nichols (1986, 1989), Gallo (1987,
1988, 1991), and Lieberson (1983). But, for Lynch (1982), Goldstein (1983),
Kramer (1983), Gunn (1985), Ault (1986), D. Altman (1986), FitzGerald (1986),
the San Francisco *A.I.D.S. Show* (Artists Involved with Death and Survival)
(Adair and Epstein 1986), and others, AIDS is the story of crisis and heroism in
the gay community. In the tabloids, AIDS has become the story of Rock Hudson
("ROCK IS DEAD," ran the headline in the *London Sun* on 3 October 1985, "THE
HUNK WHO LIVED A LIE"), Liberace, and other individuals. A documentary film
about the Fabian Bridges case, a young man with AIDS in Houston, is called
Fabian's Story. For Mains, AIDS interrupts the adventure story of leather sex, a
"unique and valuable cultural excursion" (1985, 178). And, in Thom Gunn's
(1985) poem "Lament," AIDS is a story of change and the death of friends. The
stories we tell help us determine what our own place in the story is to be.
FitzGerald writes that the "new mythology" about AIDS in the San Francisco
gay community—that many gay men are changing their lives for the better—
was "an antidote to the notion that AIDS was a punishment—a notion that . . .
lay so deep as to be unavailable to reason. And it helped people act against the
threat of AIDS" (1986, 62). But, for Mohr, this new mythology—in which the
loving relationship replaces anonymous sex—is a dangerous one: "The relation
typically is asked to bear more than is reasonable. The burden on the simple
dyad is further weighed down by the myth, both romantic and religious, that
one finds one's completion in a single other. White knights and messiahs never
come in clusters" (1986, 56).

4. Articulate voices had taken issue with the CDC position from the beginning, warning against the public health consequences of treating AIDS as a "gay
disease" and separating "those at risk" from the so-called general population.
See, e.g., comments by Gary MacDonald, executive director of an AIDS action
organization in Washington: "I think the moment may have arrived to desexu-
alize this disease. AIDS is not a 'gay disease,' despite its epidemiology. . . . AIDS
is not transmitted because of who you *are,* but because of what you *do.* . . . By
concentrating on gay and bisexual men, people are able to ignore the fact that
this disease has been present in what has charmingly come to be called 'the
general population' *from the beginning.* It was not spread from one of the other
groups. It was *there*" ("AIDS: What Is to Be Done?" 1985, 43).

One can extrapolate from Bleier's observation that questions shape answers
(1986, 4) and suggest that the question, Why are all AIDS victims sexually active

homosexual males? might more appropriately have been, are all AIDS victims sexually active homosexual males? It is widely believed (not without evidence) that federal funding for AIDS research was long in coming because its chief victims were gay or otherwise socially undesirable. Black describes a researcher who made jokes about *fagocytes* (phagocytes), cells designed "to kill off fags" (1986, 81–82). Secretary of Health and Human Services Margaret Heckler was only one of many officials who expressed concern not about existing AIDS patients but about AIDS's potential to spread to the "community at large" (with the result that Heckler was called "the Secretary of Health and Heterosexual Services" by some activists in Gay Men's Health Crisis in New York [see "AIDS: What Is to Be Done?" 1985, 51]).

There is evidence that the "gay disease" myth interferes with diagnosis and treatment. Many believe that AIDS may be underdetected and underreported in part because people outside the "classic" high-risk groups are often not asked the right questions (physicians typically take longer to diagnose AIDS in women, e.g.). Health professionals and AIDS counselors sometimes avoid the word *gay* because, for many people, this implies an identity or a lifestyle; even *bisexual* may mean a lifestyle. Although *homosexually active* is officially defined as including even a single same-sex sexual contact over the past five years, many who have had such contact do not identify themselves as homosexual and therefore as being at risk for AIDS. Nancy Shaw (1985, 1986) suggests that, for women as well, the homosexual/heterosexual dichotomy confuses diagnosis and treatment as well as the perception of risk. Murray (1985), Patton (1985a), and Pally (1985) all argue that AIDS is a "women's issue" and should receive more attention in feminist publications (and see COYOTE 1985; Switzer 1986; and Zones 1986). The persistence and consequences of the perception that AIDS is a disease of gay men and IV drug users are documented in a number of recent publications, notably Leishman (1987) and "Science and the Citizen" 1987. CDC interviews with members of two heterosexual singles clubs in Minneapolis documented that, as of late 1986, this already-infected population had made virtually no modifications in its sexual practices (CDC 1986a). DiClemente et al. (1986) found that many adolescents in San Francisco, a city where public health information about AIDS has been widely disseminated, were not well informed about the seriousness of the disease, its causes, or preventive measures.

5. Minson (1981) and Weeks (1985) analyze the evolution of homosexuality as a coherent identity. Bayer (1981) and Bayer and Spitzer (1982) document the intense and acrimonious "contests for meaning" during the *American Psychiatric Association's 1970s* debates over the official classification of homosexuality.

6. On the reclassification in 1986 of the CDC's 571 previously "unexplained cases," see Nichols (1986), and Associated Press (1986). Formerly classified as *none of the above* (i.e., outside the known high-risk categories), some of these cases were reclassified as heterosexually transmitted.

7. Even after consensus in 1984 that AIDS was caused by a virus, there continued to be conflicting views on transmission and different explanations for the epidemiological finding that AIDS and HIV infection in the United States were appearing predominantly in gay males. One view holds that this is essentially an artifact ("simple mathematics") created because the virus (for whatever reason) infected gay men first and gay men tend to have sex with each other. The second is that biomedical/physiological factors make gay men and/or the "passive receiver" more easily infected. A third view is that the virus can be transmitted to anyone but that certain cofactors encourage the development of infection and/or clinical symptoms. For more information, see Cahill (1983), Gong and Rudnick (1986), Krim (1985, 4), Leibowitch (1985, 72–73), and Leishman (1987). Many scientists suggest that, whatever sex the partners may be, infection, as Fain (1985) put it, "requires a jolt injected into the bloodstream, likely several jolts over time, such as would occur with infected needles or semen. In both cases, needle and penis are the instruments of contagion." Since women have no penises, they are "inefficient" transmitters. For more detailed discussion, see Bolognone and Johnson (1986) and Treichler (1988a).

8. Brandt (1987) and Walkowitz (1983) review the long-standing equation of prostitutes with disease and the conceptual separation of infected prostitutes (and other voluntarily sexually active women) from "innocent victims" (see also Douglas [1975] 1982; Eckholm 1985; COYOTE 1985; Shaw 1986, 1988; and Shaw and Paleo 1987).

9. Discussions of AIDS and heterosexual transmission in Africa include Patton (1985b), Osborn (1986), Marx (1986b), Lieberson (1986), Hosken (1986), Feldman (1987), L. Altman (1985b), Treichler (1988a), and "New Human Retroviruses" (1986).

10. Congressman William Dannemeyer, October 1985, during a debate in the Massachusetts Legislature on a homosexual rights bill (quoted by Langone 1985, 29).

11. In the gay community, the first reaction to AIDS was disbelief. FitzGerald quotes a gay physician in San Francisco: "A disease that killed only gay white men? It seemed unbelievable, I used to teach epidemiology, and I had never heard of a disease that selective. I thought, They are making this up. It can't be true. Or if there is such a disease it must be the work of some government agency—the F.B.I. or the C.I.A.—trying to kill us all" (1986, 54). In the San Francisco *A.I.D.S. Show* (Adair and Epstein 1986), one man is said to have learned of his diagnosis and at once wired the CIA: "I HAVE AIDS. DO YOU HAVE AN ANTIDOTE?"

12. For an example of the view that, although the virus is the sine qua non for AIDS, the syndrome actually *develops* "chiefly in those whose immune systems are already weak or defective," see Lieberson (1986, 43). For broader

discussion of public health issues in relation to scientific uncertainties and questions of civil liberties, see Bayer (1985), Silverman and Silverman (1985), and Matthews and Neslund (1987).

13. L. Altman (1985a) and Black (1986) discuss changes in scientific terminology as a result of gays' objections; *sexually promiscuous* generally shifted, e.g., to *sexually active* or *contact with multiple sex partners*. A new classification system for AIDS and AIDS-related symptoms (presented-and-agreed on at the Second International AIDS Conference in Paris, June 1986) is based on the diverse clinical manifestations of the syndrome and its documented natural history without using presumptive terminology like *pre-AIDS*. Jan Zita Grover's (1986) useful review of *Mobilizing against AIDS* (Nichols 1986) points out a number of problematic terms and assumptions that occur repeatedly in Nichols's book and other scientific writing on AIDS: (1) the term *AIDS victim* presupposes helplessness (the term *person with AIDS* or *PWA* was created to avoid this), prevention and cure are linked to a conservative agenda of "individual responsibility," sex with multiple partners and/or strangers is equated with promiscuity, and "safe" sexual practices are conflated with the cultural practice of monogamy; (2) "caregivers" are differentiated from "victims," scientific/medical expertise from other kinds of knowledge, and "those at risk" from *"the rest of us"*; and (3) existing inequities in the health-care system are noted but not challenged. Dobrow (1986) notes the dramatic and commercial appeal of the common "cultural images" in popular press scenarios of AIDS.

14. The *Journal of the American Medical Association* study is quoted by Langone to support the "vulnerable anus" hypothesis: "It is not unlikely that these prostitutes had multiple partners during a very short period of time, and performed no more than perfunctory external cleansing between customers" (Langone 1985, 49). But reports from prostitutes in many countries, summarized in the June 1985 *World Wide Whores' News*, indicate familiarity with AIDS as well as concern with obtaining better protection from infection and better health care (see also COYOTE 1985).

15. The concept of *saturation* did not last long in public AIDS discourse. For one thing, it presented the picture of a population as a passive mass, absorbing virus to capacity until the virus overflows and moves on to a new population. The instrumental image is troublesome but also inaccurate, for it suggests that a given population is homogeneous, has uniform "absorbency," and takes no steps to reduce or prevent infection (and that the rest of the world stands by while the saturated population dies off). More useful, perhaps, is a concept of circles or networks of sexual/social contact, where the density of viral prevalence better predicts the infectability of the uninfected without assuming discrete, self-contained populations. Still, in later proposals for drug and vaccine testing, comparable concepts were evoked: the desire for a "virgin population," for instance.

16. Although Lieberson insists that a "heterosexual pandemic (comparable to Africa's) has not occurred in the United States" and criticizes those who suggest that it is going to (1986, 44), current data based on tests for HIV among 1986 army recruits (nongay non–drug using, so far as researchers could determine) argue for increasing heterosexual transmission (Redfield et al. 1986). For discussion and analysis, see L. Altman (1985a), D. Altman (1986), Marx (1986a), Osborn (1986), Patton (1985b), Hosken (1986), and Feldman (1987). See also Potterat et al. (1987). It has been suggested that malnutrition plays an important role in the rapid spread of AIDS in Africa. Worldwide, malnutrition is commonly associated with acquired immune deficiency, while poverty is the factor most consistently associated with disease in general.

17. We must even, perhaps, identify with the virus, an extraordinarily successful structure that has been comfortably making the acquaintance of living organisms for many more millions of years than we have. A virus that enters the human bloodstream and circulates through the body may ultimately negotiate with the host some mutually livable equilibrium. The relation may be a close one: it is difficult to separate the effects of the virus from those of the body's defenses; and any poison intended for the guest may kill the host as well. Any given species, including human beings, may sometimes prove to be an inhospitable, even unnatural host. To speak teleologically for a moment, it is obvious that to kill the host is not in the microorganism's best interests; this sometimes happens, however, when a virus adapted to a nonhuman host shifts, through some untoward turn of events, to the human body. Although, from our perspective, HIV is indeed virulent, killing quickly, in fact the long latency between infection and the appearance of clinical damage provides plenty of time—often years—for the virus to replicate and infect a new host. For the time being, we are sufficiently hospitable for this virus to live off us relatively "successfully"; if mutation occurs, our relation to the virus could evolve into something relatively benign or mutually disastrous.

18. This interview, conducted by Philip Horvitz in Berkeley in 1985 (and scrutinized, it's said, like the Watergate transcripts to find out what Foucault knew and when he knew it), concludes as Foucault enters the BART station: "Good luck," he tells Horvitz. "And don't be scared!" The interview is titled "Don't Cry for Me, Academia."

19. Although Check writes that "it sometimes appears that the only risk group that hasn't raised a ruckus is the IV drug users, who are not organized" (1985, 28), a few commentators are beginning to draw attention to this critical problem: Barrett (1985), Joseph (1986), Byron (1985), Shaw and Paleo (1987), and Clines (1987). Finally, aware that many drug addicts were avoiding information centers as well as medical authorities, the Gay Men's Health Crisis in New York took responsibility for going to shooting galleries, clinics, and drug treatment centers to provide AIDS education and training to drug users, who in

turn could work with other drug users. (For an update, see Friedman et al. [1992].)

Works Cited

Adair, Peter, and Rob Epstein, producers. 1986. *The A.I.D.S. Show — Artists Involved with Death and Survival.* San Francisco: Direct Cinema Ltd.

"AIDS: What Is to Be Done?" 1985. Forum, *Harpers*, October, 39–52.

Altman, Dennis. 1986. *AIDS in the Mind of America.* New York: Doubleday.

Altman, Lawrence K. 1985a. "Heterosexuals and AIDS: New Data Examined." *New York Times*, 22 January, 19–20.

———. 1985b. "Linking AIDS to Africa Provokes Bitter Debate." *New York Times*, 21 November, 1, 8.

Associated Press. 1986. "571 AIDS Cases Tied to Heterosexual Causes." *Champaign-Urbana News-Gazette*, 10 April, A–7.

Ault, Steve. 1986. "AIDS: The Facts of Life." *Guardian*, 26 March, 1, 8.

Barrett, Wayne. 1985. "Straight Shooters: AIDS Targets Another Lifestyle." *Village Voice*, 5 November, 14–18.

Bayer, Ronald. 1981. *Homosexuality and American Psychiatry: The Politics of Diagnosis.* New York: Basic.

———. 1985. "AIDS and the Gay Community: Between the Specter and the Promise of Medicine." *Social Research* 52, no. 3 (Autumn): 581–606.

Bayer, Ronald, and Robert L. Spitzer. 1982. "Edited Correspondence on the Status of Homosexuality in DSM-III." *Journal of the History of the Behavioral Sciences* 18:32–52.

Black, David. 1986. *The Plague Years: A Chronicle of AIDS, the Epidemic of Our Times.* New York: Simon and Schuster.

Bleier, Ruth. 1986. *Science and Gender.* London: Pergamon.

Bolognone, Diane, and Thomas M. Johnson. 1986. "Explanatory Models for AIDS." In *Social Dimension of AIDS: Method and Theory*, ed. Douglas A. Feldman and Thomas M. Johnson. New York: Praeger.

Brandt, Allan M. 1987. *No Magic Bullet: A Social History of Venereal Disease in the United States since 1880.* New York: Oxford University Press.

Byron, Peg. 1985. "Women with AIDS: Untold Stories." *Village Voice*, 24 September, 16–19.

Cahill, Kevin M. 1983. *The AIDS Epidemic.* New York: St. Martin's.

Camus, Albert. [1947] 1948. *The Plague.* Translated by Stuart Gilbert. New York: Modern Library.

Centers for Disease Control (CDC). 1986a. "Positive HTLV-III/LAV Antibody Results for Sexually Active Female Members of Social/Sexual Clubs—Minnesota." *Morbidity and Mortality Weekly Report* 35 (14 November):697–99.

———. 1986b. "Update: Acquired Immunodeficiency Syndrome—United

States." Supplement, *Morbidity and Mortality Weekly Report* 35, no. S1 (12 December).

Check, William A. 1985. "Public Education on AIDS: Not Only the Media's Responsibility." Special supplement, *Hastings Center Report* 15, no. 4 (August):27–31.

Clines, Francis X. 1987. "Via Addicts' Needles, AIDS Spreads in Edinburgh." *New York Times,* 4 January, 8.

COYOTE. 1985. Background paper for 1985 *COYOTE Convention Summary.* San Francisco, 30 May–2 June.

DiClemente, Ralph J., Jim Zorn, and Lydia Temoshok. 1986. "Adolescents and AIDS: A Survey of Knowledge, Attitudes and Beliefs about AIDS in San Francisco." *American Journal of Public Health* 76, no. 12:1443–45.

Dobrow, Julie. 1986. "The Symbolism of AIDS: Perspectives on the Use of Language in the Popular Press." Paper presented at the annual meeting of the International Communication Association, May, Chicago.

Douglas, Colin. [1975] 1982. *The Intern's Tale.* Reprint, New York: Grove.

Douglas, Paul Harding, ed. 1989. *AIDS: Improving the Odds, 1988.* New York: Columbia Gay Health Advocacy Project.

Eckholm, Erik. 1985. "Prostitutes' Impact on Spread of AIDS Debated." *New York Times,* 5 November, 15, 18.

Fain, Nathan. 1985. "AIDS: An Antidote to Fear." *Village Voice,* 1 October, 35.

Feldman, Douglas A. 1987. "Role of African Mutilations in AIDS Discounted." Letter to the editor, *New York Times,* 7 January, 18.

FitzGerald, Frances. 1986. *Cities on a Hill: A Journey through Contemporary American Cultures.* New York: Simon and Schuster/Touchstone.

Friedman, Samuel R., Meryl Sufian, Richard Curtis, Alan Neigus, and Don C. Des Jarlais. 1992. "Organizing Drug Users against AIDS." In *The Social Context of AIDS,* ed. Joan Huber and Beth E. Schneider. Newbury Park, Calif.: Sage.

Gallo. Robert C. 1987. "The AIDS Virus." *Scientific American,* January, 47–56.

———. 1988. "HIV—the Cause of AIDS: An Overview of Its Biology," Mechanisms of Disease Induction, Introduction, and Our Attempts to Control It." *Journal of Acquired Immune Deficiency Syndromes* 1 (December): 521–35.

———. 1991. *Virus Hunting: AIDS, Cancer, and the Human Retrovirus.* New York: Basic.

Goldstein, Richard. 1983. "Heartsick: Fear and Loving in the Gay Community." *Village Voice,* 28 June, 13–16.

Gong, Victor, and Norman Rudnick, eds. 1986. *AIDS: Facts and Issues.* New Brunswick, N.J.: Rutgers University Press.

Grover, Jan Zita. 1986. "The 'Scientific' Regime of Truth." *In These Times*, 10–16 December, 18–19.

Gunn, Thom. 1985. *Lament*. Champaign, Ill.: Doe.

Hall, Stuart. 1992. "Cultural Studies and Its Theoretical Legacies." In *Cultural Studies*, ed. Lawrence Grossberg, Cary Nelson, and Paula A. Treichler. New York: Routledge.

Horvitz, Philip. 1985. "Don't Cry for Me, Academia." *Jimmy and Lucy's House of K* 2 (August):78–80. Interview with Michel Foucault.

Hosken, Fran P. 1986. "Why AIDS Pattern Is Different in Africa." Letter, *New York Times*, 15 December, 13.

Institute of Medicine and National Academy of Sciences. 1986. *Confronting AIDS: Update 1988*. Washington, D.C.: National Academy Press.

Jaret, Peter. 1986. "Our Immune System: The Wars Within." *National Geographic*, June, 702–35.

Joseph, Stephen C. 1986. "Intravenous-Drug Abuse Is the Front Line in the War on AIDS." Letter to the editor, *New York Times*, 22 December, 18.

Kramer, Larry. 1983. "1,112 and Counting." *New York Native*, March, 14–27.

Krim, Mathilde. 1985. "AIDS: The Challenge to Science and Medicine." Special supplement, *Hastings Center Report* 15, no. 4:2–7.

Kulstad, Ruth, ed. 1986. *AIDS: Papers from "Science," 1982–1985*. Washington, D.C.: American Association for the Advancement of Science.

Langone, John. 1985. "AIDS: The Latest Scientific Facts." *Discover*, December, 27–52.

Latour, Bruno, and Steve Woolgar. [1979] 1986. *Laboratory Life: The Construction of Scientific Facts*. Reprint, Princeton, N.J.: Princeton University Press.

Leibowitch, Jacques. 1985. *A Strange Virus of Unknown Origin*. Translated by Richard Howard. New York: Ballantine.

Leishman, Kate. 1987. "Heterosexuals and AIDS: The Second Stage of the Epidemic." *Atlantic*, February, 39–58.

Lieberson, Jonathan. 1983. "Anatomy of an Epidemic." *New York Review of Books*, 18 August, 17–22.

———. 1986. "The Reality of AIDS." *New York Review of Books*, 16 January, 43–48.

Lynch, Michael. 1982. "Living with Kaposi's." *Body Politic* 88 (November):1–5.

Mager, Donald. 1986. "The Discourse about Homophobia, Male and Female Contexts." Paper presented at the annual meeting of the Modern Language Association, December, New York.

Mains, Geoff. 1985. *Urban Aboriginals: A Celebration of Leathersexuality*. San Francisco: Gay Sunshine.

Marx, Jean L. 1984. "Strong New Candidate for AIDS Agent." Research News, *Science* 230 (4 May):146–51.

———. 1986a. "AIDS Virus Has New Name—Perhaps." News and Comment, *Science*, 9 May, 699–700.

———. 1986b. "New Relatives of AIDS Virus Found." Research News, *Science*, 11 April, 540.

Matthews, Gene W., and Verla S. Neslund. 1987. "The Initial Impact of AIDS on Public Health Law in the United States—1986." *Journal of the American Medical Association* 257 (6 January):344–52.

Minson, Jeff. 1981. "The Assertion of Homosexuality." *m/f* 5–6:19–39.

Mohr, Richard. 1986. "Of Deathbeds and Quarantines: AIDS Funding, Gay Life and State Coercion." *Raritan*, Summer, 38–62.

Murray, Marea. 1985. "Too Little AIDS Coverage." Letter to the editor, *Sojourner* 10, no. 9 (July):3.

"New Human Retroviruses: One Causes AIDS ... and the Other Does Not." 1986. *Nature* 320 (3 April):385.

Nichols, Eve K. 1986. *Mobilizing against AIDS: The Unfinished Story of a Virus.* Cambridge, Mass.: Harvard University Press.

———. 1989. *Mobilizing against AIDS: Newly Revised and Enlarged.* Cambridge, Mass.: Harvard University Press.

Office of Technology Assessment. 1985. *Review of the Public Health Service's Response to AIDS: A Technical Memorandum.* Washington, D.C.: U.S. Government Printing Office.

Osborn, June E. 1986. "The AIDS Epidemic: An Overview of the Science." *Issues in Science and Technology* 2, no. 2:40–55.

Pally, Marcia. 1985. "AIDS and the Politics of Despair: Lighting Our Own Funeral Pyre." *Advocate*, 24 December, 8.

Panem, Sandra. 1985. "AIDS: Public Policy and Biomedical Research." Special supplement, *Hastings Center Report* 15, no. 4 (August):23–26.

———. 1988. *The AIDS Bureaucracy: Why Society Failed to Meet the AIDS Crisis and How We Might Improve.* Cambridge, Mass.: Harvard University Press.

Patton, Cindy. 1985a. "Feminists Have Avoided the Issue of AIDS." *Sojourner* (October):19–20.

———. 1985b. *Sex and Germs: The Politics of AIDS.* Boston: South End.

Potterat, John J., et al. 1987. "Lying to Military Physicians about Risk Factors of HIV Infections." Letter to the editor, *Journal of the American Medical Association* 257, no. 13 (3 April):1727.

Redfield, Robert R., et al. 1985. "Heterosexually Acquired HTLV-III/LAV Disease (AIDS-Related Complex and AIDS): Epidemiologic Evidence for Female-to-Male Transmission." *Journal of the American Medical Association* 254: 2094–96.

————. 1986. "Female-to-Male Transmission of HTLV-III." *Journal of the American Medical Association* 255:1705–6.

Relman, Arnold. 1985. "Introduction." Special supplement, *Hastings Center Report* 15, no. 4:1–2.

Saussure, Ferdinand de [1916] 1986. *Course in General Linguistics*. Translated by Roy Harris. Chicago: Open Court.

Schwartz, Harry. 1984. "AIDS in the Media." Appendix to *Science in the Streets: Report to the Twentieth Century Task Force on the Communication of Scientific Risk*. New York: Priority.

"Science and the Citizen." 1987. *Scientific American* 256, no. 1 (January):58–59.

Shaw, Nancy S. [Nancy E. Stoller]. 1985. "California Models for Women's AIDS Education and Services." San Francisco: San Francisco AIDS Foundation. Report.

————. 1986. "Women and AIDS: Theory and Politics." Paper presented at the annual meeting of the National Women's Studies Association, June, University of Illinois at Urbana-Champaign.

————. 1988. "Preventing AIDS among Women: The Role of Community Organizing." *Socialist Review* 18, no. 4 (October/December):76–92.

Shaw, Nancy S., and Lyn Paleo. 1987. "Women and AIDS." In *What to Do about AIDS: Physicians and Health Professionals Discuss the Issues,* ed. Leon McKusick. Berkeley: University of California Press.

Silverman, Mervyn F., and Deborah B. Silverman. 1985. "AIDS and the Threat to Public Health." Special supplement, *Hastings Center Report* 15, no. 1:19–22.

Sonnabend, Joseph. 1985. "Looking at AIDS in Totality: A Conversation." In *New York Native* 129:7–13.

Switzer, Ellen. 1986. "AIDS: What Women Can Do." *Vogue,* January, 222–23, 264–65.

Treichler, Paula A. 1988a. "AIDS, Gender, and Biomedical Discourse: Current Contests for Meaning." In *AIDS: The Burdens of History,* ed. Elizabeth Fee and Daniel M. Fox. Berkeley: University of California Press. Reprinted in *American Feminist Thought at Century's End: A Reader,* ed. Linda S. Kaufman. Cambridge: Basil Blackwell, 1993.

————. 1988b. "AIDS, Homophobia, and Biomedical Discourse: An Epidemic of Signification." *Cultural Studies* 1, no. 3:263–305. Reprinted in *AIDS: Cultural Analysis/Cultural Activism,* ed. Douglas Crimp. Cambridge, Mass.: MIT Press, 1988.

U.S. House. 1984. *Acquired Immune Deficiency Syndrome: Hearing before the Subcommittee on Health and the Environment of the Committee on Energy and Commerce.* 98th Congress, 2d session, 17 September.

Walkowitz, Judith. 1983. *Prostitution and Victorian Society: Women, Class, and the State.* New York: Cambridge University Press.

Watney, Simon. 1994. *Practices of Freedom: Selected Writings on HIV/AIDS.* Durham, N.C.: Duke University Press.

Weeks, Jeffrey. 1985. *Sexuality and Its Discontents: Meanings, Myths and Modern Sexualities.* London: Routledge and Kegan Paul.

Zones, Jane Sprague. 1986. "AIDS: What Women Need to Know." *National Women's Health Network News* 11, no. 6 (November–December):1, 3.

Chapter 8

The Occult of True Black Womanhood

Ann duCille

Introduction by Claudia Tate

In "The Occult of True Black Womanhood," Ann duCille signifies on the title of
Barbara Welter's influential "The Cult of True Womanhood,"[1] to ask, "Why
have black women become the subjected subjects of so much contemporary
scholarly investigation?" DuCille combines her rigorous readings with her characteristic witty critical acuity and an uncompromising exposure of scholarly
affect—her own and others. She acknowledges the pleasure and anxiety that the
recent focus on the cultural work of African American women has engendered
in the academy. The attention has been astounding, as a cursory survey of the
tables of contents and the covers of scholarly journals and publishers' promo-
tional brochures will reveal.

In "The Occult of True Black Womanhood," duCille identifies tactics that
commodify black feminist studies into trendy "PC" exhibitions rather than legitimate scholarly investigations. In her critique—itself a rigorous model for cultural
studies—she uses literary interpretive practices to examine the cultural and
intellectual issues involved in the identity politics at the center of black women's
studies. Rather than employ the familiar tactics of presenting an impressionistic
hypothesis that arises from unstated presumptions and a few popular works by
black women, duCille's essay evolves from reading widely and deeply in primary
and secondary materials, literary and nonliterary: among them, autobiography,
biography, letters, scholarly studies, and literary anthologies. Understanding black
feminist studies, as duCille demonstrates, requires an immersion in a number of
fields—here nineteenth- and twentieth-century feminist criticism, American and
African American studies, social and literary history, as well as popular culture.
DuCille draws on diverse methodological sources: her use of deconstruction,

for example, can be seen in her attention to the ways in which scholarly work reproduces the very social and political hierarchies it attempts to unravel; cultural studies in her use of scholarly texts to consider the current academic posture toward black women, which has produced such texts; feminist studies as well as critical race theory in her consideration of the ways in which the literary academy has appropriated and commodified the figure of the black female writer. Amid this heterogeneous critical practice, duCille anchors her critique using the interpretive tool popularized by the New Criticism of the postwar era—namely, close reading—which she turns to various scholars writing about the figure of the black female writer. In paying particular attention to the textual moments in which white critics like Jane Gallop, Adrienne Rich, and John Callahan reveal their own personal motives for working on African American letters, duCille powerfully demonstrates how the black woman writer has become a fetish object to be marketed, consumed, and discarded. By using these multiple analytical frameworks and practices, duCille poses a series of questions to call our attention to how these "new" critical discourses routinely rend the black female academic engaged in black feminist studies into a "hyperstatic alterity"—the quintessential other who designates a scholarly region better explored by those who do not share her identity. As duCille points out, such a viewpoint would lead us to believe that "black culture is more easily intellectualized (and canonized) when transferred from the danger of lived black experience to the safety of white metaphor, when you can have that 'signifying black difference' without the difference of significant blackness."

Neglect has made African American cultural studies in general into a rich scholarly area—a veritable gold mine. Now that its wealth has been discovered, the field lies vulnerable to the colonizing enterprises of those needing quick publications. As duCille relates, "Often the object of the game seems to be to reinvent the intellectual wheel: to boldly go where in fact others have gone before, to flood the field with supposedly 'new scholarship' that evinces little sense of the discipline's genealogy." In this type of academic appropriation, a new breed of explorers sets out to "map" a presumably uncharted territory by disregarding, even disavowing, the scholarship of those who came before. Or these new explorers relegate their precursors to footnotes much like a new leader ostracizes (or imprisons) opponents. DuCille's essay stands as a model in opposition to such strategies. Not only does the essay construct an argument for criticizing them, but it also undermines such tactics by offering instead a thoroughgoing engagement with a multiplicity of works both within and outside black feminist studies.

Black feminist studies is not the only field at risk of such colonizing ventures. The great demand for quick publications for professional advancement has made all academic areas vulnerable to plunder. Combined with the privileging of theory over historicizing, this demand encourages interlopers "to crank texts through the theory grinder to create 'new' readings," often by compromising historical fact as well as scholarly integrity.[2] But because black feminist studies has been long neglected and trivialized, it is uniquely susceptible to both trendy critical restatement and the suspension of the rules for "doing institutional business," as duCille explains.

Let me be very clear here: duCille is not arguing for the academic privileging of what one scholar has called "black blacks" (and neither am I).[3] To the contrary, duCille makes two important points. First, she calls attention to how various recent academic enterprises commodify black women and their works as "sacred text[s]" for everyone else to possess as the signs of their racial and gender impartiality. But rather than engage in serious dialogues with black women academics and the works of African American women, both have become fetishized as objects to be invoked, like name-dropping, in hip discourses of postmodern multiculturalism. Such acts of fetishization allow us to forget that black feminist studies evolved out of the historical inequities generated by racism, sexism, and classism that have predetermined many aspects of our lives. Second, duCille offers some general procedures—what I'd like to designate broadly as critical methodologies—for preserving the integrity of black feminist studies. It is this part of the essay that is essential for future scholars to heed if this field (and for that matter academic scholarship in general) is to continue to develop rather than merely exist as a site for ready exploitation.

According to duCille, we need to rely on the professionalism that has been customary in other academic areas. Therefore, we need to insist that scholars of black feminist studies be familiar with the extensive discourses that constitute this field. DuCille offers a utopian vision that ought be a methodological goal for cultural studies in general, one that minimally expects all scholars to know as much about "minority discourses" as scholars of color are required to know about so-called dominant cultures. I offer a modified vision: if scholars of African American literature were expected to know as much about this field as they have to know even incidentally about British and white American literature, there would be no "occult" of either black feminist criticism or African American cultural studies.

NOTES

1. Barbara Welter, "The Cult of True Womanhood, 1820–1860." *Dimity Convictions: The American Woman in the Nineteenth Century.* Athens, Ohio: Ohio State University Press, 1976.

2. Here, I quote my colleague Ann Kelley who gives a pet peeve (that many of us share) particularly vivid expression.

3. DuCille uses Gayatri Spivak's term from "In Praise of *Sammy and Rosie Get Laid*" from *Critical Inquiry* 31–32 (1989), 80–88.

Truth is, I never thought I'd see the day when people would be interested in hearing what two old Negro women have to say. Life still surprises me. So maybe the last laugh's on *me.*

—Annie Elizabeth ("Bessie") Delany, *Having Our Say*

•   •   •

Hurstonism and Black Feminism

In her foreword to the 1978 reprint of *Their Eyes Were Watching God,* Sherley Anne Williams tells of first encountering Zora Neale Hurston and *Their Eyes* as a graduate student enrolled in a two-semester survey of black poetry and prose. "Afro-American literature was still an exotic subject then," Williams writes, "rarely taught on any regular basis."[1] She goes on to describe how she and her classmates fought over the pitifully few copies of African American texts, long out of print, that they were able to beg or borrow from musty basements, rare-book collections, and reserved reading rooms. When it finally became her turn to read *Their Eyes,* Williams says she found in the speech of Hurston's characters her own country self and, like Alice Walker and many others, became Zora Neale's for life.

Originally published in *Signs* 19 (Spring 1993), University of Chicago Press, © 1994. All rights reserved. Reprinted by permission. The version we are publishing is from *Skin Trade* (1996).

For those of us who came of intellectual age in the late sixties and early seventies, Williams's discovery of Zora Neale is an almost painfully familiar textual encounter of the first kind. Though Hurston was not the first black woman writer I encountered or claimed as my own (that was Ann Petry), it was during this same period, 1971, that I too discovered Zora. I was introduced to her work by my friend and fellow graduate student, Gayl Jones. When I began my teaching career a few years later at Hamilton College in New York, Gayl was again generous enough to lend me her well-worn copy of *Their Eyes*. Only a lingering fear of being prosecuted for copyright infringement prevents me from detailing how I went about sharing among the dozen or so students in my seminar, none of whom had heard of Hurston, the fruits that bloomed within the precious, tattered copy of *Their Eyes Were Watching God*.

Twenty-five years later, African American literature courses and black women writers are again exotic subjects. They are exotic this time out, however, not because they are rarely taught or seldom read, but because in the midst of this multicultural moment, they have become politically correct, intellectually popular, and commercially precious. Once altogether ignored as historical and literary subjects or badly misfigured as magnanimous mammies, man-eating matriarchs, or immoral Jezebels, black women—that is, certain black women—and their texts have been taken up by the academy, invoked by the intellectual elite as well as the scholarly marginal. Currently in print in several editions, *Their Eyes Were Watching God* has become quasi-canonical, holding a place of honor on reading lists in mainstream history courses, in social science, literature, and American studies, as well as in those more marginalized disciplines, African American studies and women's studies. Much the same holds true for Walker's *The Color Purple* and Morrison's *Beloved*, each of which has been awarded a Pulitzer Prize for fiction (with Morrison's oeuvre winning her the Nobel Prize for literature in 1993 as well).

It is important to note that black women critics and scholars have played a crucial role in bringing to the academic fore the works of "lost" writers such as Hurston and Nella Larsen and in opening up spaces within the academy both for the fiction of contemporary African American women writers and for the study of women of color more generally. Though I am usually suspicious of efforts to define benchmarks and signposts, there are a number of important essays, anthologies, and monographs that can be rightly claimed as the founding texts of contemporary black feminist studies. Toni Cade's anthology *The Black Woman*

(1970), for example—which showcased the prose and poetry of writers such as Nikki Giovanni, Audre Lorde, Paule Marshall, Alice Walker, and Sherley Anne Williams—stands as a pivotal text along with critical essays and literary, historical, and sociological studies by Barbara Smith, Barbara Christian, Frances Beal, Joyce Ladner, Jeanne Noble, Darlene Clark Hine, Angela Davis, Frances Foster, Filomina Chioma Steady, Sharon Harley and Rosalyn Terborg-Penn, and Mary Helen Washington.[2]

While keepers of culture have given the lion's share of credit for the development of black literary and cultural studies to male scholars such as Houston Baker, Henry Louis Gates, and Cornel West, Mary Helen Washington has been a key player in efforts to define and institutionalize the fields of African American literature and black feminist studies for more than twenty years.[3] Among my most precious possessions is a tattered copy of the August 1974 issue of *Black World*, which contains an article by Washington called "Their Fiction Becomes Our Reality: Black Women Image Makers." In this article, one of the first pieces of black feminist criticism I discovered (and in others that began appearing in *Black World* in 1972), Washington reviewed the work of black women writers such as Gwendolyn Brooks, Maya Angelou, Ann Petry, and Toni Cade Bambara, as well as Walker, Marshall, and Morrison.

Much the same can and must be said of Barbara Christian and Barbara Smith, whose essays on African American women writers began appearing in print in the mid and latter 1970s. Christian's first book, *Black Women Novelists: The Development of a Tradition, 1892–1976* (1980), which brilliantly analyzed the work of black women writers from Frances Harper to Walker, remains a foundational text: "the Bible in the field of black feminist criticism," according to Michele Wallace.[4] Nor have nearly twenty years dulled the impact and significance of Barbara Smith's "Toward a Black Feminist Criticism" (1977), a widely reprinted, often anthologized black lesbian feminist declaration that gave name, definition, and political persuasion to the perspective from which Bambara, Washington, and others had been writing.[5] Smith's work in literary criticism and that of her sister Beverly Smith in the area of black women's health have played crucial roles in developing the fields of black feminist and black lesbian studies.

Within the realm of literary studies alone, the names on even a partial list of pioneering black feminist scholars are, as Houston Baker has said, legion: Deborah McDowell, Nellie McKay, Hortense Spillers, Gloria

Hull, Patricia Bell Scott, Cheryl Wall, Valerie Smith, Mae Henderson, Gloria Wade-Gayles, Thadious Davis, Trudier Harris, Frances Smith Foster, Hazel Carby, Joyce Joyce, and Claudia Tate, as well as Christian, Washington, Smith, and many others.[6] Both as an inspiration to aspiring writers and as an editor at Random House in the 1970s, Toni Morrison has played a particularly dramatic role in opening up spaces for critical attention to African American women.

As a beneficiary of their research and writing, I am anxious to give credit where it is long overdue, but this chapter is not intended as a praisesong for black women scholars, critics, and artists or as a review of the literature they have generated.[7] Instead I would like to examine some of the consequences of the current explosion of interest in black women as literary and historical subjects. Among the issues I explore are the ways in which this interest—which seems to me to have reached occult status—increasingly marginalizes both the black women critics and scholars who excavated the fields in question and their black feminist "daughters" who would further develop those fields.

What does it mean, for instance, that many prestigious university presses and influential literary publications regularly rely not on these seasoned black women scholars but on male intellectuals—black and white—to review the manuscripts and books of young black women just entering the profession? What does it mean for the black female professoriate that departments ask powerful senior black male scholars to referee the tenure and promotion cases of the same black women scholars who have challenged these men in some way? What does it mean for the field in general and for junior African Americanists in particular that senior scholars, who are not trained in African American studies and whose career-building work often has excluded black women, are now teaching courses in and publishing texts about African American literature and generating "new scholarship" on black women writers? What does it mean for the future of black feminist studies that a large portion of the growing body of scholarship on black women is now being written by white feminists and by men whose work frequently achieves greater critical and commercial success than that of the black female scholars who carved out the field?

My questions are by no means new; nor do I claim to have any particularly insightful answers. I only know that as one who has been studying the literature and history of black women for almost thirty years and teaching it for more than twenty, I have a burning need to work out my own ambivalence and, at times, animosity over the new-found enthusiasm for these fields that I think of as my own hard-won territory. It is a little like the parent who tells the child she is about to reprimand that "this hurts me more than it hurts you." But lest anyone think this an easily authored Portnoy's complaint in blackface—yet another black womanist indictment of white feminists who can do no right and men who can do only wrong—I want to make explicit my own uneasy antagonism.

Elsewhere I have argued against territoriality, against essentialism, against treating African American studies as the private property of what Gayatri Spivak calls "black blacks."[8] Yet questions of turf and appropriation persist, despite my best efforts to intellectualize them away. Here again my dilemma is neither new nor mine alone. The modern version of the ageless argument over who owns the sacred text is at least as old as the work of the white anthropologists Melville and Frances Herskovits, dating back to the 1920s and reaching a controversial peak in 1941 with the publication of *Myth of the Negro Past,* a study of African cultural retentions scorned by many black intellectuals. It was in the fifties, however, that white scholars began to loom large in black historiography and literary criticism, often receiving within the academy a kind of attention that the pioneering work of many black historians and critics had not enjoyed. The black historian Darlene Clark Hine noted in 1980 that "most of the highly-acclaimed historical works were, with few exceptions, written by white scholars." In fact, the legitimization of black history as a field proved a "bonanza for the [white] professional historians already in positions [as university professors and/or recognized scholars] to capitalize from the movement."[9]

Some 130 years ago, Harriet Jacobs was able to publish her life story only with the authenticating stamp of the well-known white abolitionist Lydia Maria Child. "I have signed and sealed the contract with Thayer & Eldridge, in my name, and told them to take out the copyright in my name," Child wrote in a letter to Jacobs in 1860. "Under the circumstances *your* name could not be used, you know."[10] The circumstances were of course the conditions of slavery under which Jacobs had lived for most of her life and from which she had not completely escaped. Now, as then, it often seems to take the interest of white scholars to legitimize African American history and literature or such "minority discourses" as postcoloniality and multiculturalism.

• • •

I Once Was Blind, But Now I See

By and large, it is only those who enjoy the privileges of white skin who can hold matters of race at arm's length. The white theorist Jane Gallop, for instance, can say that "race only posed itself as an urgent issue to me in the last couple of years,"[11] but race always has been an urgent issue for Mary Helen Washington, Barbara Christian, and Barbara Smith— indeed for most black feminist critics. Gallop can say that she didn't feel the need to discuss race until the focus of her work shifted from French poststructuralist theory to American feminist literary criticism. But Gayatri Spivak and other third-world women know only too well the fallacies and consequences of treating race as something only other (nonwhite) people own and racism as a problem peculiar to the United States. As Spivak writes: "In the matter of race-sensitive analysis, the chief problem of American feminist criticism is its identification of racism as such with the constitution of racism in America. Thus, today I see the object of investigation to be not only the history of 'Third World Women' or their testimony but also the production, through the great European theories, often by way of literature, of the colonial object."[12]

The colonial object is furthered not only by the canonical literature of the west, but also by would-be oppositional feminists who continue to see whiteness as so natural, normative, and unproblematic that racial identity is a property only of the nonwhite. Unless the object of study happens to be the othered, race is set outside immediate consideration, at once extratextual and extraterrestrial. Despite decades of painful debate, denial, defensiveness, and color-consciousness raising, "as a woman" in mainstream feminist discourse all too often continues to mean "as a white woman." The philosopher Elizabeth Spelman calls this thoroughly internalized myopia the "Trojan horse of feminist ethnocentrism."[13] Indeed, for women of color who are asked to prove their feminism by placing gender before race, the exclusionary ethnocentrism of such innocent constructions as "women and minorities" is both as hollow and as loaded as the Greeks' wooden horse.

But there is a somewhat more convoluted point to make here. In the same conversation referred to above, Jane Gallop says that African American women have become for her what French men used to be: the people she feels inadequate in relation to and tries hardest to please in her writing. This fear of black feminists "is not just idiosyncratic," Gallop believes—not just hers alone—but a shared anxiety among white women academics. She traces her own awareness of this anxiety to what she calls a "non-encounter" with the black feminist Deborah McDowell, who teaches at the University of Virginia, where Gallop once gave a talk: "I had hoped Deborah McDowell would come to my talk: she was there, she was the one person in the audience that I was really hoping to please."[14] Gallop goes on to explain that in her lecture she read from the manuscript that became *Around 1981: Academic Feminist Literary Theory* (1992), after which someone in the audience asked if she was discussing any black feminist anthologies in her study. "I answered no and tried to justify it, but my justifications rang false in my ears," she replies, continuing:

> Some weeks later a friend of mine showed me a letter from McDowell which mentioned my talk and said that I was just doing the same old thing, citing that I was not talking about any books edited by black women. I obsessed over McDowell's comment until I decided to add a chapter on Pryse and Spillers's *Conjuring*. I had already vowed not to add any more chapters out of fear that I would never finish the book. As powerful as my fear of not finishing is, it was not as strong as my wish for McDowell's approval. For McDowell, whom I do not know, read black feminist critic.

Gallop ends her commentary on what might be called "the influence of anxiety" by noting that McDowell ("read black feminist critic") has come to occupy the place of Jacques Lacan in her psyche in much the same way that "emphasis on race has replaced for [her] something like French vs. American feminism."

It is interesting that while she wanted McDowell's approval, like the white child who insults its mammy one moment and demands a hug the next, Gallop seemed to expect approval without having to do the one thing most likely to win it: include McDowell and other black women scholars in the category of feminist theorists or treat black feminist critics as colleagues to be respected, not feared.

Gallop's confessional narrative—and McDowell's nonspeaking part in it—is troubling. Among other things, these remarks seem to exoticize, eroticize, anomalize, and masculinize (if not demonize) Deborah McDowell and the whole category of "black feminist critic." Just what are the implications of conflating white French men and black American women as thorns in the side of white feminists, as Father Law? Gallop's transference is all the more vexed because she and her collaborators define "the men"—them—as "the enemy" throughout their conversation. In fact, as Nancy Miller puts it, where feminist criticism and French male theorists meet, the result is a "David and Goliath thing, with little Jane Gallop from Duluth taking out her slingshot to use on the great man."[15]

Not-so-little (academically speaking) Jane Gallop wields words like a slingshot; but McDowell, daunting as her scholarly accomplishments are, is no Goliath. There is a very different power relation at work. McDowell, whom I believe Gallop means to honor, is actually diminished by a narrative that casts her somewhere between monster and mammy: demanding, demeaning, impossible to please, but at the same time possessing irresistible custodial power and exotic allure as the larger-than-life racial other.

I rush to add that mammy is my metaphor, not Gallop's. There is nothing in Gallop's commentary that defines McDowell as anything other than "black feminist critic"—nothing that describes her work or explains why she looms so large in Gallop's psyche while writ so small in her text. McDowell, the black feminist critic, is never anything other than *the other* in "Criticizing Feminist Criticism." Race enters the conversation of these three white feminists only through the referenced bodies of objectified black women, and only at those moments when the speakers tally their sins of omission against women of color and their irritation at being chastised or, as they say, trashed for those exclusions.

Spurred by McDowell's criticism, Jane Gallop did indeed add the Pryse and Spillers anthology *Conjuring* to her study of feminist theory, with interesting results. Provocative if tentative, Gallop's critique is most incisive where it attends to the tensions between the different organizing principles set out in the anthology's introduction and afterword. Her study is, for me, most engaging where it attempts to explain that *Conjuring* comes with its own deconstruction.

As Gallop reads it, Marjorie Pryse's introduction argues for a continuum of black women writers—a single, unified tradition rooted in magic, folk wisdom, and "ancient power." Hortense Spillers's afterword, on the other hand, emphasizes cross-currents and discontinuities—differences within a tradition that is itself always in flux. Gallop concludes that Pryse frames and Spillers reframes. Even as Spillers's afterword turns the reader's expectations inside out, Pryse's introduction

> corresponds to and evokes in the reader, at least in the white female academic, a fantasy which orients our reading of black women. I want the conjure woman; I want some ancient power that stands beyond the reaches of white male culture. I want black women as the idealized and exoticized alternative to European high culture. I want some pure outside and am fool enough to think I might find it in a volume published by Indiana University Press, with full scholarly apparatus.[16]

This is a difficult passage to digest, especially when the author later admits that she was disappointed that the book was so academic and that she had attributed its particularly erudite essays, with their classical allusions, to critics she imagined to be white. Surely Gallop does not mean what she seems to say here. Is she really admitting in print that she expected a critical anthology subtitled *Black Women, Fiction, and Literary Tradition*—a book edited by two university professors, one of whom has long been regarded as a dean of black feminist criticism—to be other than scholarly, literate, and sophisticated?

To be fair, I think Gallop's tone is meant to be ironic, to point out— and maybe to poke fun at—the essentializing fantasies of "the white female academic" who desires the other to be other, who brings to the text of the other a different set of assumptions, who expects to leave high theory behind when she goes slumming in low culture. Hers is a dangerous strategy, but it seems to be popular among white readers of "black texts," who feel compelled to supplement their criticism with exposés of their former racism (or sexism) in a kind of I-once-was-blind-but-now-I-see way. (It worked for the composer of "Amazing Grace," a reformed slave trader.) I will have more to say about this strategy in a moment, but for now I want to linger over what is for me more a critique of "the white female academic" than of *Conjuring*.

Gallop is subtly telling us that she, as a white woman reader, wanted to find in this black book the exotic black female other, a "new delight," the "spice" to liven up the dull dish of western culture she usually consumes. "Since I am a white academic," she writes, "what sort of fantasy not only renders those attributes contemptible but, from an imagined identification with some righteous outside, allows me to cast them as aspersions on others?" In this instance, Gallop's exoticizing movements are not entirely unselfconscious, as they seem to be in "Criticizing Feminist Criticism." As her self-reflective question suggests, her essay is underpinned by an implicit critique of the primitivist expectations that "the white female academic" (I would be more generous and say *some* white female academics) brings to the reading of texts by or about black women.

Even more interesting, however, is Gallop's contention that Pryse's introduction evokes those desires in the reader. She says that reading *Conjuring* for a second time, even knowing that Spillers's corrective essay lay ahead, she still nearly gave in to the introduction's romantic vision of black female folk. "In this chapter I wanted to transmit this illusory take on the anthology," Gallop writes, "because I consider this illusion central to *our* reading of black women. *We* must confront *our* wish to find this ancient power, this pure outside of academic culture, before *we* deconstruct or correct *our* illusion."[17] In other words, the reader needs to absorb Pryse's framing before Spillers's reframing can take effect.

I'm not quite sure how this follows: why do we need this critical *felix culpa*, this happy slip into what Gallop describes as the folk fantasies of Pryse before *we* can be rescued by the refined vision of Spillers? Perhaps my failure to follow Gallop's logic here stems from her use of "we" and "our," which is at least as problematic as my own. I am not part of her "we," and she is not part of mine. Pryse's introduction did not evoke in me as a reader the kind of desires Gallop evidently assumes it evokes in her universal "we."

What happens if we add to Gallop's notion of the framing/reframing, idealizing/realizing, "good cop/bad cop" routine of the coeditors the fact that Marjorie Pryse is white and Hortense Spillers is black? What does it mean, then, that Spillers both brings up the rear, has the last word, and "deconstructs or corrects" not only Pryse's romantic vision of a black female folk but the primitivist expectations of "the white female academic"? Can one correct where there has been no error? Perhaps because she does not quite dare to play critical hardball with those she seems to take to be two black feminist critics, Gallop bends over backward to soft-pedal the very ideological disjuncture she has so astutely identified. If the coeditors are simply playing out a well-rehearsed routine, as Gallop concludes, why has Pryse positioned herself as the essentializing, idealizing white woman academic and left the corrective black feminist criticism to Spillers?

Gallop's reading of editorial matters in *Conjuring* unwittingly punctuates my point about the dangers of a critical mode that demeans its subject in the very act of analyzing it. It is of course no better for me to use Gallop (or Pryse) as a metonym for white feminist critics than it is for Gallop to use Deborah McDowell. Yet the wide-eyed illusions Gallop attributes to Pryse's introduction and the myopia of her own remarks in "Criticizing Feminist Criticism" demonstrate precisely why it remains so difficult for some black feminists to entrust the texts of our familiar to the critical caretaking of white women (and men) for whom black women are newly discovered foreign bodies, perpetually other.

The Driving Miss Daisy Crazy Syndrome

Yet. Still. And but. If a Ph.D. in English literature is not a title deed to the African American text, neither is black skin. Romantic fantasies of an authentic, cohesive, magical, ancient, all-knowing black female folk are certainly not unique to white academics. Some might argue that the issue is not simply the color or culture of the scholar but the kind, quality, and cultural competence of the scholarship. The black historian Carter Woodson reportedly welcomed the contributions of white scholars, "so long as they were the products of rigorous scholarship and were not contaminated by the venom of racial bias."[18] Unfortunately, biases are ideologically inscribed and institutionally reproduced and are not easily put aside—not even by the most sensitive and the most well-intentioned among us. I think, for example, of Adrienne Rich.

Long a fan of Rich's poetry, I was rather late in coming to her prose. *Of Woman Born: Motherhood as Experience and Institution* (1986), originally published in 1976, was more than a dozen years old before I gave myself the pleasure of reading it. For once, though, my timing couldn't have been better: I discovered this essential book at a critical moment in my life and in the development of my feminism—on the eve of my fortieth birthday, as I wrestled with the likelihood of never having a child. Rich's brilliant analysis of motherhood as an instrument of patriarchy helped me come to terms with the constructedness of what I had been reared to believe were natural maternal instincts, without which I was no woman. But for all that Rich's book gave me, it also took something away; and that, ironically and perhaps a little unfairly, has come to mean almost as much to me as what it gave.

For a moment in the penultimate chapter of this passionate and painful critique of motherhood, Rich turns her remarks toward the black woman who helped to raise her. To this nameless woman Rich assigns the designation "my Black mother." "My Black mother was 'mine,' " she writes, "only for four years, during which she fed me, dressed me, played with me, watched over me, sang to me, cared for me tenderly and intimately." Rich goes on to describe the physical presence of her black mother, from whom she "learned—*nonverbally*—a great deal about the possibilities of dignity in a degrading situation" (my emphasis). Unaware of the degrading situation she is creating herself, she continues: "When I began writing this chapter I began to remember my Black mother again: her calm, realistic vision of things, her physical grace and pride, her beautiful soft voice. For years, she had drifted out of reach, in my searches backward through time, exactly as the double silence of sexism and racism intended her to do. She was meant to be utterly annihilated."[19]

To the silences of sexism and racism Rich adds a third: the silence (and the blindness) of feminism. Like Jane Gallop wanting to praise Deborah McDowell, Adrienne Rich no doubt means to honor the woman who cared for her as a child. But the flow of her prose should not disguise the paternal arrogance of her words or mask the annihilating effect of her claim on the being she resurrects as "my Black mother." Silent and nameless in Rich's book, "my Black mother" has no identity of her own and, in fact, does not exist beyond the nurture she gave exclusively to the young Adrienne.

" 'Childless' herself, she *was* a mother," Rich writes of her objectified subject. Her attempt to thrust motherhood on a childless black domestic worker is all the more ironic because of what she claims for all women in the introduction to the anniversary edition of the book: "the claim to personhood; the claim to share justly in the products of our labor, not to be used merely as an instrument, a role, a womb, a pair of hands or a back or a set of fingers; to participate fully in the decisions of our workplace, our community; to speak for ourselves, in our own right."[20] Even in the midst of her own extended criticism of the objectification of women as mothers, Rich has objectified someone she can see only in the possessive case. "My Black mother" is a role, a pair of hands; her function is to "nonverbally" instruct the white child in the ways of the world, even as she cannot speak "in [her] own right."[21]

The child may be father of the man in poetry, but frequently when white intellectuals reminisce about blacks from their past, it is black mammy (metaphorically speaking, even where the mammy figure is a man) who takes the ignorant white infant into enlightenment. Often as the youthful, sometimes guilty witness to the silent martyrdom of the older other, the privileged white person inherits a wisdom, an agelessness, even a racelessness that entitles him or her to the raw materials of another's life and culture but, of course, not to the other's condition.

Such transformative moves often occur in the forewords, afterwords, rationales, and apologia white scholars affix to their scholarly readings of the black other—discussions that just may protest too much, suggesting a somewhat uneasy relationship between author and subject. These prefaces acknowledge the "outsider" status of the authors—their privileged positions as white women or as men—even as they insist on the rightness of their entry into the fields of black literature and history.

Gerda Lerner offers such a rationale in her preface to *Black Women in White America:* "Black people at this moment in history need above all to define themselves autonomously and to interpret their past, their present and their future." Having called upon the black physician to heal her/himself, Lerner then goes on to explain her own presence in the operating room:

> Certainly, historians who are members of the culture, or subculture, about which they write will bring a special quality to their material. Their understanding and interpretation is apt to be different from that of the outsider. On the other hand, scholars from outside a culture have frequently had a more challenging vision than those closely involved in and bound by their own culture. Both angles of vision are complementary in arriving at the truth about the past and in finding out "what actually happened."[22]

A more challenging vision? Why does the perspective of the white scholar reading "the black experience" represent a more challenging vision?

Lerner is not alone in prefacing her work with such a claim. I am reminded of the opening chapter of John Callahan's *In the African-American Grain: Call-and-Response in Twentieth-Century Black Fiction.* Here Callahan takes us on a sentimental journey through his Irish American youth, which was affected not only by his being likened to niggers—"Do you know the definition of an Irishman?" the eight-year-old Callahan is asked by a much bigger Italian boy. " 'A Nigger turned inside-out.' "—but also by the black male protectors who taught him "a great deal about the hard work of becoming a man." The teaching tools used by one of these guardians—Bill Jackson, chauffeur for the insurance company at which Callahan worked while in college—include a "prolonged silent challenge" after Callahan calls him a black bastard and his "trickster's way" of teaching certain lessons.[23]

Like Adrienne Rich, Callahan describes his black guide as "silent," even as he credits the chauffeur with teaching him many things "essential to [his] own evolving voice and story." Indeed Bill Jackson, the stereotypical black trickster, remains silent as he is used by Callahan to claim not only his own Irish American voice but entitlement to African American fictions of voice: fictions that "connect and reconnect generations of Americans—African-American, yes and preeminently, but all others too, Irish-Americans like me, for instance—with those past and present oral traditions behind our evolving spoken and written voices."

Here again, to my mind, a critical posturing that means to celebrate a literature demeans it. Callahan's words suggest that we are all brothers not only under the skin but under the book jacket. The white scholar understands "the African-American experience" not in its own right, not on its own terms, but because he can make it like his own. With his voice he can translate another's silence. Bill Jackson's silence is telling, but so too is his profession. It is altogether fitting that Jackson is a chauffeur, for indeed it all invokes what I call the *Driving Miss Daisy* syndrome: an intellectual sleight of hand that transforms power and race relations to make best friends out of driver and driven, master and slave, boss and servant, white boy and black man.

When Callahan overhears the company vice-president lumping together Irish and African Americans as "contemptible, expendable lower caste," he wishes for the strength and skill of a black football player he admires to help him speak up for himself (though apparently not for the other contemptibles). "My fate linked to African-Americans by that Yankee bank officer," Callahan writes, "I became more alert and sympathetic to black Americans my own age and younger who, though cursed, spat upon, and beaten, put their lives and voices on the line to uphold the law of the land and integrate public schools in the South."

Am I to applaud this declaration of allegiance and understanding? No, the claim of fellow feeling and universality—of linked fates and shared voice—makes me profoundly angry and mars my reading of what is actually a fine book. In the end, Callahan's personal narrative, like Rich's, takes symbolic wealth from the martyred, romanticized black body but retains the luxury of ignoring its material poverty. Twenty-five years later, John Callahan is a university professor while, as he tells us in his introduction, Roy Fitch—the protective black mailroom manager under whom he once worked—"looks after" a building near the "plebeian end" of the town green. If we peel away the euphemisms, will we find that Fitch, former mailroom manager, is now a janitor or a security guard for a building near the rundown section of town? Intent as he is on using Fitch to tell his own success story, Callahan does not comment on the historical irony of their relative positions. Nor does he grasp the implications of his own storytelling. "Don't climb no mountain on my back," he recalls Fitch saying to him years before, in response to his awkward attempt to apologize for yet another racial slur. Had Callahan understood the significance of Fitch's words—were he as good at interpreting speech as silence—he could not have written the introduction he did.

However troubling Rich's and Callahan's apologies may be to me as a black woman reader, the white scholar Missy Dehn Kubitschek acknowledges an indebtedness to the latter: "My admiration for 'Who You For?,' " she writes in the preface to *Claiming the Heritage: African-American Women Novelists and History*, "led me to consider voicing my own simultaneously social and psychic travels as a prelude to this study of African-American women's novels."[24]

Following Callahan's lead, Kubitschek opens her study with "A Personal Preface," in which she offers a first-hand account (complete with family history) of how she as a white woman and a British Victorianist came to write a book about African American women novelists. Briefly told, one of the principal players in her disciplinary conversion was her grandmother, a long-time armchair racist, who changed her mind after watching a television program about the "dangerous urban black ghetto" of East St. Louis. Mediated through the medium of television, urban blacks became objects of pity for Mrs. Dehn rather than fear. The possibilities of her grandmother's "impossible" change of heart at such an advanced age were "seismic" for Kubitschek, who was a graduate student at the time and who found in that conversion the seeds of her own.

But other transformative encounters lay ahead for Kubitschek, which not only helped her to get over her family's racism but over her own as well. Arriving early for work one morning in the basement office of the English department, Kubitschek was terrified first by hearing a male voice and then by the sudden appearance of a black man. Reading the horror writ large across her face, the man, a construction worker apparently also early on site for renovating the building, "quickly" and "quietly" explained that he just wanted to use the phone. "Of course, I had been afraid before I had seen that he was black," Kubitschek writes. "Rape is always a threat to women, always a possibility." But seeing his black skin heightened her fear, she admits, and revealed her racism. Because she had recently read Richard Wright's "Big Boy Leaves Home," she knew the historical implications of her reaction. " 'Race' ceased to be something that had constructed other people, especially blacks," as she began to understand herself as a racial as well as a gendered being.

Rape is truly a threat to women, particularly to a woman alone with a man. Black man, white man, green man from Mars, I too would have been afraid in Kubitschek's shoes. Her fear feels more legitimate to me than the white liberal guilt that no doubt leads her to call her fear racism and to apologize for it in a preface to a book about African American women writers. Through yet another troubling sleight of text, Kubitschek's articulated awareness of her former racism becomes the authorizing agent behind her strange metamorphosis from British Victorianist to African Americanist.

I know I should be more patient, more sisterly, more respectful of other people's discoveries. I know my bad attitude comes from what in this instance might be called the arrogance of black privilege: after all, I—whose earliest childhood memories include finding a snake in our mailbox shortly after we moved into an all-white neighborhood and being called "nigger" on my first day at school—did not learn my racial consciousness from reading Richard Wright's "Big Boy Leaves Home" as an adult. But I mean my criticism as a kindness. Perhaps if I can approximate in words what is so offensive about these *Driving Miss Daisy* confessionals, I will do the field and all those who want to work in it a genuine favor. Perhaps if I can begin to delineate the difference between critical analysis that honors the field and guilty rhetoric that dishonors it, I can contribute something positive to the future production of scholarship on African American women. Unfortunately, the words don't come easily and the heart of what's the matter is a difficult place to reach. How do you tell people who don't get it in the first instance that it is only out of the arrogance of white privilege or male prerogative that they find it an honor for a black woman to be proclaimed their black mother or their black friend or their black guardian or their black conscience?

It would be a mistake, however, to imply that these gestures are solely the product of white privilege. For my money, the occult of true black womanhood has generated few more troubling renderings of African American women writers and critics than that offered by Houston Baker in *Workings of the Spirit: The Poetics of Afro-American Women's Writing*. Having largely ignored black women as cultural producers throughout his long and distinguished career, Baker takes them up in *Workings*. And like Missy Dehn Kubitschek, for whom the writing of African American women is a kind of survival kit,[25] Baker tells us in his conclusion that a traumatic experience led him to seek solace in the "expressive resistances of Afro-American women's talking books."

> The texts of Afro-American women writers became mine and my friend's harrowing but sustaining path to a new, common, and, we thought, empowering discourse and commitment. To "victim," in my friend's semantics, was added the title and entitlement "survivor." Are we not all only that? Victim/Survivors?[26]

Both Kubitschek and Baker seem unaware of the ways in which their survival-kit claims to black texts can reinscribe African American women writers and their characters as magnanimous mammies who not only endure, like Faulkner's Dilsey, but whose primary function is to teach others to do the same. Though Baker is certainly entitled to tell his story, using personal tragedy to claim entitlement to the texts of black women makes me distrust not his cultural competence, perhaps, but his gender sensibility—his ability to handle with care the sacred text of me and mine.

But I was made suspicious of *Workings of the Spirit* long before I got to its conclusion. Baker also includes an introduction that calls attention to himself as outsider. He begins by acknowledging the prior claims and the "cautious anxieties" of black feminist critics such as Barbara Smith, Barbara Christian, and Mary Helen Washington, who mined the "provinces of Afro-American women's expressivity" that he is just now entering. A "blackmale" scholar "will find cause to mind his steps in a demanding territory," he asserts, his province/metropole metaphor confirming him in the very role he wants most to avoid—that of colonizing, come-lately "blackmale" critic. Such diction is a small example of what seems to me a major problem with *Workings of the Spirit:* the hierarchical relation between what he inevitably treats as master (male) and minor (female) narrative traditions.

Rather than building on the work of black women scholars who excavated the field, Baker either ignores or dismisses what he implies is their historical (as opposed to theoretical) feminist criticism in favor of his own masculinist theorizing. Male figures such as Douglass, Du Bois, Wright, and Ellison are the oracles against which black women's expressivity and cultural fidelity are measured. In *Workings's* third chapter, for instance, to get to Baker's reading of Morrison's *Sula*, you first have to wade through thirty pages on Wright. The attention to Wright (and other male artists and intellectuals) is justified, Baker argues, because "classic Afro-American male texts" provide a touchstone from which "to proceed by distinctions" in exploring the provinces of black female expressivity.

Like much of the new "new scholarship" that has come out of the occult of true black womanhood, Baker's book fails to live up to its own postmodern, deconstructive principles. It achieves neither inversion nor subversion; black women writers and the black feminist critics who read them remain fetishized bodies set against analytical white or superior male minds. As objects of investigation in such studies, black women are constructed in terms of their difference from or (in the name of sisterhood) similarity to the spectator, whether the spectator is a black male theorist or a white feminist critic. In other words, the black woman is made only more other by the male theorist or by the "white female academic" who views the subject from a position of unrelinquished authority.

Baker is of course free to disagree with black women scholars (as we frequently do with one another), but his failure to value their critical insights undermines his effort to enter into dialogue. His privileging of male subjects in a book about black women writers becomes an act of silencing and makes his text the victim of its own intentional phallacy: his stated wish to avoid appropriating the work and images of African American women through a "blackmale" gaze.

His essential and, I think, essentializing metaphors—black women as "departed daughters" and "spirit workers"—together with the uncontextualized photographs of black women interspersed throughout the book, raise questions about the gaze, about specularization and objectification, that Baker does not address or, I suspect, even see. This is too bad, especially after Mae Henderson—one of the black feminist critics Baker faintly praises for her "fine theorizing"—called his attention to the problem in criticizing an earlier essay that was the prototype for

Workings of the Spirit. The danger, she warned, "is not only that of essentializing but of reinforcing the most conventional constructs of (black) femininity." Henderson was troubled in particular by the "*specularity* of [Baker's] rather spectacular theory" of black female spirituality. She cautioned him to rethink his treatment of black women in terms that would not objectify and idealize them.[27]

Despite Henderson's incisive critique and her pointed admonition, *Workings of the Spirit* continues the specularization of black women that its prototypical essay began. The book's complementary phototext, in fact, evokes precisely what Henderson called "the male activity of scopophilia." Largely unremarked except for occasional captioned quotation from Baker's written words, the images of black women interspersed throughout the text objectify graphically those whom the book objectifies linguistically. But in another example of Baker's strategic deployment of women, this objectification is made *okay* by the author's claim that the phototext is the handiwork not of senior blackmale theorist Houston Baker but of junior female scholars Elizabeth Alexander and Patricia Redmond. This is Baker's final point:

> The phototext is the artistry of two young scholars. Their complementary text is a rich enhancement of the present work, and I cannot thank Elizabeth Alexander and Patricia Redmond enough for their collaboration. It seems to me that the intertextuality represented by their effort makes the present work more engaging than it would otherwise have been. My initial idea was that such a text would comprise a type of countercurrent of signification, soliciting always my own words, qualifying their "maleness." What emerged from the labors of Redmond and Alexander, however, is a visualization of an Afro-American women's poetics. Eyes and events engage the reader/viewer in a solicitous order of discourse that asks: "Who reads here?"[28]

If these photos could indeed ask such a question, their answer would probably be: "A man." Baker wants the photos to speak for themselves of "the space, place, and time of Afro-American women," but it is unclear how they can do that in the midst of what is *his* project. Whose project the phototext is becomes even clearer when we know that Alexander and Redmond were graduate students assigned by Baker to collect pictures. The image presented as the "parting shot" of the book is of a young black woman, her mouth open wide as if in a scream. I wonder what it means that the black woman depicted in midscream is literally, physically, clinically mute.

I am not quite certain where to go from here. I find myself oddly drawn to (gulp) William Faulkner. The griefs of great literature, Faulkner said in his Nobel Prize acceptance speech, must grieve on universal bones. I realize that I've heard this before, and not just from Faulkner. The self-recognition generated by the literature of the ennobled other is the essence of Callahan's professed link to African American "fictions of voice" and the medium of Baker's and Kubitschek's claims to the texts of black women. And they are not alone. As Hazel Carby points out, women's studies programs and literature departments have often used reductive readings of black women (either long-suffering or triumphantly noble) to fill in the gaps in their otherwise Eurocentric or Anglocentric curricular offerings. "In spite of the fact that the writing of black women is extraordinarily diverse, complex, and multifaceted," she writes, "feminist theory has frequently used and abused this material to produce an essential black female subject for its own consumption." Carby also suggests that for many white students and faculty the black female subject and cultural texts by and about African Americans have become "fictional substitutes" for any kind of "sustained social or political relationships with black people."[29]

This is precisely the function that black writers such as Toni Morrison, Alice Walker, and Gayl Jones seem to serve for three white academics, who claim to identify closely with the depictions of physical and psychic abuse in these author's fiction. As they explain: "We, as white feminists, are drawn to black women's visions because they concretize and make vivid a system of oppression." Indeed, they continue, "it has not been unusual for white women writers to seek to understand their oppression through reference to the atrocities experienced by other groups."[30] For these feminists, as for Baker and Kubitschek, the lure of black women's fiction is, at least in part, its capacity to teach them how to endure, how to understand not the complex experiences of black women but their own.

Is this use of black women's texts a bad thing? If Faulkner is right— if it is the writer's duty to help humankind endure by reminding us of our capacity for courage and honor and hope and pride and compassion and sacrifice and survival—black women writers have done the job very well. The griefs of African American women indeed seem to grieve on universal bones—"to concretize and make vivid a system of oppression." But it also seems that in order to grieve universally, to be concrete, to have larger meaning—the flesh on these bones must always be white or male.

This, then, is the final paradox: to be valid—to be true—black womanhood must be legible as white or male; the texts of black women must be readable as maps, indexes to someone else's experience, subject to a seemingly endless process of translation and transference. Under the cult of true black womanhood, the colored body, as Cherrie Moraga writes, is "thrown over a river of tormented history to bridge the gap,"[31] to make connections that enable scholars working in exhausted fields to cross over into the promised land.

The trouble is that, as Moraga points out, bridges get walked on over and over again. To be a bridge—walked on and passed over, used up and burned out, publishing while perishing—characterizes the condition of many black women scholars. Neither academia nor mainstream feminism has paid much attention to the crisis of black female intellectuals. But the issue is much on the minds of African American women, caught as we are in the throes of a repressive political climate that would lay the nation's ills on the backs of poor black "welfare queens," on the one hand, and overeducated elite black "quota queens," on the other. Even as welfare mothers are told to go out and get jobs, working women are blamed for the disintegration of the home and the erosion of family values that are figured as the real cause of crime and all other social problems. The status of black women in America seems all the more tenuous in light of certain "events" such as the Thomas-Hill hearings, the media-fed campaigns to discredit Lani Guinier and former Surgeon General Joycelyn Elders, and the recent deaths of a number of black female scholars and artists, including Audre Lorde (Hunter College), Sylvia Boone (Yale), Phyllis Wallace (MIT), and Toni Cade Bambara.

So serious are these issues that the lot of black women in the university became the subject of a national conference held at MIT in January 1994. Called "Black Women in the Academy: Defending Our Name, 1894–1994," this conference, the first of its kind, drew over two thousand women—most of them black—from across the country. Robin Kilson and Evelynn Hammonds, the conference organizers, said that they were overwhelmed by the response to their initial call for papers.

Expecting to host a small gathering of perhaps two hundred people, they found themselves bombarded by hundreds of abstracts, letters, faxes, and phone calls from black women anxious for a forum in which to discuss the hypervisibility, emotional quarantine, and psychic violence of their precarious positions in academia.[32]

I do not mean to imply that all black women scholars see themselves as what Hurston called "tragically colored," but I think it safe to say that these testimonies are a plaintive cry from black women academics who see themselves consumed by exhaustion, depression, loneliness, and a higher incidence of such killing diseases as hypertension, lupus, cancer, diabetes, and obesity. But it also seems to me that Jane Gallop's anxieties about African American women and Houston Baker's desire for dialogue with black women scholars are also plaintive cries. In different ways and with different consequences, we all experience the pain and disappointment of failed community.

As much as I would like to end on a positive note, I have little faith that this generation of scholars—black and nonblack, male and female—will succeed in solving these problems. We are too set in our ways, too alternately defensive and offensive, too much the products of the white heterosexist society that has reared us and the Eurocentric educational system that has trained us. Training may be the critical factor, however—the only way out of the occult of true black womanhood—in terms of both the cultural competence we must bring to the field and the professional guidance we must give to the students we bring into the field. If ever there came a day when all scholars were forced by the systems that educate them to know as much about "minority discourses" as scholars of color are required to know about so-called dominant cultures, perhaps black women would no longer be exotic commodities, and African American studies would indeed be everybody's business as usual.

NOTES

1. Sherley Anne Williams, in Hurston's *Their Eyes Were Watching God* (Urbana: University of Illinois Press, 1978), p. vi.

2. See e.g. Frances Beal, "Double Jeopardy: To Be Black and Female," in Robin Morgan, ed., *Sisterhood Is Powerful* (New York: Random House, 1970), pp. 340–352; Toni Cade [Bambara], *The Black Woman* (New York: New Amer-

ican Library, 1970); Angela Davis, "Reflections on the Black Woman's Role in
the Community of Slaves," *Black Scholar* 3 (1971), 3–15, and *Women, Race
and Class* (New York: Random House, 1981); Joyce Ladner, *Tomorrow's To-
morrow: The Black Woman* (New York: Doubleday, 1972); Mary Helen Washington, "Zora Neale Hurston: The Black Woman's Search for Identity," *Black
World* (August 1972), 68–75, and "Their Fiction Becomes Our Reality: Black
Women Image Makers," *Black World* (August 1974), 10–18; Barbara Christian,
Black Women Novelists: The Development of a Tradition (Westport, Conn.:
Greenwood, 1980) and *Black Feminist Criticism: Perspectives on Black Women
Writers* (New York: Pergamon, 1985); Frances Foster, "Changing Concepts of
the Black Woman," *Journal of Black Studies* (June 1973), 433–452; Jeanne
Noble, *Beautiful, Also, Are the Souls of My Black Sisters* (Englewood Cliffs:
Prentice-Hall, 1978); Sharon Harley and Rosalyn Terborg-Penn, eds., *The Afro-
American Woman: Struggles and Images* (New York: Kennikat, 1978); Bonnie
Thorton Dill, "The Dialectics of Black Womanhood," *Signs* 4 (1979), 543–555,
and "Race, Class, and Gender: Prospects for an All-Inclusive Sisterhood," *Fem-
inist Studies* 9 (1983), 131–150; Barbara Smith, "Toward a Black Feminist
Criticism," *Conditions Two* 1 (1977); Darlene Clark Hine, *When the Truth Is
Told: A History of Black Women's Culture and Community in Indiana, 1875–
1950* (Indianapolis: National Council of Negro Women, 1981); bell hooks, *Ain't
I a Woman: Black Women and Feminism* (Boston: South End Press, 1981);
Filomina Chioma Steady, ed., *The Black Woman Cross-Culturally* (Cambridge:
Schenkman, 1981); Gloria Hull, Patricia Bell Scott, and Barbara Smith, eds., *All
the Women Are White, All the Men Are Black, But Some of Us Are Brave* (Old
Westbury, New York: Feminist Press, 1982).

3. For whatever it may suggest about the crisis and the production of the
black intellectual, it is interesting to note that the scholarly work of Baker, Gates,
and West has been lauded in cover stories and feature articles in such
publications as the *New York Times*, the *Boston Globe*, *Newsweek*, and *Time*.
I recall seeing only one article on Mary Helen Washington, in the "Learning"
section of the Sunday *Boston Globe* (although there may have been others). The
article is dominated by a stunning picture of Washington, with a caption describing her as a scholar-teacher who "helps restore sight to the 'darkened eye' of
American literary tradition." Despite this fitting and promising caption, the
article has remarkably little to say about Washington's actual scholarship and
its impact on American literary studies. See Elizabeth Weld, "The Voice of Black
Women," *Boston Globe*, February 14, 1988, pp. 98, 100.

4. Michele Wallace, *Invisibility Blues* (New York: Verso, 1990) p. 184.

5. Cheryl A. Wall, ed., *Changing Our Own Words: Essays on Criticism,
Theory, and Writing by Black Women* (New Brunswick: Rutgers University
Press, 1989), pp. 4–5.

6. See Houston A. Baker Jr., *Workings of the Spirit: The Poetics of Afro-*

American Women's Writing (Chicago: University of Chicago Press, 1991) p. 10. Most of the black feminist critics listed by Baker have produced essays and books too numerous to name. In addition to their own writings, several of these scholars have made tremendous contributions to the fields of African American and black feminist literary studies through their editorial work on a number of important projects. See e.g. Trudier Harris and Thadious Davis, eds., *Afro-American Writers from the Harlem Renaissance to 1940, Dictionary of Literary Biography*, vol. 51 (Detroit: Gale Research), and Beacon Press's Black Women Writers Series, ed. Deborah McDowell.

7. For such a review of the critical literature, see Hazel Carby, *Reconstructing Black Womanhood: The Emergence of the Afro-American Woman Novelist* (New York: Oxford University Press, 1987), and Wall's introduction to *Changing Our Own Words*, pp. 1–15.

8. Gayatri Chakravorty Spivak, "In Praise of *Sammy and Rosie Get Laid*," *Critical Quarterly* 31–32 (1989), 80–88.

9. August Meier and Elliot Rudwick, *Black History and the Historical Profession, 1915–1980* (Urbana: University of Illinois Press, 1986), p. 294; Darlene Clark Hine, "The Four Black Historical Movements: A Case for the Teaching of Black History," *Teaching History: A Journal of Methods* 5 (1980), 115, quoted in Meier and Rudwick.

10. Harriet Jacobs, *Incidents in the Life of a Slave Girl, Written by Herself* (1861), ed. Jean Fagan Yellin (Cambridge: Harvard University Press, 1987), p. 246.

11. Jane Gallop, Marianne Hirsch, and Nancy K. Miller, "Criticizing Feminist Criticism," in Hirsch and Evelyn Fox Keller, eds., *Conflicts in Feminism* (New York: Routledge, 1989), p. 363.

12. Gayatri Chakravorty Spivak, *In Other Worlds: Essays in Cultural Politics* (New York: Routledge, 1988), p. 81.

13. Elizabeth Spelman, *Inessential Woman: Problems of Exclusion in Feminist Thought* (Boston: Beacon Press, 1988), p. 13. Echoing the complaint that women of color have leveled for some time (at least since Sojourner Truth's public query "Ain't I a woman?" first asked more than 140 years ago), Spelman argues that holding their own experiences to be normative, many white feminists historically have given little more than lip service to the significance of race and class in the lives of women.

14. Gallop, Hirsch, and Miller, "Criticizing Feminist Criticism," pp. 363–364.

15. Ibid., p. 358.

16. Jane Gallop, *Around 1981: Academic Feminist Literary Theory* (New York: Routledge, 1992), p. 169.

17. Ibid., p. 170; my emphasis.

18. Quoted in Meier and Rudwick, *Black History*, p. 289.

19. Adrienne Rich, *Of Woman Born: Motherhood as Experience and Institution*, 10th anniversary ed. (New York: Norton, 1986), pp. 254–255.

20. Ibid., p. xxviii.

21. In the anniversary revised edition of *Of Woman Born*, a more reflective Adrienne Rich attempts to adjust her vision in light of 1980s concerns. To her discussion of "my Black mother" she appends a footnote: "The above passage overpersonalizes and does not, it seems to me now, give enough concrete sense of the actual position of the Black domestic worker caring for white children." Even ten years later, Rich has failed to recognize that she is talking about another woman—another woman who is not her black mother but a laborer whose role as mammy is also constructed.

22. Gerda Lerner, ed., *Black Women in White America: A Documentary History* (New York: Random House, 1972), pp. xviii, xix; my emphasis.

23. John F. Callahan, *In the African-American Grain: Call-and-Response in Twentieth-Century Black Fiction*, 2nd ed. (Middletown: Wesleyan University Press, 1989), pp. 5, 9. Later quotations from pp. 10, 21, 8.

24. Missy Dehn Kubitschek, *Claiming the Heritage: African-American Women Novelists and History* (Jackson: University Press of Mississippi, 1991), p. xii. Later quotations from p. xxi.

25. In the final moments of her personal preface, we learn that it was actually the survival strategies embedded in black literature that ultimately led Kubitschek to the work of African American women writers. "The stories that constitute African-American literature say that oppression kills and that people survive oppression," she tells us. "Wanting to know more about survival brought me here" (p. xxiii).

26. Baker, *Workings of the Spirit*, pp. 208–209.

27. Mae Henderson, "Commentary on 'There Is No More Beautiful Way: Theory and the Poetics of Afro-American Women's Writing,' " by Houston Baker, in Baker and Patricia Redmond, eds., *Afro-American Literary Studies in the 1990s* (Chicago: University of Chicago Press, 1989), p. 159.

28. Baker, *Workings of the Spirit*, p. 212.

29. Hazel Carby, "The Multicultural Wars," in Gina Dent, ed., *Black Popular Culture* (Seattle: Bay Press, 1992), p. 192.

30. Patricia Sharpe, F. E. Mascia-Lee, and C. B. Cohen, "White Women and Black Men: Different Responses to Reading Black Women's Texts," *College English* 52 (1990), 146.

31. Cherrie Moraga, "Preface," in Moraga and Gloria Anzaldua, eds., *This Bridge Called My Back: Writings by Radical Women of Color* (New York: Women of Color Press, 1981), p. xv.

32. For a report on the conference, see Saidiya Hartman, "The Territory Between Us," *Callaloo* 17.2 (1994), 439–449. It was especially poignant that the opening address was delivered by Lani Guinier. Under a gag order from the

White House, she was prohibited from responding to her critics—from defending her name—while her nomination was pending, despite the opposition's flagrant misrepresentation of her views. Noting that her written work had been repeatedly taken out of context and otherwise distorted, Guinier quipped that her experience gave new meaning to the term "publish or perish": she did both.

Part Three

Nationalism Reconsidered

Chapter 9

The Mass Public and the Mass Subject

Michael Warner

Introduction by Russ Castronovo

Michael Warner does not investigate novels or other genres of fiction in his essay, which moves from eighteenth-century civic virtue to less than "virtuous" desires in the late twentieth century to penetrate Ronald Reagan. Instead, he brings tools of literary analysis to bear on political theory, arguing that the notion of the public is itself a fiction. As the story goes, an ideal public sphere invites qualified individuals to participate in a realm of open debate and rational exchange. But this fiction—one could just as easily call it a political theory—has rarely, if ever, approximated reality because the abstract and disinterested public it imagines nowhere exists. People are just too particular, their identities too striated by such cultural determinations as race, class, sexuality, or gender, to inhabit the general "we" that is too often the main and only unit of democracy.

Despite its historical unreality, the public sphere is a fixture in political theory that guarantees liberty by dedicating the inhabitants of a city-state, as writers such as Machiavelli and Rousseau would have it, to classical republican virtues that make each person impartially interested in the general liberty of all. No doubt any genuine commitment to the *polis* seems the stuff of fantasy, now even more so in an era of global existence. Still, the use of political theory provides an important methodological tool: an account of the public sphere drives Warner's essay because it holds out, often at a very great distance, the "possibility" of "emancipation." The problem, however, is that the fiction of a public "we" also creates a host of injurious effects that stigmatize individuals precisely for their particular affiliations and endowments that make them distinctive to one another. Because of this contradiction, Warner tempers his fascination with the historical unreality of the public sphere by examining the historical reality that has prevented those not blessed with the unmarked identity of white, middle-class manhood from sharing in the rewards and satisfactions of public life.

But the historical reality that Warner juxtaposes to the ideal public sphere is nothing like what usually counts as history. Can an analysis whose references include early rag-sheets like the *Spectator,* the avant-odd filmmaker John Waters (*Pink Flamingos, Hair Spray*), and *Barbie Magazine* qualify as either "real" (read serious) or "historical"? But if one's concern is the bodies so often prevented from achieving self-abstraction, their bearers consequently disqualified from public life, one has little choice but to proceed as Warner does and look at cultural texts that to many might seem justifiably on the outer limits of academic consideration. Do not adjust your television set: although the picture of a citizenry that Warner transmits via these texts may seem unfamiliar, the images of vulnerability and disaster that both constitute and compel this citizenry are seemingly everywhere around us in the form of scandals (for example, the indiscretions of elected officials) and spectacular scenes of technology gone horribly awry (for example, downed airplanes, derailed trains, collapsed bridges). As opposed to the rational disinterest of a theoretically ideal public sphere, this sensational interest in the erotic and the catastrophic burdens both the famous and the anonymous mass with particularity against which citizens enjoy the privileges of abstraction normally reserved for more empowered identities. This indulgence in what some may consider potentially salacious and morbid episodes may not strike the abstract "we" as the most healthy or well-adjusted set of interests but, for Warner, it works to explain how individuals reconcile the impossible pressures of abstraction with the specific facts of their densely lived historical bodies.

This difficult relationship between concrete self and abstract collective body is suggested by the essay's title, in which "and" operates as both conjunction and disjunction to point up the intimacy as well as estrangement between the "mass subject" and the "mass public." On the one hand, insofar as the public recognizes us, it does so because of our "virtues," that is, for our ability to transcend the putatively annoying and petty considerations of our bodies and status. On the other hand, these considerations are neither annoying nor petty but instead are the very qualities that make us distinctive and promote a sense of belonging. The trouble is that such signs of distinction also saddle us with what Warner calls "the humiliating positivity of the particular." Such contradictions vex the public sphere, making it at once the place of utopian promise and the site of political injury. These divisions haunt the democratic subject as well, producing a self-alienation in which individuals abject their own particularities—closeting their sexuality, loathing their ethnic heritage, feeling shame for their class background—as something other than a part of themselves.

Not the most encouraging picture, yet one cannot overlook the notes of pleasure that run through the essay. While the bizarre historicization of political theory here invites a sense of dismay, Warner several times marks "rhetorical analysis" as central to his interpretative arsenal. Rhetorical analysis is aimed at domains both broader and more specific than the literary. If we are to understand not only fiction but also fictions of the public sphere, we need to deploy methodological tools that do not abide strict disciplinary boundaries. At a fundamental level, attention to rhetoric is pivotal since the abstract subjects who enter the public sphere do so by voicing opinions from the disembodied vantage point that print culture provides. But at a less immediately calculable level, examination of the language that a child uses to imagine a highway pileup of toy cars, especially when that child is John Waters, is not without its enjoyment. The child's impish pleasure is Poe-like in its perverseness, which intentionally disregards social norms for perhaps no other reason than to disregard those norms. But in case we do need a reason, Warner reads this juvenile act of simulated destruction as a political parable of sorts, expressive of the citizen's relationship to the larger public body. The palpable irony involved in the application of Waters's *Shock Value* to democratic theory is more than just humorous; irony opens up a gap that allows us to reflect irreverently as well as critically on the hallowed "we" of the public. Or, take what is perhaps the essay's most iconoclastic pleasure, the "powerful fantasy of violating Reagan's anus": here again, pleasure exerts a force that scandalizes, not Reagan the man, but the dynamics of popularity that made Reagan a public figure seemingly invincible to criticism. In this respect (or is it disrespect?), fantasy is not relegated to the private but instead constitutes a subversive meditation on the logic of the public sphere that protects certain citizens while exposing others to harm and humiliation.

Disrespect may be the point of Warner's combined use of political theory, playful historicism, and rhetorical analysis. Insofar as disrespect entails critical thinking, that's the payoff of "The Mass Public and the Mass Subject."

———————— ■ ————————

The Egocrat coincides with himself, as society is supposed to coincide with itself. An impossible swallowing up of the body in the head begins to take place, as does an impossible swallowing up of the head in the body.

The attraction of the whole is no longer dissociated
from the attraction of the parts.
        —*Claude Lefort,* "The Image of the Body
        and Totalitarianism"[1]

During these assassination fantasies Tallis became increasingly obsessed with the pudenda of the Presidential
contender mediated to him by a thousand television
screens. The motion picture studies of Ronald Reagan
created a scenario of the conceptual orgasm, a unique
ontology of violence and disaster.
        —*J. G. Ballard,* "Why I Want to Fuck
        Ronald Reagan"[2]

As THE SUBJECTS of publicity—its hearers, speakers, viewers, and doers—
we have a different relation to ourselves, a different affect, from that
which we have in other contexts. No matter what particularities of
culture, race, and gender, or class we bring to bear on public discourse,
the moment of apprehending something as public is one in which we
imagine, if imperfectly, indifference to those particularities, to ourselves.
We adopt the attitude of the public subject, marking to ourselves its
nonidentity with ourselves. There are any number of ways to describe
this moment of public subjectivity: as a universalizing transcendence, as
ideological repression, as utopian wish, as schizocapitalist vertigo, or
simply as a routine difference of register. No matter what its character
for the individual subjects who come to public discourse, however, the
rhetorical contexts of publicity in the modern Western nations must
always mediate a self-relation different from that of personal life. This
becomes a point of more than usual importance, I will suggest, in a
period such as our own when so much political conflict revolves around
identity and status categories.

Western political thought has not ignored the tendency of publicity to
alter or refract the individual's character and status. It has been obsessed
with that tendency. But it has frequently thought of publicity as distorting, corrupting, or, to use the more current version, alienating individuals. The republican notion of virtue, for example, was designed exactly

to avoid any rupture of self-difference between ordinary life and publicity. The republican was to be the same as citizen and as man. He was to maintain continuity of value, judgment, and reputation from a domestic economy to affairs of a public nature. And lesser subjects—noncitizens such as women, children, and the poor—were equally to maintain continuity across both realms, as nonactors. From republicanism to populism, from Rousseau to Reagan, self-unity has been held to be a public value, and publicity has not been thought of as requiring individuals to have discontinuous perceptions of themselves. (Hegel, it is true, considered the state as a higher-order subjectivity unattainable in civil society. But because he considered the difference both normative and unbridgeable within the frame of the individual, a historical and political analysis of discontinuous self-relations did not follow.)

One reason why virtue was spoken about with such ardor in the seventeenth and eighteenth centuries was that the discursive conventions of the public sphere had already made virtuous self-unity archaic. In the bourgeois public sphere, talk of a citizen's virtue was already partly wishful. Once a public discourse had become specialized in the Western model, the subjective attitude adopted in public discourse became an inescapable but always unrecognized political force, governing what is publicly sayable—inescapable because only when images or texts can be understood as meaningful to a public rather than simply to oneself, or to specific others, can they be called public; unrecognized because this strategy of impersonal reference, in which one might say, "The text addresses me" *and* "It addresses no one in particular," is a ground condition of intelligibility for public language. The "public" in this sense has no empirical existence and cannot be objectified. When we understand images and texts as public, we do not gesture to a statistically measurable series of others. We make a necessarily imaginary reference to the public *as opposed to* other individuals. Public opinion, for example, is understood as belonging to a public rather than to scattered individuals. (Opinion polls in this sense are a performative genre. They do not measure something that already exists as public opinion, but when they are reported as such, they *are* public opinion.) So also it is only meaningful to speak of public discourse where it is understood as the discourse of a public rather than as an expansive dialogue among separate persons.

The public sphere therefore presents problems of rhetorical analysis. Because the moment of special imaginary reference is always necessary, the publicity of the public sphere never reduces to information, discussion, will formation, or any of the other scenarios by which the public sphere represents itself. The mediating rhetorical dimension of a public context must be built into each individual's relation to it, as a meaningful reference point against which something could be grasped as information, discussion, will formation. To ask about the relation between democracy and the rhetorical forms of publicity, we would have to consider how the public dimension of discourse can come about differently in different contexts of mediation, from official to mass-cultural or subcultural. There is not simply "a" public discourse and a "we" who apprehend it. Strategies of public reference have different meanings for the individuals who suddenly find themselves incorporating the public subject, and the rhetorics that mediate publicity have undergone some important changes.

Utopias of Self-Abstraction

In the eighteenth century, as I have argued elsewhere, the imaginary reference point of the public was constructed through an understanding of print.[3] At least in the British American colonies, a style of thinking about print appeared in the culture of republicanism according to which it was possible to consume printed goods with an awareness that the same printed goods were being consumed by an indefinite number of others. This awareness came to be built into the meaning of the printed object, to the point that we now consider it simply definitional to speak of printing as "publication." In print, understood this way, one surrendered one's utterance to an audience that was by definition indefinite. Earlier writers might have responded with some anxiety to such mediation or might simply have thought of the speaker-audience relation in different terms. In the eighteenth century the consciousness of an abstract audience became a badge of distinction, a way of claiming a public disposition.

The transformation, I might emphasize, was a cultural rather than a technological one; it came about not just with more use of print but rather as the language of republicanism was extended to print contexts as a structuring metalanguage. It was in the culture of republicanism, with its categories of disinterested virtue and supervision, that a rhetoric of print consumption became authoritative, a way of understanding the publicness of publication. Here, for example, is how the *Spectator* in 1712 describes the advantage of being realized in the medium of print:

> It is much more difficult to converse with the World in a real than a personated Character. That might pass for Humour, in the *Spectator*, which would look like Arrogance in a Writer who sets his Name to his Work. The Fictitious Person might contemn those who disapproved him, and extoll his own Performances, without giving Offence. He might assume a Mock-Authority; without being looked upon as vain and conceited. The Praises or Censures of himself fall only upon the Creature of his Imagination, and if any one finds fault with him, the Author may reply with the Philosopher of old, *Thou dost but beat the Case of* Anaxarchus.[4]

The Spectator's attitude of conversing with the world is public and disinterested. It elaborates republican assumptions about the citizen's exercise of virtue. But it could not come about without a value placed on the anonymity here associated with print. The Spectator's point about himself is that he is different from the person of Richard Steele. Just as the Spectator here secures a certain liberty in not calling himself Richard Steele, so it would take a certain liberty for us to call the author of this passage Richard Steele—all the more so since the pronoun reference begins to slip around the third sentence ("those who disapproved *him*"). The ambiguous relation between Spectator and writer, Steele says, liberates him. The Spectator is a prosthetic person for Steele, to borrow a term from Lauren Berlant—prosthetic in the sense that it does not reduce to or express the given body.[5] By making him no longer self-identical, it allows him the negativity of debate—not a pure negativity, not simply reason or criticism, but an identification with a disembodied public subject that he can imagine as parallel to his private person.

In a sense, however, that public subject does have a body, because the public, prosthetic body takes abuse for the private person. The last line of the passage refers to the fact that Anaxarchus was pommeled to death with iron pestles after offending a despotic ruler. In the ventriloquistic act of taking up his speech, therefore, Steele both imagines an intimate violation of his person and provides himself with a kind of prophylaxis against violation (to borrow another term from Berlant). Anaxarchus was not so lucky. Despite what Steele says, the privilege that he obtains over his body in this way does not in fact reduce to the simple body/soul distinction that Anaxarchus' speech invokes. It allows him to think of his public discourse as a routine form of self-abstraction quite unlike the ascetic self-integration of Anaxarchus. When Steele impersonates the philosopher and has the Spectator (or someone) say, "Thou dost but beat the case of Anaxarchus," he appropriates an intimate subjective benefit of publicity's self-abstraction.

Through the conventions that allowed such writing to perform the disincorporation of its authors and its readers, public discourse turned persons into a public. At points in *The Structural Transformation of the Public Sphere*, Jürgen Habermas makes a similar point. One of the great virtues of that book is the care it takes to describe the cultural-technical context in which the public of the bourgeois public sphere was consti-tuted. "In the *Tatler*, the *Spectator*, and the *Guardian* the public held up a mirror to itself. . . . The public that read and debated this sort of thing read and debated about itself."[6] It is worth remembering also that *per-sons* read and debated this sort of thing, but in reading and debating it *as* a public, they adopted a very special rhetoric about their own person-hood. Where earlier writers had typically seen the context of print as a means of personal extension—they understood themselves in print es-sentially to be speaking in their own persons—people began to see it as an authoritative mediation. That is clearly the case with the Steele pas-sage, and pseudonymous serial essays like the *Spectator* did a great deal toward normalizing a public print discourse.

In the bourgeois public sphere, which was brought into being by publication in this sense, a principle of negativity was axiomatic: the validity of what you say in public bears a negative relation to your person. What you say will carry force not because of who you are but despite who you are. Implicit in this principle is a utopian universality that would allow people to transcend the given realities of their bodies and their status. But the rhetorical strategy of personal abstraction is both the utopian moment of the public sphere and a major source of domination. For the ability to abstract oneself in public discussion has always been an unequally available resource. Individuals have to have specific rhetorics of disincorporation; they are not simply rendered bod-iless by exercising reason. And it is only possible to operate a discourse based on the claim to self-abstracting disinterestedness in a culture where such unmarked self-abstraction is a differential resource. The subject who could master this rhetoric in the bourgeois public sphere was im-plicitly, even explicitly, white, male, literate, and propertied. These traits could go unmarked, even grammatically, while other features of bodies could only be acknowledged in discourse as the humiliating positivity of the particular.

The bourgeois public sphere claimed to have no relation to the body image at all. Public issues were depersonalized so that, in theory, any person would have the ability to offer an opinion about them and submit that opinion to the impersonal test of public debate without personal hazard. Yet the bourgeois public sphere continued to rely on features of certain bodies. Access to the public came in the whiteness and maleness that were then denied as forms of positivity, since the white male qua public person was only abstract rather than white and male. The contradiction is that even while particular bodies and dispositions enabled the liberating abstraction of public discourse, those bodies also summarized the constraints of positivity, the mere case of Anaxarchus, from which self-abstraction can be liberating.

It is very far from being clear that these asymmetries of embodiment were merely contingent encumbrances to the public sphere, residual forms of illiberal "discrimination." The difference between self-abstraction and a body's positivity is more than a difference in what has officially been made available to men and to women, for example. It is a difference in the cultural/symbolic definitions of masculinity and femininity.[7] Self-abstraction from male bodies confirms masculinity. Self-abstraction from female bodies denies femininity. The bourgeois public sphere is a frame of reference in which it is supposed that all particularities have the same status as mere particularity. But the ability to establish that frame of reference is a feature of some particularities. Neither in gender nor in race nor in class nor in sexualities is it possible to treat different particulars as having merely paratactic or serial difference. Differences in such realms already come coded as the difference between the unmarked and the marked, the universalizable and the particular. Their own internal logic is such that the two sides of any of these differences cannot be treated as symmetrical—as they are, for example, in the rhetoric of liberal toleration or "debate"—without simply resecuring an asymmetrical privilege. The bourgeois public sphere has been structured from the outset by a logic of abstraction that provides a privilege for unmarked identities: the male, the white, the middle class, the normal.

That is what Pasolini meant when he wrote, just before his murder, that "tolerance is always and purely nominal":

In fact they tell the "tolerated" person to do what he wishes, that he has every right to follow his own nature, that the fact that he belongs to a minority does not in the least mean inferiority, etc. But his "difference"— or better, his "crime of being different"—remains the same both with regard to those who have decided to tolerate him and those who have decided to condemn him. No majority will ever be able to banish from its consciousness the feeling of the "difference" of minorities. I shall always be eternally, inevitably conscious of this.[8]

Doubtless it is better to be tolerated than to be killed, as Pasolini was. But it would be better still to make reference to one's marked particularities without being specified thereby as less than public. As the bourgeois public sphere paraded the spectacle of its disincorporation, it brought into being this minoritizing logic of domination. Publicness is always able to encode itself through the themes of universality, openness, meritocracy, and access, all of which derhetoricize its self-understanding, guaranteeing at every step that difference will be enunciated as mere positivity, an ineluctable limit imposed by the particularities of the body, a positivity that cannot translate or neutralize itself prosthetically without ceasing to exist. This minoritizing logic, intrinsic to the deployment of negativity in the bourgeois public sphere, presents the subjects of bodily difference with the paradox of a utopian promise that cannot be cashed in for them. The very mechanism designed to end domination is a form of domination.

The appeal of mass subjectivity, I will suggest, arises largely from the contradiction in this dialectic of embodiment and negativity in the public sphere. Public discourse from the beginning offered a utopian self-abstraction, but in ways that left a residue of unrecuperated particularity, both for its privileged subjects and for those it minoritized. Its privileged subjects, abstracted from the very body features that gave them the privilege of that abstraction, found themselves in a relation of bad faith with their own positivity. To acknowledge their positivity would be to surrender their privilege, as for example to acknowledge the objectivity of the male body would be feminizing. Meanwhile, minoritized subjects had few strategies open to them, but one was to carry their unrecuperated positivity into consumption. Even from the early eighteenth century, before the triumph of a liberal metalanguage for consumption, commodities were being used, especially by women, as a kind of access to publicness that would nevertheless link up with the specificity of difference.[9]

Consumption offered a counterutopia precisely in a balance between a collectivity of mass desires and an unminoritized rhetoric of difference in the field of choices among infinite goods. A good deal of noise in modern society comes from the inability to translate these utopian promises into a public sphere where collectivity has no link to the body and its desires, where difference is described not as the paratactic seriality of illimitable choice but as the given constraints of preconscious nature. Where consumer capitalism makes available an endlessly differentiable subject, the subject of the public sphere proper cannot be differentiated. It can represent difference as other, but as an available form of subjectivity it remains unmarked. The constitutional public sphere, therefore, cannot fully recuperate its residues. It can only display them. In this important sense, the "we" in "We the People" is the mass equivalent of the Spectator's prosthetic generality, a flexible instrument of interpellation, but one that exiles its own positivity.

From the eighteenth century we in the modern West have inherited an understanding of printing as publication, but we now understand a vast range of everyday life as having the reference of publicity. The medium of print is now only a small part of our relation to what we understand as the public, and the fictitious abstraction of the Spectator would seem conspicuously out of place in the modern discourse of public icons. So although the bourgeois public sphere continues to secure a minoritizing liberal logic of self-abstraction, its rhetoric is increasingly complicated by other forms of publicity. At present the mass-cultural public sphere continually offers its subject an array of body images. In earlier varieties of the public sphere it was important that images of the body *not* figure importantly in public discourse. The anonymity of the discourse was a way of certifying the citizen's disinterested concern for the public good. But now public body images are everywhere on display, in virtually all media contexts. Where printed public discourse formerly relied on a rhetoric of abstract disembodiment, visual media, including print, now display bodies for a range of purposes: admiration, identification, appropriation, scandal, etc. To be public in the West means to have an iconicity, and this is true equally of Qaddafi and of Karen Carpenter.

The visibility of public figures for the subject of mass culture occurs in a context in which publicity is generally mediated by the discourse of consumption. It is difficult to realize how much we observe public images with the eye of the consumer. Nearly all of our pleasures come to us coded in some degree by the publicity of mass media. We have brand names all over us. Even the most refined or the most perverse among us could point to his or her desires or identifications and see that in most cases they were public desires, even mass-public desires, from the moment that they were that person's desires. This is true not only in the case of salable commodities—our refrigerators, sneakers, lunch—but also in other areas where we make symbolic identifications in a field of choice: the way we bear our bodies, the sports we follow, or our erotic objects. In such areas our desires have become recognizable through their display in the media, and in the moment of wanting them, we imagine a collective consumer witnessing our wants and choices.

The public discourse of the mass media has increasingly come to rely on the intimacy of this collective witnessing in its rhetoric of publicity, iconic and consumerist alike. It is a significant part of the ground of public discourse, the subjective apprehension of what is public. In everyday life, for one thing, we have access to the realm of political systems in the same way that we have access to the circulation of commodities. Not only are we confronted by slogans that continually make this connection for us ("America wears Hanes," "The heartbeat of America"); more important, the contexts of commodities and politics share the same media and, at least in part, the same metalanguage for constructing our notion of what a public or a people is. When the citizen (or noncitizen—for contemporary publicity the difference hardly matters) goes down to the 7–Eleven to buy a Budweiser and a Barbie Magazine and scans from the news headlines to the tabloid stories about the Rob Lowe sex scandal, several kinds of publicity are involved at once. Nevertheless, it is possible to speak of all these sites of publicity as parts of a public sphere, insofar as each is capable of illuminating the others in a common discourse of the subject's relation to the nation and its markets.

In each of these mediating contexts of publicity we become the mass-public subject, but in a new way unanticipated within the classical bourgeois public sphere. Moreover, if mass-public subjectivity has a kind of singularity, an undifferentiated extension to indefinite numbers of individuals, those individuals who make up the "we" of the mass public subject might have very different relations to it. It is at the very moment of recognizing ourselves as the mass subject, for example, that we also recognize ourselves as minority subjects. As participants in the mass subject, we are the "we" that can describe our particular affiliations of class, gender, sexual orientation, race, or subculture only as "they." This self-alienation is common to all of the contexts of publicity, but it can be variously interpreted within each. The political meaning of the public subject's self-alienation is one of the most important sites of struggle in contemporary culture.

• • •

Self-Abstraction and the Mass Subject

Part of the bad faith of the *res publica* of letters was that it required a denial of the bodies that gave access to it. The public sphere is still enough oriented to its liberal logic that its citizens long to abstract themselves into a privileged public disembodiment. And when that fails, they can turn to another kind of longing, which, as Lauren Berlant shows, is not so much to cancel out their bodies as to trade in for a better model. The mass public sphere tries to minimize the difference between the two, surrounding the citizen with trademarks through which she can trade marks, offering both positivity and self-abstraction. This has meant, furthermore, that the mass public sphere has had to develop genres of collective identification that will articulate both sides of this dialectic.

Insofar as the two sides are contradictory, however, mass identification tends to be characterized by what I earlier called noise, which typically appears as an erotic-aggressive disturbance. Here it might be worth thinking about a genre in which the display of bodies is also a kind of disembodiment: the discourse of disasters. At least since the great Chicago fire, mass disaster has had a special relationship to the mass media. Mass injury can always command a headline; it gets classed as immediate-reward news. But whatever kind of reward makes disaster rewarding, it evidently has to do with injury to a *mass* body—an already abstracted body assembled by the simultaneity of the disaster somewhere other than here. When massive numbers of separate injuries occur, they fail to command the same fascination. This discrepancy in how seriously we take different organizations of injury is a source of never ending frustration for airline executives. They never tire of pointing out that, although the fatality rate for automobiles is astronomically higher than for airplanes, there is no public panic of supervision about automobiles. In the airline executives' interested exasperation, that seems merely to prove the irrationality of journalists and congressmen. But I think this fondness of the mass media for a very special kind of injury makes rigorous sense. Disaster is popular because it is a way of making mass subjectivity available, and it tells us something about the desirability of that mass subject.

John Waters tells us in *Shock Value* that one of his hobbies in youth was collecting disaster coverage. His all-time favorite photograph, he claims, is a famous shot of the stadium collapsing at the Indianapolis 500, a photograph he proudly reproduces. But despite his pride in the aura of perversion that surrounds this disclosure, he is at some pains to point out that his pleasure is a normal feature of the discourse. "It makes the newspapers worth the quarter," he writes, and "perks up the local news shows." What could be the dynamic of this link between injury and the pleasures of mass publicity? Waters stages the intimacy of the link in the following story about his childhood, in what I think of as a brilliant corruption of Freud's *fort/da* game:

> Even as a toddler, violence intrigued me. . . . While other kids were out playing cowboys and Indians, I was lost in fantasies of crunching metal and people screaming for help. I would sweet-talk unsuspecting relatives into buying me toy cars—any kind, as long as they were new and shiny. . . . I would take two cars and pretend they were driving on a secluded country road until one would swerve and crash into the other. I would become quite excited and start smashing the car with a hammer, all the while shouting, "Oh, my God, there's been a terrible accident!"[10]

Exactly what kind of pleasure is this? It isn't just the infantile recuperation of power that the *fort/da* game usually represents. The boy Waters, in other words, is not just playing out identification and revenge in the rhythm of treasuring and destroying the cars.

Nor is Waters simply indulging the infantile transitivism of which Lacan writes: "The child who strikes another says that he has been struck; the child who sees another fall, cries."[11] In fact, Waters's pleasure in the scene seems to have little to do with the cars at all. Rather, it comes about largely through his identification with publicity. Not only does Waters have access to auto disaster in the first place through the public discourse of news; he dramatizes that discourse as part of the event. Whose voice does he take up in exclaiming, "Oh, my God, there's been a terrible accident!"? And just as important, to whom is he speaking? He turns himself into a relay of spectators, none of whom are injured so much as horrified by the witnessing of injury. His ventriloquized announcer and his invisible audience allow him to internalize an absent witness. He has been careful to imagine the cars as being on "a secluded country road," so that his imaginary audience can be anywhere *else*. It is, in effect, the mass subject of news.

In this sense, the story shows us how deeply publicity has come to inform our subjectivity. But it also reveals, through Waters's camp humor, that the mass subject's absent witnessing is a barely concealed transitivism. The disaster audience finds its body with a revenge. Its surface is all sympathy: there's been a terrible accident. The sympathetic quality of its identification, however, is only half the story since, as Waters knows, inflicting and witnessing mass injury are two sides of the same dynamic in disaster discourse. Being of necessity anywhere else, the mass subject cannot have a body except the body it witnesses. But in order to become a mass subject it has left that body behind, abstracted away from it, canceled it as mere positivity. It returns in the spectacle of big-time injury. The transitive pleasure of witnessing/injuring makes available our translation into the disembodied publicity of the mass subject. By injuring a mass body—preferably a really massive body, somewhere—we constitute ourselves as a noncorporeal mass witness. (I do not, however, mean to minimize Waters's delirious perverseness in spelling out this link between violence and spectatorship in mass subjectivity. The perverse acknowledgment of his pleasure, in fact, helps him to violate in return the minoritizing disembodiment of the mass subject. It therefore allows Waters a counter-public embodied knowledge in the mode of camp.) The same logic informs an astonishing number of mass publicity's genres, from the prophylaxes of horror, assassination, and terrorism, to the organized prosthesis of sports. (But, as Waters writes, "Violence in sports always seemed so pointless, because everyone was prepared, so what fun could it possibly be?"[12]) The mass media are dominated by genres that construct the mass subject's impossible relation to a body.

In the genres of mass-imaginary transitivism, we might say, a public is thinking about itself and its media. This is true even in the most vulgar of the discourses of mass publicity, the tabloid pasttime of star puncturing. In the figures of Elvis, Liz, Michael, Oprah, Geraldo, Brando, and the like, we witness and transact the bloating, slimming, wounding, and general humiliation of the public body. The bodies of these public figures are prostheses for our own mutant desirability. That is not to say that a mass imaginary identification is deployed with uniform or equal effect in each of these cases. A significant subgenre of tabloid publicity, for instance, is devoted not to perforating the iconic bodies of its male stars but rather to denying them any private power behind their iconic bodies. Johnny Carson, Clint Eastwood, Rob Lowe, and others like them are subjected to humiliating forms of display not for gaining weight or having cosmetic surgery but for failing to exercise full control over their lives. By chronicling their endless romantic/matrimonial disasters, publicity keeps them available for our appropriation of their iconic status by reminding us that they do not possess the phallic power of their images— we do.

In this respect, we would have to say that Ronald Reagan stands in partial contrast to these other male icons of publicity. He does not require a discourse of star puncturing because he seems to make no personal claim on the phallic power of his own image. His body, impossible to embarrass, has no private subject behind it. The gestures stay the same, undisturbed by reflection or management. Reagan never gives a sense of modulation between a public and private self, and he therefore remains immune to humiliation. That is why it was so easy for news reports to pry into his colon without indiscretion. His witless self-continuity is the modern equivalent of virtue. He is the perfect example of what Lefort calls the egocrat: he coincides with himself and therefore concretizes a fantasy-image of the unitary people. He is popularity with a hairdo, an image of popularity's popularity.

The presentation of Reagan's body was an important part of his performance of popularity. J. G. Ballard understood that as early as 1969 in a story entitled "Why I Want to Fuck Ronald Reagan." In that story every subject of publicity is said to share the secret but powerful fantasy of violating Reagan's anus. In sharing that fantasy, Ballard suggests, we demonstrate the same thing that we demonstrate as consumers of the Kennedy assassination: the erotics of a mass imaginary. Like Waters's perverse transitivism, Ballard's generalized sadistic star cult theorizes the public sphere and ironizes it at the same time. His characters, especially in *Crash*, are obsessed with a violent desire for the icons of publicity. But theirs is not a private pathology. Their longing to dismember and be dismembered with Ronald Reagan or Elizabeth Taylor is understood as a more reflective version of these public icons' normal appeal. In the modern nations of the West, individuals encounter in publicity the erotics of a powerful identification not just with public icons but also with their popularity.

It's important to stress, given the outcome of such a metapopularity in the realm of policy, that the utopian moments in consumer publicity have an unstable political valence. Responding to an immanent contradiction in the bourgeois public sphere, mass publicity promises a reconciliation between embodiment and self-abstraction. That can be a powerful appeal, especially to those minoritized by the public sphere's rhetoric of normative disembodiment. Mass subjectivity, however, can result just as easily in new forms of tyranny of the majority as it can in the claims of rival collectivities. Perhaps the clearest example now is the discourse on AIDS. As Simon Watney and others have shown, one of the most hateful features of AIDS discourse has been its construction of a "general public."[13] A spokesman for the White House, asked why Ronald Reagan had not even mentioned the word "AIDS" or its problems until late in 1985, explained, "It hadn't spread into the general population yet."[14] In pursuit of a public demanded by good professional journalism, the mass media have pursued the same logic, interpellating their public as unitary and as heterosexual. Moreover, they have deployed the transitivism of mass identification in order to exile the positivity of the body to a zone of infection; the unitary public is uninfected but threatened. In this context, it is heartbreakingly accurate to speak of the prophylaxis held out by mass publicity to those who will identify with its immunized body.

Hateful though it is to those exiled into positivity by such a discourse, in a sense everyone's relation to the public body must have more or less the same logic. No one really inhabits the general public. This is true not only because it is by definition general but also because everyone brings to such a category the particularities from which they have to abstract themselves in consuming this discourse. Of course, some particularities, such as whiteness and maleness, are already oriented to that procedure of abstraction. (They can scarcely even be imagined as particularities; think for example of the asymmetry between the semantics of "feminism" and "masculinism.") But the given of the body is nevertheless a site of countermemory, all the more so since statistically everyone will be mapped into some minority or other, a form of positivity minoritized precisely in the abstracting discourse with which everyone also identifies.

So in this sense, the gap that gay people register within the discourse of the general public might well be an aggravated form, though a lethally aggravated form, of the normal relation to the general public. I'm suggesting, in other words, that a fundamental feature of the contemporary public sphere is this double movement of identification and alienation:

on one hand, the prophylaxis of general publicity; on the other hand, the always inadequate particularity of individual bodies, experienced both as an invisible desire within a visible body and, in consequence, as a kind of closeted vulnerability. The centrality of this contradiction in the legitimate textuality of the video-capitalist state, I think, is the reason why the discourse of the public sphere is so entirely given over to a violently desirous speculation on bodies. What I have tried to emphasize is that the effect of disturbance in mass publicity is not a corruption introduced into the public sphere by its colonization through mass media. It is the legacy of the bourgeois public sphere's founding logic, the contradictions of which become visible whenever the public sphere can no longer turn a blind eye to its privileged bodies.

For the same reasons, the public sphere is also not simply corrupted by its articulation with consumption. If anything, consumption sustains a counterpublicity that cuts against the self-contradictions of the bourgeois public sphere. One final example can show how. In recent years, graffiti writing has taken a new form. Always a kind of counterpublicity, it has become the medium of an urban and mostly black male subculture. The major cities each devote millions of dollars per year to obliterate it, and to criminalize it as a medium, while the art, world moves to canonize it out of its counterpublic setting. In a recent article Susan Stewart argues that the core of the graffiti writers' subculture lies in the way it has taken up the utopian promise of consumer publicity, and particularly of the brand name. These graffiti do not say "U.S. out of North America," or "Patriarch go home," or "Power to the queer nation"; they are personal signatures legible only to the intimately initiated. Reproduced as quickly and as widely as possible (unlike their canonized art equivalents), they are trademarks that can be spread across a nearly anonymous landscape. The thrill of brand name dissemination, however, is linked to a very private sphere of knowledge, since the signature has been trademarked into illegibility. Stewart concludes,

> Graffiti may be a petty crime but its threat to value is an inventive one, for it forms a critique of the status of all artistic artifacts, indeed a critique of all privatized consumption, and it carries out that threat in full view, in repetition, so that the public has nowhere to look, no place to locate an averted glance. And that critique is paradoxically mounted from a relentless individualism, an individualism which, with its perfected monogram, arose out of the paradox of all commodity relations in their attempt to

create a mass individual; an ideal consumer; a necessarily fading star. The independence of the graffiti writer has been shaped by a freedom both promised and denied by those relations—a freedom of choice which is a freedom among delimited and clearly unattainable goods. While that paradise of consumption promised the transference of uniqueness from the artifact to the subject, graffiti underlines again and again an imaginary uniqueness of the subject and a dissolution of artifactual status *per se*.[15]

The graffiti of this subculture, in effect, parodies the mass media; by appearing everywhere, it aspires to the placeless publicity of mass print or televisualization. It thus abstracts away from the given body, which in the logic of graffiti is difficult to criminalize or minoritize because it is impossible to locate. ("Nowhere to look, no place to locate an averted glance" exactly describes the abstraction of televisualized space.) Unlike the self-abstraction of normal publicity, however, graffiti retains its link to a body in an almost parodic devotion to the sentimentality of the signature. As Stewart points out, it claims an imaginary uniqueness promised in commodities but canceled in the public sphere proper. Whenever mass publicity puts its bodies on display, it reactivates this same promise. And although emancipation is not around the corner, its possibility is visible everywhere.

Obviously, the discursive genres of mass publicity vary widely. I group them together to show how they become interconnected as expressing a subjectivity that each genre helps to construct. In such contexts the content and the media of mass publicity mutually determine each other. Mass media thematize certain materials—a jet crash, Michael Jackson's latest surgery, or a football game—to find a way of constructing their audiences as mass audiences. These contents then function culturally as metalanguages, giving meaning to the medium. In consuming the thematic materials of mass-media discourse, persons construct themselves as its mass subject. Thus the same reciprocity that allowed the *Spectator* and its print medium to be mutually clarifying can be seen in the current mass media. But precisely because the meaning of the mass media depends so much on their articulation with a specific metalanguage, we cannot speak simply of one kind of mass subjectivity or one politics of mass publicity. Stewart makes roughly the same observation when she remarks that the intrication of graffiti, as a local practice, with the systemic themes of access—"access to discourse, access to goods, access to the reception of information"—poses a methodological problem, "calling into question the relations between a micro- and a macro-analysis: the insinuating and pervasive forms of the mass culture are here known only through localizations and adaptations."[16]

Nevertheless, some things are clear. In a discourse of publicity structured by deep contradictions between self-abstraction and self-realization, contradictions that have only been forced to the fore in televisual consumer culture, there has been a massive shift toward the politics of identity. The major political movements of the last half century have been oriented toward status categories. Unlike almost all previous social movements—Chartism, Temperance, or the French Revolution—they have been centrally about the personal identity formation of minoritized subjects. These movements all presuppose the bourgeois public sphere as background. Their rallying cries of difference take for granted the official rhetoric of self-abstraction. It would be naive and sentimental to suppose that identities or mere assertions of status will precipitate from this crisis as its solution, since the public discourse makes identity an ongoing problem. An assertion of the full equality of minoritized statuses would require abandoning the structure of self-abstraction in publicity. That outcome seems unlikely in the near future. In the meantime, the contradictions of status and publicity are played out at both ends of the public discourse. We, as the subjects of mass publicity, ever more find a political stake in the difficult-to-recognize politics of our identity, and the egocrats who fill the screens of national fantasy must summon all their skin and hair to keep that politics from getting personal.

NOTES

1. Claude Lefort, "The Image of the Body and Totalitarianism," in his *Political Forms of Modern Society,* ed. John B. Thompson (Cambridge: MIT Press, 1986), p. 306.

2. J. G. Ballard, *Love and Napalm: Export U.S.A.* (New York: Grove Press, 1972), pp. 149–151.

3. The arguments condensed here can be found in full form in *The Letters of the Republic: Publication and the Public Sphere in Eighteenth-Century America* (Cambridge: Harvard Univ. Press, 1990).

4. [Richard Steele], *Spectator,* no. 555, in Angus Ross, ed., *Selections from the Tatler and the Spectator* (New York: Penguin, 1982), p. 213.

5. Lauren Berlant, "National Brands/National Body: *Imitation of Life,*" Hor-

tense Spillers, ed., *Comparative American Identities* (New York: Routledge, 1990), pp. 110–140.

6. Jürgen Habermas, *The Structural Transformation of the Public Sphere* (Cambridge: MIT Press, 1989), p. 43.

7. The point here about the character of gender difference has been a common one since de Beauvoir's *The Second Sex* (1949); its more recent extension to an analysis of the bourgeois public sphere is in Joan Landes, *Women and the Public Sphere in the Age of the French Revolution* (Ithaca: Cornell Univ. Press, 1988).

8. Pier Paolo Pasolini, *Lutheran Letters,* quoted in Douglas Crimp, "Strategies of Public Address: Which Media, Which Publics?" *Discussions in Contemporary Culture,* vol. 1, ed. Hal Foster (Seattle: Bay Press, 1987), p. 33.

9. Timothy Breen, "Baubles of Britain," *Past and Present* 119 (May 1988): 73–104.

10. John Waters, *Shock Value* (New York: Dell, 1981), p. 24.

11. "Aggressivity in Psychoanalysis," *Ecrits,* trans. Alan Sheridan (New York: Norton, 1977), p. 19.

12. Waters, *Shock Value,* p. 26.

13. Simon Watney, *Policing Desire: Pornography, AIDS, and the Media* (Minneapolis: Univ. of Minnesota Press, 1987), pp. 83–84 and passim.

14. Jan Zita Grover, "AIDS: Keywords," *October* 43 (1987): 23. This issue has since been reprinted as *AIDS: Cultural Analysis, Cultural Activism,* ed. Douglas Crimp (Cambridge MIT Press, 1988).

15. Susan Stewart, "Ceci Tuera Cela: Graffiti as Crime and Art," in John Fekete, ed., *Life after Postmodernism: Essays on Value and Culture* (New York: St. Martin's, 1987), pp. 175–176.

16. Stewart, "Ceci Tuera Cela," p. 163.

Chapter 10

Traditional Narrative
Contemporary Uses, Historical Perspectives

Elaine A. Jahner

Introduction by Arnold Krupat

Although Native American literatures still remain the red sheep, as it were, of the multicultural, diversity-university, it is fortunately the case that since the early 1990s, more (and more sophisticated) critiques of Native poetry, fiction, and autobiography written in English have begun to appear. But few literary scholars have turned their attention to the texts that derive from *oral traditions*—texts, that is to say, that are transcriptions and translations of stories, songs, chants, and speeches historically, and in many cases presently, *performed* in indigenous languages. Elaine A. Jahner notes "the important specialized work of the last two decades of Dell Hymes, Dennis Tedlock, Karl Kroeber, Donald Bahr, Paul Zolbrod, Barre Toelken, William Bright, Julian Rice, and Julie Cruikshank" with such materials. Of these scholars, only Kroeber, Zolbrod, and Rice are from literary studies, and their work is deeply informed by the disciplines of their colleagues.[1] Jahner's own methodology bases itself upon broad interdisciplinary competencies that include historical and ethnographic learning, as well as a multidimensional (for example, Lakota language, sociolinguistics, and discourse analysis) linguistic capability.[2]

Jahner's analysis of Lakota Stone Boy stories begins with a consideration (drawn from prior work with the Greeks, the European Middle Ages, and small-scale societies around the world) of the various functions of narrative in Native American cultures. In addition to providing entertainment, narrative also serves to instruct and (re)confirm its audience's sense of collective identity. This latter function of narrative may be of particular importance inasmuch as Native peoples remain in the paradoxical condition described by Chief Justice John Marshall when, in 1832, he referred to the tribes as "domestic dependent nations." The paradox of dependent sovereignty—sovereign nations are typically independent; sovereignty and independence are virtually synonymous—has produced the politics of sovereignty in which Native nations attempt to recuperate greater measures of independence from federal and state governments. In order to do this, it has often been necessary for tribes or nations (the terms are synonymous in the United States, although not in Africa) to demonstrate their coherent integrity as communities or collectivities. Euro-American institutions require this demonstration to be based upon historical documents, insofar as they have been preserved: treaties, deeds, records of births, deaths, marriages, and the like. But, as Jahner shows, narrative texts may also be entered into the record as evidence of communal coherence.

The genre or group of narratives Jahner focuses upon, Lakota Stone Boy stories, are especially interesting for her purposes because of their status as "origin stories" of a particular kind. Stone Boy stories, that is, do not so much tell how the world was made, as they tell how a culture became itself. They are foundational narratives in that they dramatize for a community its historical specificity or collective identity. Thus, the Constitution of the United States, in an example Jahner gives, serves as an origin story for Americans. One might also, in this regard, consider Lincoln's Gettysburg Address as an origin story, but one that reinscribes the narrative of the Declaration of Independence rather than that of the Constitution as central to who "we" Americans are.

Jahner's interdisciplinary method pays close attention to both the literary and social components of Stone Boy narratives; for her, the literary and the social are complementary and in no way at odds. To offer one example of her interdisciplinary and multifocused method of reading, we can turn to Jahner's emphasis on the fact that the mysterious woman who arrives at the beginning of all versions of Stone Boy stories is welcomed as a potential *sister* rather than a potential wife. In examining many of these stories, Claude Lévi-Strauss, founder and foremost practitioner of an ahistorical structural anthropology, concluded that "the woman's role is ambiguous"; she could be a sister, or a potential wife, or even play the role of a grandmother. While this ambiguity may be present at the level of theory, Jahner's ethnographic knowledge of Lakota culture allows her to affirm that it is not true at the level of actual practice. The story as told in local Lakota communities, she notes, places a special emphasis on the role of the sister, an emphasis that "is a western Sioux development." In a sense, then, in answer to the question, Who are the western Sioux? one might answer, That group of narrators and auditors who begin their Stone Boy stories with the arrival of a woman welcomed as a sister.[3] Such an answer—deriving from a particular sort of attention to a particular group of traditional narratives—is not only pertinent to the politics of sovereignty, but also to the cumulative body of ethnographic data "about Lakota social organization and gender roles." Further, Jahner's "close reading" throughout is of a type that has marked specifically literary analysis—a practice that should prevent us from forgetting that Stone Boy stories, in addition to their social and political functions, are, as literary narratives, aesthetically pleasing to Lakota people.

NOTES

1. Bahr, Cruikshank, Hymes, and Tedlock are anthropologists; Bright is a linguist; and Toelken a folklorist—and all are particularly interested in Native verbal expression, or to use the conventional oxymoron, *oral literature*.

2. It is worth pointing out that grammars, dictionaries, exercise books, both in print and via computer software, for learning any one of a number of Native languages are currently more abundant and more available than in years past. An interested student *can* presently find the materials for learning Lakota or Navajo or Mohawk.

3. In the same way one might answer the question, Who are the Americans? by saying, They are a community that believes that all men are created equal, and the government of the people, by the people, and for the people shall not perish from earth.

No story or song will translate the full impact of falling
or the inverse power of rising up.
—Joy Harjo, "A Postcolonial Tale"

KARL KROEBER'S new book *Artistry in Native American Myths* reminds us that the study and teaching of traditional oral narratives represent what is possibly the most complex and yet the most promising aspect of American Indian Studies. The complexities derive from two primary issues. First, traditional status generally implies performance restrictions

From *Studies in American Indian Literatures* 11:2 (Summer 1999). Reprinted by permission of the author.

related to patterns of communal authority and these sometimes prohibit presentation to a general audience. Secondly, even for those texts deemed appropriate for audiences outside the community of origin, we have so little reliable interpretive material that discussion of a narrative's significance easily strays into formalistic rigidities, bland generalities or private appreciation, although books like Kroeber's have been of significant help in countering these tendencies. As we expand the body of commentary on oral literary texts, we inevitably question the history of our discipline and the history of the texts we study, with the latter being by far the more difficult to address. Even some of the simplest narratives show such intriguing traces of ancient sources that anyone sensitive to the compulsions of the past gets drawn into speculations about historical understandings of a text. Yet the move from present observation of a narrative's status to historical reconstruction of its past significance is one that the intellectually cautious recognize as a perilous exercise even though the exigencies of current politics add their considerable weight to sheer historical curiosity and imaginative delight as arguments for facing up to the task.

Educators at all levels seem to be in agreement over the need for more consistently organized ongoing collective efforts that would help us use the important specialized work of the last two decades, such as that of Dell Hymes, Dennis Tedlock, Karl Kroeber, Donald Bahr, Paul Zolbrod, Barre Toelken, William Bright, Julian Rice and Julie Cruikshank, most of whom quite sensibly base most of their analyses on texts that they themselves have collected and have seen performed. Christopher Vecsey in his book *Imagine Ourselves Richly* competently surveys the many academic approaches to the study of oral literatures and he illustrates the first stages of comparative historical analysis that ethnologists and linguists made possible earlier this century through their extensive recording of texts from all over the continent. If we engage in some sheer wishful thinking, freed just for the moment from our usual concerns about practical difficulties, we can take our cue from the title of Vecsey's book and imagine our subdiscipline richly, with different communities (academic or political) implementing the best that can be learned from each of the scholars mentioned above and also from the less well-known ones not listed in my abbreviated disciplinary roster, who have certainly done their own important ground-breaking work. As long as we are just imagining, we can plan to use all this impressive scholarly detail with the pedagogical awareness and immediacy that Greg Sarris talks about in his final chapters of *Keeping Slug Woman Alive.* And we should definitely imagine tapping into the power that characterizes the writings of poets and novelists so that critical discussions can become explicit demonstrations of attitudes toward language that we have learned from them. Finally, we need to link up with the developing intellectual debates led by people like Robert Warrior and Jace Weaver.

Such unbridled imagination in relation to research and pedagogy has a definite, practical purpose because only idealistically bold envisaging of what might be possible will keep alive our vision of collective opportunities. But sooner rather than later, we have to return to the practical matters we had briefly set aside in favor of letting a vision of possibilities emerge. What follows here is one kind of mapping within a general framework that could allow us to situate the more specialized endeavors in reference to each other and in relation to extra-literary issues as part of an effort to open the critical discussion to a broader range of voices and positions. I am also setting up some tentative but precisely informed moves into historical analysis in the second part of this article where I illustrate how elements of one tale represent links in the associative networks of meaning, inferential presuppositions and artistic strategies that we still call "culture" even as we question virtually all the term has meant in the past.

Generalities are easy enough to come by. It is more difficult to justify them within the cross-currents of debates about the aims of cultural analysis and the appropriate authority of any given analyst. That is why my initial general proposals and the subsequent detailed illustration occur within my own adaptations of the framework set forth by Brian Stock in his 1990 book *Listening for the Text: On the Uses of the Past.*[1] Stock's work is well-known in the field of Medieval Studies. My reasons for bringing it into American Indian narrative studies are primarily strategic. The last fifty years have resulted in so much theorizing about textuality and culture in so many disciplines that situating oneself within the general field requires some careful mapping, hence my use of Stock's work as a practical strategy for keeping my own theoretical digressions to an absolute minimum while recognizing that theoretically informed alertness to abstract disciplinary formations is an indispensable backdrop to our work. Stock's initial observations sum up the current situation in American Indian Studies as effectively as they characterize other contexts. "The oralities and literacies of the past," he says, "are regularly made the subject of inquiries by linguists, philosophers, theologians, anthropologists and historians. But there is no common methodology, and the methods developed in one discipline are not always recognized in others" (141).

Stock may be underestimating the cross-disciplinary utility of developments in discourse analysis which address cognitive process in relation to narrative structure, but that does not take away from the value of his strategies for studying the historical development of textual communities.[2] For all its apparent simplicity, his approach to textual communities involves a focus on the local community within a general perspective that accommodates well-articulated, slight shifts in the positions of several of the century's leading thinkers, while remaining quickly recognizable in terms of what we are already doing in relation to American Indian narratives. A textual community is "a group in which there is both a script and a spoken enactment and in which social cohesion and meaning result from the interaction of the two" (100). The "script" is the problematic notion here, not because of the oral/written dichotomy but because of what it implies about a community's uses of texts to constitute communal identity and because of the difficulties in understanding the history of that usage. What I propose here is necessarily and definitely a departure from what medievalists do and from what most folklorists and anthropologists have been doing with archived texts, although Dennis Tedlock pointed the way with his first published work on Zuni dynamics of textual interpretation.[3] I propose an approach to cultural thinking that allows us to work with a generically diverse body of narratives in relation to other cultural artifacts from a definite historical period. Transcriptions of texts will necessarily have varying degrees of validity as a consequence of collection procedures. Nevertheless, we can compensate to some extent through the manner in which we use a range of different narratives and other cultural artifacts so that they become commentaries on each other and thereby reveal some verifiable elements of a historical interpretive dynamic.

What makes this general approach so useful is the explicit focus on social cohesion and meaning as deriving from a continuing interactional dynamic. Therefore, our critical concern is with that dynamic. Without getting too far sidetracked by all that is implied by a philosophically overdetermined term like "meaning," I want to quote Stock's carefully reasoned position, one to which I will return when I begin to address the place of custom in relation to our commentary on definite texts and their history within communities. Stock addresses the interpenetration of text and behavior:

> Meaning comes first. A text, proposed by one member of a group, is understood by others in a similar way . . . one text has given rise to another, the second being a combination of the original and an interpretation. It is the second that influences behavior. . . . We understand ourselves, Ricoeur correctly notes, "by the long detour of signs of humanity deposited in cultural works." Yet there are still longer detours: for example, the manner in which our preexisting values, sense of meaning, and education are shaped by experience, or the manner in which memory, reminiscence, and the unconscious play out roles in our everyday lives, compelling us, as Freud stresses, to enact dramas whose ultimate meaning may be hidden from us. (109)

The assumption that narrative works to generate social cohesion by enacting the cognitive principles that grant coherence to relations among changing variables is one of those givens of social theory that only becomes useful through tracing the concrete effects of its development. In an American Indian context, the politics of dependent sovereignty give a definite pragmatic edge to the need to develop methods of historically precise documentation for a process of maintaining distinctive textual communities.[4] And, as we all know only too well, precise documentation is considerably complicated by the nature of the historical records. Therefore, we can start (have, in fact, already started) by asking a series of elementary questions, documenting our answers and going from there to other kinds of studies. What kinds of texts currently function in this manner? How do different textual communities achieve overlapping boundaries so that individuals can claim membership in more than one? What kinds of communal agreements create the pragmatic conditions that enable a group to function as a narrating community? That last question points to the originary authority of local communities and the processes of self-reflection that sustain communities. We always have to go back to that local base.

• • •

Legal questions of sovereignty are all, to some degree, questions about the boundaries of communities that maintain distinctive identities by way of reference to distinctive origins. Here I am not necessarily referring only, or even primarily, to historical or geographical origins. I am using the concept of origins in its philosophical and in its legal sense to refer to a specific symbolic economy with verifiable social consequences. Such usage allows us to connect many different kinds of analysis back to the political context of debates over sovereignty and a community's own means of determining the dynamics of inclusion and exclusion. And I turn to a legal scholar to make the necessary connections between narrative analysis, communal boundaries and legal studies. His observations are so staggering in their implications that they more than make the case for any abstract claims that I, using various scholars, may be advancing about the utility of working with the idea of textual communities.

Milner S. Ball, a professor of American constitutional law, has analyzed the American constitution, the origin narrative for American civil rights, from the perspective of Indian land claims and his astonishingly honest conclusion is a call to interpretive legal action, a fact he clearly recognizes. "The American story of origins fundamentally excludes tribes and denies them voice.... I hope I am wrong" (2300).[5] His response is radical indeed. He argues for revisions of American constitutional law that would allow for inclusion of "multiple concepts of origin in legal paradigms." Undoubtedly, experts in constitutional law can and would find many ways to challenge this idealistic proposal. But whether or not any such fundamental change in constitutional interpretation ever occurs, the fact that he has articulated his arguments opens the way for lesser claims that can turn on a court's understanding of what the term "origins" signifies. Therefore, a constitutional lawyer's choice of how to demonstrate origins turns out to have considerable practical interest for all of us in American Indian Studies.

. . .

The implied conjunction between legal analysis of narrative and ethnographic studies gives a definite, pragmatic focus to studies of textual communities, using the term "pragmatic" in its narrow linguistic as well as its broader philosophical senses, with the narrow linguistic focus referring to the verifiable features of meaning controlling a context of interpretation. Whether we start with an example of traditional art or a tale, we have to demonstrate how that example reflects both symbolic foundations and a history of changing interpretations. Whatever example of expressive culture is designated as "originary" in a legal sense must be one that also exists as evidence of a contemporary textual community. Therefore, the authority of the local community is the deciding factor in making that selection from among the material or verbal artifacts of history. The selection process, itself, becomes an exercise in sovereignty and it implies an educational process whereby the local community achieves its own critical understanding of what can be accomplished through the self-reflexive activity that is the concomitant of critical thought.

With all these possibilities in mind, we can return to Stock's characterizations of the dynamic involving texts and the historical consequences of that process which distinguishes one community from another. "The normal hermeneutic activity is the experience of the text along with individual interpretations. In the textual community . . . there is a similar process at work, but here the interpretive variants are derived from thought and life, the forms of life having the same spontaneity as verbal glosses on a written text. Each community creates its culture, subjectively perceiving and objectively constructing new texts" (111–112).

Documenting various facets of this process is a task for which we, as a subdiscipline, have already developed rigorous and appropriate techniques. The task is well begun, but now we need to recruit more members if we are to study not just a text in context, but multiple texts interacting in the same context, all of them adding a dimension of significance to the others, each dimension attesting to the historical status of ideas at work in a particular place. How we might achieve an agreed-upon division of organized labors is a discussion that goes well beyond my purposes in this article, but my proposal here is that one currently neglected facet of the task involves the study of archived texts, most of them collected at the end of the nineteenth century and the beginning of the twentieth. Flawed though these texts may be, separated from most of the necessary contextual data, they nevertheless represent a window to the past, and in conjunction with currently vital texts that are their own kind of commentary on the older versions, these remnants are crucial elements of intellectual traditions.

With that observation I move from general schemes to the concrete detailing of a process whereby texts and "forms of life" comment on each other, generating new texts and keeping ancient texts in living relation to historical destinies. For illustrative purposes I am using a Lakota text, namely the Stone Boy story, which I have studied, translated, taught, and just plain puzzled over for more than thirty years now, and to which I keep returning out of a genuine sense of responsibility to the extraordinary range and evocative power of this tale.[6] But my reasons for coming back to the tale go well beyond the subjective facts of long familiarity and interest in it. The most convincing reason for using this particular text is that some of its episodes have an unbroken history of performance in Lakota communities.[7] Therefore, we have transcriptions that allow us to compare texts recorded in different Sioux communities. Also, the plot type has wide intertribal distribution so we can also engage in more broadly based comparisons as we try to discern which elements indicate a specifically Lakota symbolic economy.[8] The way this tale sums up features of belief proves it to be an origin tale in every sense of that term. It exhibits the generative cognitive principles that lie at the origins of the symbolic system and its event structure prefigures the articulation of these same principles in the social system and in ceremonial act, so we have a good body of concrete evidence about the way received narrative forms were used and adapted historically. When Lakota people claim this tale as evidence of the connection between their way of life and their landscape, they are making a claim that narrative analysis supports as historically legitimate. What I illustrate here is only one facet of the text's significance, only one set of conjunctions between narrative action and social understanding; therefore, a plot summary is enough to allow me to make my initial points even as I recognize how little such summary suggests about the nature of the text in question.

Four brothers live together. One day a woman comes to their tipi and just stands there. They discuss her presence, decide that she will be their elder sister and invite her in. She brings with her a large bag. They offer her food but she refuses to eat. All but the youngest brother go out for the day's work. Then the youngest turns into a bird in order to observe the woman. She opens her bag and takes out what is needed for her gruesome art of placing heads on a shield. He overhears her talk about how the brothers' hair will find their place in the design she is crafting, and he warns his brothers that their new elder sister is up to no good. They try to escape and one by one she kills all but the youngest, who follows the advice of a bird about how to kill her. Then he brings his brothers back to life in a sweat lodge. They return home. Soon, another woman arrives. In spite of their nervousness about women who come from outside to stand at their doorway, they proceed just as they had done the first time. This woman eats when she is given food; she opens her bag and starts making moccasins for the brothers. She is the perfect

elder sister. But she also adds new elements to the household requirements, and when the brothers go off to bring her what she needs, they
do not return. The sister fears that they have been killed. As she sings a
mourning dirge, she looks for something to suck on and finds a shiny
white pebble that she puts in her mouth and accidentally swallows. Stone
Boy is born. When he grows up, he asks why she grieves and when he
learns of his absent uncles, he sets out on an obstacle-ridden journey to
find them and gain their release from his father. Grandmother figures
give him the necessary powers. After struggling for the lives of his uncles
(in one extraordinary version this struggle is with his father), he brings
the brothers back to their sister, his mother. Then occurs the episode in
which Stone Boy rides a sled downhill, placing himself behind four white
buffalo girls. On the way down the hill, he crushes the girls, provoking
their father the Crazy Buffalo to attack him. To ward off the attacking
buffalo, Stone Boy builds four concentric palisades around the tipi. The
buffalo break all but the last before admitting that Stone Boy's is the
greater power and that the buffalo will subject themselves to it.

Most versions of the story end at this point, but one telling postscript
given by Left Heron ends the episode with a commentary that gives us a
rare and extraordinary historical commentary on how people understood the tale.

> The woman who is not a wife, but is a mother, goes to the sky, not as a
> wife but as a sister. Jack Rabbit and Eagle came and said [to Stone Boy]
> "You are too powerful" and prayed for him to leave the earth. [Stone
> Boy] asked his relatives where they wanted to go. The six uncles became
> the seven sister star constellation; three were part of the head and one
> served as the tail. Then he asked his mother and she became the North
> Star, but [Stone Boy] decided to stay on earth to help. (McKeel)

As we work out connections between this narrative and the history of
the Sioux on the Great Plains, we find a remarkable coincidence between
narrative shifts and historical adaptation, a coincidence that I propose is
radical in that it is bound to distinguishing historical features of Lakota
life. And the episode that I want to use to illustrate this is, at first glance,
the very one which would seem to negate all the claims that I have just
made because it is a highly conventionalized episode that seems to refer
only to the most ordinary and universal of human relationships about
which one assumes little of interest can be said. I am referring to the
opening motifs that precede Stone Boy's heroic action, the episode of the

woman coming to that male household and her subsequent adoption as a sister. As we survey the available Sioux variations, we begin to see what features of the episode occurred with highest frequency among the western Sioux and that gives us the first clues that get us beyond "seems" into what proves to be a historical drama generating the social and narrative conventions, giving them a form that repetition sculpted into an elegant summation of a way of life.

For purposes of close analysis of this introductory event, we need more than mere summary and I quote the first few segments of my own translation of George Sword's version, noting that the presentational units shown here were determined by pause markers in the original text. Part of what strikes me about Sword's text is the way his shortest units seem to carry the most condensed social significance. Is this coincidence or is it evidence that Sword's performance style accommodated an audience's need for moments of reflection as convention opened ever outward toward expanding horizons of belief?

Four young men lived together,
    One of them was called Hakela.
    Suddenly, outside, they heard someone who came and stood, so they told Hakela to look. He peeked out.

There was a young woman, a most beautiful young woman. The front part of her hair was bound and she had a great big bag. Like that she came and stood. Hakela saw her and he said, "Brothers, a young woman is there; she has arrived and she is standing; the front part of her hair is bound and she has a bag." That's what he said.
    And the oldest brother, that very one, said this, they say,
    "Invite her into the tipi. We have no woman who can be a sister, so she can be our elder sister," he said.
    So Hakela peeked out and said, "Sister, come in. Our oldest brother says we have no elder sister so you can be our sister." So the woman said, "yes" and she settled down in their home.
    They gave her food but she didn't eat. She just sat there. So they tell.
(Walker, *Lakota Myth* 89–90)

Whatever variations we may find in the introductory motifs, all the rest of the action of the tale follows from the brothers carrying out their newly acquired roles as men who could become brothers-in-law if only they could survive the dangers posed by relatives they don't even know, can't possibly know in a world still coming into being. They get the help they need from their nephew, once he comes from the sky by way of the second adopted elder sister, the one whose actions (and art) open the social unit outwards toward new possibilities, unlike the first one who turns it inward, refuses the intermediacies represented by art, and decorates her shield with the heads of the brothers. Without question, though, this is an episode about the role of a sister, usually an elder sister, and comparison of different Lakota versions suggests that while the mode of the woman's arrival is variable (Bad Wound's version has the younger brother stubbing his toe and the sister coming forth from that brotherly gestation, but this version, too, elaborates the brothers' determination to keep her as a sister), the consistent emphasis on this particular kinship role is a western Sioux development.

The evidence becomes even more compelling when the comparisons are extended to other tribes and we note that the plot type is predictably introduced with an episode that shows how a woman becomes the agent of localization in a world without spatial or temporal orientation. The woman, who is the feminine addition to the elementary and exemplary household, always acquires a relational designation as a preliminary condition of her founding action and that relational role is the clue we need if we are to follow features of gender categories through their narrative orchestration in different tribes. If we turn to the most famous and theoretically based comparatist of them all, Claude Lévi-Strauss, we find that he zeroes in on the episode, labeling the role of the woman as "the invariant feature of the group."[9] From his structuralist point of view, the woman's role is ambiguous and that ambiguity is seen as the potential for transformations allowing different cultures to realize the figure according to the terms of their own system. The woman could be a potential wife, an old stranger who assumes or otherwise acquires a grandmother role, a young stranger who is designated as an older or a younger sister, a sister who is a biological sibling, even a sister-in-law. But if the role is ambiguous from a structuralist perspective that seeks evidence of stable elements within a hemispheric system, it is anything but so from the perspective of the local community. The way a specific social group develops this variable element appears to be just the kind of strong evidence we look for as we try to understand how definite communities shaped a story's received or borrowed elements, giving them the fit required by the local belief system. Whatever role this woman plays in a community's narrative heritage, she prefigures the woman's place. Her work bag is one every woman will open.

Certainly in a Lakota context the fact that the woman is consistently an adopted sister, usually an elder sister, turns out to be the realization that says it all, that makes this relational term into the means whereby all the basic principles of the symbolic order are given dynamic realization in different domains of expressive culture. If such commentary seems like typically overstated academic rage for order, we find it to be mere sober summary when we validate it with George Sword's statements of late nineteenth-century beliefs. In a text specifically intended to teach the fundamentals of Lakota belief, Sword clearly refers to the four brothers as the Four Winds, their tipi as the world, and the good elder sister as Wohpe, the woman from the sky whom Finger, another of Sword's contemporaries, identifies as the bringer of the White Buffalo Calf Pipe. (See Walker, *Belief* 103–104, 109–112 and *Myth* 58–89.) Once these connections are in place, anyone who has even the slightest familiarity with Lakota thought can recognize that the conventional nineteenth-century introduction to the Stone Boy story really does evoke the foundations of the entire belief system. And that gives considerable weight to the question about the woman's status as adopted elder sister rather than as wife. Calculating the social logic from the position of the elder sister shifts many received anthropological notions about Lakota social organization and gender roles, but it is a direction that promises a way out of the rigidity of previous impositions of external models of social structure on internal dynamics.[10]

Before going beyond the generic requirements of the narrative world, we do well to survey the western Sioux narrative tradition for more pervasive evidence of how the elder sister role operates within the narrative system. Survey proves the pivotal role of the adopted sister within the discursive world of the old ohunkakan, the Lakota category for ancient tales from an era before the current historical world. In those tales, the adopted sister, generally the elder sister, presents the brothers with a series of options about how to negotiate with the world outside the microcosm of their own social unit. These negotiations are the action that brings society into being. Lakota ohunkakan develop the consequences deriving from four of these options: 1) the sister is stolen and the sister as captive requires that the brothers negotiate relationships with the captors; 2) the brothers are captured in their quest to find what the sister needs, and the captive brothers establish sister's son and brother's captors in a relationship requiring negotiation (the Stone Boy plot option); 3) the sister's husband is captured and the captive brother-

in-law establishes the brothers in opposition to sister's husband's captors; 4) an adopted brother tries to become a husband and the sister as
captive within the family unit establishes brothers as enemies to each
other. This last option is the Sioux mythic explanation for inclement
weather. The North Wind wants to rape the adopted sister; she hides
under her robe to escape and has to remain there; her robe covers the
earth and from beneath she sends up vegetation when the sun shines.
The sister's progeny are plants. (See *Dakota Texts* and *Lakota Myth*.)

   In all these narratives we see that the consequences of brother/sister
relationships develop mythic categories, lining up the possibilities, not in
terms of male and female oppositions but in terms of oppositions between categories represented by differently classified male figures who
achieve their social position through their relationship with the sister,
who consistently acts as a mediating agent. While the general pattern
undoubtedly has validity for many Native American groups, the particularities point toward details of historical development.

   How can we set up the move from narrative pattern to the actuality
of social life, a move that allows for the possibility of using narrative
evidence for historical purposes?[11] We should quickly note, as ethnographers consistently have, that even outside the symbolic constructs of the
old ohunkakan, the Sioux gave primacy to brother/sister relationships.
We also need to note that within the ceremonial system, two ceremonies
are said to be the direct requirements of the White Buffalo Cow Woman;
the first is the Hunka ceremony, normally performed for young girls,
which altered the kinship system for one generation. Therefore, any
woman, no matter the order of her birth, could be someone's elder sister.
The second was the puberty ceremony for women, which enacted
the fact that all women were younger sisters of White Buffalo Cow
Woman. Simple acknowledgment, though, is just the first step in a
process that expands into a social logic linking the symbolic realm with
social organization to create an associational matrix that gives definite
reference to abstractions like "symbolic economy." And if we are to get
closer to historical detail, we need to turn to the ceremonial action that
made young Lakota women into younger sisters of the White Buffalo
Cow Woman.

   Here again, for purposes of historical scholarship, I insist on a distinc-
tion between the ceremony itself and the texts that are evidence of how
Lakotas chose to explain ceremonies at a particular historical moment.
Texts that represent a tradition of commentary on ceremonial action are

indispensable sources for evidence of cognitive features indicating a tradition of interpretation, or we might say, a tradition of internal criticism and philosophical reflection with its own local structure and rules. Thus, we are looking at a local educational system. We are looking at how a community created its texts about its own ceremonial identity. If we turn to the women's puberty ceremony, we find texts and some crucial cognitive clues that give defining detail to the emerging picture of the adopted elder sister as figuring all that constituted Lakota gender categories. Turn-of-the-century texts reveal the detail and the dynamic by which all women become younger sisters of the White Buffalo Cow Woman, who aligns and assigns all relationships in Lakota culture. The Sioux taught that kinship itself was her gift to the people.[12] In other words, without the possibility of ceremonial recognition and reorganization, biological consanguinity is meaningless. We find all this ringingly endorsed when, at the end of the ceremony, the leader said to the young girl, "You are now a woman. The buffalo woman is your oldest sister. Go out of this lodge" (DeMallie 252).

The theme of newness in conjunction with that command to action "go out of this lodge," is one that can be brought back to the underlying structure of interpretation that links ceremonial and narrative understanding. The ceremony requires a new tipi, a new dress, a new breechclout, even a new ceremonial order since individual holy men presiding over it sought a vision to learn the exact order for each ceremony. The young woman was literally taken out of her tipi, her old dress, her former relationships. She was brought ceremonial step by ceremonial step to the center of a new tipi, where she was given a new dress, a new role, a new point of interiority from which to act. Then, she was taken outside again at the end of the ceremony after her father had thrown the new breechclout outside the ceremonial space. And that gesture announces the next stage of externalization/internalization for which she is now ready—namely marriage and motherhood (*Lakota Belief and Ritual* 251). Her relationship to her elder sister inaugurates a spiraling series of stepping across thresholds that choreograph woman's gender roles according to an underlying theme of location, transformation and translocation, a point to which I will return.

Once we recognize how the elder sister role operates as the pivotal point of contact between belief, ceremonial organization and social organization, we are in position to appreciate the fact that for the Lakotas the coming of the White Buffalo Cow Woman with the Sacred Pipe is a

historical event. Lakota belief is definite on this point, just as the tradition is definite in its distinctions between a mythic temporality about
which little is known and a historical one for which each group must
account in terms that prove the group's continuing identity in relation
to the facts of individual agency. The basic premise of Lakota identity is
the historical fact of a way of life that began a specified number of
generations ago with the gift of the Sacred Pipe that makes them who
they are. The presence of the Pipe is the fact that channels older mythic
significance, like that found in the Stone Boy story, into the ordinary
forms of life and historical action. The difference in discursive modality
marks a crucial cognitive intentionality. One might argue that we are
still within the realm of belief, not empirical historical fact, but there is
absolutely no doubt that with this belief we have the cognitive basis for
historical action on the part of Lakota people who perceive themselves
as Lakotas because ceremonial action marks them as younger sisters and
brothers of White Buffalo Cow Woman.

In switching from the content of a single event to local elaboration on
the significance of the elder sister role, I may seem to have abandoned
the artistry of the tale, indeed the very idea of a narrative construct, in
order to insist on the condensed social significance of a few opening
moves. And, to some extent, that effect may be an inevitable consequence of the argument on behalf of history, which requires some
straightforward justification. Nevertheless, I want to insist yet again on
the important distinction between historical and/or sociological fact and
the narratives that arise from the collective process of making the experience of that facticity operative and memorable, and I want to repeat
that what I seek to illustrate is the range of texts that are indirect
commentaries on each other because they arise from similar collective
strategies for memorializing meaning. I can illustrate this interplay of
texts and advance my commentary on the plot of my reference tale by
picking up on the name of the hero with its many resonances in Lakota
belief.

In keeping with my emphasis on textual dynamics, I want to address
beliefs about stone by looking at the presentational structure as well as
the content of a nineteenth-century Lakota text written by Thomas Tyon,
who was explaining why stone is perceived as sacred. He does not start,
as he could have, with reference to beliefs or narratives about stone.
Instead, he launches the presentation with an actual experience. Something happens—a man dreams of stone. We should not go too quickly

past Tyon's concrete opening move. His structural point of departure is that event whereby belief enters history when it becomes a definite motive in the life of a known individual. Tyon then talks about the customary action that follows from the dream experience and he establishes the link between these dreams and the Yuwipi Society that brought together men with similar spiritual experiences. Concrete social organization follows from dream experience. Men act and their actions are the collective interpretation of the meaning of stone's sacredness within history.

Human action is, of course, the stuff of continuing narrative, and the fact that a man's narrative of his own deeds was an indispensable part of his cultural authority is further evidence of continuing narrative genesis, with each new autobiographical tale serving as a commentary on every other tale about the same powers. After describing how dreams about stone lead to the formation of a society, Tyon proceeds to another ordinary event that would account for that society's performing its social role. At this stage, Tyon gets remarkably specific. "So it is that if someone loses a horse, he might make a feast for the Rock dreamer." The ensuing ceremony is performed for the purpose of finding what is lost and the detail of Tyon's text makes ordinary curiosity into commentary on the continuing action of an ancient text. "So the rocks tell about whoever stole the horse, even the name and the place. They come to report everything, they say" (Walker, *Lakota Belief and Ritual* 154). We can here recall that Left Heron's gloss on the ending of the Stone Boy tale identifies the power of Stone Boy with that of the stone in the Yuwipi Ceremony. Stone locates what is lost. The elder sister locates stone within Lakota ceremonial life. Textual realizations of the process locate individual experience within the discursive space of a textual community. Or, to put it in more simple and direct terms, telling about Stone Boy keeps everything in place. And, as the tale tells us, his mother is the means by which it was possible to think about things having a place, and we come back to thinking about how gender works in the context we are explicating.

• • •

This ordinary drama of Great Plains life is an act of localization.[13] Woman transforms and places, or it may be more accurate to say that she transforms and replaces. What comes from elsewhere is brought into her space and given agency therein. Stone Boy comes from the sky; the buffalo comes from afar; men arrive from another unrelated household.

The man standing outside the woman's tipi (as occurred in courting practice) seems like the reversal of the initial situation found in our tale where the women arrive at the tipi of the four brothers. But that seeming takes no account of the way arrivals are the occasion of crossings and translocations, movement in and out of demarcated space, which transforms the significance of that space as women "turn" the forms they make. With this observation we can note again that the mythic women who arrive at the brothers' tipi have their work bags with them. They arrive ready and willing to do their particular art and once they are inside the tipi, it is theirs. The life of the social unit flows from their achieving their art and that always involves a process of bringing inside what has been outside the social unit, the tiyospaye. The first sister, of course, reverses that process. She takes what is inside and places it on the other side of life; she stops action, immobilizes the brothers. The second one shows that woman's transformative action, her art, localizes by centralizing. She knows that mediation is transformation that shifts life forms from sphere to sphere. Lakota life advances by a continuing process of interiorization and exteriorization in which men and women change their respective positions so that each turning makes or unmakes life. Detailing this summation would continue to expand the importance of that mythic sister who swallows a clear white stone as she mourns the adopted brothers who have gone off to get her what she needs. The stone comes from the sky to the human community and brings the brothers back home before he sends them, the buffalo daughters, and his mother back to the sky.

In the interests of an economy that is certainly not symbolic, namely the economy of a single article, we need to side-step commentary on other features of the tale and cut to the ending and the final role of the mythic elder sister. Left Heron's coda to the story, quoted above, tells us that Stone Boy sends his mother to the sky where she is the North Star, the pivot around which all else is measured, just as the elder sister role is the pivotal one in the kinship structure. The North Star enables people to make those calculations that let them find their way in the geographical landscape, and the elder sister lets them find their way in the spiritual and relational landscape. At this point, I can end what is designed to suggest possibilities for using archived texts in relation to historical and cultural analysis by emphasizing again how a textual dynamic achieves consonance with a social one, not, I believe, because one is abstracted from the other but because each creates the other within that other dynamic which is history and which inevitably requires new referents, new agents by which to maintain meaning.

At various stages of this demonstration, I have clearly been in critical territory previously explored by others in the field of American Indian narrative study. Just as I have been concerned to show an interplay of texts that sets up the terms of interpretation, each for the other, I am concerned to show how different critical projects open out, each upon the other. Dennis Tedlock was the first among us to draw attention to the hermeneutic process occurring through oral performance. His article "The Spoken Word and the Work of Interpretation in American Indian Religion" is certainly one of the essential articles for the field. In the preceding illustration, I have been demonstrating that we can expand the range of texts that we use to show how any community maintains its own tradition of interpretation. This argument for expansion of textual analysis in a given specific locale is one of the practical consequences of the emphasis on textual communities. The textual commentaries I use all come from responsible Lakota leaders at the same period of history; the historical mapping of authoritative transmission represents another neglected task. Transmission reveals the genealogy of authority. The historical reality of that transmission is every bit as essential to understanding a group as the propositional content of any narrative, historical or otherwise. The period of history on which this article concentrates is one of upheavals in this genealogy. The individuals quoted in this brief article—people like Sword, Left Heron, Tyon, Bad Wound and Finger—engaged in soul-searching about how knowledge should be preserved and transmitted, and that experience is now part of any interpretation of material they left us.[14]

· · ·

Motives for historical study are many, but political necessity certainly has priority. The body of critical analysis linking literature to law is, happily, growing. Julie Cruikshank's article "Negotiating with Narrative" is another of those basic works that are creating the boundaries of a field of study that emphasizes the role of audience. She notes that the practice of allowing members of communities to introduce their own terms into land claims negotiations is definitely an advance. Yet, she says, "there are risks . . . even when they share terminology, indigenous people may understand these terms to have meanings very different from those attributed by government negotiators for whom such language has become routine." She goes on to ask, "And what messages does the language of indigenous narrative carry to multicultural audiences?" (57–58). Her questions justify this entire exercise.[15]

I could go on with a process of demonstrating how people in our field are already doing the work that lets us map textual communities that have definite geographical locations. Beyond that place in space, they have definite epistemological boundaries that are rarely exclusive. Obviously, people normally belong to multiple textual communities, but some historical process, affecting several domains of expressive culture, has to be the generative source of performed enactments of belonging to these communities. My purpose, as stated at the beginning of this exercise, is to build more bridges between existing bodies of scholarship, so that our scholarship related to texts within communities can acquire some of the pragmatic edge that communities need to assure the future identities they choose, with the emphasis once again firmly on the choices of the communities. People in academic positions could work with definite communities to designate the body of texts that the community views as public evidence of communal identity. The process of developing an interpretation of that body of texts will involve scholars from various disciplines because interpretation is simply one more phase in adjusting meaning to different audiences and some audiences are defined by institutions with particular rhetorical requirements. Academic interpretations have no more or less authority than those occurring outside the academy. Their authority is simply different, adapted to particular strategic purposes.

My own work in cognitive style was originally motivated by an apparent gap between historical archived materials and contemporary performance. I believed that the right kind of look at what was happening with contemporary narrative would reveal a cognitive continuity that might not be immediately evident at the propositional level but which nevertheless represented a traditional communal process. The hypothesis certainly allowed me to find more artistry in the contemporary materials than would otherwise have been possible. Whether or not such work could reveal the operation of tradition at the level of style remains, in my opinion, an idea worth pursuing. The indispensable first stage of such a demonstration requires historical analysis of the sort I begin here but have pursued in detail well beyond what is indicated here. The next stages would involve juxtaposing the patterns revealed by all that detail to what is found in contemporary materials. Clearly such tasks require considerable time and effort, and that is another argument for collaborative efforts. As a subdiscipline, we have made impressive advances in the last twenty-five years. The questions now are, "where can we go from here?" and "what kind of plurality is signified by 'we'?"

NOTES

1. Baltimore: Johns Hopkins U P, 1990.

2. The many works of Teun van Dijk and his associates have been developing models for scientific study of narrative pragmatics in relation to propositional structures. The models strategize notions of narrative competence in relation to performance. The research that is generally categorized as ethnography or sociology of communication has applied many theoretical principles of discourse analysis to American contexts, with Dell Hymes' ground-breaking work making the connection with Native American narratives. See in particular "The Ethnography of Speaking" in T. Gladwin and W. C. Sturtevant, eds., *Anthropology and Human Behavior,* p 13–53. Washington DC: Anthropological Society of Washington, 1962.

An excellent introductory text in the field is Alexandra Georgakopoulou and Dionysis Goutsos' *Discourse Analysis.* Their sketch of future agendas for the field includes the observation that each analytic method is but prelude to "a broad-based approach that applies to language any and all roads to understanding, including introspection, experimentation, theorizing, and above all careful observation of the myriad discourse practices within social and cultural practices. Discourse analysis needs to be able to combine the rigorous, disciplined and systematic investigation with the attention and sensitivity to the personal and the particular" (184).

3. "The Spoken Word and the Work of Interpretation" in Kroeber, *Traditional Literatures of the American Indian: Texts and Interpretations.* Lincoln: U of Nebraska P, 1981.

4. The connection between narrative analysis and claims of sovereign status is recognized by a number of scholars in the field of international law. An especially helpful analysis is that given by Andrew Carty in *Was Ireland Conquered? International Law and the Irish Question.* (123).

•   •   •

5. See Milner S. Ball, "Stories of Origin and Constitutional Possibilities," *Michigan Law Review* 87.8 (1989)

6. Karl Kroeber also discusses this text in *Artistry in Native American Myths*. He, too, sees the myth as important to understanding historical process. His discussion covers far more features of the tale than I do in this article.

7. See Martha Warren Beckwith, "Mythology of the Oglala Dakota"; Eugene Buechel et al., *Lakota Tales and Texts*; Deloria, *Dakota Texts*; Marie L. Mc-Laughlin, *Myths and Legends of the Sioux*; Ronald Theisz, *Buckskin Tokens: Contemporary Oral Narratives of the Lakota*; Gilbert Walking Bull, *Ohu-ka-kan*; and Clark Wissler, "Some Dakota Myths."

8. The question of what constitutes a legitimate basis for comparison runs like a fault line through all my references to comparative research. In the interests of critical economy, I believe that we can start with the notions of tale type and motifs that allow us access to the bibliographical work of historic-geographic tradition. That basis for comparison will not get us very far, though, in considering the cognitive themes that bind different genres. Claude Lévi-Strauss, of course, recognized that inadequacy and aimed for a more abstract basis in systematic transformations. But his approach moves so quickly to high level abstractions that it bypasses the intermediate stages by which individuals and communities adjust received forms to their own uses, the very stages that interest me here. Still, all of these early efforts to find a basis for comparison provide indispensable tools for first-stage scanning.

•   •   •

9. The entire chapter entitled "Three Adornments" in *The Origin of Table Manners* is devoted to this narrative complex. Lévi-Strauss touches on Arapahoe, Crow, Gros Ventre and Omaha versions. He used Bad Wound's Sioux version, which, according to Sioux terms, is exceptional. The woman is a sister but not necessarily an elder sister and she does not arrive at the tipi from the world beyond. Nevertheless, Lévi-Strauss does pick up on the connections between the type and the significance of women's quill work, just as he perceives that issues of location and translocation are somehow involved. The details of these broad-based intercultural themes can only be worked out through close analysis of a single culture's expressive forms. Using the structuralist comparative data, though, supports my contention that the presentational units in Sword's version of the story represent highly compressed significance.

10. What I propose regarding kinship studies is radical but not entirely without precedent. Differentiating between a social structural approach to kinship (genealogical, precisely integrated) and a cultural approach (broadly defined to include symbolic interpretations) Raymond DeMallie argues that each provides "entirely different kinds of understandings of kinship systems" (143) with the latter being more particularistic because it does not begin with the imposition of an outside framework. He notes that "for the Sioux, kinship is an active force,

the act of relating. They understand their own kinship system to be in striking contrast to the static nature of American kinship . . ." (132).

• • •

11. The historiographer Hans Kellner has summarized some of the questions that historians now share with narratologists, questions that reveal some of the issues for which narrative analysis can yield information to the advantage of both historical and literary understanding. "If the processes of the historical imagination are specifically literary only in the final stages of creation, however, I have argued in this book that they are everywhere linguistic, shaped and constrained from the start by rhetorical considerations that are the 'other' sources of history. The immortality of facts is dependent upon the conventions of discourse governing the culture that accepts their authority, which is to say, the authority of the process by which they are constituted. This authority is an important form of the cultural power to be sure, and the basis of the human sciences, but it is a tenuous sort of immortality indeed. In the first place, facts themselves are invariably constituted by communities through defining, naming parts, sorting these designated objects, devising conceptions of the relations between them, distinguishing oppositions and contraries, selecting beginnings and endings, eliding gaps, evaluating relative importance among objects that will differ from existing objects in detail while resembling them in kind" (325–326).

12. See DeMallie, "Kinship and Biology in Sioux Culture," in *North American Indian Anthropology*. Norman: U of Oklahoma P, 1997.

13. Some detailing of semantic fields emphasizes the significance of this comment. The term *tan* is a contraction of *tancan* or body. It is also a reference to the severed half of the buffalo hide. There is a metonymic transfer at work whereby a body exists as half of something. (Themes of twins take on particular significance in this context.) The potential for confusion between phonemics and morphemics is real. Nevertheless, at the risk of such confusion, I point out that the term for sister's husband is *tanhan* and the temptation to transliterate that as the body standing up continuously in a definite place is evident from the arguments of this paper. Marriage localizes the other half. People inclined to think in terms of dualisms are bound to appreciate this evidence of a body divided in half but brought together again in the individual household (itself literally half of the buffalo) by way of marriage. This is especially intriguing since there is so little evidence of dualism in Lakota sociology.

14. Some information about each of these leaders is included in *Lakota Myth* in relation to the presentation of their tales, including George Sword's life and texts.

15. See "Negotiating with Narrative: Establishing Cultural Identity at the

Yukon International Storytelling Festival" in *American Anthropology* 99.1 (1997).

Works Cited

Ball, Milner. "Stories of Origin and Constitutional Possibilities." *Michigan Law Review* 87.8 (1989).

Beckwith, Martha Warren. "Mythology of the Oglala Dakota." *Journal of American Folklore* 43 (1930):430.

Buechel, Eugene, et al. *Lakota Tales and Texts.* Ed. Paul Manhart. Pine Ridge, SD: Red Cloud Indian School, 1978.

Carty, Andrew. *Was Ireland Conquered? International Law and the Irish Question.* Chicago and London: Pluto Press, 1996.

Cruikshank, Julie. "Negotiating with Narrative: Establishing Cultural Identity at the Yukon International Storytelling Festival." *American Anthropology* 99.1 (1997).

Deloria, Ella. *Dakota Texts.* New York: G. E. Stechert and Co., 1932. 87–95.

DeMallie, Raymond. "Kinship and Biology in Sioux Culture." *North American Indian Anthropology.* Norman: U of Oklahoma P, 1997.

Georgakopoulou, Alexandra, and Dionysis Goutsos. *Discourse Analysis.* Edinburgh U P, 1997.

Hymes, Dell. "The Ethnography of Speaking." *Anthropology and Human Behavior.* Ed. T. Gladwin and W. C. Sturtevant. Washington DC: Anthropological Society of Washington, 1962. 13–53.

Kellner, Hans. *Language and Historical Representation.* Madison: U of Wisconsin P, 1989.

Kroeber, Karl. *Artistry in Native American Myths.* Lincoln: U of Nebraska P, 1998.

———. *Traditional Literatures of the American Indian: Texts and Interpretations.* Lincoln: U of Nebraska P, 1981.

Lévi-Strauss, Claude. *The Origin of Table Manners.* Chicago: U of Chicago P, 1978.

Lowie, Robert. "The Assiniboine." *Anthropological Papers of the American Museum of Natural History* 4.1 (1910).

Mathiot, Madeline. *An Approach to the Cognitive Study of Language.* Bloomington: Indiana U P, 1968. 2.

McKeel, H. Scudder. Field Notes, Summer of 1931, White Clay District, Pine Ridge Reservation, South Dakota. Archives of the Department of Anthropology, American Museum of Natural History, New York.

McLaughlin, Marie M. *Myths and Legends of the Sioux.* Bismarck: Bismarck Tribune Co., 1916. 179–97.

Sarris, Greg. *Keeping Slug Woman Alive.* Berkeley: U of California P, 1993.

Skinner, Alison. "Plains Ojibway Tales." *Journal of American Folklore.* xxxii.280.

Stock, Brian. *Listening for the Text: On the Uses of the Past.* Baltimore: Johns Hopkins U P, 1990.

Tedlock, Dennis. "The Spoken Word and the Work of Interpretation in American Indian Religion." *Traditional Literatures of the American Indian: Texts and Interpretations.* Ed. Karl Kroeber. Lincoln: U of Nebraska P, 1981.

Theisz, Ronald. *Buckskin Tokens: Contemporary Oral Narratives of the Lakota.* Aberdeen, SD: North Plains Press, 1975.

Van Dijk, Teun. *Some Aspects of Text Grammars.* The Hague: Mouton and Co., 1972.

Vecsey, Christopher. *Imagine Ourselves Richly.* New York: Crossroads Press, 1988.

Walker, James R. *Lakota Belief and Ritual.* Ed. Raymond DeMallie and Elaine Jahner. Lincoln: U of Nebraska P, 1980.

———. *Lakota Society.* Ed. Raymond J. DeMallie. Lincoln: U of Nebraska P, 1982.

———. *Lakota Myth.* Ed. Elaine Jahner. Lincoln: U of Nebraska P, 1983.

Walking Bull, Gilbert. *Ohu-ka-kan.* Dallas, OR: Itemizer Observer Press, 1975.

Wissler, Clark. "Some Dakota Myths." *Journal of American Folklore* 20 (1907). 199.

———. *Mythology of the Blackfoot Indians.* Lincoln: U of Nebraska P, 1995.

Chapter 11

The Stakes of Textual Border-Crossing

Hualing Nieh's Mulberry and Peach *in Sinocentric, Asian American, and Feminist Critical Practices*

Sau-ling C. Wong

Introduction by David Palumbo-Liu

The landscape of American literary studies has shifted dramatically over the past decade—its geographic parameters have broadened as notions of "American" identity have begun to accommodate not only the changing cultural and historical borders of the United States proper, but also the expansion of U.S. cultural production into the spaces into which the United States has historically encroached. Similarly, the United States itself has been apprehended as increasingly (and more complexly) inhabited by diverse populations that press notions of "multiculture" past the usual limits of understanding—rather than being constituted simply as a "plurality" of cultures, these new formations are understood as intricately and variously connected, disjoined, interwoven (in both transitory and enduring ways). Indeed, this formation applies both to the cultures at the margins of the perceived core and to the core itself.

As these formations capture our critical attention, they demand new methodological perspectives if we are to grasp this complexity, rather than reduce it to conform to one or another preexisting model. Sau-ling Wong's essay takes as its object Hualing Nieh's transnational narrative *Sangqing yu Taohong* or *Mulberry and Peach* and demonstrates how such a text, which may be understood within the newly expanded rubric of American studies, may also be configured variously under different interpretive regimes. This is not simply an exercise in hermeneutic indecidability, for the focus is not (only) on showing how this text may produce multiple readings, but rather to demonstrate how this text's production, distribution, and circulation evince its multiple trajectories, audiences, and historical embeddedness. By incorporating studies of marketing, publishing houses, editorial practices, and classroom and critical reception, Wong shows how the novel's various incarnations illustrate both the fluid movement of the text among different audiences and the material histories that anchor it particularly.

Specifically, Wong's essay crosses the boundaries among autobiography, biography, and autobiographical fiction, to engage the ways this literary text not only exerts tremendous pressure on such limits and their truth regimes, but also how the production of the text itself calls for specific modes of representation: how is the writing subject constructed transnationally, historically, and in various political contexts? Which "truth" is conveyed at the forefront of different agendas of meaning making? How do different methods of reading and interpretation yield different insights, and how might they exclude others?

Wong's subject, a Chinese language novel largely composed in Iowa, requires such questions about crossing from "Asian" to "Asian American." She describes in careful detail the publication history of *Mulberry and Peach* in Taiwan, Hong Kong, mainland China, and, finally, in English translation in the United States and Great Britain. Each of these sites of publication, Wong argues, implicates the novel in a new set of cultural and political conflicts, a phenomenon that Wong unravels by showing how the literal, physical writing appeared in different forms in each instance. Building on this publication history, Wong juxtaposes these "discursive locations" against one another so as to uncover the way in which they influence a reading of the text. In doing so, Wong is able to reveal complexities about the text itself, particularly its treatment of gender, as well as about how these locations influence the interpretive act of reading.

Attending to the material conditions of this novel's publication forces Wong to engage the diasporic model of Asian culturalism that includes writers and readers living throughout the world. However, Wong does not argue that such globalism effaces nationalism entirely, nor does it preclude the novel from being enlisted in politically motivated agendas. Diaspora, she reminds us, reinforces notions of descent and homeland. In contrast, the institutionalization of Asian American studies is predicated upon the belief of "claiming" America—and therefore would insert *Mulberry and Peach* into U.S. literary traditions. Wong's essay insists upon the necessity of critics being aware of how these often conflicting agendas bear upon the same literary text. In this instance, it means understanding how Nieh's novel, originally written in Chinese, can function in both "Chinese" and "Asian American" literary studies, and what this fact tells us about the authority of nationalist and diasporic labels to govern the reading of literature.

The attention that Wong pays to the classroom as a site of reception and criticism plays a crucial role in her methodological strategy. Rather than bracketing the study of literature in higher education as irrelevant to the text itself, she carefully describes how she and her students have approached the text in ways that resituate it. She demonstrates convincingly that the notion of "the classroom" is itself unjustifiably reductive, for she notes how the same text might be read significantly, even radically, differently, depending on the way it is framed by the course title, the pedagogical goals of the instructor, and the composition of the student body. Attention to such nuances is particularly useful to teachers of literature, as it reminds us that our assumptions are often out of sync with the interests, perceptions, and knowledge base of our students. Moreover, it reminds us that we cannot ignore the role that the participants in the classroom experience—both teachers and students—have in constituting the experience of the literary.

Parallel to these shifting contexts are the different incarnations of the novel: Wong shows us how advertising, packaging, book jackets, and publication house all weigh upon the novel and inflect it with a different tenor and tonality. It may be read as a national allegory (of one of "two Chinas," a transnational feminist text, an American ethnic text, and so on). In sum, Wong's essay is itself an exemplary instance of creating a series of approaches around a complex literary text: the text proves resistant to any one method, and forces us instead to recognize it through multiple optics. In doing so, it animates its own historicity and multiple situatedness. "Classification," Wong writes, "is never innocent." But she does not suggest that we can disentangle ourselves from that process; instead, she hopes that we can learn from it.

——————— ▬▬▬▬ ———————

IN AN ERA WHEN, in Elaine H. Kim's succinct formulation, "the lines between Asian and Asian American . . . are increasingly being blurred" (Kim 1992, xiii), what happens when a literary text of "Asian" provenance crosses national, political, linguistic, and cultural borders and ends up being claimed by a variety of critical (and pedagogical) practices, including but not limited to those in Asian studies and Asian American studies? What stakes are involved in such claims? How are feminist concerns inserted, if at all, in these processes? To explore these questions, my essay examines the protean publication and reception history of the novel known in Chinese as *Sangqing yu Taohong* and in English as *Mulberry and Peach: Two Women of China,* by the writer known in Chinese as Nieh Hualing and in English as Hualing Nieh.[1]

This last sentence, deliberately awkward, is meant to underscore the inherent instability of the subjects ("persons" as well as "subject matter") implicated in transnational practices. As Shu-mei Shih remarks on the multiple name changes undergone by border-crossing women like herself, Nieh, or Theresa Hak Kyung Cha, author of *Dictee* (Shih 1992, 3): "Each name and each language evok[e] a different aspect of one's self, a different life, a different story, a different time and space. And yet the contradiction is that they also coexist at the same time." Shih's statement is a truism, but one that, far from conferring comfort because of its familiarity, compels constant, often distressing, negotiations of meaning. As such, it provides a thought-provoking induction into the problematics of Asian/Asian American crossing.[2]

A Synopsis and Brief Publication History of Sangqing yu Taohong/Mulberry and Peach

In the synoptic convention favored by book reviewers, one could say that Nieh's novel is "about" a woman who lives through some of the most harrowing traumas in recent Chinese history and ends up suffering from what is clinically known as multiple personality disorder or dissociative identity disorder: she is split into Sangqing or Mulberry and Taohong or Peach.[3] Her story begins in 1945, when she is 16, and ends (textually, at least) in 1970. During this period she traces a geographical trajectory evoking the political upheavals that have dislocated numerous Chinese. Because the protagonist's journey originates in China and continues on to the United States, even by the most mechanical criterion of "physical setting," the novel could be understood as a text spanning the Chinese and the Chinese American, the Asian and the Asian American.

In Part One of the novel, on the eve of China's victory over the Japanese invaders, Mulberry is stranded in a boat along with other refugees in a Yangtze River gorge. In Part Two, on the eve of Communist victory over the Nationalists in 1949, Mulberry enters the besieged city of Beijing to marry Shen Chia-kang, the man to whom she has been betrothed since childhood. In Part Three, covering 1957 to 1959, Mulberry is in Taiwan, hiding out in an attic with Chia-kang, now a fugitive from the law for embezzlement, and with Sang-wa, their daughter. In Part Four, the protagonist is alone in the United States as an illegal alien; she is pregnant from an affair with a Chinese professor and cannot decide whether or not to have an abortion. By now the identity dissociation has occurred; there is evidence that Peach has been wandering across the American continent and eventually "kills off" her primary identity. Each of the four sections is supposed to be an excerpt from Mulberry's diary, introduced by a letter to the U.S. immigration service written by a mocking, teasing, and defiant Peach. Framing all this are a *xiezi* or prologue and a *ba* or epilogue.

The above bare-bones account can, I think, be agreed upon by readers in both languages, but its simplicity is achieved by eliding details of the novel's many textual metamorphoses. The book's tortuous publication history resonates uncannily with the physical and psychological traversals experienced by the protagonist, which in turn echo the author's own ordeals not so much in biographical detail as in spirit. Born in Wuhan in 1925, Nieh was uprooted numerous times during her formative years as a result of the Japanese invasion and the unremitting Nationalist-Communist strife. After fleeing to Taiwan in 1949, Nieh became the literary editor of a dissident publication. When her superiors were arrested in 1960 for criticizing Chiang Kai-Shek's repressive rule, she had to flee again, this time to the U.S. *Sangqing yu Taohong* was written in Iowa.[4] It was first serialized in Taiwan's *United Daily News* in 1970, but had, by Part Three, drawn such vicious political and moralistic attacks (for veiled satire of the Nationalist regime and for "pornographic" accounts of Peach's sex life) that the editors were forced to terminate the serialization. The ban on *Sangqing yu Taohong* was not lifted until after the death of Chiang Ching-kuo, Chiang Kai-shek's son and successor.[5]

It was left to Hong Kong, then a British colony caught in but not committed to either side of the Nationalist-Communist conflict, to provide the relative neutrality needed for *Sangqing yu Taohong* to first see the light of day in its entirety. Hong Kong's *Ming Pao Monthly* took up the serialization, and the novel finally appeared in book form in 1976, published by Youlian chubanshe.[6] The second edition was published by

Zhongguo qingnian chubanshe in Beijing in 1980, after the resumption of diplomatic relations between the People's Republic of China and the United States. But this is a drastically expurgated version, with a number of changes, including the deletion of Part Four, initiated by the press but acceded to by the author.[7] On the mainland, the unexpurgated version appeared in 1989 and again in 1996.[8]

As for the English version, in 1981 an English translation by Jane Parish Yang (with Linda Lappin), *Mulberry and Peach: Two Women of China,* was simultaneously published by New World Press in Beijing and Sino Publishing Company in New York. New World Press unilaterally made some changes to the typescript, despite reassurances to the author that the project, being intended for non-Chinese audiences, was politically safe.[9] The altered version appeared in Great Britain in 1986, published by The Women's Press in London. In 1988 Beacon Press of Boston, using the original typescript, reissued *Mulberry and Peach* as part of its "Asian Voices" series (which included titles by both Asian and Asian American authors). Beacon later dropped the title for unsatisfactory sales, but the Feminist Press at The City University of New York republished it in 1998.[10]

As can be seen even from this brief factual account, it is impossible—quite simply, inaccurate—to talk about Nieh's novel as if it were a single text. The unauthorized changes in English are relatively minor, but in Chinese the unexpurgated and expurgated editions of *Sangqing yu Taohong* diverge drastically. When the censor's "suggestions" were acquiesced to by the author, however reluctantly, the cut version cannot simply be placed outside the "true intentions" of the author. For the author's desire to see her book published on the Chinese mainland, which was strong enough to override protectiveness toward her creation, was part of her "intentions" too. Add to this the fact that Nieh implemented certain changes to the English translation to assist the Anglophone reader—such as the subtitle, *Two Women of China,* a well-intentioned but misleading misnomer, or "dramatis personae"-type lists summarizing the main characters in each section—[11] and the questions of fidelity and equivalence usually obtaining with translations are raised to the n-th degree. In short, Nieh's novel must be recognized as an unstable textual complex that traverses multiple national, political, linguistic, and cultural borders.

While it is safe to say that contemporary works of literature seldom generate variants matching *Sangqing yu Taohong/Mulberry and Peach* in convolution, I suggest that Nieh's textual choices, where they existed, are not merely "idiosyncratic." In other words, I don't believe that her authorial decisions can be reduced to matters of individual personality, much less of artistic integrity. Rather, if Nieh endorsed or at least tolerated changes to her novel, she did so in response to certain historical circumstances that have irreversibly problematized the notion of the Chinese subject. It is precisely such historical circumstances that have made for the current surge of interest in the Chinese diaspora. At the same time, the case of the unauthorized alterations points to the ways in which Nieh's novel itself problematizes the notion of the Chinese subject. Hence its distinctly unwelcoming reception by Chinese authorities on both sides of the Taiwan Straits, relaxed only very recently.

Assignment of Discursive Locations

In a thoughtful review of the Beacon edition of *Mulberry and Peach*, Kirk Denton raises the question of how to classify the novel and its author, given their extensive border-crossings:

> The genesis of *Mulberry and Peach* raises some questions about literary hermeneutics . . . . For those of us who study modern Chinese literature, the question begs: is Nieh Hualing a Chinese writer, a Taiwanese writer, or an overseas Chinese writer? Drawing from such diverse literary traditions as she does, based on which tradition are we to view her novel? . . . But perhaps we should see her novel in a larger context [of the literature of exile]. (Denton 1989, 137)

Denton poses his questions as scholarly and disciplinary ones. But his query is predicated on a broader understanding: that classification is never innocent. As David Perkins has observed with regard to literary taxonomies, "a classification is also an orientation, an act of criticism" (Perkins 1992, 62). Each classificatory label not only brings forth expectation-setting contexts and intertexts, but also signals a discursive location constituted by recognizable political and cultural assumptions and underwritten by interested institutions (universities, publishers, etc.). Reading practices will differ according to where one places the text. While Denton's terms are understood to function in a United States academic context, their implications are generalizable.

Modern Chinese literature leaves the nation-state unspecified; however subliminally, this label hints that cultural commonalities could (and should?) transcend political differences. Thus what appears to be a "national" label ("Chinese") could in geopolitical terms be already "transnational," involving, just as the publication history of Nieh's novel does, three political entities of which two have the full trappings of the nation-state. Denton's loose usage of Taiwanese writer to cover both transplanted mainlanders and native-born Taiwanese would be more vehemently contested today, given the growing strength of Taiwanese nativism. Still, this label recognizes not only the powerful presence of mainland-origin writers of Nieh's generation and beyond, but also the peculiarities of the island's post-1949 cultural development. Depending on one's purposes, the label could be "regional" or incipiently "national." The term overseas Chinese writer, privileging shared origin over the specificities of current locations, connotes centripetalism. The defining distinction is between *guonei* ("within the country"—nation-state again unspecified) and *haiwai* ("overseas"). The literature of exile label places Nieh's novel in a "world literature" location; while the concept of exile appears to be centrifugal and border-transcending, it actually recuperates the notion of a legitimating political and cultural center, as I will presently argue.

Even without addressing the issues of expurgation and translingualism, Denton has been struck by the range of discursive locations that Nieh's novel could occupy. I would like to further the analysis initiated by Denton by adding two items to his list: Anglo-American feminist literature and Asian American literature. The relevance of the former is evident from the sponsorship of feminist publishers in both Britain and the United States; the germaneness of the Asian American label is less obvious, perhaps even far-fetched to many, yet could certainly be established "empirically" beyond the matter of chapter setting.[12] In the following section, outlining my evolving relationship with *Sangqing yu Taohong/Mulberry and Peach* as a teacher and analyzing the critical scholarship on the novel, I will tease apart questions raised when these two additional discourses are taken into account.

Critical (and Pedagogical) Practices

Born and raised in Hong Kong until I came to study in the United States at age 20, I first read *Sangqing yu Taohong* in Chinese when it appeared in Hong Kong's *Ming Pao Monthly*. In the early 1980s, I began a "professional relationship" with Nieh's novel, using excerpts (the Prologue and Part Four, both set in the United States) in an undergraduate course on Chinese immigrant literature offered by the Asian American Studies Program, Department of Ethnic Studies, at the University of California, Berkeley. Chinese immigrant literature here refers to writings in Chinese by first-generation writers about their life in the United States; the course was designed to serve Chinese-literate, recent immigrant students.[13]

The fact that such a course was initiated by the Asian American Studies Program is, in itself, significant. As a discipline under the ethnic studies rubric, Asian American studies began with an activist commitment to "local" (as opposed to "homeland," i.e., "Asian in Asia") politics; an emphasis on the experiences of American-born, Anglophone Asians; and a strong anti-Orientalist agenda that, in extreme cases, led to a studied avoidance of Asian connections by cultural critics.

However, by the late 1970s and early 1980s, the numbers of first-generation Asian students at UC Berkeley had become large enough to prompt greater attention to their curricular needs; hence the immigrant literature course. This was one of the first signs of the blurring of Asian and Asian American that has become such a part of the intellectual climate of the 1990s. Tellingly, Chinese immigrant literature did not attract the interest of East Asian studies at the time, perhaps because of the former's marginality to the Sinological core of "great traditions."[14]

Throughout over a decade of teaching and discussing *Sangqing yu Taohong/Mulberry and Peach* in various institutional environments, I have come to be struck more and more forcefully by the novel's protean nature, its radical uncontainability. "The same book" has been claimed by different critical and pedagogical practices in the same institution— in my case, by the same person. And each time it was taught or read in a new setting, something different about it emerged into the foreground. The potential for contradiction in such a situation is immense, and it all came to a head for me when, after years of interpreting *Sangqing yu Taohong* as a coherent allegory on the tragic fate of the modern Chinese and teaching it as such in my Chinese immigrant literature course, I was presented with persuasive readings of *Mulberry and Peach* in papers, conversations, and in-class remarks, by Asian American graduate students who expressed little interest in the "Chinese" aspects of the text.[15]

"Chineseness": The Chinese Nation and/or Chinese Peoplehood

I was in good company when I taught *Sangqing yu Taohong* to my immigrant students as an allegory about "the tragic fate of the modern Chinese." The overwhelming majority of published criticism (in both Chinese and English) on Nieh's novel treats it as an allegory of the Chinese nation and/or Chinese peoplehood, with Leo Ou-fan Lee's reading of the deconstructive potential of diaspora being a notable exception (Lee 1994, 229–31).

The ambiguity of and/or in the above statement arises from the novel itself, which shifts focus ceaselessly, often barely perceptibly, from one to the other. We might say that, artistically, "Chineseness" is a richly productive, if painful, concept for Nieh. Perhaps the productiveness comes precisely from the pain—from the impossibly snarled relationships between the Chinese nation-state (of course, the immediate question is "which?"), the "Chinese people" or *zhonghua minzu* (how far and how long can this already ineffable entity be stretched under diasporic conditions?), and the *zhongguoren*, the individual onto whom "Chineseness" has been indelibly inscribed, to her endless grief. In what I call Sinocentric allegorical readings of the novel, the "Chineseness" of the protagonist is regarded as the most crucial determinant of her life; the tragedies of the modern Chinese nation-state (chief among them internal strife ending in political division) as either responsible for or symbolized by her personal calamities; and dislocation from China proper as an irreparable trauma.[16]

Such readings are easy to support. For one thing, Nieh herself has offered explicit suggestions on how to read her novel as a symbolic enactment of injuries sustained by the modern Chinese nation and a lamentation over the Jew-like fate of the diasporic Chinese. In her preface to the 1980 edition in Chinese, tellingly entitled "Langzi de beige" ["The wanderer's lament"], she draws attention to the recurrent images of imprisonment in the four parts of the novel, each marking a crisis in recent Chinese history. Even specific characters and textual details are carefully explicated. For example, she states that the Peach-flower Woman and Boatman in Part One represent the refreshing "primitive life force" of *zhonghua minzu*, and that the news clippings in Part Three "reflect Taiwan society" (Nieh, 1980a, 3–4).

Indeed, bracketing for the moment the question of the novel's uncontainability, on one level one could decode an almost schematic design structuring the meticulously chosen details of the allegory. For example, each passenger on the refugee boat can be demonstrated to embody a type of response to the approach of "modernity" via the nation-state. Space limitations preclude a fully worked out exegesis of the novel; suffice it to say that, despite its deep investment in the last century or so of Chinese history, *Sangqing yu Taohong* also evokes a mythic *zhonghua minzu* based on a sense of primordial and continuous cultural membership predating and indeed transcending the modern nation-state. The most obvious example is the name Sangqing, the mulberry being a sacred tree symbolizing Chinese civilization (it feeds the silkworm that produces silk). Taohong, though associated with a primitive life force by Hualing Nieh herself, can hardly be construed as devoid of cultural connotations. Rather, the peach flower is no less Chinese than the mulberry, being replete with centuries of allusions ranging from the erotic (as in the phrase *taohuayun*) to the utopian (as in Tao Yuanming's Taohuayuan ji) to the tragic (as in Kong Shangren's Taohuashan). These and numerous other references to Chinese legend and folklore construct a sense of peoplehood endowed with far greater nobility and resilience than the modern nation-state, which, in being vulnerable to splitting at all, has betrayed its unsuitableness as a first principle. Yet for Nieh the latter still partakes of the inviolability of the former, both being enfolded in a notion of "Chineseness" capable of calling forth the most fervent passions.

Sinocentric Allegorical Readings from the Chinese Mainland

This equivocation about "Chineseness"—which, I again emphasize, is "ideological" and not a matter of Nieh's individual confusion—allows *Sangqing yu Taohong* to be shaped into nation-serving master narratives. It should come as no surprise that once the novel was published on the mainland, critics there have been well-nigh unanimous in reading the novel as solely or primarily a nationalist narrative.[17] Furthermore, since from the mainland's official point of view, the nation means the People's Republic of China, Nieh's novel has been constructed by some as pro-People's Republic, well-intentioned if somewhat wanting in revolutionary class consciousness. Essays in an anthology dedicated to Nieh's works (Li and Chen 1990) are typical of this approach. Despite minor reservations, *Sangqing yu Taohong* is affirmed as a politically courageous and insightful work whose imperfections can be understood and tolerated given the author's obviously ex-centric location—outside the mainstream of Chinese history, here identified with the People's Republic of China. The very fact that Nieh sacrificed Part Four of *Sangqing yu Taohong,* however reluctantly at heart, for the opportunity to publish it on the mainland betrays a belief that her "real" audience is the numerical majority of Chinese in "China proper."[18] In her 1980 preface to the expurgated edition, Nieh writes (Nieh 1980a, 6–7; my translation):

> I greatly admire *guonei* ["inside the nation," referring to those on the mainland] writers for their concern for the people; they write for the people. For me, a writer in exile, where could I find the people? I only had artistic demands to sustain me. Now that *Sangqing yu Taohong* can be introduced to *guonei* readers, I have begun to have doubts about myself. From now on, for whom should I write? What kind of works should I write?

One gathers that for Nieh, at least at this point in her life and career, being ex-centric is considered an anomalous, pathology-inducing condition which must be redeemed by a return to the center, to within the borders of the nation, to *guonei.*

Sinocentric Allegorical Readings from Exilic/Diasporic Locations

A Western-educated *haiwai* or "overseas" critic might detect a party-line predictability in the mainland interpretations of *Sangqing yu Taohong,* with their vulgar-Marxist and social realist, not to mention "patriotic," demands on the writer. By contrast, reception to *Sangqing yu Taohong* outside of the People's Republic might appear free of propagandistic freight. An examination of the book jackets of the various Chinese editions yields a thought-provoking contrast. The cover of the expurgated mainland edition shows a red background, a simplified map of southeastern China and Taiwan in black, and a white bird in flight over the Taiwan Straits, its right wing tip brushing the island. Evoked are both the dove of peace and the Princess Bird in the Epilogue, the latter's pebble-dropping now construed as a valiant effort to bring out reunification. (The Sisyphean connotations of the labor would have to be brushed aside to make this heroic reading possible.) On the other hand, the covers of the Youlian (Hong Kong), Huahan (Hong Kong), and Hanyi seyan (Taiwan) editions all have "neutral" graphic designs.[19] Thus the non-mainland publishers seem to perceive the book quite differently, more as an aesthetic object than as an instrument of partisanship.

It might be habitual for many non-mainland critics to rest the analysis on such a contrast. But I suggest that most *haiwai* criticism on *Sangqing yu Taohong*, notwithstanding its non-official discursive venues, its vocabulary of aesthetic autotelism, and its dissociation from an obvious nationalism, shares with its mainland counterpart a fundamental similarity: Sinocentrism.

Perhaps the best known and most widely cited piece of *haiwai* criticism on Nieh's novel is Pai Hsien-yung's essay, "The Wandering Chinese: The Theme of Exile in Taiwan Fiction."[20] Pai, himself a revered master of fiction, is among the first to appreciate the ambition and vision of *Sangqing yu Taohong*. Citing C. T. Hsia's oft-quoted phrase, "obsession with China," he contextualizes Nieh's novel in a centuries-old Chinese tradition of intellectuals exiling themselves from corrupt regimes, and observes that Nieh has designed the novel "as a fable of the tragic state of modern China, whose political schizophrenia is analogous to the chaotic world of the insane." The novel employs "personal dissolution as a paradigm for political disintegration"; "[i]n creating the fragmented world of the schizophrenic, Nieh Hua-ling has allegorized the fate of modern China in all its tragic complexity" (Pai 1976, 210, 211). In short, the tragedy of the protagonist is homologous to the tragedy of China.[21]

The "literature of exile" under which Pai classifies *Sangqing yu Taohong*, far from transcending nation (as it may first appear to do), is very much a literature about nation. For the concept of exile is constituted by the concept of nation. It is the failures of the nation-state—to unify warring factions, to forge a tolerable form of government, to nurture and protect its citizens, to honor its cultural creators—that compel exile.[22] While Pai has never succumbed to the facile fantasy that return to the homeland will undo the exile's grief, neither has he considered putting down roots on non-Chinese soil—*luodi shenggen*, to cite L. Ling-Chi Wang's typology on Chinese American identity—a viable possibility (L. Wang 1994). In the exilic tradition, there is only the dichotomy between rootedness and deracination.

"Chineseness" Deconstructed: Some Asian American Readings

What happens when the notion of Chinese peoplehood becomes radically disjoined from the notion of the Chinese nation-state, whether the latter is considered to be in its "natural" state of plenitude, or in an interim of weakness and internecine strife? This is the question posed when *Sangqing yu Taohong,* translated as *Mulberry and Peach,* becomes incorporated into Asian American literature, which counts putting down roots where one resides—*luodi shenggen*—among its foundational principles. Established Asian American cultural criticism holds that once Asians move away from Asia for whatever reason, it is no longer tenable to fixate on Asia as center. Instead of preserving Asian cultures (a doomed enterprise anyway, given how the Asia left behind is not static but continues to change), they and their descendants can and should develop peculiarly Asian American identities and cultures that recognize the "here and now" of their historical particularities.

From this perspective, a political exile is on the same footing as (that is, neither more noble nor more tragic than) an economic migrant seeking a better livelihood. Such an estimation is clearly at odds with Pai's sense of the self-banished intellectual's unique historical burden. An Asian American consciousness also wreaks havoc on the sacrosanct status of Asian origin, and for that reason might seem outlandish to the point of heresy to many Asians on Asian soil, especially to rulers with a vested interest in expanding their political control or attracting economic capital. With regard to Chinese Americans, both the Communist and the Nationalist regimes have had a long tradition of treating them as *huaqiao*—Chinese sojourners—whose ultimate loyalty should be to the *zuguo* or ancestral land (L. Wang 1995). When *huaqiao* do not show signs of returning to the center, the tendency is to construe them (compassionately) as having been prevented from doing so, or (reproachfully) as having been seduced by the materialism or spurious freedoms of their land of residence. *Wangben,* to forget one's origin, is among the most self-righteously deployed insults one person of Chinese ancestry could hurl at another.

Sinocentric sentiments are not shared by the students of Asian American literature whose work first forced, then inspired me to rethink what kind of book Nieh's novel is. When they read *Mulberry and Peach* in the frame of the United States, a nation-state other than the People's Republic of China, the Republic of China, or else a posited unified

China, patterns initially startling to me emerged. Furthermore, given the strong background in feminism of many of these young scholars, such a deconstruction is closely tied to the issue of gender. The intertexts they deployed for Nieh's novel were not Qu Yuan or Lu Xun or Yu Li-hua, but Sui Sin Far, Frank Chin, and Theresa Hak Kyung Cha; their concerns were women's bodies, performativity of gender and ethnicity, women's madness and illness as fact and trope, gothic images of decay and confinement (J. Chiu 1999; Chen 1998; Nguyen 1997; M. Chiu 1996). Such patterns eventually led me to a radical deconstruction of "Chineseness."

A fascinating case in point concerns Part Four, set in the United States. In a Sinocentric reading, when Mulberry reappears as the wandering Peach, she can be said to have become a tragic symbol of the Chinese people in diaspora. A "stateless" illegal alien hounded by the U.S. immigration service, she sleeps around with an assortment of men (apparently "making her living" that way); her sexual restlessness may be a trope for the Chinese people's inability to replace their lost nation with a worthy and suitable object of allegiance. However, her pregnancy (by a fellow Chinese) might be a sign of hope: despite her vacillations over abortion, the ending of the novel remains ambiguous, thus leaving room for some kind of future, however vaguely envisioned, for *zhonghua minzu*, that sense of abiding Chinese peoplehood on which exilic/diasporic consciousness depends as a last spiritual resort. In a Sinocentric frame, the United States functions as the backdrop to the Chinese protagonist's inner morality play, a mere signifier to an assortment of spiritual ills. It is thus an ahistorical "place," or rather non-place. For all intents and purposes, when return to a Chinese center is foreclosed, Mulberry/Peach might have fallen off the face of the earth. (Which accounts for the very conceivability of excising Part Four altogether.)

Pai Hsien-yung again provides the exemplary statement: "With all her traditional values and ethics shattered, Peach Pink [Pai's translation of Taohong] plunges into moral and sexual anarchy, soon sinking to her spiritual nadir and becoming half-mad" (Pai 1976, 211). Madness and anarchy are here postulated as the opposite of having cultural values; if they take an American shape at all (in Pai's terms, "hitchhiking along the American freeways, getting picked up by whatever man comes her way"), it is incidental. In a similar vein, Li Li notes that by going primitive, "Taohong becomes a liberated person, but then she is no longer a Chinese person or any other kind of person" (Li 1983, 408).

That Peach might be an "Americanized" person is ruled out—her promiscuity is merely symbolic of reversion to a primeval state as an ineffec-
tual solution to a Chinese spiritual crisis. "American" details like her
hanging out with hippies are there to serve that symbolic end.

In contrast, in the "America-claiming"[23] type of readings that some
of the Asian American students engage in, it is China that fades into
vagueness, while the United States clarifies into sharp focus as a place
with its own history. For example, when *Mulberry and Peach* was discussed in my seminar on transnational narratives by Asian American
women, my interpretation (following Nieh) of Peach as a primitive life
force was immediately challenged.[24] Students raised pointed questions
along the following lines: If Peach symbolizes a primitive life force, are
we saying it is prediscursive? Is such a thing even theoretically possible,
considering how thoroughly one is interpellated from the moment of
birth? If, for the sake of argument, we accept the idea of a primitive life
force, a kind of tabula rasa, doesn't it ironically leave Peach more vulnerable to assimilation? Look at her participation in '60s counterculture
and the sexual revolution, look at her acquisition of white feminist
discourse about control over her own body (the abortion issue)—aren't
these culturally inscribed, and once marked, how can they signify a
primitive life force, which by definition transcends historical marking?
In short, though at times their observations might have been articulated
at the expense of Chinese historicity, it is clear that the students insisted
on the availability, indeed inescapability, of alternative systems of value
and behavior in diasporic locations, and refuse to derive meaning solely
from Chinese "origin." On this point, they would have agreed with
David Palumbo-Liu's recent analysis of diasporic and ethnic identification: "Despite the diasporic subject's identification with the home it left
behind, and despite any attempt to freeze time and fix space, the diasporic subject must give itself up to the temporal and historical as it is
resituated in a new sociopolitical sphere" (1999, 347). As Palumbo-Liu
notes, it is no accident that the American narrative in *Mulberry and
Peach* is propelled by the figure of the immigration agent: "It is his
interrogation that marks the intervention of the state in the construction
of ethnic identity and attests to its need to recuperate that fugitive subject
into its political field" (347).

The contrast between Sinocentric and Asian American readings of
Part Four raises a provocative possibility. The former, despite some
critics' professions of distaste for nation-statist power, are premised on

a yearning for the coincidence of such power with the Chinese people's mandate (however defined), such that just dominion over the "ancestral land" would render exile and diaspora unnecessary. On the other hand, without glossing over the extent to which some strands of Asian American criticism have played into the United States's nation-building myths (see critiques by, for instance, Campomanes 1992; Fujikane 1996), one might consider Asian American discourse by definition minoritarian. Asian America, a quasi-geographical term frequently used by Asian Americanists, refers to a cultural space with neither territorial claims nor state underwriting. To paraphrase that well-known aphorism on the distinction between a standard language and a dialect, one might say that Asian America is a "cultural nation" without an army and a navy. The validity of "Asian Americanness" as a culturally viable and vitalizing concept assumes—depends on—departure from the Asian origin and marginalization by its "official" culture, as well as minoritization by hegemonic American culture. Asian American critical practices are sustained by the very lack of an army or a navy, whereas Sinocentric ones are informed by (at least haunted by) the notion of an army and a navy, even if these happen to be absent or in the "wrong hands" at the moment. This statement is not about the relative powerfulness of individual critics, nor does it imply that Sinocentric critics are personally complicit in upholding the nation-state. Rather, the point is that the two groups' conceptualizations of "Chineseness" are quite distinct, emanating as they do from vastly disparate political situations.

When and Where Women Enter

Reading without the filtering lens of Sinocentric thematics, as some of my Asian American students do, one may find feminist issues readily foregrounded. Perhaps a mistrust of nation-state narratives encouraged by the notion of "Asian Americanness" has allowed gender-inflected details to emerge from the deeper shadow of "Chineseness." A host of intriguing questions then present themselves. For example, why has the author chosen a woman to be the representative Chinese subject, when the customary pattern in modern Chinese literature is to assign this role to a male, especially a male intellectual?[25] Is gender merely incidental, as implied by the majority of Sinocentric analyses positing a "universal" Chinese subject with unspecified gender? If the desired "natural" state of grace were restored, making the Chinese people and the Chinese nation one, would the female protagonist's insanity-inducing sufferings have been salved?

Textual details in *Sangqing yu Taohong/Mulberry and Peach* suggest an emphatic "no" to this question. When the protagonist's female gender is taken seriously, widely received views on the meaning of the novel begin to fracture. Both Pai Hsien-yung and a number of mainland critics begin their plot summaries with Sangqing's innocence (Pai 1976, 210; Li and Chen 1990, 339; 367; 375; 378; 396),[26] but textual evidence paints no such picture. Mulberry has never had an innocent childhood; rather, she is haunted by memories of abuse and violence, much of it caused by institutionalized oppression of women. Patriarchy-sanctioned promiscuity abounds (multiple concubines and mistresses, legalized rape of maid-servants, and so on); only it is not called promiscuity, a label reserved for condemning "loose women," but Confucian tradition.

I read the critics' fabrication of an unblemished origin for Sangqing/Taohong as bespeaking a desire to preserve the notion of an ideal *zhonghua minzu* victimized by history (as if this *minzu* were not made up of people who enact history, as if history were some inexplicable natural disaster). On this point anti-Communist and pro-Communist readers converge: both are silent about certain "unspeakable" aspects of history that would have marred such a reassuring narrative. For the former, the "unspeakable" is how the Nationalists lost the civil war despite massive U.S. aid; for the latter, it is the kind of fate someone like Sangqing—from the gentry class, with a record of sexual misconduct, and indifferent to politics—would have met had she stayed on the mainland. An all-purpose word, "tragedy," enables one to fast-forward history, skipping the manifold reasons why contemporary Chinese subjects have been scattered. Perhaps Sinocentrism needs a narrative of modern Chinese history as a coherent story of the fall, and such a narrative can only be achieved by projecting innocence and health onto Mulberry (the Virgin) while assigning sin and anguish to Peach (the Whore).

The question then arises of how the woman's body, especially the woman's sexuality, has been used to serve the task of narrating nation—a question that has been fruitfully explored by Lydia Liu in a "modern Chinese literature" context (Liu 1994). Following Liu, I contend that in the vision set forth in Nieh's novel, the interests of nation and the interests of women are, more often than not, at odds with each other, and that the crises of nation are typically a contest between patriarchal structures in which women have no say. For example, in Part One, when the Refugee Student tries to rally his fellow passengers with a stirring, patriotic, anti-Japanese song, he raises one of Peach-flower Woman's blouses, which the wind blows into a suggestive shape like ample breasts. This image recalls Cynthia Enloe's analysis of how women (and their sexuality) have typically functioned to support the nation-state (Enloe 1989, 54).[27] But while Peach-flower Woman serves the metaphorical needs of nation, she has been excluded from its political structure through imposed illiteracy: she can't even write her own name, and so can never take part in the kind of signature campaign advocated by the Student. As Part One is about to end with the news of Chinese victory over Japan, Nieh leaves us with this striking image of three generations of men clinging to, and gratifying themselves on, Peach-flower Woman's reclining body: her baby sucking noisily at her breast, and the Refugee Student and the Old Man at her feet, each smoking a cigarette stuck between her toes.

In another inspired image (narrated by the Old Man) with the Rape of Nanking as setting, a Chinese man and a naked Japanese soldier (a would-be rapist) are shown tussling absurdly over a Chinese woman (the Chinese man's newly wedded wife). The former yanks at the latter's tiny penis while the latter bites the Chinese man's neck, but the fight is broken up by a German member of the International Relief Committee in Nazi uniform, whose sleeve insignia sends the Japanese soldier fleeing. Thus are the grand narratives of nation, stories capable of justifying world wars and rousing armies of patriots to action, reduced to a farcical scuffle between inept and insecure men, whose power is derived from accoutrements rather than from any inherent strength. Meanwhile, the woman in whose name the fight is fought is left out of the picture. (She eventually becomes crazed from repeated trauma.)

In setting forth feminist interventions in an Asian American context, I am not arguing for an Asian American exceptionalism, suggesting that Asian American critics have a monopoly on feminist insights. What I do want to submit is that for border-crossing texts like Nieh's novel, the concept of "Asian Americanness" might provide a catalyst for deconstruction by dislodging "Chineseness" from its place of honor, and that one result of such a process is to create the room for women's concerns to emerge. Of the Chinese-ancestry critics whose work I have consulted so far, only Leo Ou-fan Lee, as touched on above, has identified a productive potential for "decipher[ing]" and "deconstruct[ing" "the master narrative of modern Chinese history" in the protagonist's border-crossings (Lee 1994, 230).[28] He does not, like Pai, regard removal from Chinese soil as an unmitigable disaster.

However, his outlook is recognizably different from an Asian American critic's in that a shadowy Sinocentrism remains in his advancement of the notion of "Chinese cosmopolitanism"—a combination of "a fundamental intellectual commitment to Chinese culture and a multicultural receptivity" "beyond the parameters of what is known as Chinese American ethnic or minority discourse" (Lee 1994, 229). The suggestion is that in today's world, one might be in a better position to be a Chinese subject (that is, have more freedom to practice the essential components of Chinese culture damaged by totalitarianism) or even be a better Chinese subject (such as, be more equipped to be critical of a regime's excesses) away from Chinese-ruled nation-states. While Lee and the Asian American students both question the "natural" authority of the Chinese nation, he retains a belief in Chinese peoplehood not shared by them.

Conclusion

My necessarily brief essay has left many intriguing and important questions unexplored. For the purposes of this anthology, chief among them are two related issues: first, how precisely discursive activity is articulated with material conditions, and second, whether my analysis overlooks the possibility of some kind of rapprochement between Sinocentric, Asian American, and feminist critical practices.

I have highlighted an orientational commonality between the various Sinocentric readings of *Sangqing yu Taohong/Mulberry and Peach,* but to arrive at this focus I have had to simplify both Asian studies and Asian American studies, not to mention feminist studies (addressed in my essay only through the students' readings). As a number of scholars have reminded us (for example, Hu-DeHart 1991; Mazumdar 1991; Chow 1993), the fields of Asian and Asian American studies have separate and complex institutional and discursive histories. I did not tease apart exactly how, under the Sinocentric rubric, critics variously located vis-à-vis "China" are embedded in—and have their readings made possible by—a matrix of economic relations and political/bureaucratic structures. Nor did I show how, within the Asian American context, changing demographics in the academy (both faculty and students) and in institutional job market forces have made for a time-lagged interest in Chinese-language works on American life such as Nieh's novel. Perhaps examining the case of Nieh's novel alongside another well-known border-crossing text enjoying time-lagged critical attention, Theresa Hak Kyung Cha's *Dictee* (which is, however, in English), might foster more nuanced understandings of diaspora, postmodernism, globalization, postcoloniality, and a host of related notions currently interfacing with both Asian and Asian American studies.

The fact of existing interfaces raises the possibility of some sort of fusion or synthesis—of reconciling contradictions and eliminating all blind spots through an attempt to delineate, take into account, and respect as many critical practices as can be enumerated. To return to Elaine Kim's remark with which I began this essay, there have, after all, been many observable signs of increasing traffic between Asian and Asian American (identities, cultural productions, institutional entities, etc.). Furthermore, theoretically certain combinations of interests are certainly entertainable; thus a Chinese-nationalist outlook and a feminist one need not be mutually exclusive, although at the present moment Sinocentric readings of *Sangqing yu Taohong/Mulberry and Peach* tend to be short on feminist subjectivity and long on Chinese subjecthood, and although the most trenchant feminist critiques I have encountered occurred in an Asian American context through the mediation of Anglo-American feminism.

Yet as I argued above, the tangled publication and reception history of the novel has already cast serious doubts on the concept of author as self-consistent artistic orchestrator, and the case of Part Four has demonstrated that the author herself may not be able to provide the ultimate authorized/authoritative analysis of what her work means. While in one sense *Sangqing yu Taohong/Mulberry and Peach* is an impeccably crafted allegory, in another sense it self-deconstructs relentlessly, its form (deliberately fragmented as it is in good high-modernist manner) inadequate to the task of ordering contending historical forces into a singular narrative. In addition to the factor of change over time, this unruliness of the material accounts for the shifts in Nieh's own focus from one preface to another of her various editions, highlighting now universality, transcendence, and the human condition; now the peculiar tragedy of Chinese history; now the hermetic purity of the dictates of art.[29] If the "source" of the novel herself, encapsulated in Nieh's single body, mind, and history, cannot be unified, one might reasonably ask if diverse critical and pedagogical practices, each with its own material investments and corps of individual practitioners, could be. If nothing else, the selective, manageable, and "interested" focus required of any institutionalized endeavor would make an all-encompassing presentation impossible.

The case of Part Four even suggests that there might be some basic incommensurability between the Sinocentric readings and the Asian American ones, traceable to political differences between the respective discursive and material locations that subtend them. If so, this would be an incommensurability that could not be mitigated by soft-pedaling geopolitical anchorage for the concept of nation and by appealing to the transcendent, comprehensive, and difference-dissolving potential of transnationalism. Metaphorizing national boundaries, insisting that they need not be taken literally since what matter are cultural boundaries, would not allow one to arrive at a less contradiction-ridden reading of Part Four. Nor could valorization of border-bursting multiplicity be taken as the final lesson: the protagonist is radically multiple but also in the end, by all accounts, mad. The language of mutual exchange, support, understanding, and recognition is typically used to invoke the promise of Asian/Asian American intercourse. But while not dismissing the desirability of widening circles of acceptance, I would like to proffer the protean (and still metamorphosing) career of *Sangqing yu Taohong/ Mulberry and Peach* as a case study in the need to attend to historical situatedness.

Acknowledgments

This essay is a slightly condensed and modified version of the essay of the same title published in *Orientations: Mapping Studies in the Asian Diaspora,* edited by Kandice Chuh and Karen Shimakawa (Durham: Duke University Press, 2001). I thank the editors of this volume, and the good offices of David Palumbo-Liu, for the opportunity to present this version here; the editors' suggestions for revision, as well as patience and support, are much appreciated.

I am profoundly grateful to Hualing Nieh for generously granting me lengthy interviews in March 1996, and for sharing with me her collection of various editions of *Mulberry and Peach,* reviews and critical essays, and documents related to its publication history.

Special thanks are due the many colleagues who have provided astute and helpful comments on drafts of this essay, among them, Kandice Chuh, Rachel Lee, Colleen Lye, David Palumbo-Liu, Karen Shimakawa, and the participants, too numerous to name, of the 1996 University of Washington workshop on the *Orientations* anthology project. Shu-mei Shih kindly shared her unpublished manuscript on Nieh's novel. I greatly appreciate the thoughtful comments made by students in my Spring 1996 seminar, especially Eliza Noh and Sandra Oh; and the compelling analyses offered by my former dissertation advisees (now esteemed colleagues) Tina Chen, Jeannie Chiu, Monica Chiu, and Viet Thanh Nguyen. Without their provocative insights this essay would not have been written.

NOTES

1. Depending on the romanization system used, the author's surname is sometimes spelled *Nie;* the given name, sometimes hyphenated as *Hua-ling.* The last name of her late husband, poet Paul Engle, is sometimes appended to her surname. Page numbers for quotations from the novel refer to the 1998 Feminist Press edition; additional publication information is provided and discussed in the text of the essay.

2. I am indebted to Shih for permission to quote from her unpublished paper.

3. The Chinese names literally mean "mulberry green" and "peach red" (or "peach pink"). For convenience, the English names of the protagonist will be used in this essay unless the context calls for Chinese.

4. Nieh was hired as a consultant by the Iowa Writers' Workshop in 1964. Nieh and Engle founded the International Writing Program at the University of Iowa in 1967. Nieh is still living in Iowa City.

5. In 1988, *Sangqing yu Taohong* was published in full by Hanyi seyan chubanshe in Taiwan.

6. In Hong Kong, another edition of the full Youlian version was published by Huahan wenhua shiye gongsi in 1986.

7. At the time, all the mainland publishers were under direct government control. In her interview with the author, Nieh noted that given the political and cultural conditions in China at the time, it would have been impossible to publish *Sangqing yu Taohong* at all if the cuts hadn't been made.

8. Published by Chunfeng wenyi chubanshe and Beijing's Huaxia chubanshe

(as part of its "haiwai huanwen zuojia xilie" or "overseas Chinese language writers series"), respectively. The place of publication of the Chunfeng edition was not provided by Nieh.

9. New World Press, which specialized in foreign language publications, was under government control, like all publishers on the mainland at the time.

10. Besides English, *Sangqing yu Taohong* has been translated into many languages, among them Dutch, Hungarian, and Croatian. These lie beyond the scope of this essay and the limited compass of my literary knowledge, but would certainly make for a fascinating project in comparative reception studies.

11. Nieh added the subtitle out of a concern that Anglophone readers might find the terms "mulberry" and "peach" rather unintelligible, since these plants evoke entirely different associations in English than in Chinese.

12. As examples of prima facie "empirical" support for this view, I point to not only the novel's publication by Beacon Press in its "Asian Voices" series (which included both Asian and Asian American writers), but also its inclusion in Cheung and Yogi (1988), a bibliography of Asian American literature that is standard in the field, and the fact that the novel received a Before Columbus Foundation American Book Award in 1990, nominated by Shawn Wong, a veteran Asian American writer and anthologizer. For a related discussion on discursive placement, see Ma (1998).

13. Chinese American historian and activist L. Ling-Chi Wang must be credited with having the foresight and initiative to offer this course when he was chair of the Department in the early 1980s. I am deeply indebted to him for encouraging me to teach and study this body of literature at a time when it was considered inordinately marginal in the American academy. Note that the Prologue and Part Four are the excerpts from Nieh's novel selected in Li (1983), a key anthology on this body of literature.

14. This marginality was something of which the (at best moderately educated) early immigrant writers of the *Songs of Gold Mountain* were acutely aware; see Wong (1991).

15. I also thank University of California colleagues who have taught the book in both "Chinese" and "non-Chinese" contexts for contributing to my reconsideration of *Mulberry and Peach* by sharing their experiences of the novel—Professors Norma Alarcon, Lydia Liu and Genaro Padilla (Berkeley), and Shu-mei Shih (Los Angeles).

16. Note that while I use the feminine pronoun here, in most Sinocentric allegorical readings the gender of the Chinese subject is unspecified. This will be examined in a later section of my essay.

17. Such a view of *Sangqing yu Taohong* is considerably bolstered by analyses of other pieces in Nieh's *oeuvre*, in particular, the short story "Wang Danian de jijian xishi" ("The Several Blessings of Wang Danian"] in the collection of the same name (Nieh 1980b), and the novel *Qianshan wai shui changliu*

(the title is translated as *Lotus* or *Far Away: A River* (Nieh 1984). Note that in the Li and Chen anthology of critical essays, Lu and Wang (1990), with its greater interest in gender issues, represents an exception to the celebration of nation.

18. Remember that the first edition appeared in Hong Kong, then a British colony, which was not "Chinese soil" even though the population was (and is) overwhelmingly Chinese. Remember also that the ban in Taiwan against *Sangqing yu Taohong* was not lifted until eight years later.

19. They are, respectively, four wide, vertical bands of color; a photograph of green grass and pink flowers; and an all-over floral ground. Interestingly, the latest mainland edition (Beijing: Huaxia, 1996) seems to have adopted the "aesthetic" approach to cover design.

20. The widely cited English version was published in the United States in 1976; a Chinese version appeared in *Ming Pao Monthly* (Jan. 1970). In this essay quotations are from the English version.

21. In this essay, Pai makes a distinction between these modern Chinese exile writers, for whom "the individual's fate is inevitably bound up with the national destiny of China," and European exile writers who universalize the human condition (Pai 1976, 207). In a post-Tiananmen reassessment of the relevance of *Sangqing yu Taohong*, which has enjoyed an upsurge of interest especially in Eastern Europe, Pai negates this difference somewhat by linking the Chinese tradition of *Shijing* and *Chuci* to the Western tradition of Mann, Hesse, Solzhenitsyn, Kundera, and others; his focus, as in Edward Said's essay "Reflections on Exile" (Said 1990), is now "the world" (Pai 1989). But the larger scope of Pai's recent analysis will not invalidate my point about exilic literature's ultimate preoccupation with nation.

22. Denton notes that the literature of exile is "based on a paradox: the longing for freedom from one's past and the psychological need to define one's self in terms of the past" (Denton 1989, 137).

23. "Claiming America," a term attributed to Maxine Hong Kingston, is now taken in Asian American cultural criticism to refer to establishing the presence of Asian Americans in the United States.

24. I am indebted to the students in my Spring 1996 seminar for their stimulating discussions of *Mulberry and Peach,* especially to Eliza Noh and Sandy Oh for their comments on Part Four.

25. Well-known examples, heroic or antiheroic, range from (late Qing) Liu E's Lao Can to (May Fourth) Lu Xun's Ah Q and Ba Jin's Gao brothers of the *Family* trilogy, to (more recently, in 1960s–1970s *liuxuesheng wenxue,* or "literature of the sojourning students," set in the United States) Pai Hsien-yung's Wu Hanhun and Yu Li-hua's Mou Tian-lei.

26. To simplify documentation, authors in the Li and Chen anthology will not be listed separately.

27. I am indebted to Rachel Lee for drawing my attention to Enloe's analysis here.

28. Note for the record that the Asian American students cited in this essay didn't appear to have read Lee when they came up with their deconstructive readings.

29. For example, while Nieh (1980a) provides detailed historical readings, Nieh (1988) speaks emphatically of the novel's relevance to the human condition in general, even appearing to find sensitivity to specific events in Chinese history reprehensible. The former preface implies that artistic concerns are solipsistic, but the latter adopts the tone of an uncompromising writer at the service of her art.

Works Cited

Campomanes, Oscar V. 1992. "Filipinos in the United States and Their Literature of Exile." In *Reading the Literatures of Asian America*. Ed. Shirley Geoklin Lim and Amy Ling. Philadelphia: Temple Univ. Press. 49–78.

Cha, Theresa Hak Kyung. 1982. *Dictee*. New York: Tanam Press.

Chen, Tina. 1998. "Sights Unseen: Acts of Impersonation in Asian American Representation." Ph.D. diss. University of California, Berkeley.

Cheung, King-Kok and Stan Yogi. 1988. *Asian American Literature: An Annotated Bibliography*. New York: Modern Language Association.

Chiu, Jeannie. 1999. "Uncanny Doubles: Nationalism and Repression in Asian American Literature and African American Literature." Ph.D. diss. University of California, Berkeley.

Chiu, Monica. 1996. "Illness and Self-Representation in Asian American Literature." Ph.D. diss. Emory University.

Chow, Rey. 1993. "The Politics and Pedagogy of Asian Literatures in American Universities." In *Writing Diaspora: Tactics of Intervention in Contemporary Cultural Studies*. Bloomington: Indiana Univ. Press. 120–43.

Denton, Kirk. 1989. Review of *Mulberry and Peach: Two Women of China* by Hualing Nieh, *Journal of the Chinese Language Teachers' Association* 24.2: 135–38.

Enloe, Cynthia. 1989. *Bananas, Beaches and Bases: Making Feminist Sense of International Politics*. Berkeley: Univ. of California Press.

Fujikane, Candace Lei. 1996. "Archipelagos of Resistance: Narrating Nation in Asian American, Native Hawaiian, and Hawaii's Local Literatures." Ph.D. diss. University of California, Berkeley.

Hu-DeHart, Evelyn. 1991. "From Area Studies to Ethnic Studies: The Study of the Chinese Diaspora in Latin America." In *Asian Americans: Comparative and Global Perspectives*. Ed. Shirley Hune et al. Pullman: Washington Univ. Press. 5–16.

Hune, Shirley, et al., eds. 1991. *Asian Americans: Comparative and Global Perspectives*. Pullman: Washington University Press.

Kim, Elaine H. 1992. Foreword. In *Reading the Literatures of Asian America*. Ed. Shirley Geok-lin Lim and Amy Ling. Philadelphia: Temple Univ. Press. xi–xvii.

Lee, Leo Ou-fan. 1994. "On the Margins of Chinese Discourse: Some Personal Thoughts on the Cultural Meaning of the Periphery." In *The Living Tree: The Changing Meaning of Being Chinese Today*. Ed. Wei-ming Tu. Stanford: Stanford Univ. Press. 221–38.

Li Kailing and Chen Zhongshu, eds. 1990. *Nie Hualing yanjiu zhuanji* [An anthology of studies of Nie Hualing]. N.p.: Hubei jiaoyu chubanshe.

Li Li, ed. 1983. *Haiwai huaren zuojia xiaoshuo xuan* [Selected fiction by overseas Chinese writers]. Hong Kong: Sanlian.

Liu, Lydia. 1994. "The Female Body and Nationalist Discourse: The Field of Life and Death Revisited." In *Scattered Hegemonies: Postmodernity and Transnational Feminist Practices*. Ed. Inderpal Grewal and Caren Kaplan. Minneapolis: Univ. of Minnesota Press. 37–62.

Lu Shiqing and Wang Jinyuan. 1990. "Lun *Sangqing yu Taohong*." In *Nie Hualing yanjiu zhuanji* [An anthology of studies of Nie Hualing]. Ed. Li Kailing and Chen Zhongshu. N.p.: Hubei jiaoyu chubanshe. 522–34.

Ma, Sheng-mei. 1998. "Immigrant Subjectivities and Desires in Overseas Chinese Literature: Chinese, Postcolonial, or Minority Text?" In *Immigrant Subjectivities in Asian American and Asian Diaspora Literatures*. Albany: State Univ. of New York Press. 93–129.

Mazumdar, Sucheta. 1991. "Asian American Studies and Asian Studies: Rethinking Roots." In *Asian Americans: Comparative and Global Perspectives*. Ed. Shirley Hune et al. Pullman: Washington Univ. Press. 29–44.

Nguyen, Viet Thanh. 1997. "Writing the Body Politic: Asian American Literature and the Contradictions of Democracy." Ph.D. diss. University of California, Berkeley.

Nieh, Hualing. 1980a. "Langzi de beige (qianyan)" [The wanderers' lament (preface)]. In *Sangqing yu Taohong*. Beijing: Zhongguo qingnian chubanshe. 1–7.

———. 1980b. *Wang Danian de jijian xishi*. Hong Kong: Haiyang wenyishe.

———. 1984. *Qianshan wai, shui changliu*. Sichuan: Renmin chubanshe.

———. 1988. "*Sangqing yu Taohong* liufang xiaoji (dai xu)" [A brief account of Sangqing yu Taohong's exile (in lieu of a preface)]. In *Sangqing yu Taohong*. Taipei: Hanyi seyan chubanshe. No page.

———. 1998. *Mulberry and Peach: Two Women of China*, trans. by Jane Parish Yang with Linda Lappin. Afterword by Sau-ling Cynthia Wong. New York: The Feminist Press at The City University of New York.

———. Interview with author. Iowa City, Iowa, 22–23 March 1996.

Okihiro, Gary Y., et al., eds. 1995. *Privileging Positions: The Sites of Asian American Studies.* Pullman: Washington State Univ. Press.

Pai, Hsien-yung. 1976. "The Wandering Chinese: The Theme of Exile in Taiwan Fiction." *Iowa Review* 7: 2–3. 205–12.

———. 1989. "Shiji de piaobozhe: zhongdu *Sangqing yu Taohong.*" *Jiushi niandai yuekan* 12. 93–95.

Palumbo-Liu, David. 1999. *Asian/American: Historical Crossings of a Racial Frontier.* Stanford: Stanford Univ. Press.

Perkins, David. 1992. *Is Literary History Possible?* Baltimore: Johns Hopkins Univ. Press.

Said, Edward. 1990. "Reflections on Exile." In *Out There: Marginalization and Contemporary Cultures,* ed. by Russell Ferguson et al. New York: The New Museum of Contemporary Art and Cambridge, MA: The MIT Press. 357–66.

Shih, Shu-mei. 1992. "Re-membering a Self: Nieh Hualing's *Mulberry and Peach* and Theresa Hak Kyung Cha's *Dictee.*" Paper presented at the Univ. of California, Los Angeles, 8 April.

Tu, Wei-ming, ed. 1994. *The Living Tree: The Changing Meaning of Being Chinese Today.* Stanford: Stanford Univ. Press.

Wang, L. Ling-Chi. 1994. "Roots and the Changing Identity of the Chinese in the United States." In *The Living Tree: The Changing Meaning of Being Chinese Today.* Ed. Wei-ming Tu. Stanford: Stanford Univ. Press. 185–212.

———. 1995. "The Structure of Dual Domination: Toward a Paradigm for the Study of the Chinese Diaspora in the United States." In *Thinking Theory in Asian American Studies.* Ed. Michael Omi and Dana Takagi. A special issue of *Amerasia Journal.* 21: 1 and 2. 149–69.

Wong, Sau-ling Cynthia. 1991. "The Poetics and Politics of Folksong Reading: Literary Portrayals of Life under Exclusion." In *Entry Denied: Exclusion and the Chinese Community in America, 1882–1943.* Ed. Sucheng Chan. Philadelphia: Temple Univ. Press. 246–67.

———. 1993. *Reading Asian American Literature: From Necessity to Extravagance.* Princeton: Princeton Univ. Press.

Chapter 12

Americanization
What Are We Talking About?

Rob Kroes

Introduction by Paul Lauter

In "Americanization: What Are We Talking About?" Rob Kroes offers an entry point into several key questions related to the increasing internationalization of American literary studies. First, he raises the issue of how or indeed whether the work of European and other overseas scholars can gain a meaningful audience within the American studies community and what that might mean to a definition of the fields of literary and cultural studies. Second, he illustrates the differing intellectual contexts through which scholars from overseas can view the subject matter of American culture, society, and politics. And, to reverse the movement somewhat, he offers a theory about how the materials that constitute American culture are appropriated and rearticulated in cultural communities outside the United States. Third, he addresses the implications of globalization, and the increasing concerns about them, for the study of American culture. Finally, he illustrates how permeable disciplinary boundaries generally taken to separate fields like literary study, cultural anthropology, and history have become; indeed, he suggests ways in which tomorrow's literature students— even more than today's—will of necessity be conversant with disciplines "outside" their own.

Few issues within American literary studies are as contentious as those charged by an imperative toward internationalizing the work of the field. In part, this drive seems to me a result of the development within American studies— rooted in the antiwar movement of the 1960s—of a critique of American imperialism and the need to understand the impact of imperial politics on culture both at home and abroad. More important, perhaps, internationalization of the study of American culture probably derived from the globalization of that culture itself, from the ways in which phenomena from hip-hop and performance art to the Ali-Foreman "rumble in the jungle" to the stories of Junot Díaz could no longer be comprehended within national paradigms. Not surprisingly, then, an internationalized American studies reflects the growing worldwide conflict over globalization, represented by names like Seattle, Quebec, and Genoa. It need hardly be said that the events of September 11, 2001, and their aftermath emphasize further still the need to understand the interactions of American culture and society with the rest of the world.

While there is consensus about the desirability and even inevitability of inter-nationalizing American studies, disagreement remains about the character of the intellectual work implied in the term "internationalization," as well as about the implications for institutions like American studies programs, English departments, and organizations like the American Studies Association. Some argue that the objects of study of the field called "American literary studies" need to change, that internationalization necessarily implies a shift in focus from the culture and society of the United States itself, perhaps to comparative study of, say, slave narratives or of magical realism. In some areas of the world, notably Asia, the study of the United States constitutes an alternative way of reflecting on local issues and conditions, such as the lack of democratic political options (as was the case in Indonesia) or the effects of large-scale hydroelectric projects on people, economic growth, and ecology (as in Nepal). Similarly, the study of texts such as Melville's "Benito Cereno" and *Typee* enables non-American students—such as those I once taught in Spain—to consider how definitions of civilization, savagery, citizenship, and the like are framed in their own *polis*. Here, the concern is the implications of U.S. experience for development, policy, and daily life and culture in very different national venues.

But, of course, as Kroes points out, in such interactions, American culture undergoes a sea change, becoming "other people's property." He examines how in Europe now, American popular culture comes to lead a different life and serve purposes distinct from those for which it might initially have been created. For instance, my Spanish students focused their initial response to Stephen Spielberg's film *Amistad* on the meaning of "Spanish" in the American imaginary, how the filmmaker deploys Latino characters in his other work, and the ways in which anti-immigrant sentiment plays out even in otherwise progressive films. Some efforts at internationalization have had as their goal not a shift in the objects of study but in the attention given to the range of intellectuals throughout the world investigating the United States. Kroes brings to bear on the subject matter of American culture a range of writers and of experiences generally unfamiliar to many American literary practitioners. To be sure, most Americanists have become familiar with Frankfurt school intellectuals, with Walter Benjamin, and with French theorists like Foucault and Derrida. Relatively fewer will have used the work of Ulf Hannerz, Reyner Banham, or even a figure as significant as Johan Huizinga. In other words, the text-milieu in which Kroes works is meaningfully different from mine . . . or most of yours. This has both the advantage of extending the horizon of relevant theory and likewise its disadvantage—which is to say, it illustrates both the importance and one of the difficulties of reading overseas cultural theorists.

Kroes's primary concern, however, is to devise a theory that enables a richer understanding of the flow of cultural power between "centers" and "peripheries," especially as these shift over time. The center-periphery paradigm is familiar to literary scholars concerned with texts marginalized by virtue of their subject matter or their origins in communities of color or in the working class. Kroes offers a distinctive approach by means of the analogy he draws to the uses of creolized languages in the "periphery." This analogy offers a potent model for the study of earlier (that is, before the late twentieth century) America as a colonial culture: in the areas of the "periphery" like America, he writes, "creolization" invested cultural elements with new meanings. Kroes's paradigm helps to illuminate how African American modernist writers such as Claude McKay, Countee Cullen, and Jean Toomer deploy traditional forms—the sonnet, the nursery rhyme, the sketch—in their revolutionary work; he himself cites the ways in which the generation of Van Wyck Brooks, Waldo Frank, and Randolph Bourne challenged the culture of "genteel highbrows" on behalf of "America's vibrant vernacular culture." Kroes's theory of creolization enables an account of American culture that richly integrates elements long marginalized by virtue of race, national origin, gender, and the like, precisely because such elements have proven to be critical to the processes of creolization he describes as characteristic of American culture. Equally important, he focuses our attention less on the problem of the objects of study, or on the intellectual worlds within which American literary studies proceed at home or abroad, than on the cultural dynamics implied in such terms as "colonization," "imperialism," or, indeed, "globalization." And he suggests—contra Frankfurt school pessimism—how forms of culture—high, low, and in between—come to be reappropriated and in the process reinvigorated in the ongoing, and never stilled, struggles over hegemony.

A PARADIGM SHIFT has been underway in cultural anthropology during the last several years. The Swedish cultural anthropologist Ulf Hannerz has been foremost among those who hold that the dominant perspectives in their field of endeavor have increasingly lost touch with the contemporary world.[1] Hannerz makes the point that colleagues in the various social sciences—historians, anthropologists, sociologists, economists, and political scientists—have been developing theories that have kept abreast with the increased interdependence among human societies in this world. Those theories tend to focus on the lines of economic and political interwovenness that stretch across the globe and that have produced worldwide patterns of societal subordination. According to the various ideological perspectives of the observer, this subordination may be conceived of in terms of interdependence and inequality or, more radically, in terms of exploitation and subjection. Whatever the precise ideological view, the world is seen as divided between centers of economic and political power that have subordinated the rest of the world as a mere periphery.

Such a globalization has taken place culturally as well. One can distinguish centers for the production of meaning that have subjected the rest of the world to their semiotic auspices. According to Hannerz, cultural anthropologists have so far failed to account for the effects of this cultural globalization on the recipient periphery. Like true cultural archivists, they have hurried to chart the cultural diversity of the world before it becomes too late, before the last indigenous cultures fall prey to the Coca-colonization of the world. Hannerz makes two accusations against his colleagues: either they tend to ignore processes of cultural globalization, pretending that the local communities that are the object of their study are still untouched in a time and space entirely their own, or they see globalization as a process of cultural homogenization, eroding all cultural diversity and therefore unworthy of their expert attention. Hannerz begs to differ. As he sees it, cultural anthropologists have the special responsibility of bringing their talents of cultural empathy to bear on the situation of people and societies that find themselves at the margins of the world system. Thus, anthropologists can hope to gain an insight into the ways in which people at the so-called periphery undergo cultural bombardment from a distant and alien world.

In this context Hannerz uses the term *creolization*. It is a felicitous metaphor inspired by the changes that languages undergo when, far from their cultural home base, they have to serve as the means of communication among groups of diverse geographical and cultural origins. In a process attendant on the increased economic and political interlinking of human societies across the globe, many cultural meeting grounds have come into existence where the cultural heritage of each of the parties involved has undergone a transformation. Creolization as a linguistic phenomenon is a case in point. Thus, languages from "center" cultures, such as Spanish, French, Portuguese, and English, have served as the mold for the creole languages of the Caribbean; thus also, at the southern end of the African continent, Dutch has been creolized into Afrikaans. The languages of the center countries in creolized versions allowed meaningful exchange among people from the world's "periphery." The center countries were instrumental in uprooting these people in the first place and in bringing them together, through colonization, the slave trade, and migration.

The metaphor of creolization is a felicitous one because it takes the structural transformations of languages in the melting pot of the world's periphery as an illustrative case of the more general processes of cultural change that take place there. Linguistically, creolization refers to the reduction of the structural complexity of a language in the sense that strict rules of grammar, syntax, and semantics prevailing in the parent country lose their controlling force. Words no longer obey the structural discipline of spelling, inflection, conjugation, gender, syntactic order, connotation, and denotation; they align themselves more freely and more simply. Away from the parent country, at the meeting ground of alien cultures, no authority figure is in place to rap a person over the knuckles for saying "I is" and "we be" or, even more to the point, "I is, therefore we be."

What could the notion of creolization mean when transferred to cultural forms other than language? It must have to do with the simplification of their structural principles, with their "grammar," "syntax," and "semantics." Every parent country always has an arsenal of means of cultural reproduction and preservation, in institutions of education and in the social control of everyday life, but beyond its span of control these means have no effect. Such areas are free from the cultural syntax that orders cultural matters hierarchically in the parent country, as high or low, "done" or "not done," or as Nancy Mitford would have it, "U or non-U."[2] There the grammar that defines the proper form of cultural conventions and rituals of social intercourse collapses. There, finally, the cultural semantics of the parent country can be cut adrift, allowing cultural forms and meanings to interact freely, beyond any meddling of the parent country's semantic authority.

In all these respects the parent country's structural mold collapses, with the consequent liberation of cultural forms and meanings from their prescribed patterns of interlinkage. In the wake of the worldwide political and economic expansion first of Europe and then of America, their cultures have also spread across the globe. In many ways these cultures have been cut adrift from the authoritative sway of the parent countries. The inhabitants of the world's periphery, not unlike beach-combers, are scavenging along the tide line of Western expansion, appropriating its flotsam and jetsam. They feel free to rearrange the order and meanings of what they collect. They turn things upside down, beads turn into coinage, mirrors into ornaments. Syntax, semantics, and grammar become jumbled. At the same time, however, in their selective appropriation people at the periphery create their own environment, doing so under their own auspices. They are their own free agents. In roughly this way one could make sense of the metaphor of cultural creolization.

This line of argument suggests a somewhat malicious reading of what we might call the rules of transformation of the American culture. Many European observers have been struck, if not dumbfounded, by the American tendency to disassemble cultural forms into their component parts and to rearrange them freely into new patterns. Americans do not follow European rules of syntax in dealing with the culturally high and low, in their undaunted recycling of the low and their unacademic achievement of the sublime through reassemblage. They take liberties with accepted European cultural grammar; in their cultural "aphasia" they show a freedom from rules of cultural spelling that can render surprisingly new formations. Whereas cultural forms always appear in a particular hue to Europeans, the Americans do not shrink from taking hue-turns, subverting the established order of hue and nonhue. If Europeans are spelling-bound—so to speak—by rules of grammar, Americans tend to question the rules. Their mental mold is inclined to conceive of cultural structures as open-ended. If their state is a federation, it is never in solid state; new states can always be added. When they build, their skyscrapers are not self-contained forms. They could have been higher, and they might as well have been lower. A unity of style, rules of scale and proportion, has given way to the freedom of selective appropriation from European cultural repertoires. One single building in America can look like a veritable catalog of European building conventions, in a mad mélange of era and locus. When writing music composer Charles Ives could play with the idea that "if you can have two 3ds, major or minor, in a chord, why can't you have another one or two on top of it?" To him it was as natural as thinking, "If three bases in baseball, why not four or five?"[3]

This cast of mind, which struck Johan Huizinga as being antimetaphysical and which others such as John Blair have described in terms of the logic of replaceable parts,[4] could perhaps best be compared to a catalytic converter. In their selective appropriation of the European cultural heritage, Americans have tended to dissect patterns of traditional and organic cohesion while feeling free to rearrange the component parts into new wholes. They enjoy a freedom from academicism, from cultural orthodoxy, that has struck many European observers. Whereas Huizinga called it an antimetaphysical bent of mind, Tocqueville and others saw it in connection with the egalitarian ethos in America. The two views are not necessarily compatible. The democratic impulse may have led Americans to dissolve the membranes that in Europe separated the high from the low, the trivial from the sublime, but what remains is never solely a desecrated Europe, robbed of its metaphysical grandeur. In America, in the great Whitmanesque tradition, there is always some celebration of democratic equality, of the recognition of the sublime in the trivial, which is far from being antimetaphysical. The American cultural tradition has its moments of transcendence, its moments of rapture toward its own creative potential, and the object could be the great experiment of their republican order, technical marvels like the Brooklyn Bridge, the illumination of Niagara Falls, or the creation of a nocturnal cityscape through commercial neon signs—they are all equally moments of a confrontation with the sublime.[5] Not only have Americans broken the European cultural syntax and grammar, they have also changed Europe's cultural semantics. Whenever Europeans made fun of American enthusiasms for the low and vulgar, their reaction was born of ignorance. They weighed an American aesthetics against European standards, as if these would apply equally to America.

Perhaps at this point an alternative view suggests itself. As I pointed out before, there is the somewhat facetious possibility of conceiving of the rules of transformation that characterize the American cultural mold as the outcome of creolization. It is more than a little facetious because it implies a view of America as a country at the periphery of a Eurocentric world. This hardly characterizes the present century—the "American century"—in which the United States has come to constitute a potent center of political, economic, and above all, cultural radiance. The case might well be argued for earlier periods of America's national existence, however. For a long time America did find itself at the tide line of the European expansion. Then the flotsam and jetsam of foreign cultures that had been cut adrift through the agency of the European expansion washed ashore in random order. Settlers from Europe, slaves from Africa, and poor immigrants from peripheries elsewhere in the world came together to fill the empty space of America. The setting was one of a cultural deracination and contact, which naturally made for creolization.

Umberto Eco once referred to America as "the last beach of European culture." His point was made tongue-in-cheek. Although the authentic version of European culture was crumbling in Europe, prey to the erosive forces of time, acid rain, and exhaust fumes, America was serving as the repository of the European heritage, which was reproduced in a thousand replicas, enlarged or reduced, in plastic or plaster, juxtaposing King Lear and King Kong, Rimbaud and Rambo, Plato and Puzo. These echoes from Eco render a caricature more than a real-life portrait of America, yet his tirade does have its points. In a sense Eco, too, is referring to creolization, and more than only European cultures have been involved in the process.

There has always been a clear dividing line among the people who washed ashore at Eco's "last beach." There were those who resembled Robinson Crusoe, representing as they did the culture of the Anglo-Saxon parent country. Large numbers were more like "good man Friday," however, cut adrift from their own cultural moorings and taken in tow by their new masters. Whereas they were like Friday's child, working hard for a living, the Crusoes were like Sunday's child. They enjoyed positions of social, economic, and cultural authority. They were the branch directors in America on behalf of the parent culture of England. They constituted the replica of the center at the periphery. They were the true guardians of a cultural continuity that would keep them oriented toward England.

But Friday's children, no matter how subservient and lowly, have never been passively and exclusively subjected to the cultural hegemony of their masters. As the cultural history of American subservience has taught us (e.g., in the work of Herbert Gutman or Eugene Genovese), slaves and immigrants alike have managed against all odds to create their own cultural environments, freely drawing on cultural repertoires that could be traced either back to their homelands or to their new social setting in America. It always meant that cultural elements, regardless of origin, underwent creolization. They were divested of the control systems that prevailed in the parent country; they were rearranged into new patterns, and they assumed new meanings. Thus, under conditions of slavery or of life at the frontier, varieties of Christianity sprang forth that emphasized emotionalism rather than dogmatic nuance. In a context of commercial mass media Christianity appeared in the guise of a televangelism, calling on its audience "to come to Jesus" as if it were a matter of buying the latest model Chevrolet. European forms of music, such as marching music, European musical instruments, and European standards on how to play them underwent drastic creolization in that American musical idiom par excellence, jazz. In the case of the parent country's language—English—things were no different. Among the slave population, in black urban ghettos, in ethnic neighborhoods, on the shop floor, and on the street, vernacular forms of English developed that differed in pronunciation and vocabulary, in syntax and semantics. In all those speechmaking settings English gained a freedom from outside control, as well as a vernacular vitality, that later on, in the endless recycling of American culture, gave its flavor to ethnic literature, ethnic movies, and American popular music. The international appeal of American English, as of so many other forms of American popular culture, must be tied to these ingredients of freedom and looseness. Although America may have moved all the way from the periphery to the center of our present-day world system, it has never lost its early habits of creolization.

As I already pointed out, however, in every country at the periphery there are always replicas of the distant center country, local branch offices staffed by the center's representatives. I called them collectively the Sunday's children of America. They are the local managers of the interests of the home country, politically and economically but also culturally. Lawrence Levine's book *Highbrow/Lowbrow: On the Emergence of Cultural Hierarchy in America* assumes its full meaning against this background. What he describes as the gradual assertion of elitist cultural standards in nineteenth-century America can be seen as a movement of resistance against the creolization of culture. When earlier in the century Shakespeare, Verdi, and Beethoven in a great many forms of blithe bastardization had been appropriated by the general populace, a social elite of Sunday's children rallied to turn the tide. Under such elite auspices theater, opera, and music were once again restored to their holy status of high art and drawn within the exclusive domain of elitist tastes. In this forcible assertion of standards that were quintessentially European, the elite reaffirmed the cultural dominion of the home country, turning America into a mere province of England, if not Europe. This trend most strongly exerted itself in the heyday of a cultural Victorianism that held sway in America as strongly as it did in England. Against this genteel hegemony of an established bourgeoisie a younger generation of cultural rebels, such as Van Wyck Brooks, Waldo Frank, and Randolph Bourne, rose up in anger and protest. Brooks challenged the genteel highbrows to face up to America's vibrant vernacular cultures. Bourne called on his compatriots to cut the umbilical cord that tied the country to England and that would forever doom it to remain a mere provincial echo of Europe. Ironically, in much of their feverish search for an authentic and truly American culture, they tended to overlook much cultural creativity in the America of their time. In their views of an American equivalent of high art, they unconsciously still toed the line of European conceptions concerning a hierarchy of cultural forms. Time and time again this pattern would repeat itself among later American critics of American culture. But that is a different story.

If the authenticity of American culture consists in its picaresque tradition of creolization, its freedom from genteel control, its freedom to borrow, to cut up and hybridize, we are back once again at what I called the rules of transformation of American culture. European observers have always had an intimation of these rules, even if their response was one of disgust and rejection. Their opprobrium mostly went toward what they found lacking in America: there was no soul, depth, warmth, or authenticity. Underlying their reaction was an unwillingness or inability to conceive of American culture in terms of its "Otherness," of its difference from the structural logic of European cultures. They weighed America against European standards and found America wanting. To the extent that their diagnosis went beyond this litany of estrangement, they still cast their discourse in terms of absences, of things missing in America. As they saw it, America lacked the European sense of the historical and organic cohesion of cultures. Up to a point that observation was relatively astute. The European critics of American culture noticed the effects of a modularizing, fragmenting cast of mind in every cultural domain. Education, for instance, was no longer the continued, time-consuming appropriation of a "body of knowledge"; the transfer of knowledge in America had been disassembled into a range of disconnected modules. Europeans noticed the same characteristics in American sports and games; American football in particular was a prime illustration of this fragmenting attitude. In architecture, literature, constitutional thought and institutions, industrial production, the semiotics of advertising and political messages, the use of radio and television time—everywhere the European observer could recognize the transforming logic of disassemblage and reassemblage, the logic of a catalytic converter.

So far I have chosen to relate this molding force to a history of cultural creolization in America. In this view America's historical position at the tide line of the European expansion, at the periphery of a Eurocentric world, would have trained its inhabitants in their particular ways with culture. That may well be the case, yet it seems to be less than the whole truth. Other readings begin to suggest themselves when, for instance, one enters the Library of Congress. There, on opposite sides of the entrance hall, are two bibles on display. One is the result of monastic endeavor, a product from the age of individual craftsmanship. The other is a Gutenberg bible, an early product of the printing age, the age of mechanical reproduction. An explanatory note gives the following information:

> The Gutenberg Bible is the first great book printed in Europe from movable metal type. It is therefore a moment which marks the turning point in the art of bookmaking, and consequently in the transition from the Middle Ages to the modern world. Through the invention of printing it became possible for the accumulated knowledge of the human race to become the common property of every man who knew how to read—an immense forward step in the emancipation of the human mind.

> The printing of this Bible was probably completed late 1455 at Mainz, Germany. To Johann Gutenberg, who lived from about 1400 to 1468, the credit is usually given for inventing the process of making uniform and interchangeable metal types and for solving the many other problems of finding the right materials and methods of printing.

The text continues, but what is of relevance to my story here is in the quoted passage. Confronted with these two bibles, which the accompanying note puts into historical context, the visitor has a brief moment of delusion. He or she may feel briefly like a latter-day Menno Ter Braak, Johan Huizinga, or André Siegfried and like them may feel tempted to look at these two bibles in terms of the contrast between Europe and America. Huizinga's longing for what is "old and silent," Siegfried's elevation of the individualism and the creative spirit of the artisan, and Ter Braak's evocation of Europeanism seem to be embodied in the first of the two bibles. Next to it, the Gutenberg bible appears as almost American, an impression that is reinforced by the accompanying note. Its choice of words breathes an American spirit of optimism and a belief in progress, in the ongoing democratization of humanity. More specifically, however, its use of phrases like "movable metal type" or "the process of making uniform and interchangeable metal types" seems to place the invention of printing in a characteristically American framework. Are not uniformity and interchangeability precisely the attributes of an American cast of mind against which so many European critics have cried out in protest?

Such a view is soon rejected. Incontrovertibly both bibles have their origins in Europe; they are both products of European culture. Nor can it be denied that with the advent of modernity, a spirit of catalytic conversion captured people's minds in Europe, ruthlessly factoring a metaphysical world into its physical components. Newton dissected metaphysical concepts like motion and stasis in terms of measurable physical forces. John Locke reduced the mystery of social order to the level of the rational calculation of individual interest. Adam Smith robbed social production of its hallowed luster of individual craftsmanship by taking the organic process of production apart into its separate constituent activities. Karl Marx stripped his teacher Hegel's worldview of its metaphysical features by "turning it upside down" and conceiving of world history as the result of clashing class interests.

Such considerations should caution us against opposing "America" to "Europe." Everything that strikes European observers of America as the expression of a modularizing cast of mind is really not more than a radical version of trends that are indigenous to Europe. America thus shows us, in "pure culture," so to speak, only what Europe has never quite managed to bring to full fruition. In Europe there have always been powerful, entrenched forces of opposition to the demystification of the world.

This reading of America as the country where cultural trends that in Europe will be forever stunted could fully come into their own is not without precedent. In the 1950s consensus historians in America further developed an essentially Tocquevillean idea. As they saw it, a liberalism that can be traced back to John Locke had sunk roots in America more deeply than anywhere in Europe, unopposed as it had been by rival ideologies, in a setting that was free from the European dialectics of class. Also, more recently, Baudrillard in his style of apodeictic aphorism maintained that America is the one truly modern nation. Unencumbered by the debris of the European past, a spirit of modernity established itself in America. Europe has never been able fully to replicate itself in America. From the selective transplants of parts of Europe's many societies and cultures a new organism developed that has its own rules of growth and development. Creolization, then, is only one metaphor that can help us to grasp America's rules of culture.

America at the Center

In our century the tables have been turned. America has irresistibly moved toward center stage, while Europe finds itself on the receiving end of a wave of American culture that washes across the globe. That leads me to questions that have harrowed many cultural observers in Europe for many years: the questions of Europe's exposure to a pernicious Americanism and of the attendant Americanization of Europe's cultures. In alarm or exhilaration Europeans have been pointing to an influx of American cultural products, tangible or abstract, goods or ideas. "America" is a presence in our lives, a part of our imagination, to a greater extent than ever before. In that sense our lives unmistakably have undergone an Americanization. We have acquired a set of cultural codes that allow us to understand American cultural products, to appreciate them, and to consume them as if we were Americans. We have no more trouble deciphering American messages—be they commercials, television programs, or Hollywood movies—than does the average American. That is not naturally so. We have had to get the hang of it. Time and time again generations in Europe have parted ways in their appreciation of American culture. Time and time again younger generations in Europe have had to explain to their elders what was so appealing about jazz music, about Laurel and Hardy, about blue jeans and sneakers, about Western movies. Principles of form and of narrative technique, contexts of association—we all have had to make them our own.

Of course, we were never complete outsiders, fully uninitiated. To the extent that America holds up a phantasm, a dreamworld, to the extent that it conjures up a world of freedom, without inhibitions and constraints, we are reading a leaf from our own book. The European imagination had already invented a mythical West before America was discovered. To a certain extent America has merely kept our collective dreams alive. Even today it still holds up before our eyes a gigantic screen for the projection of fantasies that are European as much as they are American. It provides a repertoire for identification with epic worlds that derive their attraction from the fact that America is conceived as a non-Europe, that it provides a counterpoint to our culture, a utopian realm for our dreams of escape. That is precisely why America has never been a consensual matter in Europe. What to some may appear as a repertoire for identification and creative escapism appears to others as the repertoire for their indictment. Anyone who truly cares about the European store of cultural conventions will tend to look on America as the distorting mirror of our culture. Conventions have been torn asunder, hierarchies turned upside down, and connections broken. On the rear balcony of Amsterdam streetcars we no longer find Ter Braak's newspaper boy, immersed in the reading of a musical score, deciphering the code of Europe's cultural heritage. Now there stands a boy with his Walkman turned on, removed from Europe, in total surrender to the raptures of American mass culture. Those around him are reduced to the status of strangers on their own turf, beset by an American culture that as a rhythmic hiss prevents them from reading their newspaper. Newspaper boy, where have you gone?

America's culture has become an unavoidable presence. Its reception knows many varieties. There is the form of an unreflected aping, as almost a miniplayback show on television. Little girls of seven mimic their idols, up to the minutest details of pronunciation and expression, yet they have no inkling of what the words are about. Does that make their aping mindless? I say it does not. What is happening is an act of cultural appropriation, an experiment in creative identification with their admired examples. Creative identification is the key word. Whether it is little girls of seven or European jazz musicians, the French *cinéphiles* of

Cahiers du cinéma, or someone like the Dutch columnist J. L. Heldring (who once confessed his admiration for the American soap opera *Dallas*), the admiration and identification always involve the contrapuntal aspects of the American culture compared to Europe's, its freedom from academic constraint, its professionalism in the production of a vernacular culture.

Often there is an element of nostalgia in our admiration, of a return to adolescent dreams when the world was still one of endless potential. America as a realm of dreams has preserved that quality. It still holds out the option of an escape from what we have become. America in that sense is a country that in its cultural production has refused to grow up and to assume a fixed form and shape. It is a Disneyland where suddenly we are again as young as our children. Every enjoyment of American culture now always takes us back to a remembered America, to the early rapture that we felt while discovering jazz, when we were Elvis Presley fans, or when we stopped in our street in silent admiration of one of America's dream cars. There is a paradox here: our imaginary return to a remembered adolescence always makes us more keenly aware that we have grown older. But American culture could not be bothered; it rushes on, forever young.

There are those who argue the opposite case. They call America's contemporary culture postmodern, because as they see it, the country has lost its innocence and sense of invention. It has become aware of its own underlying rules of transformation, of its modularizing penchant, its freedom to fragment and rearrange. In this view America has grown old in the weary awareness that everything has already been done, that every experiment has already been tried. America has seen through the secret of its own vitality, losing its élan in the process. Nothing much remains to American culture other than endlessly to quote itself, as merely an ironic gesture, in a conscious recycling of cultural clichés. A European cultural critique that always has tended to see little more than the cliché in American culture now seems to have gained a foothold in America.

Nonetheless, this is nothing more than a repetition of what has previously happened in America. There have always been cultural elites who in the critique of their own culture have let themselves be guided by European standards while remaining blind to what went on before their very eyes in terms of cultural vitality and innovation. Today things seem to be no different. Those who, within the walls of academia in America, keep chattering about postmodernism, poststructuralism, and deconstructionism have set out to subject the entire range of America's cultural forms to deconstruction. Theirs is a quest for the tacit premises, if not the conventional stereotypes, that have turned American culture into a potent means for the oppression of cultural Others, such as women, blacks, American Indians, and other ethnic minorities. To the extent that they examine the repertoire of American culture, it is with a view to deconstructing the cliché.

There is an irony in all this. In their busy deconstruction of American cultural forms, the postmodernists are in fact pursuing a more radical version of the rules of transformation underlying American culture. To the extent that American culture has moved in the direction of canonization, with lists of great books and great authors, of the Great White Whale and the Dead White Males, the deconstructionists have ruthlessly broken the reigning consensus, bringing a renewed and further splintering to the American cultural tradition. Under their hands American literature has splintered into manifold American literatures from which emerges a whole host of voices and stories that had been ignored in the established academic canon. This modularization and fragmentation of America's cultural past seems to be a worthy latter-day illustration of the American way with culture. If one chooses to call it postmodernism, then most likely America has been postmodern from the beginning.

Nevertheless, we should not forget that all this commotion is limited mostly to the ivied domain of American universities. Outside the walls, unhampered by any weary sense of postmodernism or by the existential quest of the deconstructionists, there is still an innocence and a freshness of cultural creation that show no signs of a midlife crisis. There the endless recycling of street culture, of popular culture, of mass culture, of cliché and collage, of high and low, of kitsch and art, is still proceeding apace in an unreflective forward surge. There are moments of transcendence, as there always have been. The film *Pretty Woman*, for instance, is a prime example of the sort of romance, if not fairy tale, that Hollywood's dream factories churn out endlessly. At the behest of the directors of the Disney studio the story has a happy ending. The male protagonist, played by Richard Gere, appears as the knight in shining white armor about whom his love, a cheap street hooker, has been dreaming. The story is over and the audience gets ready, contentedly, to leave the theater. In a final scene, on a Hollywood sidewalk, a roving black character that we remember from the opening shots reappears. Once again we hear his voice, and with the camera wandering off to the capital letters HOLLYWOOD high above Beverly Hills—a classic icon of America—he repeats what he keeps hollering all day: "This is Hollywood. This is the city of dreams. This is the place where dreams come true." The film ironically deconstructs itself. A cliché regains its cutting edge. If this is postmodernism, so be it.

America has replicated itself into icons, clichés of itself that leave their imprint everywhere, on T-shirts, in commercial images, and in our heads. They have lost their lifelines to America and circulate as a free-floating visual lingua franca. Several years ago the English historian Reyner Banham published an interesting piece entitled "Mediated Environments."[6] The piece appeared in a volume that set out to explore the impact of American culture on Europe for a range of cultural domains. Banham asked whether America's architecture had exerted a noticeable influence on Europe. He arrived at a rather surprising conclusion. With a few notable exceptions European architectural environments show little imitation of American examples. To the extent that America has left any traces at all, it is in our collective imagination. Through a host of mediating agencies—among which are the modern mass media—our heads have soaked up a range of images of the America that Americans have built, the skylines of Manhattan, Chicago, and Houston and street scenes from San Francisco and Los Angeles. We have seen them in newspaper photographs, in films, and on television. When we go to America for the first time, we have moments of recognition, of déja vu. We remember the places in America not only as places in our heads but also as fragments of television news and movies that we have seen in Europe. We remember how old we were then, in whose company we were. America has become a part of our individual life histories. It calls forth recollections that are solely ours and that Americans can never share. Their culture has become other people's property.

The word *mediation,* which Banham uses and which occurs in many other studies of America's cultural radiance, should be central to any treatise on Americanization. America reaches us through a great many media of transmission. Every single one of them affects the context of our perception. American pop music, when interspersed by the inane babble that Dutch disc jockeys have borrowed from their American confreres; assumes a different guise. The deejay may have modeled his role after American examples, but he remains hilariously Dutch: "Veronica is er voor JOU!" American news flashes are accompanied by Dutch voices. While watching footage of the recent Los Angeles riots, viewers hear a Dutch schoolmaster's voice pontificate, "Los Angeles is burning. America is burning." It is the voice of the moral censor. It is Dutch preaching rather than information and analysis. There is the undertone of "what happens there can never happen to us."

We are always the last link in these chains of mediation, the final recipients of messages from America. In that position we are never purely and only passive, gradually losing our Dutchness while becoming ever more American. We make room for "America" in a context of meaning and significance that is ours. If, along with so many Americans, we opposed the war in Vietnam, we could join them in protest against that war; at the same time, however, the suppressed recollection of war atrocities that the Dutch themselves had perpetrated at the time of Indonesian decolonization could resurface and for the first time provoke a public debate in the Netherlands. If in England and the Netherlands groups of young people began to make music in idioms that drew on American blues and rock music, they were not simply the agents of an American cultural imperialism. They wrote their own lyrics, they made their own music, and they gave vent to sentiments that were their own. They, as well as their fans, recognized themselves in the music. They created a cultural space of their own to which they gave sense and meaning. Dutch-language classics in the genre, such as "Kom van dat dak af" or "Oerend hard," gave an added twist to the borrowed musical idiom that further illustrated the processes of mediation that were at work.

Even in the early years of Dutch television, when the medium could still function as a social bonder, assembling family members, friends, and neighbors in front of the television screen, a number of Dutch television productions were modeled after American examples. Television quiz shows became popular, and the word *quiz* itself entered into the Dutch language, along with the word *quizmaster*. Some quizmasters acquired a fame and popularity that made them the first Dutch examples of the American phenomenon of the "television personality," enjoying the transient fame promised by Andy Warhol. I recently asked my students whether they remembered the name of Theo Eerdmans. There was an embarrassed silence. They had never heard of the man. As others will remember, however, he was one of Holland's first television personalities, the highly popular quizmaster of a show on the socialist broadcasting station, VARA. My point here is that, in spite of all the echoes of the American example, no viewer at the time would have been aware of the American origin of the program. Eerdmans was the epitome of Dutchness. Instead of Dutch television becoming Americanized, American models had been Dutchified.

We are at the tide line of the waves of American culture that wash across the globe. Their impact will become stronger with the impending revolution in mass-communication techniques. Satellites will be revolving around the earth oblivious to the alarmist and highly paternalist attempts at patrolling our cultural borders, at preserving our national cultures as members of parliament and ministers of culture see them. As inhabitants of a cultural world periphery, it is our turn now to devise a daring creolization of what reaches us from faraway centers of the global culture industry. Old chimeras of a leveling, eroding, homogenizing American mass culture reappear. The Netherlands has already coined a new term for the process: *vertrossing*. It does not translate easily into English, and doing so would require a full exposé on the peculiarities of the Dutch mass-media setting.[7] That is precisely as it should be. The concept of Americanization has through mediation turned into *vertrossing;* it has been given a Dutch twist, even though the word, given its critical edge, seems to deny this. Paradoxically, it is a highly appropriate metaphor not for a process of Americanization but for the reverse process of Dutchification. Only Netherlanders can grasp the full reverberation of what the term implies. We may call it mediation; we may also call it creolization. Whatever we call it, there is a resilience to the old European cultures that refuses to be washed away easily.

NOTES

1. See, for example, U. Hannerz, "American Culture, Creolized, Creolizing," in E. Åsard, ed., *American Culture, Creolized, Creolizing*, 7–30 (Uppsala: Swedish Institute for North American Studies, 1988); Hannerz, "Culture between Center and Periphery: Towards a Macro-anthropology," *Ethnos* 54 (1989): 200–216; Hannerz, *Cultural Complexity* (New York: Columbia University Press, 1992).

2. N. Mitford, ed., *Noblesse Oblige: An Enquiry into the Identifiable Characteristics of the English Aristocracy* (London: Atheneum, 1986).

3. J. Kirkpatrick, ed., *Charles E. Ives Memos* (New York: Norton, 1972), 120, 121.

4. J. Blair, *Modular America: Cross-Cultural Perspectives on the Emergence of an American Way* (Westport, Conn.: Greenwood, 1988).

5. David Nye has further elaborated this point in *The Technological Sublime in America* (Cambridge, Mass.: MIT Press, 1995).

6. R. Banham, "Mediated Environments, Or: You Can't Build That Here," in C. W. E. Bigsby, ed., *Super-Culture: American Popular Culture and Europe,* 69–83 (London: Paul Elek, 1975).

7. Without trying fully to remove the mystery, let me simply say that the word *vertrossing* ("trossization") derives from the acronym T.R.O.S., the name of a Dutch broadcasting licensee. Set up as a pirate station transmitting from the North Sea, it successfully filed for legal status when, in the aftermath of the cultural tremors of the late 1960s, the Dutch airwaves were no longer the sole preserve of the established broadcasting corporations. Their cozy oligarchy had been the outcome of an earlier grand compromise in Dutch pacification politics going back to the interwar years. T.R.O.S. and Veronica—another former pirate—entrenched themselves as the unrepenting purveyors of mass culture, catering to the lowest common denominator of mass tastes. Against the old Catholic, Calvinist, Socialist, and Liberal networks and their self-imposed civilizing mission toward their respective "flocks," the new networks were seen by assorted guardians of culture as a fifth column operating behind the lines of the Dutch defensive perimeter of the national culture, disseminating a pernicious American mass culture. Thus, in the paternalist indictment of these broadcasting upstarts, the word *vertrossing* became the Dutch equivalent of a process of Americanization, although in fact, as I have argued, through mediation and selective appropriation, the result can more appropriately be understood as Dutchification. Ironically, and unwittingly, the word *vertrossing* seems to illustrate this latter point rather aptly.

About the Contributors

Lauren Berlant is Professor of English and the Director of the Center for Gender Studies at the University of Chicago. She is the author of *The Anatomy of National Fantasy: Hawthorne, Utopia, and Everyday Life* (1991); *The Queen of America Goes to Washington City: Essays on Sex and Citizenship* (1997), *Intimacy* (2000); and, with Lisa Duggan, *Our Monica, Ourselves: Clinton, Scandal, and Affairs of State* (2001), as well as essays on pain, trauma, and "women's culture" in the United States.

Russ Castronovo is the author of *Necro Citizenship: Death, Eroticism, and the Public Sphere in the Nineteenth-Century United States* (2001) and *Fathering the Nation: American Genealogies of Slavery and Freedom* (1995). He is the Jean Wall Bennett Professor of English and American Studies at the University of Wisconsin at Madison.

Wai Chee Dimock is Professor of English and American Studies at Yale University. She is the author of two books: *Empire for Liberty: Melville and the Poetics of Individualism* (1988); and *Residues of Justice: Literature, Law, Philosophy* (1996). She has also coedited a volume of essays, *Rethinking Class,* and is now at work on a new project, *Literature for the Planet,* on global readers of Dante.

Ann duCille is the William R. Kenan Professor of the Humanities at Wesleyan University, where she chairs the African American Studies Program and directs the Center for African American Studies. She is the author of *The Coupling Convention: Sex, Text, and Tradition in Black Women's Fiction* (1993) and *Skin Trade* (1996).

Michael A. Elliott is Assistant Professor of English at Emory University. He is the author of *The Culture Concept: Writing and Difference in the Age of Realism* (2002).

Frances Smith Foster is the author of *Witnessing Slavery: The Development of Ante-Bellum Slave Narratives* (1979) and *Written by Herself: Literary Production by African American Women, 1746–1892* (1993), and has edited recent editions of works by Frances E. W. Harper and Harriet Jacobs. She is Charles Howard Candler Professor of English and Women's Studies at Emory University.

Elaine A. Jahner is Professor of English and Native American Studies at Dartmouth College. She is the editor of *Lakota Myth* (1983) and the coeditor (with Raymond DeMaillie) of *Lakota Belief and Ritual* (1980). She has published numerous articles on Native American literature and on cross-cultural literary criticism. Her forthcoming book *Spaces of the Mind: Narrative and Community* explores both oral and written narratives in relation to specific Native American and immigrant communities.

Rob Kroes is Chair of the American Studies program of the University of Amsterdam. He was President of the European Association for American Studies (1992–96). He is the author, coauthor, or editor of over thirty books. His most recent publications include *If You've Seen One, You've Seen the Mall: Europeans and American Mass Culture* (1996); *Predecessors: Intellectual Lineages in American Studies* (1998); and *Them and Us: Questions of Citizenship in a Globalizing World* (2000).

Arnold Krupat's books include *The Voice in the Margin: Native American Literature and the Canon* (1989), *Ethnocriticism: Ethnography, History, Literature* (1992), and *The Turn to the Native: Studies in Criticism and Culture* (1997). His most recent book is *Red Matters: Native American Studies* (2002). With Brian Swann he has edited *I Tell You Now: Autobiographical Essays by Native American Writers* (1987), and a follow-up volume, *Here First: Autobiographical Essays by Native American Writers* (2000) which won the Wordcraft Circle of Native American Writers and Storytellers' Award for Creative Prose in 2001. He teaches literature in the Global Studies Faculty of Sarah Lawrence College.

Paul Lauter is A.K. & G.M. Smith Professor of Literature at Trinity College (Hartford). A former president of the American Studies Association (USA), he is General Editor of *The Heath Anthology of*

American Literature. His most recent book *is From Walden Pond to Jurassic Park: Activism, Culture, and American Studies* (2001).

Marilee Lindemann is Associate Professor and Associate Director of graduate studies in English at the University of Maryland. She is the author of *Willa Cather: Queering America* (1999), and has edited Cather's *Alexander's Bridge* (1997) and *O Pioneers!* (1999).

W. T. Lhamon, Jr., teaches American Studies at Florida State University, where he is University Distinguished Teaching Professor and George M. Harper Professor of English. He is the author of *Raising Cain: Blackface Performance from Jim Crow to Hip Hop* (1998) and the editor of *Jump Jim Crow: Lost Plays, Lyrics, and Street Prose of the First Atlantic Popular Culture* (2002). He recently republished, with a new preface, his *Deliberate Speed: The Origins of a Cultural Style in the American 1950s* (1990, rpt. 2002). His next book, on fetish theory and vernacular culture, will be called *Secret Histories*.

Christopher J. Looby is Professor of English at the University of California, Los Angeles. His publications include *Voicing America: Language, Literary Form, and the Origins of the United States* (1996) and *The Complete Civil War Journal and Selected Letters of Thomas Wentworth Higginson* (2000).

David Palumbo-Liu is Professor of Comparative Literature and Director of the Program in Modern Thought and Literature. He has published on topics from medieval Chinese literature to contemporary race and ethnic studies, Asia Pacific American studies, cultural studies, social theory, and diaspora studies, and on the work of Rorty, Lyotard, and Paul Gilroy. His most recent book is *Asian/American: Historical Crossings of a Racial Frontier* (1999).

Roy Harvey Pearce is Professor Emeritus of American Literature of the University of California at San Diego. His works include *Savagism and Civilization: A Study of the Indian and the American Mind* (originally published in 1953 as *The Savages of America*), *The Continuity of American Poetry* (1961), and *Historicism Once More: Problems and Occasions for the American Scholar* (1969).

Lora Romero is the author of *Home Fronts: Domesticity and Its Critics in the Antebellum United States* (1997). She taught at Stanford University and the University of Texas at Austin. She died in 1997.

Ramón Saldívar holds the Hoagland Family Chair in the School of Humanities and Sciences at Stanford University. He is the author of *Figural Language in the Novel: The Flowers of Speech from Cervantes to Joyce* (1984), a study of the authority of meaning in the novel. His second book, *Chicano Narrative: The Dialectics of Difference* (1990), is a history of the development of Chicano narrative forms. Presently, he is working on a project on Chicano modernity and transnational poetics, tentatively entitled *Transnational Identities and Border Knowledge: The Poetics of Américo Paredes.*

Carroll Smith-Rosenberg is Alice Freeman Palmer Professor of History, University of Michigan, as well as a professor in the Women's Studies Program and the American Culture Program. She is the author of *Disorderly Conduct: Visions of Gender in Victorian America* (1985) and *Religion and the Rise of the American City* (1971), and is completing a study of the constitution of a national identity during the debates over the ratification of the American Constitution, entitled *Federalist Capers.*

Werner Sollors teaches Afro-American Studies and English at Harvard University and is the author of *Neither Black Nor White Yet Both: Thematic Explorations of Interracial Literature* (1997) and of *Beyond Ethnicity: Consent and Descent in American Culture* (1986). Among the volumes he has edited are *The Multilingual Anthology of American Literature: A Reader of Texts with English Translations* (with Marc Shell, 2000); *Multilingual America: Transnationalism, Ethnicity, and the Languages of American Literature* (1998); and *Theories of Ethnicity: A Classical Reader* (1994).

Claudia Stokes is Assistant Professor of English at Trinity University. She is currently writing a book on the origins of the discipline of American literary history.

Claudia Tate taught at Princeton University and authored *Domestic Allegories of Political Desire: The Black Heroine's Text at the Turn of the Century* (1992); and *Psychoanalysis and Black Novels: Desire and the Protocols of Race* (1998). She edited *Black Women Writers at Work* (1983), *The Works of Katherine Tillman Davis* (1991), and

The Selected Works of Georgia Douglas Johnson (1997). She died in 2002.

Paula A. Treichler teaches in the College of Medicine, Institute of Communications Research, and Women's Studies Program at the University of Illinois, Urbana-Champaign. Her most recent book is *How to Have Theory in an Epidemic: Cultural Chronicles of AIDS* (1999).

Priscilla Wald is Associate Professor of English at Duke University and Associate Editor of *American Literature*. She is the author of *Constituting Americans: Cultural Anxiety and Narrative Form* (1995) and is currently at work on a book about contagion, genetics, and the figure of the human carrier.

Michael Warner is Professor of English at Rutgers University. His most recent works include *Publics and Counterpublics* (2002), *The Trouble with Normal: Sex, Politics, and the Ethics of Queer* (1999), and *American Sermons: The Pilgrims to Martin Luther King* (1999). He is also the author of *The Letters of the Republic: Publication and the Public Sphere in Eighteenth-Century America* (1990) and the editor of *Fear of a Queer Planet: Queer Politics and Social Theory* (1993).

Laura Wexler is the author of *Tender Violence: Domestic Visions in an Age of U.S. Imperialism* (2000) and, with Sandra Matthews, *Pregnant Pictures* (2000). Currently she is at work on a book about American cultural memory and the St. Louis World's Fair of 1904. She teaches American Studies and Women's and Gender Studies at Yale University.

Sau-ling C. Wong is a Professor in the Asian American Studies Program, Department of Ethnic Studies, University of California, Berkeley. She is the author of *Reading Asian American Literature: From Necessity to Extravagance* (1993) editor of Maxine Hong Kingston's *The Woman Warrior: A Casebook* (1999); and coeditor (with Stephen H. Sumida) of *A Resource Guide to Asian American Literature* (2001). She has published extensively on Asian (especially Chinese) American literature.

Index of Names